THE RAVEN, THE DOVE, AND THE OWL OF MINERVA

The Creation of Humankind in Athens and Jerusalem

MARK GLOUBERMAN

The Raven, the Dove, and the Owl of Minerva

The Creation of Humankind in Athens and Jerusalem

UNIVERSITY OF TORONTO PRESS
Toronto Buffalo London

Toronto Buffalo London
www.utppublishing.com

ISBN 978-1-4426-4505-9

Library and Archives Canada Cataloguing in Publication

Glouberman, M.
The raven, the dove, and the owl of Minerva : the creation of humankind in Athens and Jerusalem / Mark Glouberman.

Includes bibliographical references and index.
ISBN 978-1-4426-4505-9

1. Theological anthropology – Biblical teaching. 2. Philosophical anthropology – Greece – History. 3. Philosophy, Ancient. I. Title.

BT702. G56 2012 233 C2012-904946-8

This book has been published with the help of a grant from the Canadian Federation for the Humanities and Social Sciences, through the Awards to Scholarly Publications Program, using funds provided by the Social Sciences and Humanities Research Council of Canada.

University of Toronto Press acknowledges the financial assistance to its publishing program of the Canada Council for the Arts and the Ontario Arts Council.

Canada Council for the Arts Conseil des Arts du Canada

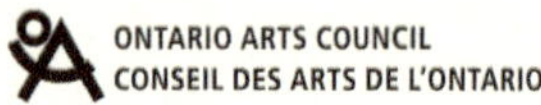

University of Toronto Press acknowledges the financial support of the Government of Canada through the Canada Book Fund for its publishing activities.

Of the priest what can be said? As with all priests his mind had become clouded by the illusion of its proximity to God.

Cormac McCarthy, *The Crossing*

Contents

Preface and Acknowledgments

The main burden of this book is to extract and to defend the Hebrew Bible's view of men and women as (in my slightly specialized usage) human beings, the view that in my view is the heart of the Western sense of what it is – and what it means – to be a man or a woman on earth.

A key part of the extraction and defence consists in wresting the text from those who are generally regarded as having ownership of it. This I do by establishing that the 'religious' aspects of the biblical narrative, the aspects that cause secular people to see a rather distorted image and likeness of themselves when they look into the Bible, are not what they seem. Another key part targets a powerful group of external opponents, the philosophers.

The philosophical style of thinking, the intellectual basis of Greece's contribution to the West, a massive contribution of which science is a central component, is hostile to what the Bible teaches about men and women. I argue that opposition to the Bible from the side of philosophy is due to an internal disciplinary bias. A subthesis that assists me here, since it puts the early philosophers of Greece into a dialectical relationship with those behind Scripture, giving us a glimpse of the fitting room in which the straitjacket is being zipped and buckled onto the view of the latter, is that what the Bible advances is present in the Greece of the time too, though only very sketchily. As I see it, the wisdom of a few Hellenic Solomons was wasted by the Hellenic Socrateses.

In respect of self-knowledge, the thesis, in sum, is that it's דע את עצמך not γνῶθι σεαυτόν.

I was trained professionally in the modern Academy. How did I get to Jerusalem? In neither instance as part of my philosophical activity,

I have twice found myself in proximity to the more easterly star of the binary system known as 'Athens and Jerusalem.' Right through high school I attended, in Montreal, an educational institution half of whose curriculum was devoted to Jewish subjects. There, in grade three, I became, as the Hebrew phrase has it, a 'bridegroom of Genesis,' beginning the study of the Bible with a solemn ceremony of initiation and dipping over the next nine years into quite a few of the writings of the Tanakh. Several years after completing graduate studies I returned to those texts. (I was at this time on the faculty at Ben-Gurion University of the Negev, in Beer Sheva. According to the Bible, it was in Beer Sheva that Abraham dug a well and planted a tamarisk.) A chance encounter early in the 1980s with Robert Sacks's 'The Lion and the Ass,' a verse-by-verse commentary on the Book of Genesis serialized in the journal *Interpretation*, seeded a more concentrated interest. As to the Jerusalemite strain on the Athenian side of the binary: instructing over the last dozen or so years in a number of non-philosophical liberal arts subjects has afforded me the opportunity to study Homer's epics and the plays of the Athenian tragedians. Repeated reading of the *Iliad* alerted me to the fact that Achilles is something of a Hellenic Abraham, God, something of a Hebrew Athena; Homer, then, something of a Greek Moses.

It's a happy accident that a story that plays an emblematic role in what follows is the extra-Torah scriptural portion that I chanted at my Bar Mitzvah. I can imagine the dismayed reaction of the teachers from whom I learned, many of them rabbis, to my 'take' on the exciting contest on the Carmel between Elijah and the prophets of Baal, as narrated in 1 Kings. 'Were you,' I can hear them asking from across the chasm of years, 'paying attention?' On the other hand, since most of them bore witness, a few on their flesh, to the inferno stoked by the modern prophets of Baal, perhaps they would be receptive, even approve. As the case may be, the reading of the episode that I offer, a reading on which Elijah bests the idolaters by guile, epitomizes what I understand to be the core biblical teaching about the condition of men and women, viz., that though, *pace* the Baalites, they are on their own in a universe into which they do not fit and that has no care for them, they can nonetheless find meaning for their lives, meaning anchored in their difference. Superfluous to belabour, this is not what stereotypically devout inheritors of the Bible perceive in chapter-and-verse. Nor, equally, is it how they understand themselves. But, again, the 'religious' content of the Bible is (like Elijah on the Carmel) deceptive. Like training wheels on a bicycle, that content is a device for getting the conception of men and women as human beings up and running on its own. Doesn't God say so much to Jacob? 'Know that I am with you and will keep you wherever you go . . .; for I will not leave you until I have done what I have promised you' (Genesis 28:15). Otherwise put: 'I, whose name is "I am," *will* leave you once you can stand – even if you limp – on your own two feet; once, that is, your sense that you are what I am is stable.'

Have the fortuities of autobiography placed me advantageously to tackle the issues? To say that they have isn't to say that the result, if it comes anywhere near the truth, cannot be improved. It is only to say that the result could scarcely have been produced had I not been exposed early to the Bible, exposed later to philosophy, and exposed quite a bit later to the classics. As to why the exposures came to interact as they did, on that I must profess myself, as most of us must in regard to how we got personally and intellectually to where we find ourselves, clueless.

I believe myself to have been fortunate in the fortuities. I know myself to have been fortunate in those in contact with whom I have worked out these matters.

A perceptive interlocutor, Bill Barthelemy was often better able to see the shape of the argument than I could. With Chaim Tannenbaum, an ideal conversational partner for combining keen understanding of technical philosophy and great sensitivity to the nuances of the Bible, I have had the privilege and pleasure of agitating the central issues of the book. My oldest friend as per ordinary usage, Leonard Angel, continues, as befits his very apt surname, to be a messenger of insights about matters scriptural; about other matters too. Over many of the texts that are the woof of the essay I puzzled in the company of Rob Crawford. In these pages I draw not only on his conceptual penetration but also on his sharp wit.

Three who were my colleagues in Beer Sheva lent a hand with *my* tamarisk: Yuval Lurie's insightful book *Cultural Beings: Reading the Philosophers of Genesis* supplied a vital push; Adi Parush's essays on Greek theatre and related matters classical, models of broad scholarship and analytic precision, proved very helpful; over the years Haim Marantz has been an unflagging source of encouragement.

My eagerness to persuade those in my wider circle is at its most intense in regard to Berel Rodal. Though I have not brought my good friend Harold Rich around, his vigorous resistance to the position that I take on biology and culture forced me to sharpen my formulations.

Norman Simms's provocative writings on Judaism taught me a lot. In his capacity as editor of the journal *Mentalities/Mentalités* Professor Simms has also been receptive to several products of my ruminations. In this matter of editorial receptivity I am immensely grateful to Professor Adi Zemach, who for many years presided over *Iyyun, The Jerusalem Philosophical Quarterly*; grateful in equal measure to Eva Shorr, *Iyyun*'s Associate Editor.

For support that facilitated the research I am indebted to the officials of Kwantlen Polytechnic University's Office of Research and Scholarship and to the faculty members who man (and woman) the relevant committees. I was helped along the way by David Bates, Mazen Guirguis, Ed Hundert, Len Husband, Peter Loptson, Linda Schwartz, and Doran Smolkin. To all of them I express thanks.

The book is dedicated, with love and admiration, to my wife, Chava.

THE RAVEN, THE DOVE, AND THE OWL OF MINERVA

The Creation of Humankind in Athens and Jerusalem

Introduction: Athens *and* Jerusalem

The account in Genesis 1 of the world's creation is immediately followed, in Genesis 2, by another, different, account. If God (the creator in both cases) made two worlds, in which world do we find ourselves, and where in the world is the other one?

In the first of the Bible's[1] two accounts of the beginning, God blesses the denizens of the deep alone among non-human creatures. Why this benediction of the fish? No obvious respects come to mind in which by contrast with sub-human mammals fish relevantly resemble men and women, and the narrative does not draw attention to any unobvious respects.

Why is 'good' the only adjective used in Genesis 1 to describe how the creation strikes the creator? If a lamb could talk, we would not expect 'good' from its mouth as the jaws of a lion sever the jugular. Does he who made the lamb see things entirely from the perspective of the big cat? Suppose you were the prey. Would you pray reverently to a deity who said 'Amen' to that?

Why, in the continuation of Genesis 2's account of the coming into being of the world, don't the man and the woman in the Garden of Eden immediately eat of the tree of eternal life? Wouldn't *you* have made a beeline? To say that the pair, lacking knowledge, are too stupid to understand the offer is to imply that they are being set up for a fall. For not only are the smarts forbidden them but once they partake of the fruit of the tree of knowledge God bars access to the other tree.

How is it that Cain, cursed to a life of wandering after killing Abel, forthwith settles, resuming in the land of Nod the very activity God's cold response to which had caused him to rise up against his brother in the first place? Are God's curses toothless?

Why does the dove return to Noah's ark but not the raven? More than a week passes before the dove, sent out a second time, finds a place to land. That's a long stretch for a bird on the wing. Should the raven not have perished? Yet ravens are still with us.

And why does Moses, according to tradition the transmitter of God's word, stutter?

Why (moving westwards now from the Bible's catchment area, and starting a series of questions about Greece with another case of abnormal orality) does Zeus swallow his pregnant wife and himself give birth at term to Athena?

The Greek gods frequently take their pleasure with creatures of flesh and blood. But why does the chief Olympian deity broker a monstrous marriage between Thetis, a god, and Peleus, a mortal?

Why, at the start of Homer's *Iliad*, doesn't Priam, king of Troy, recognize Agamemnon, chief of the Greeks, or Odysseus, a high-profile fighter? The war has been raging – has it not? – for nearly a decade. Didn't Odysseus head a high-profile embassy some years prior to the outbreak of hostilities to sue for Helen's repatriation?

Odysseus escapes from Polyphemus the Cyclops through what we are supposed to see as an exercise in trademark ingenuity. But though a proper conclusion to Odysseus's epic journey depends on his freeing himself and at least some of his men, he could not have known in advance what question the neighbouring monoculars would ask when, roused by the blinded monster's bellows from within the cave, they come to scope out the commotion. Doesn't Odysseus escape the Cyclopean isle by sheer luck?

In the tragic play by Sophocles that bears her name, Antigone says that she would not have defied Creon had the edict banned a son's burial, or a daughter's, rather than prohibited the sprinkling of earth on a brother. If she advocates for family values over and against civic ones, is this not a distinction without a difference?

Why does Oedipus, in *Oedipus the King*, not notice the absurdity of his connecting his name with his having solved the riddle of the Sphinx? He *knows* that he was called 'Oedipus' long before he encountered the monster.

Did Oedipus solve the riddle? If he did, why do all those troubles assail him afterwards? How is it, anyway, that the riddle, much easier than the one about the chicken crossing the road, had baffled so many for so long? If Thebes is Sophocles's version of Gotham or Chelm, what lesson could the Sphinx's prolonged terrorizing of the Thebans teach?

The puzzles will seem an assortment. But each of them is provoked by an aspect of the relevant text that bears on the conception of men and women as human beings.

Appreciating that this last sentence contains a specialized usage, the reader will ask a series of questions. 'How exactly do you mean "human being"? Aren't we all human beings? What other (non-fanciful) conception is there?' As I employ the phrase, to characterize a person as *a human being* is to assign to the person's life, understood to be finite and terminating, value of a kind (we might at this early stage call the kind 'intrinsic') the possession of which makes it reasonable always to try to snatch from eternity a few days more of life regardless of what fills the days and no matter the cost. For the man or the woman who regards himself or herself as a human being it is therefore reasonable to try to extend his or her life just for the sake of that life, and reasonable for like-minded others to assist the effort to do so, even to make the effort independently if the man or the woman (who may be an infant) is himself or herself incapable.

The conception of men and women as (in the explained sense) human beings is, we see, not without alternatives. Among people currently on the human merry-go-round some as level-headed and as well-informed as any who ride the wooden horses might harbour doubts as to whether they are human beings. Those whose doubts rise to the status of convictions might profess a (non-suicidal) desire to dismount. Is a man or a woman whom the doubts nag questioning the behaviour, *moral* behaviour, systematic non-performance of which draws the charge of inhumanity – keeping promises, extending a helping hand to the halt, and feeding the hungry? Would a man or a woman who acts on the desire and gets off the carrousel turn uncaring of others once feet touch ground? Not necessarily. All that can safely be inferred is that the man or the woman is open to conceiving himself or herself differently (or is taking steps to conceive himself or herself differently) than most among us conceive ourselves.

The assignment of (what I have preliminarily called) intrinsic value to their (finite) lives is a strong sign that the men and the women who do the assigning or approve it conceive themselves as human beings. Though the assignment is only one of several conditions that must be satisfied in order that the phrase truly apply, it is so central a condition that men and women encountered in the world who subscribe to some other view of themselves are apt to be men and women who do not attach to their lives the kind of value that most of us attach to ours, and men and women who for purposes of analysis or clarification are envisaged as not thinking of themselves as human beings are apt to be envisaged as differing specifically in that wise.

The category of the human is a *cultural* category. As the dominant *Western* cultural category, it has real world competitors. The category of men and women is by contrast *biological*. For competitors we must trek to the counterfactual worlds of science fiction – for example, the comic book world of the 1950s in which silicon replaces carbon as the elemental basis of life and hence in which if our counterparts have feet they literally have feet of clay.

The conception of men and women as human beings, the conception dominant in the West, is my subject matter. My interest in the conception has two foci. One focus is the conception's gestation and origin and early history, its nature and structure; the other, the presuppositions of the conception's possibility – all as described, expressed, elaborated, defended, and contested in representative writings that have made it down to us from archaic and ancient Greece, and in the Bible, which took shape at roughly the same time east of that cultural Eden and which despite being pretty much the only literary remain is certainly the representative writing of *its* catchment area.

What is the content of the human conception? How does it relate to other conceptions that men and women, past and present, have had or have of themselves? Is it reasonable for anyone to think of himself or herself as a human being?

These questions, connected with the first focus of interest, make up one of two sets of questions to be tackled in the coming pages. In answering the questions of this set, I lean heavily on the Bible. The Bible is more than just a rich seam of material about the human conception, more than just an especially penetrating dig into the conception's core. It is *the charter document* of men and women who consider themselves human beings. (A lot of the emotional heat is due to the fact that the Bible injects the conception into a hostile and uncomprehending environment. The biblical enterprise is remedial and proselytizing, not coolly analytic. The Bible writers are, so to speak, on a crusade. Those who find the Bible's deity unappealing because of what looks like hard-wired irascibility would do well to budget for the fact.) This identifies a basic thesis of the book: the Bible is at core a humanist tract. By the time the puzzles concerning the Bible have been solved, its non-religious character will have become clear. ('Non-religious' is not self-explanatory. The meaning at this juncture is minimal: 'free of commitment to a realm beyond the realm of everyday experience.') Is it the case, then, that the Bible is not what it seems? The question isn't rhetorical. Perhaps the Bible seems as it does – and 'seems as it does' of course means 'seems as it does *to us*' – because of the viewpoint that we occupy. It is not in the least controversial that the Bible's target audience does not consist of latter-day secularists. About latter-day secularists the Bible's writers know nothing. The Bible's writers are out to criticize pagans and those attracted to pagan ways; criticize them and if possible influence them to change. Yet in an anachronistic manner that they would never allow to pass in other contexts, readers of the Bible who bring their secularism to Holy Writ almost invariably see God as fulminating against the god-less when in actuality *qua* god-less the god-less are of God's party. For, equally obviously, God is, or those who speak for God are, fulminating precisely against the (pagan) gods and those who speak for them. 'I am the Lord your God . . .; you shall have no other gods before me' (Exodus 20:2–3, Deuteronomy 5:6–7). More simply put: you shall be god-less. In biblical terms, what is it to depart pagan ways? What is it to reject those 'other gods'? The answer that I defend is this. It is to embrace human ways.

I lean heavily on the Bible in answering the questions of the last paragraph but one. I lean no less heavily on central literary works of archaic and classical Greece. Specifically, several ways are compared in which men and women as these works present them to us think of their natures and of what their lives mean. The portrayals in these works of members of our kind who conceive themselves otherwise than as human beings and of members of our kind who share only part of the human self-conception help us winnow the essentials. Homer's *Iliad*, the most important of the texts to be looked at, dramatizes the emergence of the human ensemble – through a mixture of personal humiliation and exposure to wrenching suffering, the epic's protagonist, Achilles, who does not initially think of himself as a human being, comes up with the rudiments of such a conception – in a fashion that might even track an actual historical development. If it does track such a development, the *Iliad* supplies a genetic line on the self-conception that most of us in these parts share, the self-conception for which the Bible stands and whose fall would mark *its* fall.

This identifies another basic thesis: the conception of men and women as human beings is inchoately present in archaic and classical Greece. Solutions to the set of puzzles about Greece that was advanced at the start will help make *this* clear. Present within Greek culture is, then, a strain of thinking harmonious with the thinking that is expressed in a much fuller way in the Bible. 'If this is the case, why do the two cultures seem so different, one a culture of faith, the other, of reason?' It's an excellent question. Answering it will identify a third basic thesis.

I referred to 'the presuppositions' of the conception of men and women as human beings: the presuppositions of a cultural self-conception such as this one. Are culture and biology mutually irreducible? If they are, does that mean that beings with culture belong to a fundamentally different compartment of existence than beings with only biology? While the questions of the first set home in on the differentiae of the human conception among the various (cultural) conceptions, the questions of this set, questions that link to the second focus of interest, inquire into what it is that distinguishes among things in general those things that have such self-conceptions. What kind of distinction is it? Is it or is it not an *ultimate* distinction?

The answers to be offered to the latter questions are based on the Bible; on, specifically, the relations between the two biblical accounts, in Genesis 1 and Genesis 2, of the creation of men and women. (The Bible answers both questions affirmatively. Among created things men and women, and only men and women, are not purely natural; their possession of culture is what identifies men and woman as not purely natural.) The material at the heart of my treatment of the distinctive reality of men and women in the creation is encountered, then, at the very beginning of the chief Western account of the very beginning of men and women.

A couple of head scratchers erupt naturally from the preceding sketch. If the Bible is self-consciously the charter of the human conception, why look to Athens for clarification? Why not stick to Jerusalem? That is one head scratcher. Given that the issue of the special status of cultural beings in the creation is an *ontological* issue, wouldn't the place to look for answers be on the Greek side, where ontological matters are debated explicitly and in depth? More generally put: in the light of the received view of the relations between (as the idiom has it) Athens and Jerusalem, doesn't what I say confound our settled expectations? That is the other.

The first head scratcher is easily dealt with. Though the Bible *is* the charter of the human self-conception, that self-conception is presented without much of a hearing being given to alternatives, and certainly without a fair hearing being given. The Bible ties the mentioned presuppositions very closely to the specific cultural ensemble that it endorses:

the *first* individual biological man and individual biological woman whom we meet in the biblical story, the couple known to us as Adam and Eve, are human beings, and the story that their creation initiates is the human story. (My way of using 'human being' is to some degree justified, though not etymologically so, by two facts: the common noun applied to the first individual person in the Bible is, in translation, 'a man'; that first man is, culturally, a human being.) The most that the Bible gives us of alternatives is, therefore, caricature or satire or vague allusion. True, we are only likely to get positive help of the sort that we need here from the Athenian side if I am correct in my thesis that the Greek materials contain an inchoate account of the human. And the thesis is by no means self-evident. However, since the Bible itself is so narrowly focused, it is quite natural to look outside for alternatives. Roughly contemporary Greek culture is a quite natural place to look.

The other head scratcher raises issues at once deeper and more vexed. Let me describe the problem again.

The second set of questions that I listed addresses an issue of ontology. 'Ontology' names a province of philosophy. Since Plato and Aristotle – paradigm philosophers who produced their works, paradigms of philosophy, in the self-same culture that venerated Homer and that looked upon Sophocles with reverence – go on at length about the ontological issue, I anticipate the following aggressive query. 'Philosophy did not come out of Zion. In fact, it was never fully domesticated there. The discipline arose in Greece and got refined in Athens into the powerful intellectual tool that we continue to make use of today. So why look here to Jerusalem? Nor is it just a matter of clarity's beginning at home. Operating as it does in the mode of close analysis and careful reasoning, isn't Athens free of the instability endemic to the Bible's narrative mode?' The programmatic answer is that, powerful tool though Greek philosophy is, like any tool it has a built-in slant. Analytic acuity and care with the relations between one's p's and q's, intellectual merits both, are less than half the story. In its search for truth philosophy is strongly attracted to the common and the general. Inclined therefore to rise to ever higher levels of abstraction, philosophy is by nature poorly calibrated to the particular – indeed it has a tendency not to notice the particular, and even when it does notice deliberately to avert its gaze from it. (Common denominators between diverse things can always be found by climbing the ladder of abstraction: a stick of chalk is just as physical as a piece of cheese; night and day are each of them spans of time; this stick of chalk and Monday both have a beginning and an end.) On the side of Athens, to express it more technically, ontology gets subordinated to metaphysics. We see this clearly in Aristotle. Despite a resistance to Platonism (which is unashamedly metaphysical), Aristotle still handles the analysis of primary substance in terms of the more general metaphysical categories of form and matter. One feels him struggling towards something that he cannot quite reach. It is on the side of Jerusalem that the reality of men and women in their particularity is addressed, lovingly addressed I am inclined to say, the biblical narrative being a cornucopia of men and women vividly presented. The dominance of the story-telling mode over the abstractive and analytic approach is an outward expression of the underlying view that among the many distinctive creatures men and women are *distinctively distinctive* – of the view, to put it more precisely, that the distinctive reality of men and women is anchored in the particularity of each man and of each woman, a particularity that nothing else in the creation has.

We abut here that third basic thesis: philosophy is constitutionally hostile to the kind of conception of men and women that the Bible advances. If, as I say, a strain of biblical-type thought is present in Greece, it is not therefore surprising that this strain is sounded on the non-philosophical side. Neither, given philosophy's force, is it surprising that the strain is absent from the more commanding echelons of intellection. Homer and Sophocles *need* the help of thinkers of the sort behind the Bible if the trend of *their* thinking is to be brought out properly. Without a hand from such a quarter – and in their culture no hand is extended – their theme gets drowned out by the philosophical music.

Is it the case that philosophy did not arise in Jerusalem because the distinctively distinctive reality of men and women occupied its reflective types to the exclusion of all else, or was philosophical thinking *repudiated* in Jerusalem because the reflective types sensed that through its abstractions that reality would be betrayed? Possibly, the reflective types never thought about it. Not impossibly, they felt what the medieval Jewish poet and thinker Judah Halevy felt when he warned against the beguiling but sterile wisdom of the Greeks 'which has only flowers and produces no fruit' – that, in the less flowery but more contentful words of another Levite, Emmanuel Levinas, 'our Western concepts detach themselves from the concrete prematurely.' The information available to us is so scanty that we might as well flip a coin. About the Greek ensemble we have more to go on. So the counterpart question – Why on the non-philosophical side in Greece is no account like the Bible's account of men and women advanced? – seems a bit less elusive. Grounds are adducible for thinking that Plato's philosophical assumptions, assumptions that can be cited to explain his powerful opposition to the conception of men and women as human beings, respond to deep features of archaic Greek culture – features that are dimly visible in the myth-encoded theology glimpses of which we get in Homer. That suggests that the mentioned absence on the Greek side (a few feints and gestures apart) isn't entirely accidental. As the case may be, it is, I shall argue, a fact that philosophy is slanted against the conception of men and women as ontologically unusual among creatures. (Aristotle doesn't get beyond characterizing men and women as one kind of living creature. Distinctive in that sense – so are squirrels, or lizards – they are not distinctively distinctive. In this regard, Aristotle is indistinct from Darwin.)

Apart from the benefit to any inquiry of looking at more, there are, we see, a couple of *internal* reasons for addressing the two sets of questions in terms of Athens *and* Jerusalem. Let me review the reasons, amplifying on the preceding remarks in the process.

Since the first individual biological man, Adam, and the first individual biological woman, Eve, whom we meet in the biblical story are human beings, the reader can easily come away from the narrative with the impression that in the Bible's optic only children who are immature or men and women suffering from some manner of cognitive deficit do not conceive themselves so. But the Bible certainly does not subscribe to such a view. Quite accurately, the Bible advertises itself *qua* monotheistic tract as *revolutionary* in its conception of men and women. This would be false advertising if the opposition comprised only the unformed and the deformed. Due to the way that the Bible narrows its focus – deliberately I would say, because of the crusading character – the view that one gets from it is conceptually less clear than it might be. The (non-philosophical) Athenian side furnishes a corrective to Jerusalem in this regard. In writing that is roughly contemporary with the Bible, the Athenian side fleshes out a conception alternative to the one that dominates the Bible, and does so in a manner that is very respectful towards it. In supplying the conception (regarding which there is in fact a casual gesture in the biblical salute to 'the heroes that were of old, warriors of renown' [Genesis 6:4]) this Greek material enables us to see that the Bible's differentiation of culture from biology is not indissolubly tied to the specific cultural ensemble that the Bible endorses. Moreover, by offering a quasi-historical account of the emergence of the human value system, the Greek material also forces us to confront difficulties in the defence of that system that the Bible handles rather cavalierly. A good case can, I believe, be made for that system. The capacity of proponents of the Bible to make that case requires however greater explicitude about the meaning and implications of monotheism.

'Cavalier.' The devout will bristle. More relevant to my project, interpreters of Scripture will be moved to object too, as will explorers of the relations between Athens and Jerusalem. 'What distinguishes the Bible,' both will insist, 'is the supra-historical, transcendent, anchorage of its value system.'

That God plays a role in the biblical narrative is a plain fact. But *pace* the umbrage takers, the deity who looms so large in chapter-and-verse is not the Bible's ontological fulcrum, though he certainly has star billing in the Bible's drama. Nor (therefore) do the meaning and stability of core biblical claims about value ultimately depend upon God's reality. Appearances notwithstanding, the effective biblical field of operation is the (self-contained) world of men and women. With respect to the central issue of its scriptural writings, viz., our nature and destiny, Jerusalem is not the city of faith on my map of capitals. It is the city of the distinctively human. As for the Greek case, in it can be detected the seed of something like the monotheistic view, when the latter is approached as a value system rather than as a theology. In a kind of mirror image of what occurs over in Jerusalem (a mirror image reverses left and right), the system takes shape in the form of a parting of men and women from (as the Greeks conceived them) the gods. In their turn, the (non-philosophical) Athenian materials have an Achilles's heel too. The discursive content beneath their dramatic veneer is readily assimilated to armchair anthropology and fireside sociology. They are as a consequence susceptible to dismissal on the grounds of superficiality by those on the Greek side given to deeper intellection: the philosophers. The side of Jerusalem outfits (non-philosophical) Athens with a shield of theory – a Magen David, then – that serves to parry the thrusts of the assimilators and functions to deflect the darts of the dismissers. In respect of that same central issue, Athens, on the map of capitals, is not the city of reason.

In common parlance and in intellectual circles both, the phrase 'Athens and Jerusalem' functions contrastively. With respect to the central issue of both cultures, *I* therefore see these emblems of their cultures as twin cities, though not of course identical twin cities. There is more to Jerusalem than faith, and more to Athens than reason. The 'more' referred to in each case is the root conception of Western identity and the terms to think about it that, together, the two cities have bequeathed to the West, and that, together, they supply the wherewithal for defending as effectively as it can be defended – more effectively, at any rate, than either on its own can manage.

Roughly three thousand years ago, at the ragged edge of historical time, the thinking in the biological species *Homo sapiens* took a turn that made it possible for men and women to develop and self-apply the human conception. (The turn also made it possible for men and women to develop and take on board many of the various supra-tribal conceptions that have since come to dominate the globe. Speculative historians of culture speak of the super-fertile span of years that followed the mentioned turn as 'The Axial Period' or 'The Axial Age.') Most of us in *these* parts are the latest inheritors of the members of the species who first actualized the possibility.

In addition to having a structure and a history, the conception also has a politics. Along with the liberal attitudes and the democratic institutions that nowadays are its companions, the view of men and women as human beings is currently under pressure. The pressure comes from two quite different groups. Proponents of what I call 'non-reformed' conceptions of men and women make up one of the two. With a fair degree of explicitness, the more militant among these either have descended from or resist climbing aboard the human merry-go-round. Especially dangerous here are devotees of each of the three major (so-called) Abrahamic religions who insist that they have a lock on core biblical teachings when, as we shall see, they miss the basic point, which *is* to climb aboard. The second group, an influential one too, found as it is at the centre of the culture that accepts the idea of the human, is comprised of scientific naturalizers and their rearguard of Minervan owls, the philosophers. (The members of this second group might aptly be referred to as 'neo-pagans.') Without full awareness of the implications of what they are doing on the political plane, they are gnawing away at the human conception from within. It certainly seems odd that these two groups should be bedfellows. Odd or not, we shall by the end understand why *les extrèmes se touchent*.

To be sure, nothing lasts forever. That does not however make it a matter of indifference which route to the taxidermist is travelled. The prospect of the conception's going the way of the dodo is for most of us in these parts a real and present worry. Since the abandonment of the conception, as the abandonment of the way in which we think of our lives, has wide-ranging implications for how those lives are lived, the issue of what can be said for it is not of academic interest alone.

Might those applying the pressure have a point? Even if they do, that would not necessarily be game over. A point does not necessarily make a victory. To paraphrase Winston Churchill: the conception might be better in its weaknesses (assuming that the weaknesses are not lethal) than the alternatives are in their strengths. Though Churchill's point is worth remembering, I am not however of the view that the conception can be defended only in so negative a manner.

A moment ago I made use of a figure of speech involving the dodo. Dodos of flesh and blood went the way of the dodo due to an 'extinguish me' suite of characteristics. In its present incarnation the conception of men and women as human beings seems uncannily similar. Hard to export effectively, that conception tends to provoke jealousy and is friendly to those who would do it harm. Like the dodo, it is, that is, flightless, tasty, and good-natured. It may be a question of survival whether the conception can be toughened up without becoming unpalatable even to its erstwhile adherents – whether, in the image used recently by a Canadian political leader, it can be more carnivorous, less vegetarian. But how else than through knowledge can subscribers properly evaluate their commitments and, assuming that they deem this to be the right course, defend the conception against enemies and shore it up where it is vulnerable?

The conception of men and women as human beings is my subject. The project is to locate, in the central text of Jerusalem and in some of the best-known and most influential writings of Athens, the point at which men and women whom we recognize as our *semblables* were delivered onto the cultural scene; to extract from the two cultural matrices the various essential ingredients, some of which are more clearly treated on the Jerusalem side, some more effectively characterized on the side of Athens, that constitute our core self-understanding as human beings; to tease out of the biblical treatment in particular the ontological underpinnings of that core self-understanding; to explain, on a more abstract plane, why that conception is inconsistent with philosophy; and to explain why the philosophical constellation is, despite what its latest exponents think, a danger to human flourishing.

*

A poor host it is whose guests must negotiate an obstacle course before they, breathless and begrimed, are ushered into the hall. Since the preceding pages might seem more like basic training than an invitation to the dance, let me put on a more hospitable face by lowering the drawbridge, raising the portcullis, and if not quite setting out a welcome mat then at least supplying a key to the internal disposition of the structure. These, then, are the main theses.

As the Bible sees it, men and women have basic value; the life of each man and of each woman, though understood to be finite and terminating, is possessed of intrinsic worth. The view of men and women as *human beings*, the view of which this constitutes the core, is the view that the Bible advances, elaborates, and defends.

The difference between the view that biblical culture endorses and the roughly coeval Greek view – the worth of the individual man and of the individual woman, such as it is, is subordinate to something larger and more robust – has an *ontological* basis. Differences of temperament or variations in social and material conditions of life do not tell the essential part of the story of why the two cultures diverge.

The Bible's ontological position – men and women, alone among creatures, are particulars – is problematic in a culture in which the style of thinking that we call 'philosophical' (a style that arose and became increasingly prominent in Greece as myth gave way to more 'rational' thought) exerts force. For philosophy, which is committed to rationalization in terms of general metaphysical categories, cannot easily accommodate (indeed it is by nature hostile to) the particularity of the human, since the latter, as the Bible forcefully dramatizes in the story of the transgression in Eden, disrupts the former.

Through Greek culture there runs a non-philosophical strain of thinking. The composers of *this* post-mythic strain (Homer, Sophocles) are moving fitfully in the direction of a view of the sort that Jerusalem endorses *ab initio*. But such is the gravitational pull of the philosophical constellation that the principled underpinnings of the strain never get developed adequately. With the result that Homer and Sophocles look like proto-philosophers rather than (as I claim them to be) biblical thinkers *in potentia*.

The core-ism of the Bible, monotheism, is at base an upward reflection of the conception of human particularity that the Bible advances – a theologized expression, then, of what underlies the self-conception of men and women as human beings. *Qua* charter of particularity, the

Bible therefore inaugurates the characteristically 'Western' view of men and women, the view that comes to practical expression in liberal attitudes and in democratic institutions. The 'religious' appropriation of the Bible continues to do a good job masking this more basic feature.

The contrast between monotheism and (as it is misleadingly called) polytheism is, as just stated, a theological expression of the difference between the Bible's non-philosophical understanding of the reality of men and women and the philosophical style that dominates Greek thinking. Polytheism is itself a theological expression of a pagan view of things, a view that does not have room for particularity. Science as we know it and metaphysics develop from paganism/polytheism and build on several of its defining characteristics.

The biblical character whose proper name is 'God' is the vector of particularity. To the degree that particularity can be got going without God, the Bible can therefore be rewritten in a detheologized manner. And to a large degree, it can be got going in that way.

An understanding of the biblical view, and of the corresponding (non-philosophical) Greek view, has a role to play in the frame of the cultural wars that are now being played out.

1
In Defence of Perplexity

The Body of Science

Hiero was royally displeased. The crown, only recently delivered, had already lost its shine. Had the artisans debased the precious metal supplied to them for the commission? The suspicion gnawed at the Syracusan potentate. But how to figure out whether he had fallen victim to a golden fleecing? Peace of mind shattered by the very thought of the tarnished symbol of power, Hiero summoned the brain trust. He summoned Archimedes.

It came to Archimedes as, sunk in the problem, he dunked himself in the tub. Of course! The buoyancy of his body! Suppose that the material composing the headgear was alloy, a portion of it ignoble or non-metallic. Wouldn't a balancing quantity of treasury gold displace an unequal volume of liquid? 'Eureka!' he exclaimed, racing excitedly from the public bath, innocent – so the story goes – of his nakedness.

The story is quite similar to the story of the Archimedes of a later age having *his* brainwave when, as he pondered the glue of the universe, an apple from the tree against which he reclined came loose and hit him on the head. Significant for us in the amusing vignette is the way that, like Isaac Newton in the garden, Archimedes in the tub serves as a value of a physical variable. It's certainly a convenient arrangement, this, the scientist's being part of the experimental set-up. To be sure, only a very unusual investigator would leap from a roof to establish the rate of free fall or apply flame to his or her limbs to test for combustibility. Yet isn't it in a larger sense true that investigator and subject matter coincide? The body scientifical displaces according to its density and attracts in proportion to its mass. Doesn't the scientist come to know the nature of the universe by coming to know himself or herself?

Much lore has accreted around the figure of Archimedes. In its imagery, an equally famous bit of language that Archimedes is reputed to have vocalized – more this time than just an excited blurt – bespeaks an ambition usurpatory of a prerogative of no mere temporal king. 'Give me a place to stand and a lever long enough,' said he, himself again figuring in the experimental set-up, 'and I will move the earth.'

'Eureka' and 'Eheu'

Thus sayeth the Proverbist (Proverbs 30:18–19):

> Three things are too wonderful for me;
> four I do not understand:
> the way of an eagle in the sky,
> the way of a snake on a rock,
> the way of a ship on the high seas,
> and the way of a man with a girl.

Tradition has it that King Solomon authored these lines. At the risk of what the devout might therefore decry as lese-majesty, let me, for discussion's sake, debase the poetic rhythms.

> The world is wondrous, full of things at which I marvel. There is one thing in the world, though, that surpasses wonder and perplexes me utterly.

In instances of the sort first referred to, the wonder inspired is the knock on the door that gives when it swings open onto what Archimedes achieved: understanding. How about instances of the kind described in the second line of the original? Here, those in the know understand that knocking is futile. Part and parcel of the attendant attitude in such cases, 'perplexity' I am calling it, is a conviction that the cognitive El Dorado of understanding is a mirage. Bewilderment, then, for the duration. Had a Greco-Roman dramatist got hold of the Proverbist's three and four, he or she might therefore aptly have set wide-eyed astonishment, orchestrated with an Archimedean 'Eureka,' against a pensive scratching and vexed shake of the head, accompanied by a rueful Horatian 'Eheu.'

Understanding is not only a state. It is also a process through which the state is reached. Understanding, as we say, *dawns*. Come sun-up

Thursday the measure of what resisted comprehension Wednesday nightfall is sometimes taken. Should the incomprehension survive Thursday's labours, perhaps on Friday the bulb will go on. With time and trial, with a bit of luck thrown in too, could not the Proverbist's four elicit *its* 'Eureka,' thereby making a quartet of his trio?

The Book of Proverbs doesn't stand alone. Conversant with core Hebrew Scripture and imbued with its spirit, the Proverbist is a member in good standing of the communion whose articles of incorporation are the Books of Moses and, beginning with its fifth book, the Deuteronomistic History. Attention to his cultural surround positions us confidently to deny that the Proverbist rates as provisional the distinction between three and four, and at the same time to understand why he takes this line. With respect to four, bewilderment *must* in his view harden into the mentioned conviction. Positioning the Proverbist in his cultural surround also does much to neutralize the condescension that secular folk often express towards the quality of the thinking about physical reality that plays into core Scripture. It is doubly important to neutralize the condescension. The hauteur certainly makes interpretive mischief. Also, or so I am inclined to believe, it occults the truth. Too, we will gain an early appreciation that the interest of the authors of core Scripture lies elsewhere than in physical reality. Though their interest is of greater depth and of wider scope than the interest of the Proverbist, it has its focus in the same place – the distinctively human world.

Three and four the Proverbist presents as disjoint: 'Eureka' waits in the wings for the former and their ilk alone. With respect to the contents of a region of being on which men and women reflect, the region to which they in fact apply themselves most, the rod that moves the very earth lacks leverage.

For argumentation that the barrier separating three and four is impassable, much less for knockdown argumentation, one knocks in vain at the Proverbist's door. His isn't that kind of book. What the Proverbist says does however fit into the framework whose coordinates are fixed by core Scripture. If one is attuned to the ways of the Torah, from it one occasionally picks up as close to 'Q.E.D.' as an issue such as this is susceptible of.

The Proverbist and the Walrus

As a start to situating what the Proverbist says in the wider whole of which it forms a part, note that the third of the wondrous three recalls Archimedes in the tub. The density of its composing material exceeds on average the density of a volume of the surrounding water equal to the material's volume, yet the ship on the high seas stays afloat. It does so because when the cavity of the hull is factored in, the density of the whole is on average less than the density of the liquid that the whole would displace if immersed. Archimedes's insight explains the ship's bobbing on the surface and explains also why the bilge must not be allowed to rise above a certain level and why one more pallet of Pentelic marble would end up panelling Poseidon's palace.

Consider now how the items of the Proverbist's three interrelate. The eagle rides the thermals; the snake slithers through the grasses; the ship cuts the waves. True, anything can be carved into three. Take the wall staring you in the face. Though from a perceptual perspective an undifferentiated expanse of pale yellow, it can be mentally partitioned into upper, middle, and lower thirds. In preparation for wainscotting, a decorator might pencil parallel lines to give visible form to the cogitative factoring. But like Caesar's Gaul that *in partes tres omnis divisa est*, and unlike the partitioning of the wall, *Proverbs*'s parsing into heavens, earth, and watery realm isn't arbitrary. The compartmentalization is – is it not? – precisely what is found in the creation story of Genesis 1.

The compartmentalization reflects how the world manifests itself to a world dweller with eyes to see and the capacity conceptually to process the ocular stimulation. One *expects* a like partition from most cultures that orient a wide angle lens vertically at the world and formulate what is registered with a modicum of generality. In the Greek context, the opening of Hesiod's *Theogony* has Ouranos (the heavenly body) coupling with Gaia (the earthly one). Precisely 'the heavens and the earth' of the Bible's opening verse. Why then link the Proverbist's picture specifically to Genesis? A closer look at the particulars of the three sustains the claim that the parallel is not in this instance due to an inelastic or culture-invariant feature of cognitive encounter with the world. We expect any culture to set the sectors apart. Though the fact that this culture does so is not therefore remarkable, the specifics of how the sectors are staked off tell another story.

In enumerating the sectors the Proverbist is limiting himself to the natural realm as that realm appears to any man or woman strolling about in the cool of the day unconcerned about sustenance, physical safety, or the perpetuation of the species. The Proverbist is *deliberately* enforcing the limit. But the items put forward as representative constituents of the sectors are, *prima facie*, an assortment odd enough to call up Lewis Carroll's recipe for beguiling the Oysters onto the half-shell: 'shoes – and ships – and sealing wax – [and] cabbages – and kings.' Borrowing from the Walrus's list of conversation topics for bivalves, one might point to the fact that the Proverbist singles out an artefact as testimony that we have here more than just an attempt to put words to a subject's culturally uninfluenced sensory processing of the surroundings. Would not a literary type attuned to such a subject have chosen a natural thing, a fish? Although a culturally mediated explanation for mentioning the ship will presently be offered, this line of thinking is unproductive. Looking seawards from the shore, even plying the waves, one does not normally see (or expect to see) fish. A mind without an ulterior motive is far more likely to conjure up a ship when painting a mental water colour. But though this avenue of thinking is therefore a false creek, following it to the end puts the reader into the correct frame of mind. On the *qui vive* for rustlings in the rushes, he or she will be inspired to pose the following questions about the two living things listed in the first line of verse 19: the eagle and the snake.

A feathered inhabitant of the sky, certainly. We almost invariably see (and expect to see) such things as we go about our business. By contrast with ships, birds, like fish, are also not produced in factories. Why so majestic a bird as an eagle? That's one question. As for the land dwellers, would a fox or a bear not have been more natural? Though no one is surprised to find a tightly strung poetic sensibility remarking that 'narrow Fellow in the Grass,'[1] a reptile is a very odd choice coming from an uncomplicated observer – a scale odder than an eagle. Since the master of the thermals is referred to, wouldn't a lion, king of beasts, have been a more appropriate candidate from the middle region?[2] That's another question.

It's a heterogeneous mix. There is little doubt that the Proverbist is not plucking specimens at random out of the air and off the ground.[3] Casting back to the early chapters of Genesis, we can get a pretty good fix on his non-natural principle of selection.

Of the items in verse 19, the second stands out most. The reptile cannot but call up the first non-human land creature specifically mentioned in Holy Writ. By alluding to the serpent, a saliently non-natural presence in the biblical narrative, the Proverbist is indicating that the story of Genesis 2 is not telling of an earthly marvel. Whether on the rocks or in the grass, a snake is just more of nature. The beguiling serpent of Eden is outside natural history. Why should the eagle be elevated above a lesser 'winged bird' (Genesis 1:21)? This suggests an answer. God's spirit hovers 'over the face of the waters' (1:2). Accordingly, the ornithological specimen emblematic of empyreal supremacy is just what the doctor of divinity ordered to counteract the thought, sure to arise in readers of Scripture, of heaven as God's abode. The point is as before: the world of wonders is a natural place. No matter the altitude, the cognitive quest should be prosecuted in a uniform attitude. For natural explananda, seek natural explanantia.

So why a ship? The eagle corresponds to God in his heaven. The snake in Eden is a non-natural presence on earth. The immediate scriptural association of the vessel is Noah's ark. The ark, at any rate, extends the same message. No tempest tos't mariner, no merchant who must jettison goods for the sake of reaching dry land, should default explanatorily to *that* terrifying voyage across the margin of natural creation.

Three are 'too wonderful' to the Proverbist. In regard to these, the stance of perplexity is improper. Doubtless, the world contains much of the same general character as three for which the wonder does not find its 'Eureka.' The position of the Proverbist is however primarily *ontological* and only consequentially *epistemological*. The creation comprises things and occurrences that the understanding can in principle penetrate, and other things and occurrences resistant to its probings. 'Can in principle penetrate' does not mean 'has penetrated.' With respect to things and occurrences of the first class, the epistemological challenge is to catch up. But the protagonists of the Proverbist's last sector, featherless bipeds, are birds of a very different colouration than his eagle.[4]

To sum up: the word translated as 'wonder' names the proto-scientific attitude. To say this is to go beyond epistemology. It is to grant that science has a subject matter whose measure, in principle, the cognitive apparatus of the scientist can take. Providing the mimicry is continued to the end, 'Render unto Archimedes . . .' is then a suitable motto for the Proverbist's view. 'Render unto Archimedes what belongs to Archimedes. Withhold from him what does not.'

The Proverbist in Royal Society

Attention to the text inspires towards scriptural thinking about nature a more respectful attitude than prevails among casual readers of the Bible. Note in this regard that the Proverbist would have been critical even of Newton, and critical of the great man not for God's sake but for the sake of science. Pressed about the mechanism of gravitation, Newton replied testily, '*Hypotheses non fingo*.' He felt no need, he was saying, to speculate about what lies behind the appearances. (The Latin '*fingere*' seesaws between 'frame' and 'fabricate.') The equations enable the tides to be predicted, the trajectory of projectiles to be plotted. To ask more is to exit science for theology. Though much preoccupied with scanning God's mind, the Proverbist disagrees. The scientist ought in his view to have been less blasé. Though it is no doubt accidental that Newton said of hypotheses that *he* did not need them, rather than that *science* should do without, the first-person formulation is tailor-made for the Proverbist's disagreement. 'So much the worse for you.' The point might even be made that Newton is at odds with himself. To be true to the eschewal of hypotheses, should he not have said that the moon's position and the level of the oceans *co-vary*, not that the cratered body and the waters *attract*?

The philosopher John Locke, a contemporary of Newton's, endorsed a line closer to that of the Proverbist. Despite a robust scepticism as to the human mind's capacity to fathom the depths – 'Though the familiar use of things about us take off our wonder, yet it cures not our ignorance' (*Essay Concerning Human Understanding*, 3.6.9) – Locke encouraged speculation about what was transpiring on the dark side of the appearances. He himself was much attracted among hypotheses to *corpuscularianism:* material reality is at base particulate in nature, and the solid, indivisible particles act and interact in accordance with their characteristics as atoms. Had our receptive apparatus been calibrated to the micro-level, the goings on there might therefore, Locke held, have been as intelligible to us, and hence as predictable without benefit of repeated experience, as the angles of a Euclidean triangle's summing to 180°. Just so – to offer a macro-case of the sort of thing that Locke *qua* corpuscularian envisages to obtain on the micro-level – we are able immediately to 'see' that a (round) ball bearing will roll on a tilted plane, while a (cubical) block of wood will at most slide.

Corpuscularianism seems not to work in cases where Locke himself, orbiting 'the incomparable Mr. Newton,' would have been anxious for it to work. How can the principles that underlie the dynamic behaviour of sphere and cube on plane, or principles in the least like them, account for attraction across expanses of empty space? Yet in its general form, Locke's way of thinking about the world and about the mind's commerce with it still exerts a lot of pull, as testifies the case, to be enlarged upon in a moment, of the twentieth-century Newton. One might therefore flatter Locke more than he flattered himself when he described the *Essay Concerning Human Understanding* as the work of 'an under-labourer in clearing the ground a little, and removing some of the rubbish that lies in the way to knowledge.'

The General Theory of Relativity supplies an excellent latter-day example of understanding – supplies it with respect to the very Newtonian view under discussion. Relativity elicits in regard to Newtonian gravitation a perfectly Archimedean 'Eureka.'

Einstein's position can be illustrated in a location adjacent to the washroom in which you perform your ablutions. Exiting the tub, you repair to the bedchamber. The mattress, as you climb onto it, sags. *Gravity's Rainbow*, placed near the head of the bed in preparation for a soporific read, inches towards the low point of the depression. Does your belly pull the slab of printed matter? Nothing of the kind. The concavity of the mattress explains the slide. Eureka! At last, we understand the baffling business of non-contiguous and physically unconnected masses – in this case paunch and Pynchon – attracting. Masses deform the medium, space, in much the way that the body deforms the mattress. (For the illustration to work, one must abstract from the fact that the depression the body causes would be attributed to the pull of gravity. One must think geometrically.) Larger masses deform it more than do smaller ones, as many an Eve struggling to doze off next to her beefy Adam will testify. Smaller ones therefore move in the direction of larger ones. They move *downwards*, one might say, a bit figuratively. They *fall*. Other forces may counterbalance the downward movement, even overcome it. Because of its momentum the earth does not fall into the much more massive sun. Similarly, propulsive fuel can power a projectile into planetary orbit.

Spatially separated masses such as the sun and the earth are not reciprocally drawn to one another along the lines of objects tethered to the ends of a taut elastic. Not that they are reciprocally drawn to one another in a more subterranean way. Rather, gravity is to General Relativity as phlogiston is to Atomic Theory. So though Newton was wrong to cite as a reason the need to maintain a *cordon sanitaire* between theology and science, he was it turns out right to forswear hypothesizing about the mechanism of bodily attraction.

What of the Proverbist's four? The sun acts on the earth and the earth on the sun. The reciprocal influence across the empty expanse, once we get the drift of General Relativity, we understand. The mutual attraction (and repulsion) of a man and a girl? 'John and Mary? Surely you're joking.' The scriptural reverberation is patent: the allusion is to the man and the woman of Genesis 2.

The few lines quoted from Proverbs are, then, thickly intertextual. In his natural imagery of eagle, snake, and sailing ship, the Proverbist shadows the move from Genesis 1 (God hovering), through Genesis 2 (the serpent), to Genesis 7–8 (Noah, the end of the prehistoric or primordial portion of the book). With the mention of the rock on which understanding founders – that is, the man and the maid – an instantaneous shift of perception occurs, a figure–ground reversal: God the creator of everything, the temptation of the woman and the man, the mounting difficulties culminating in the slate-cleaning waters of the Flood.

The Proverbist dallied with the opposite sex. The knowledge he evinces of affairs of the body and heart could not have been procured clinically. So, *inter alia*, the Proverbist's own behaviour perplexes him. He himself is what engenders his bafflement. This again turns Archimedes upside down. It's as if the Proverbist's body, in the soak, behaved so erratically as to provide no basis for distinguishing noble from base.

Tradition has it that Proverbs is a Solomonic production. From the standpoint of the character and comportment of the king as the tradition represents them, the attribution of authorship is astute. Solomon like his father before him has the reputation of a womanizer. I shall expand on the point. Prior to doing that, let me return to Archimedes – to, more specifically, the chain of thinking of which Archimedes's constitutes a very important link.

Philosophy's Genesis

'Knowledge,' the saying goes, 'begins in wonder.' Aristotle is the saying's source. '[I]t is owing to their wonder that men both now begin and at first began to philosophise' (*Metaphysics* 982^{a}12–13). The overlap of this rendering of the Stagirite's Greek with the English-language version of Proverbs is doubly apt. Aristotle's remark accords with what the Proverbist says on the side of wonder: its cognitive completion is understanding. The remark also indicates that the remarker does not think of the road to the cognitive goal as forked. In this, Aristotle reflects, as one expects that he would, the philosophical position of Greece.

'Philosophical position.' What is philosophy? Aristotle does not say that the attitude of wonder is sufficient to lead to philosophy. His formulation does however slant in that direction. The suggestion is very much that responded to properly, the attitude will bring philosophy forth. But why might the attitude not generate the conviction spoken of earlier? Examining the standard histories of philosophy, we find bewilderment towards the world being dismissed from the very start as benighted. Perplexity is equated with confusion, which even by the Proverbist's lights has to be cleared up or overcome or eliminated, not funded with research grants. The arena of mature response has no place for perplexity. The foundation for Aristotle's internally unified treatment is laid well before he appears on the scene.

Let me quote a modern historian of philosophy's account of his subject's genesis. In identifying that which makes a style of thinking philosophical (as soon becomes apparent, 'philosophical' implies 'rational'), Jonathan Barnes's first mark is the absence of fuddled appeal to supernatural forces and magic.

> [T]he Presocratics . . . hit upon that special way of looking at the world which is the scientific or rational way. They saw the world as something ordered and intelligible, its history following an explicable course and its different parts arranged in some comprehensible system. The world was not a random collection of bits, its history was not an arbitrary series of events.
>
> Still less was it a series of events determined by the will – or the caprice – of the gods.[5]

If Barnes is right, do the Presocratics not dogmatically foreclose on a potentially viable property? As Barnes tells it, the characteristic attitude prior to the advent of philosophy is not wonder. It is bewilderment. Bewilderment is the response to the world that the earliest philosophers put behind them. Works with mythic content, scriptural works prominent among them, are typical expressions of bewilderment. The philosophers slammed those works shut and opened a new book, the Book of Nature.[6]

Working up to a section on Thales of Miletus, the person honoured in standard histories with the label 'First Philosopher,' Barnes mentions the poems of Homer and Hesiod. 'All this,' he writes, 'is myth; but it is, as it were, scientific myth' ('Precursors,' 56). The purpose of his book being through an examination of its origins to illuminate philosophy's distinctiveness, Barnes would have excluded 'all this' had it in his view lacked proto-philosophical status. Inclusion would otherwise have placed Barnes in the line that goes back to that retailer of the extra-curricular doings of and around the earliest philosophical thinkers, Diogenes Laertius. Barnes's point is that the earliest philosophers could have drawn positively from, say, the *Theogony*.[7]

Only a slug of a person is unmoved by the starry heavens above. The Proverbist is duly awed. Yet the Proverbist, no less than Barnes's philosophers, is bent on keeping the response to three from the clutches of mythopoets and mystagogues. Like the position of Barnes's philosophers, the Proverbist's considered position about the natural realm thus echoes the cheeky slogan of Las Vegas's Tourist Bureau: explanation of what happens there stays there. No horoscopy. No haruspication. Here however the truth-seeking minds part company. The Proverbist does not dismiss perplexity in regard to four as unworthy. He sees it as a legitimate reaction, one requiring a different response.

The position at philosophy's inception, as Barnes describes it, is this. From the standpoint of the nascent way of thinking, bewilderment is void of cognitive respectability. Barnes implies it to be 'irrational,' an adjective still more harshly dismissive than 'void of cognitive respectability.' Recur to the quotation three paragraphs back. In using 'or' ampliatively (as in 'common or garden') rather than to specify alternatives ('coffee or tea'), Barnes opens two-way traffic between 'unscientific' and 'irrational.' From the standpoint of the new intellectual kid on the block, this marks the Proverbist's bewilderment as infantile.

In a more extensive treatment of the origins of philosophy, Barnes strengthens this *suggestio falsi* through the use of some explicitly biblical imagery. The world of thinking of Thales and those who followed him Barnes likens to Eden.[8] To be sure, Barnes is not engaging in biblical exegesis. Still, the allusion to Genesis is revealing. What it reveals is *attitude*. Barnes is having himself some fun. But, as the saying goes, he who laughs last laughs best. The fact is that from the Bible's standpoint philosophy is, if anything, *pre*-Edenic. From Eden onwards philosophy is cognitively inappropriate to the subject matter. To see that the world, as an object of philosophical exploration, is mapped in Genesis 1 is to gain a quite different perspective on the quality of biblical thinking. It is to see that biblical thinkers have thought through what they are usually represented as never having thought of.

Proverbs is in a line that spools out from the Bible. Archimedes, for his part, is a later link in the Greek chain that Barnes is following. Let me look a bit more closely at the chain's earliest links.

Archimedes discovered a general truth about a solid's displacement of a liquid. It happens that the solid from which he learned the truth was his own body. Archimedes has a predecessor, Thales, arguably the first link in the chain, who maintains that self-knowledge generally has the same character as the self-knowledge that Archimedes acquired in the tub. As Thales saw it, men and women are no different, that is, than the Proverbist's three. Thales, as we say nowadays, *naturalizes*.

To Thales are attributed a number of general claims about nature, the best known of these being the claim that water is the basis or principle – the *arche* – of all things. The meaning of the identification is contested in scholarly forums. Could the fact that it is essential for life be the ground on which Thales counts water as basic? While no less an authority than Aristotle says so, the interpretation exacts a cost. Rocks and stones are not alive. On this reading Thales's 'all things' therefore loses the generality required for the proposition to have a footing equal to that of, say, Einstein's principle about the convertibility of mass and energy. A mildly specialized fact about the natural realm as we encounter it in the course of our perambulations is that water is pretty much the only substance to occur in liquid form. (Water is the only *carbon-free* substance to occur in liquid form at standard temperatures and pressures. Some might wish that oil, also liquid at STP, was as abundant. They should be careful what they wish. One part motor oil can pollute a million parts water. Were the hydrocarbon anywhere near as plentiful, the groundwater would poison plants and animals.) A similar sort of fact, though this one is not the preserve of specialists, is that water is encountered in our everyday environment in all three physical forms: solid, liquid, gas. Water's trinitarian character makes for the following conjecture about Thales's 'basis of all' claim: other things are yet denser or yet more rarefied versions of the same basic stuff. It confirms the conjecture that Thales's immediate successor, his co-urbanite Anaximander, identified as the basic principle – what he styled 'το ἄπειρον,' sc., 'the indefinite,' hence something common capable of assuming various more definite (phenomenal) forms.

The precise meaning of the proposition about water is contested. On the immediately preceding reading, the reading that I prefer, the proposition means that all physical things have a single (meta)physical basis. That reduction to a narrow explanatory basis is something that modern scientists try to achieve in their attempts to find a Theory of Everything. As the case may be, a different claim of Thales's – that 'all things are full of gods' (in Aristotle, *On the Soul*, 411^{a}9–10) – has greater import for present purposes. Here is Aristotle's gloss (405^{a}19–21): 'to judge from what is recorded about him [Thales] seems to have held soul to be a motive force, since he said that the magnet has a soul in it because it moves the iron.'

'Soul,' transliterated from the Greek, is 'psyche.' The magnet, according to Thales, is enpsyche-ed. (In a display of verbal agility, Barnes, calling upon the Latin, offers 'animated.') Thales does not in saying this have it in mind to implant in the lodestone that which inspires so much religious talk. Consistently with his general physicalist tendency, Thales means that what is widely regarded as a non-natural or extra-natural principle is at base nothing of the kind. This, speaking of Thales's *arche*, is H-to-O with a vengeance! An enterprise that will reduce Human to Objective.

Is the enterprise viable? That is a very large question. Our question, a historical question of smaller size, is why in Greece at this stage of human inquiry anyone should have conceived the reduction, let alone pursued it as a serious project. Isn't the characterization of the magnet as animated a pun, not a thought? Why, to transfer to the vocabulary of the scriptural document, are bewilderment and perplexity not rated as reasonable, mature responses deserving of respect and elaboration rather than relegation to the annals of befuddlement and error? Why should *philosophy* not have been dismissed as cognitively suspect, even frivolous? In Barnes's account of the emergence of philosophy we found a conversion of 'unscientific' with 'irrational' and a linkage of irrationality with explanatory appeal to the gods. That supplies the syntax of the explanation. Now the semantics.

God and the Gods

In the Greek context of which Barnes is speaking, the mentioned connections have cultural anchorage and hence can be motivated from within. While the gods in the Greek frame are supernatural, they are not extra-natural; they are not transcendent of space and time. Though deathless, the gods are still created. Since the gods are so closely associated with extra-human nature,[9] Thales's claim that all things are full of gods is less a departure than it might initially seem. The Thalean démarche hitches a ride on an extant vector at the heart of Greek culture. Using the borrowed momentum, it then boldly goes where no earlier thinker had gone. So Aristotle's promotion of wonder over bewilderment is not in that conceptual environment a repudiation of a presumptively legitimate cognitive response. The older gods are not being exorcized. They are being sanitized.

In the biblical frame, something quite different. The distinctively human is linked to the divine nearly in the way of identity. As Genesis 1 has it, men and women are 'made in [God's] image, according to [his] likeness' (26). And God is transcendent and uncreated. (The likeness would explain why the Proverbist's four is set so sharply apart from his three. Four's *arche* is irreducibly different.) From this perspective, the Greek way of thinking is more 'Eastern' than the biblical. One mark of the differential affinity is the holism that is characteristic of Greek thought, and its associated preoccupation with fate. Holism is recessive in the biblical context because God, the paradigm or model, is figured in a strong sense as a separate individual; and predetermination is not a panicky worry for those in the force field of the Bible because God, the agent *par excellence,* is more chess master of destiny than its pawn. In saying these things I am not of course reporting on God's character. Neither am I committing myself on the truth. Perhaps we should hit the panic button. Here and now, the point is restrictedly interpretive. The portrayal of God gives expression to the individualistic (antiholistic) and controller-of-fate (effective agent) self-image of those men and women who do the portraying. Note too that genealogy in the Bible is rarely linked to specific life outcomes. True enough, a biblical character is wise to avoid exiting the birth canal first. Systematically, the first to emerge are eventually overtaken. But this attack on primogeniture is a deliberate delinkage of life prospects from biology, not a claim to the effect that latecomers are made of sterner genetic stuff.

The difference drawn implies that for biblical thinking, God is *not* full of gods. On Aristotle's reading, to say that X is full of gods means that X moves other things as a magnet moves iron filings. It means that a magnet's moving iron filings is a model, no doubt an overly simply model yet a model still, of how X operates. In the biblical story, God very pointedly does not move things in that way. In the first chapter of Genesis the paradigm act of creation finds God doing things with words. As its exemplar of A-getting-B-to-do-C the Bible takes a case of the sort that makes sense primarily among men and women: asking, commanding, threatening, cajoling, begging, and so on – which puts a bit of English on the Johannine declaration that in the beginning was the word. When it comes to lodestones and what they affect, no sense at all attaches to the idea. They do not ask; nothing responds.

This difference, along with the differences immediately bound up with it, underlies many of the contrasts between the Greek and the biblical views. In particular, the differences explain why the side of bewilderment is so prominent in the biblical frame and why its development in the Greek frame assumed so different a form – expressive in the hands of those who were, like the Proverbist, sensitive to its peculiarities, dismissive in the hands of those given over to more abstract thought and inquiry. The issue between the parties is whether human reality responds to or violates Thales's 'all things' and 'everything.'

To begin to wind down this phase of discussion, let me illustrate and explain how deep the commitment to perplexity is on the biblical side, or, more precisely, how high it is. For it is heaven-high.

A Higher King's Displeasure

Hiero was royally displeased about the state of the crown. Taking instruction from Archimedes as to how he might establish its constitution, the king no doubt called for a big bowl of water and then summoned the suspected fiddlers. Like the baker encountered by Joseph in the Egyptian lock-up (another court functionary whose service had angered his ruler), the artisans certainly faced the music if in the test of their mettle they came up light.

Hiero II of Syracuse is one of several kings relevant to our discussion. Another is the King of Kings – the creator of the earth that Archimedes vaunted he could shake with a stick. This king too was royally displeased. *His* crowning glory, the world over which he held sway, had lost its shine virtually before the sun had got the hang of circling the sky. But who in *this* case had done the fiddling? God himself and no other was the brain behind the enterprise. God himself and no other had produced the design and fired up the forge. This king was sorely vexed by the state of affairs. So sorely vexed was he that after several abortive attempts with carrot and stick to set things right, he put one of his subjects (a very simple-minded and compliant one, as it happens, prepared, without asking questions, to keep to the tiller) into a tub, and consigned the rest to a watery grave.

The story of Archimedes and the crown probably contains a Troy ounce or two of truth. Hiero, a real person, was in Greek political terms a king. This 'King of Kings' talk will not however be allowed to pass as factual; not, anyway, by my readers. To bring the talk closer to earth, setting up in the process a real contrast with Hiero and Archimedes, I call upon several historical personages who, like the Pope, are traditionally represented as having accreditation from the heavenly kingdom.

The Book of Proverbs is traditionally attributed to King Solomon. Whatever its authorship (the tradition has its scholarly detractors), the core part of the Bible, as it has come down to us, *does* trace to the newly formed Israelite monarchy: to King David and to his son and heir. Not that anyone at the time envisioned a book of the sort now pored over in our seminaries and prayed from in our pews. Rather, court scribes produced written materials that, whatever their local inspiration, later lent themselves to scriptural use. Such being the case, one would expect the core part of the text to reflect the contemporary thinking of those responsible for it.[10] Certainly, the Book of Judges does just that. The pressing concern is with the issue of kingship. 'In those days,' Judges concludes (21:25), 'there was no king in Israel; all the people did what was right in their own eyes.' One would expect texts composed after the monarchy had been established, texts that narrated the run-up, to prepare for the first coronation. After all, the monarchy came into being, and a minimal historical sense will incline one to think that its emergence met a need.

Genesis asserts that men and women are made in God's likeness. Likeness is, logicians say, a *symmetrical* relation. From the likeness of men and women to God follows the likeness of God to men and women. As I see it, on a more specific level, a level that might be styled 'biographical,' God is *made in the likeness* of those founding monarchs, especially God's especial favourite, David. The claim will be defended in the sequel. For now, I want to focus on the flesh-and-blood biblical king mentioned most frequently in past pages. The actions of *this* king supply, we shall see, a conversational topic for 'oy'-sters.

'Solomonic Wisdom'

Asked what he would have from the Lord if he were given *carte blanche*, Solomon requests wisdom. Well pleased that Solomon does not solicit wealth and power, gratified that he does not express the wish that his enemies be smote, God proceeds to confer on the king 'an understanding mind to govern your people, able to discern between good and evil' (1 Kings 3:9).[11] No hyperbole puffs up the claim that men and women are from the biblical point of view uniquely God-like among creatures in their *modus vivendi*. For the life that inspired *God* was breathed into their original alone. Just so, Solomon having been invested from on high with wisdom, no exaggeration attaches to saying that, for the Bible, the son of David is uniquely God-like in understanding and discernment.

It's bad form to look a gift horse in the mouth. When the giver is God, it is, one might think, terrible form. But consider the following.

The story of the two harlots and the disputed maternity – which is told in 1 Kings 3 right after the description of the donation – is an epitome of Solomon's wisdom. By proposing to cut the infant in two, Solomon is able to identify the rightful claimant. The God-given wisdom supplies him with the wherewithal for uniting mother and child. What occurs, however, after Solomon the sapient lawgiver and sagacious dispenser of justice passes from the world? Immediately the body is united with the ground (Solomon's burial is reported in the final verse of 1 Kings 11), the ground that David united, fractures, and fractures for the duration (the cleft palace is described cheek by jowl in 1 Kings 12). The national baby that Solomon inherited from his father, the baby whose integrity had cost David so much to secure, including the death of his (ironically named) favourite son Absalom, is cut in two.

The wisdom that God confers upon Solomon, wisdom to 'govern your people,' proves politically ineffective!

This is my understanding of the story that has given us the adjective 'Solomonic.' As I see it, those behind the text are cold-eyed and critical, though realistic rather than cynical. (No wonder that the conclusion of the story of Solomon's request for wisdom douses the reader with cold water: 'Then Solomon awoke; it had been a dream' [1 Kings 3:15].) In the view of those behind the text, the perplexity about human affairs is sky-high: the wisdom that doesn't work is God's wisdom. Elevating the problem into Heaven stamps a seal of finality upon it. The problem with the united kingdom is not a local one stemming from a particular flesh-and-blood person named 'Solomon.' To say that God is in the same condition is to say that better cannot be done. And, of course, in the chapters of Genesis that present the primordial history, God's capacities, great as they are, fall short of ensuring a well-running world.

Right after the passage from Proverbs, the writer offers the following (30:20):

> This is the way of an adulteress;
> she eats, and wipes her mouth,
> and says, 'I have done no wrong.'

'Eats and wipes her mouth.' Euphemism only heightens the revulsion. Does Scripture present us with a correspondent in adultery who only magnifies the offence in the attempt to cover the tracks? Most definitely, it does. And in engineering the death of Uriah, King David violated a prior commandment into the bargain.

God's mirror image: David. God's star pupil: Solomon. Why does this model human being fail, this earthly spitting image of God? Why does this knower of good and bad fail, this divinely gifted king among the wise? The answer is in both instances as before: more than just elusive, effective understanding is illusory. 'A man and a girl?' As the fifteenth-century lyric has it, 'Believe and leave to wonder.' To regard what engenders perplexity as amenable to being fixed once and for all rather than managed piecemeal is to confuse men and women for something they are not.[12] It is to mistake men and women for the likes of eagles, snakes, and heaving ships. With respect to the jewel and pinnacle of creation, the beauty of the world, the King of Kings is no philosopher-king.

In Archimedes's story, the investigator himself is the variable. Given his wayward behaviour as Scripture conveys it, Solomon, who 'loved many foreign women' (1 Kings 11:1), is an excellent object of the Proverbist's – that is, traditionally, Solomon's – thoughts and reflections. Solomon is very much like a CEO with a roving eye on an unlimited expense account who finds himself in a distant city full of temptations. Nor, details apart, is Solomon's comportment unique. Though the credit limits of the commoner keep *our* roving in check, we could each of us I daresay look in the mirror and see an image and likeness of the king. But the resemblance between the Archimedean case and the Solomonic one – for symmetry's sake, though appropriately given the mentioned comportment, we might place Solomon in a hot tub – is structural only. In the first the reflexively curious principal understands himself: 'Eureka.' In the other, his own workings come over as a puzzle: 'Eheu.' Descendants of the king might couch the puzzled reaction in their non-classical language: 'Oy vey.'

Perplexed by his creation, God fashioned a small world: Noah's ark. A tub to place alongside Archimedes's. The first experiment had failed. Another try was to be made.

Mankind in a tub. It's an appropriate image. To be sure, the Proverbist regards the way of a ship on the seas as capable of being understood. Such understanding is what mariners, designers of vessels, and students of current affairs achieve and can be called upon to impart. This tub, and these waters, are not however natural ones.

A position taken about the earth in early Greek philosophy supplies a nice figure of the human situation, as the Bible sees it. Anaximander, Thales's successor, explained why the earth doesn't move. The earth is stationary, he said, because it is in the middle, *meteôros*. Being in the middle, the earth is in equilibrium.

What Anaximander explained (that the explanandum is imaginary does not dull the brilliance of the explanans), the Bible also explains. God, it is written, 'hangs the earth upon nothing' (Job 26:7). As an account of the position of the globe, this is hopeless. The scriptural concern is not however a physical one. The point is about the earth as the abode of men and women. It is not about the earth as a piece of the physical universe. The point is that the position of men and women cannot be plotted by the physical markers. Men and women are not like Archimedes in the tub or like Newton beneath the apple tree. They too are *meteôros* – in mid-air.

Alexander Pope penned a philosophical reflection on the human condition, *An Essay on Man*. (The quote is Epistle II ll:3–8.) Could anyone be misled by his geographical vocabulary?

> Placed on this isthmus in a middle state,
> A being darkly wise, and rudely great:
> With too much knowledge for the sceptic side,
> With too much weakness for the stoic's pride.
> He hangs between; in doubt to act, or rest,
> In doubt to deem himself a god, or beast;

Athens and Jerusalem

Archimedes laid down a trace in the public memory through, most of all, his 'Eureka.' Thales, too, is best remembered because of a specific historical event. Thales (so the story goes) foretold an eclipse of the sun in his part of the sky on, in our reckoning, 28 May 585 BCE. The prediction itself was a distillate of the new way of looking at the world, the way of Archimedes in his tub and of Newton beneath his tree. To have been able to figure out that the lunar body would displace the solar one on precisely that day in precisely that location, Thales had had painstakingly to plot movements that were recognized on a gross level to have some regularity to them, and then he had to extrapolate forward.

The starry heavens are marvellous. Thales understood them. But the story attracts present interest for another reason. Thales's uranography turns out to have been significant both for the rise of the Athens, whose cultural contributions continue to be celebrated, and also for the survival of the Jerusalem out of which the Bible, a living document too, came. This we can see if we play out a few more links of the causal chain that begins with the eclipse.

Thales's prediction had a practical application. Herodotus records (*Histories* Book One, 74) that the day of the eclipse witnessed a battle between the Medes and the Lydians. Having got wind of the occultation – Thales hailed from and operated out of Miletus, on the Aegean coast of Asia Minor, adjacent, then, to Lydia – the Lydians were able to hold their own against the foe, whose fighters were not prepared for the darkness at midday. What might have been a rout of the Lydian force thus ended inconclusively.

The stand-off kept the Medes from dominating the whole of the region. Hegemony, had they achieved it, would likely have resulted in greater internal stability. As it was, a few short decades later the Persians, a subject group within the Median orbit, rose up against the throne. With the connivance of disgruntled nobles, they gained control as Cyrus defeated the Median king Astyages in 549 BCE. Once in power, Cyrus ('The Great') justified the confidence reposed in him by extending Persian governance in all directions. The business with Lydia in the west was finished; the Babylonians to the south were subdued. When the dust had settled, Cyrus gave the Israelites, in exile in Babylon since the destruction visited upon them in 586 by the Babylonians, the green light to return to the Promised Land and to rebuild God's House, garnering for himself by this Moses-type act a series of glowing biblical press clippings unexampled for one outside the Israelite communion. (See the final verses of Isaiah 44 and the opening verses of Isaiah 45.) Jumping forward four decades to the reign of Cyrus's grandson Xerxes, we find the Athenian fleet smashing the Persian expeditionary naval force in the Strait of Salamis in 480. For, as it turned out, the numerous Persian vessels were unable to manoeuvre effectively in the cramped waters of the strait. Confusion in their battle formation gave the day to the smaller and more mobile Athenian fleet. After this famous victory, the Greeks completed the job in 479 at Plataea and Mycale.

Just as the stand-off between the Lydians and the Medes had been instrumental in the rise of Persia, so the repulse of the Persian invaders set the stage for Periclean Athens.

Thales's prediction, then, saved the Israelites and their Temple *and* constituted a link in a relatively short chain leading to, as we say, the glory that was Greece.[13]

Even ignoring the tenuousness of the causality, the story might still be blown off as froth on the grounds that the outcomes for Athens and for Jerusalem were different: on the latter side, bewilderment, on the former, understanding. That, however, is incorrect.

Perplexity is the dominant cognitive attitude in the Bible. At every turn, sources of bafflement lie in wait. On that which elicits the attitude, Scripture focuses intensely. Wonder, whose cognitive completion is understanding, applies to the extra-human realm only, and in this realm

Jerusalem is little interested. Understanding, the cognitive completion of wonder, is what philosophy, as it arose in Greece, sees as the sole proper cognitive goal. From the philosophical standpoint perplexity is in the best case romanticized wonder. In the worst case it is irrational, irredeemably so. The philosophical standpoint is not however the only Greek standpoint. A whole line of thinking on the Athenian side, a line that for us will begin with Homer and proceed through the tragedians of the classical period, focuses in the attitude of perplexity on things. A whole line of thinking here is, then, biblical in character.

What do Athens and Jerusalem stand to learn from each other? The early Church Father Tertullian posed the question. *Quid ergo Athenis et Hierosolymis*. Pressed to be explicit (and he was a dangerous man to press) Tertullian would have thundered a categorical '*Nihil*': in regard to human nature and destiny, Athens the worldly has nothing to teach Jerusalem the spiritual. The secular men and women who constitute the primary audience for *this* enterprise are likely to see the question, my question too, as, like Terutullian's, rhetorical; though, as the discussion of philosophy's Genesis has shown, *their* 'Nothing' would privilege Athens. The gospel out of Athens, the gospel of science and philosophy, is in their view the gospel truth. In the mentioned regard Athens has superseded Jerusalem.

What do Athens and Jerusalem stand to learn from each other in regard to the reality of men and women? The short answer is: 'A lot.' On the side of perplexity non-philosophical Athens and biblical Jerusalem are partners. For approaching what is distinctive about men and women from different angles and anatomizing the distinctiveness in different ways, their partnership is mutually beneficial. Extracting and amplifying what the voices on the two sides have to say and arranging them into an instructive dialogue, instructive each one to the other and both together instructive to us, is the task ahead.

Breadth and Depth

From a cultural perspective the Bible is narrowly focused on human reality, as we in the West regard that reality. The Bible conceives men and women as human beings throughout – as occupying a special place in the world, and, for having that place, as constituting an autonomous locus of primary value. Starting in the archaic age and proceeding through the classical period, the Greek documents modulate towards the same conception. Since, however, they are not focused on it *ab initio*, they range more broadly. The men and women whom we encounter in the earliest Greek materials – Homer's warriors, for example – conceive themselves differently. The very idea that their lives have intrinsic value they would find preposterous. The Greek materials thus contain the wherewithal for a more granular, diachronic or genetic-type account of some of the things that the Bible treats as baseline. Indeed, Homer in his dramatic style furnishes just such an account. It could well be that the culture to which the Bible belongs covered the same territory. But the fact (and a striking fact it is) is that from that culture all that we have in the way of written matter is the Bible, and the fact is that the Bible contains only telltale traces of what preceded, usually treating earlier cultural formations in the objectionable ('Whiggish') mode of *pre hoc ergo propter hoc*.

The cultural breadth on the Greek side is however accompanied by a lack of depth. Here the Bible does much better, penetrating the foundations of the distinctive reality of men and women. It provides a suitable basis for what might be called 'the anti-philosophical view.' I will, as I said, arrange the two voices into a dialogue. The Greek materials will be conscripted to overcome the narrowness in the Bible's representation of the cultural options; the biblical materials will be enlisted to make good a theoretical shallowness on the Greek side.

Proverbs is very much a product of reflection on men and women and their ways. I stated that like the Proverbist's interest, the interest of the writers of core Scripture is narrowly focused on distinctively human reality. How very narrowly will now be shown.

2
Man's Estate

David's Question

In counterpoint with an excited blurt from a wise man who counselled a king, lines traditionally ascribed to a wise king set the preceding chapter's agenda. To home in on the scene of core scriptural action we go back one link from Solomon along the chain of the Israelite monarchy.

David, in the book of the Bible with which *he* is traditionally credited, addresses the following question to God: 'What are human beings that you are mindful of them, mortals that you care for them?' (Psalms 8:4) On first hearing, the question sounds rhetorical. 'Why on earth should God take a positive interest?' is however inaccurate as a paraphrase. God's concern for men and women is as David sees it a fact. 'On what basis does God care?' To *that* he seeks an answer. To be sure, difficulty in identifying the basis, or problems affecting the basis identified, will sow seeds of doubt about the deity's attitude. 'Nowadays,' the novelist Kurt Vonnegut quipped, 'paranoia is an act of faith.' Retrofitting the witticism to self-regard, the cynical would even say, and say in advance, that David is deluded heavenwards to croon ''S wonderful, 'S marvelous, That you should care for me.' To get to David's answer, and in part thereby to defend him against the charge of living a fantasy, let me start off from the sceptic side.

The Greeks of the archaic and classical periods never tire of repeating: man is puny and insignificant. Here, from the *Iliad*, is a representative expression of the thought [6:171–176].[1] The speaker is Glaucus, commander of the contingent from Lycia.

> Like the generations of leaves, the lives of mortal men.
> Now the wind scatters the old leaves across the earth,

now the living timber bursts with the new buds
and spring comes round again. And so with men:
as one generation comes to life, another dies away.

The Greeks of whom we are speaking regard their own fragility and fleetingness as a reason, a *compelling* reason, for divine indifference. A scene in Book 24 of the *Iliad* [613–614] even finds Achilles making indifference sound like the lesser of the evils apt to befall men and women from on high.

So the immortals spun our lives that we, we wretched men
live on to bear such torments – the gods live free of sorrows.

'So,' the Greeks *would* ask rhetorically, 'why, except for sport, would the power who created everything, sovereign of the universe, attend to a veritable nonentity, here today and, under the species of eternity, gone later today?'

David disagrees. God is not paring his nails while men and women moil. Nor is he contriving torments to make them rue the day. Though the accuracy of the Greeks' description of the human condition cannot be disputed (we *are* a sorry lot, that's for sure), David would not however be content to put God's favourable notice on the basis of Matthew's claim (10:29) that no sparrow falls in the forest but God knows it.[2] Whatever specific reasoning might underlie David's discontent, in logic he would be right to be dissatisfied. The truth of 'B does not escape A's attention' does not underwrite 'B is significant to, that is, makes a difference to or has meaning for, A.' Nor does the inference go through if we add – what the Greeks would have resisted adding save counterfactually – that A is maximally caring. Presumably, the Gospel writer doesn't mean to imply that God sheds tears over a stone that dripping water is slowly eroding. Some things could, that is, lie in a region of indifference of – and hence be left to their own devices even by – one without a scintilla of malignance.[3]

Another point bears yet more directly on David's dissatisfaction with (as I am taking it here) the New Testament answer. Compared to God *everything* is puny and insignificant: a galaxy of a billion suns is as puny and insignificant as a mote of dust. But David is asking, specifically, about creatures such as we. He is seeking an answer that isn't reached, as the Gospel writer's (question-begging) answer is reached, by substituting 'human beings' for 'x' in 'For every value of x, God, being God, cares about x.' God's regard for us must be, distinctively, a regard *for us*, not a dusting of a favourable attitude spread about more liberally.

A gimlet-eyed consideration of the condition of men and women gives abundant reason to query the proposition that God extends to us his grace. Even allowing against the massive evidence that we are so favoured, the point in and of itself is still of little help. Were all creatures peas in a pod from the divine perspective, differing *solo numero*, God's graciousness towards men and women would be arbitrary. In his regard for us God would be much like the purblind priest of Anatole France's *Penguin Island* who, mistaking the flightless bipeds for humans, baptizes a flock of the birds. As a matter both of theology and (more important here) of scriptural interpretation, one must resist the idea that what the Bible portrays God as doing it portrays God as doing on a whim or arbitrarily, much less out of short-sightedness. The negative consequences of succumbing are profound. Assume that all the jugs in the dairy case contain the same grade of milk. Assume that they are from the same producer and have the same 'best before' date. To whom but a chromosome-damaged cretin does it make a difference which jug is lugged home from the supermarket? If the shopper ahead picks up the jug that we've eyed over his or her shoulder, we reach for another without missing a beat. The answer about caring, that is, either presupposes that God has a ground for making a distinction between humankind and the rest; or else, for likening God's warmth towards men and women to that of the shopper who picks a fight over a particular jug, it leaves David's question still shopping for an answer.

For all save the most myopic priest, separating humans from beasts isn't difficult. Unlettered men and women make the distinction, not only zoologists who have earned their stripes. The case is not however much advanced by these truths. Do dogs go about happily sniffing the cats whose paths they cross? Do they happily allow cats to sniff *them*? Beasts, that is, are proficient also. Yet one expects that God's preference is not from the Psalmist's viewpoint like that of a pet owner – let alone the pet – for, say, canines over felines. As the Psalmist sees it, it could not have gone the other way.

This locates the operative question. It is the characteristically philosophical question,[4] viz., the Socratic 'What Is X?' question. X being humankind in this case, it is the central question of philosophical anthropology.

What is it about men and women that makes us, from the Bible's perspective, an object of divine regard? This question differs from the earlier question as to why God, being God, should care for things so insignificant. Sought is an expansion of X in 'Men and women are X' that does not net, as 'X = part of the creation' nets, absolutely anything whose existence is consistent in logic with a smile on God's countenance. Sought is an expansion that explains why, because of what *they* are, not just because of what God is, *men and women alone or in some uniquely close way* are objects of heavenly concern. The expansion might be compatible with the puniness and fragility of men and women. In fact, it had better be. For puny and fragile we certainly are, more so than much else alongside which we inhabit the world, and in any case puny and fragile enough justifiably to think of ourselves that way despite that a large number of things in the world do not rise even to our limited level of stoutness.

As with the son, so with the father. Like the Proverbist, the Psalmist is immersed in and committed to core Scripture. Some might see proof of committed immersion in Psalms' having five books. But though the division *is* a reverent salute to the Pentateuch, like the division of the Homeric epics equinumerously with the letters of the Greek alphabet it is a later editorial move. Decisive evidence is however plentiful. Referring to human beings the Psalmist says in verse 6 of Psalm 8:

> You have given them dominion
> over the works of your hands;

A clear quote of Genesis 1:26.

These last lines raise our question again – in a more specific form. Could God have accorded dominion to some subhuman species? Certainly, God could have created a four-legged predator so effective as to have relegated men and women to caves and burrows. The unavoidable image here is chilling: a fanged beast whose dietary needs (or junk food cravings) only human flesh can satisfy. However, to quote the aptly named Robert Frost, 'for destruction ice is also great and would suffice.' Perhaps an insidious and fast-mutating virus is in the works as we speak. But if God had created the fanged ferocity, it would not in the biblical sense have had dominion, any more than would the deep-freeze or the bug properly be described as dominators should either of them appear on the scene. Neither would any of these come to merit the description 'dominator' if once they appeared they proceeded to extinguish human life. (Appreciating the 'would not' and the 'neither would' waits on closer analysis of the biblical idea of domination.) At any rate, a reader who is prepared to countenance the idea that God could have made dominant a subhuman or inorganic thing, or who says that when on the afternoon of the sixth day God creates humankind he *alienates* dominion from some already existing species, is deeply out of touch with how the text functions. Such a one, I shall also argue, is out of touch with the truth too.

Dogs do not sniff amicably at cats. This they do to their own – a clue to answering David's question. The basis for God's regard is, in the Bible, the likeness of men and women to God. God has regard for us because God cares about *himself*: God has self-regard.[5] Crucially, the underlying logical order here is of course the reverse. We represent God as caring in some exclusive way for us because we care for ourselves. (The Greeks do not represent the higher beings in this manner. This is what makes the Greek case of such interest for comparison and contrast.) We care for ourselves in a way that we do not care for other created things. We care *differentially* for ourselves. Our caring *can* leave home. But it begins near the hearth and for the most part does not wander very far. Consideration of cases in which we must choose ('your monkey or your life') makes this plain.

Let us take stock. Two points have been collected, one more general, one more specific. We distinguish ourselves from other elements of creation. We care for ourselves. That is the more general point. The more specific point, still to be elaborated, is that men and women dominate the rest of the creatures.

Xenophanes's Mockery

The pre-Socratic thinker Xenophanes, perhaps the first of the breed of rational theologians, asserted that if cows had religious-type belief systems the gods in their creeds would be horned and would low; as for horses, *theirs* would prohibit with neighs.[6] Think what we may of the Bishop of Hippos's mockery of the contemporary forms of religious belief, the underlying point has application to the Bible. It applies even more to the Bible than to, say, Homer, whose writings Xenophanes is, according to the doxography, sending up. The anthropomorphism of the Bible with regard to God goes right to the bottom. The biblical theological position is *theistic*. In respect of psychology God genuinely resembles men and women. God has wishes, hopes, plans. He feels the full gamut of emotions. God, in short, is a person. By contrast, the ascription of desires and plans and beliefs to the Greek deities, like the description of the westward wind as a wayward wind, is more figurative than literal.

What Xenophanes says may seem to leave the answer given to David's question in tatters. Each kind cares about itself. Like like like. If so, a cow would, *per impossibile*, answer *its* David's question differently. The bipedal response it would reject in favour of a four-legged one. Such being the case, 'we care *differentially* for ourselves' reduces to 'men and women are special *from their own viewpoint*,' and this it would seem *is* an instantiation of the more general 'for each type of thing, things of the type are, for being of the type, distinguishable from things of any other type, and behave differentially in regard to its members.' Or, as the Romans put it, *pares cum paribus facillime congregantur*.

The Bible sees something distinctively distinctive about men and women. The double-distinctiveness is explicit in the creation story – a story that the Psalmist accepts. Though in Genesis 1 men and women come into being along with the other creatures, they are not just creatures among creatures. Them, and them alone, God fashions in his image and according to his likeness. In Genesis 2 God breathes life into the man whom he makes, and into nothing else. Both cases see God sharing with or projecting onto or transferring to men and women something of himself – *his* likeness, life of the sort that inspires *him*. Men and women are, then, God-like. The distinctive distinctiveness of men and women follows directly: mankind differs from dogkind in a way that dogkind does not differ from catkind, and Adam differs from Rover in a way that Rover does not differ from Felix. It might however seem too high a price to pay to validate this result to require literal acceptance of the Genesis story. But isn't Xenophanes vindicated unless the requirement is satisfied?

We come back to the Proverbist's three and four. In this chapter a fuller defence of the distinction, of the distinction *as the Proverbist understands it*, is mounted. As a matter of interpretation, it will be shown that core Scripture is devoted almost exclusively to four. Asking for proof that the Bible's philosophical position about human nature (its *anti-philosophical* position) is correct is asking too much. Still, attention to the text substantially disables the preceding criticism. At minimum, it puts Xenophanes on the defensive.

David's question has to be answered otherwise than through instantiation. It is by ascribing to men and women a unique intimacy with God that Scripture seems to accomplish this. The task, then, is clear: it is to supply a non-instantiating answer, one anchored in the text, that does not make essential reference to God. In other words, it is to extract from the text a non-instantiating answer on which God's contribution is given a non-literal interpretation.

Confronting me here is a problem that arises from the quarter of thinkers committed to the rational, scientific, philosophical agenda, the agenda of the Proverbist's three. Such thinkers have no quarrel with the distinction between men and women, on the one side, and other elements of creation, on the other. The line between lepidoptery and anthropology is not erased. But for them the difference is not qualitative. Plainly, Darwin's 'Eureka' informs this denial, as does much else in the ongoing enterprise of science.

Even proponents of intelligent design do not comb the Bible for a refutation of Darwin. The Bible isn't that kind of book. Nor are the Greek writings to be examined of that kind. However, under the head of the Proverbist's three, biblical thought cedes to Darwin what is Darwin's. Indeed, in essential respects the Bible's origin story is compatible with Darwin's *Origin*.

To chart the lay of the land, let me offer a vignette associated with a recent engineering feat. The story concerns the tunnel under the English Channel – the Chunnel.

When the digger from the Dover side was asked to put into words what he felt upon first glimpsing his counterparts moling away *du côté de Calais, his* immortal 'A large step for mankind' was (so the story goes) 'Well, guv, the hole was just big enough to catch a soupçon of garlic.'

The Bible does its spadework in regard to human reality at the human end. Science tunnels towards human reality from the other, natural, end. Taking the extra- or the sub-human as primary, science tries to naturalize the human – to reconstitute what is *prima facie* distinctive of the human – in its own terms. Can the taste of garlic be simulated in salad cream and tomato sauce?

The issue comes down to the barbarically denominated 'distinctive distinctiveness' of men and women. Proponents of the rational, scientific conception complain that the biblical perspective is anthropocentric, and false for assigning men and women the pre-eminence. The complaint is levelled against the foundational part of the Bible – the primeval chapters of Genesis.

By way of establishing that the charge of anthropocentrism against the Bible is unfounded, I now address myself to determining the biblical stance on the 'What Is Man?' question. The Bible's answer will be teased out of core Scripture – specifically, the opening chapters of

Genesis. Consistent with the implicit references of the Proverbist's three to the region of his four, the answer falls, we will see, entirely on the latter side. The core scriptural treatment has no interest in three, though, aside from noting its existence.

In a highly encoded way, the Bible makes a point that resonates with David's own case. In the Song of Songs (another text attributed to Solomon), the lover states, referring to God (2:16).

> My beloved is mine and I am his

'David' means 'beloved.' The words, though pronounced differently, are orthographically identical. 'David' is

דוד

'My beloved' differs only by the addition of the mark of first-person possession:

דודי

A reader of the original will *see* 'David' when he or she looks at 'beloved.' So the Hebrew can be rendered: 'David is mine, and I am David's.' This captures the intimacy between David and God, on which I remarked in the preceding chapter and to which I shall return.

Focus versus Centre

Because of the pre-eminence that its story of what happened '[i]n the beginning' (1:1) accords the human sector of being, the Bible is a lightning rod for criticism from the secular, rational, scientific quarter. On the dominant view from this quarter, the sixth day is not a red letter day. Latecomers to the phylum though men and women are, they are continuous with the other living things that the creation comprises. Since business as usual is conducted on the seventh day – the series of higher organisms remains, science says, a work in progress – even those who approach Genesis with their minds wide open and with the best will in the world are therefore driven off by, as they invariably see it, the Bible's anthropocentrism.

Anthropocentrism is at odds with the cosmological and anthropological deliverances of science. But *is* the Bible anthropocentric? In the last analysis, the biblical view of the nature of men and women and the scientific view do differ. The difference does not however trace back to an antecedent and non-negotiable creedal commitment on the Bible's part to a realm of existence beyond space and time, a realm prior to the latter and with which men and women are held, uniquely so among things with feet of clay, to be on terms of intimacy. Rather, it arises out of biblical acuity to a characteristic of down-to-earth human reality that few rational metaphysicians would deem problematic.

What of the fact that the Bible gives our kind such prominence? The Bible is, to coin a term, *anthropofocal*. The narrative centrality of men and women is due in the first instance to the focus. It turns out that what emerges from within the focus does not fit with the teachings of science. But the focus itself begs no questions. If, then, the Bible seems anthropocentric, this isn't due to a dogmatic raising up of men and women. That it seems anthropocentric bespeaks in fact a blind spot in the scientific world view.

A sense of what it means to say that the Bible is (harmlessly) anthropofocused rather than (problematically) anthropocentred can be imparted as follows. You pick up a book advertised as a biography of Napoleon. Napoleon, you find, is mentioned only *en passant*. Certainly, *that* would leave you scratching your head. Is it just because publishers set an arbitrary limit on length (a book of one thousand pages might as well be infinitely long) that the biographer does not devote page 1 of the human's life to the beginning of human life at Olduvai Gorge? The book being the book *of* Napoleon, it is as it should be that everything revolves *about* the Corsican. But I daresay that in giving him pride of place no biographer commits to Napoleon's ontological centrality or claims that the eighteenth and nineteenth centuries in Europe mean more to history than, say, the age of Augustus or the reign of Charlemagne. Indeed, in a biography of a contemporary nonentity, the spotlight would be, in precisely the same fashion, on Nobody. Bonaparte would be Rosencrantz and Wellington, Guildenstern.

The Bible approaches men and women as a biographer does his or her subject: it focuses on them. It would not be at all inaccurate to describe the Bible as the authorized Western biography of men and women. Accordingly, the biblical privileging of humankind is precisely what one should expect. That this privileging reduces the Bible's truth quotient is not decided in the affirmative simply by pointing a finger at its anthropofocus.

Of two central theses to be defended here the first is that the whole of the core part of the Bible is a focused treatment of the human reality of men and women. 'The whole of the core part' means just that. In the nature that is the primary subject matter of science the narrative takes no interest. *Genesis has nothing to do with the events about which scientific cosmologists theorize – for example, the Big Bang*. The second thesis is that the point on which the Bible and science are anthropologically at odds emerges from within this focus on human reality. Though couched in the terms that are the Bible's terms ('God makes humankind in his image,' 'God breathes life into the first man'), the point is conceptually independent of theology. *It has to do with what is independently seen to be distinctive about men and women.*

The upcoming discussion is largely free of meta-interpretive matters. But to establish the first thesis the historical background of the biblical text has to be explored. The first thesis is present in a form bound up with a particular historical milieu. Here the Documentary Hypothesis about the Bible plays into my thinking. So a brief scramble through the scholarly thickets is necessary.

The Mosaic Mosaic

Even casual readers notice the roughness of the Bible's narrative texture. The Documentary Hypothesis (DH), an explanatory response to the jagged transitions, redundancies, and apparent inconsistencies, has it that the object in our possession is a scissors-and-paste job, reconfiguring elements of written sources that had lived independent lives prior to the snipping and gluing.

Quite a few versions of DH are in play. Of the number I can quote the motto of my alma mater: '*Grandescunt aucta labore*.' Given that no earlier document or fragment of document coinciding with or overlapping chapter-and-verse has ever been found, neither the quantity nor the steady build-up baffles understanding. True, the absence of external evidence imparts an odd character to the debates among proponents of conflicting versions of DH. But for a reason mentioned already in passing the general appeal of DH is not thereby weakened. Astonishingly in view both of how long its culture lasted and also of the culture's having been a literate one, aside from scratchings on potsherds and a few early correlates of 'Kilroy was here' the Bible itself is the only written thing to have survived.

DH is frequently represented, on the following basis, as a bar to the Bible's interpretability. The wish, or maybe the pressure, to include the various and sometimes poorly matching pieces constrained whoever put the text together – the redactors. (I use the plural, 'redactors,' for purely stylistic reasons. Perhaps one person did the bulk of the work.)

The reasoning is flawed. The redactors might well have configured as they did precisely because they aimed to tell a unitary story, rather than despite the desire to do so or in the absence of any interest one way or the other. Given the materials they had to work with, the narrative choppiness might be the redactors' way of achieving unity, or a by-product of the valiant attempt under the circumstances to achieve it. A mosaic fashioned from the remnants of other mosaics may have an integrity of its own, even though the tiles, sized and shaped and coloured for a different pattern and visual effect, constrain the mosaicist from the outside. Needless to say, the intentions of the redactors are unavailable to us. A decision on whether unity was their objective comes down to whether we can furnish a unitary reading that does not force us into sideshow contortions with respect to verse-and-chapter.[7]

I spoke of the redactors' wish, or the pressure on them, to include the various elements. Those who rest an anti-hermeneutic position on the Bible's patchwork character often buttress the assertion of uninterpretability by observing that *the authority* of the inherited texts tied the redactors' hands. For the reason that the texts were severally treasured, by themselves and/or by those whom they identified as their audience, they had to include even variants that contradicted one another.

To this 'every jot and tittle' point the rejoinder is not far to seek. The ascription of authority turns question begging immediately agreement is secured (and who could reasonably disagree?) that the redactors in all likelihood excluded much; much more in all likelihood than they incorporated. To take inclusion as attesting to authority of the highest order is to commit a *petitio*. In the vacuum of information that is our lot, omission counts with equal plausibility as a mark of serious lack of fit.

Roughly contemporary with the Bible, the Homeric epics supply a useful model for comparison. Myths that came down to archaic Greece are woof to the warp of Homer's rich tapestries. Since we often have several versions of the mythic stories that are woven into the epics, the extent to which Homer treats the stories with kid gloves can be checked. What emerges, as the following simple case illustrates, is that Homer, with his own tale to tell, doesn't tiptoe through the mythic entailment.

Achilles is the central character of the *Iliad*. His genetic make-up, as mapped in myth, informs the epic's theme. To be for a brief time or to be forever? That is the question. With which parental endowment, of Thetis his immortal mother or of Peleus his mortal father, will Achilles run his life's race? At the decisive turn, with which parent will he identify?

The wedding of Thetis and Peleus is alluded to more than once in the *Iliad*. The story of the solemnizing of the highly irregular union casts Paris as a key player. Here are the pertinent details.

For reasons that her name telegraphs, Eris is not invited to the nuptials. Crashing the party anyway (they should have known!), the goddess of discord tosses among the assembled a golden apple inscribed 'For The Fairest.' Athena, Aphrodite, and Hera begin forthwith to bicker. Reckoning discretion the better part of valour, Zeus, whom the three call upon to crown Miss Heaven, Eastern Mediterranean, demurs. To restore decorum to the solemnities, he proposes that Paris, who at the time is tending sheep on Mount Ida, do the judging. With Miss Earth, Eastern Mediterranean, dangled by Aphrodite before him, Paris goes Cyprian.

Evidently, Paris is sensitive to the attractions of the fair before Achilles is conceived. But in the *Iliad* Paris and Achilles are roughly the same age. The discrepancy of his plotting with mythic chronology obviously doesn't bother Homer, nor does it affect the story he tells – the story, as we shall later see, of a cultural shift from the heroic age to a more pacific phase of human existence.[8]

This is a trivial example. Or is it? Who knows how protective the Greeks of the time were of their mythic deposits? Perhaps taking such liberties opened Homer to a *fatwa*. As the case may be, the example gives onto what is unquestionably a massively substantial example – one, indeed, that tells us what the *Iliad* is about. But that is for later.

Only bad *a priori* reasons exist for ruling impossible that the Bible's redactors treated the materials they had in hand as did Homer. And the *a posteriori* argument that they did not do so runs afoul of the objections raised earlier. To be sure, we do not *know* that the redactors' practice corresponded to Homer's. We do not have the materials. Then again, we do not know otherwise.

The Text's Centre

'[T]he genesis of the biblical process is bound up with the beginnings of the monotheistic concept; both converge in the age, and presumably also the person, of Abraham.' So writes E.A. Speiser, editor of the Genesis instalment of the Anchor series on the Bible.[9] And again: 'The history of the biblical process is ultimately the story of the monotheistic ideal in its gradual evolution.'

With the view that the story congeals around the novel notion of a single deity I agree, deeply and completely agree, though it will be some time before we settle on just what, beyond the matter of sheer numerosity, is new and operative in the idea. I dissent however from a related point of Speiser's. 'Genesis,' he writes, beginning his text, 'is a book of beginnings' (xvii). As I see it, Genesis as we know it – sc., the Book of Genesis with its fifty chapters telling the story of the creation, of Noah, of Abraham, of the descent to Egypt, and so on – is a book that bears on its body the internal mark of an ending. If not for that ending, which has nothing to do with the creation, with the Flood, with the Patriarchs, with a famine in Canaan that forces a migration, neither would the book have been produced, nor would it have the character that it has.

The point here concerns DH and the identity and inspiration of the redactors. It does not concern Abraham and the spiritual currents, such as they may have been, of his age.

Among committed exponents of DH the consensus is that the cutting and pasting that produced the text that is now in our hands was executed in the decades after the Babylonians reduced Jerusalem, and that the wielders of shears and brush belonged to the Jerusalemite élite, the cream of the cream of the population and the stratum that in the effort at pacification had been skimmed off to Babylon. The view has much to recommend it. First: why *a* book? After the calamity known from the Hebrew as the *Hurban* (cognate with the Hebrew for 'sword,' the word means 'laying-waste') God's House was no longer there to serve, as it had for the preceding three centuries served, as the communion's mortar. A new centre to counteract the forces of dispersion was urgently needed.[10] The book, a portable object, was a good choice. Second: why *this* book? The redactors found themselves back in Babylon, Abraham's departure from which, in their historical lore, had starting up the national enterprise. To the faithful this was no small blow. As his part in the covenant hadn't God promised a glorious future over Jordan for the patriarch's progeny? Was it all a fiendish joke? That the best-laid schemes of men and women go awry is commonplace. Nor is it that the road to hell is paved with good intentions. Let he or she cast the first stone for whom a promise made is a promise kept. But we are not speaking here of what was understood by the affected parties to be a merely *human* undertaking. *God* had made, and several times ratified, *this* undertaking. For those unwilling to write the project off (they undertook to write it up) the challenge was not just to produce a portable centre for the scattered and dispirited people. If the sack of Jerusalem and the dispersion had delivered a deathblow to their hopes and dreams, that by itself would have rubbed salt in the wound.

The destruction and exile – by contrast with the Flood a completely human event – served as the occasion for the production of the biblical text that we possess in the form that we possess it. 'Occasion' is too weak. The calamity played more than just the *sparking* role. The serious problem that the event raised affected the *content*. The pressing need to come up with a credible response to what had taken place supplied the principle under which the available literary elements were picked and packaged. On the creedal side, the project was touch and go: soft-pedal the triumphal strain of God's promise of a future as an independent nation for the children of Israel without in the process dangerously muting the good news, even scoring a dirge.[11] The extant materials were themselves uninfluenced by what from the standpoint of *their* authors was far in the future. The challenge from a compositional perspective was daunting: produce the account without producing something that members of the communion would not recognize, and produce it out of (familiar) materials that had been composed for entirely different purposes.[12]

The beginnings described in Genesis are, then, influenced by the sense of an ending. The opening itself is configured so as to reflect the real-world breakdown that had occurred – to render that historical happening explicable and therefore, perhaps, bearable. This adjustment does not result in a serious loss of generality. Indeed, it results in what *we* perceive as greater realism, since it is not far from true in the view of most of us that things contain within themselves a principle of dissolution and/or that the idea of complete control is a myth.

What was just now said about backwards influence has to do with the Bible's tone. The claim is that what otherwise would very likely have been a triumphalism in the text akin to that sonically rendered in the opening movement of Beethoven's Ninth Symphony, an upwards and regular climb from early promise to eventual glory, is played down. Though the contemporary preoccupations of those who configured the text affected the conceptual content too, they affected it less. Which is as it should be. For the conceptual content saturated the materials that were at the heart of their way of thinking. Had the redactors been unsympathetic to the content, they would have looked elsewhere for data, even perhaps started afresh. Otherwise, the product would have been satirical. Here, it is not the personal or near personal experience of the redactors that influences how the story of much earlier happenings is told. The influence comes from their view of what Abraham, notably, had turned his back on.

What then of 'the age, and . . . the person, of Abraham'? Here too, though in this instance internally, the beginning is affected by an ending. Obviously, the monotheistic concept marks a cultural shift. The Bible, the charter document of monotheism, is the charter of, and charts, the shift. In the biblical dramatization, God invites Abraham to leave home and native land – to strike out on the monotheistic venture. The new way does not begin *ex nihilo*. Abraham has already lived half a life.

One might essay in this regard a historical biography of God along the lines of, but more embedded in fact than, what Hesiod offers in the *Theogony* about the generations of the Greek deities. Here's the briefest sketch.

The creation of the world is closely associated with the river valleys of the Tigris and the Euphrates. The text locates the Garden where the first man and the first woman come into being and dwell in their salad days relative to four rivers, the same Mesopotamian flows being two. Abraham hails from Ur, on the lower reaches of the Euphrates. In the light of these geographical coincidences it makes good sense to represent God's itinerary as an upward reflection of Abraham's. Abraham is the vector of the new way. God, its inspiration. God too strikes out from the same region, heading for 'the land that I will show you' (12:1). If not, why would the call come to Abraham rather than to someone situated elsewhere?[13] Who then is God? The biblical belief system is nothing if not an abandoning of a creedal path. Disaffection with the extant way obviously lies at the motivational core of the departure. A plausible conjecture, then, is that God is a minor deity in the Babylonian pantheon who makes a break with *his* land and *his* father's house.[14]

The point here is that monotheism, though it dominates the very beginning of Genesis *qua* story of an unchallenged deity performing an act of creation *tout seul*, has to be understood as a critical response to a creed that is a going concern. God is saying a not very fond goodbye to all that. This is less than clear from 'In the beginning.' Focusing now on what Speiser identifies as Genesis's conceptual driver, I will show that the creation story of Genesis is not just the creation story of the document that happens to be the charter document of monotheism, as the Big Bang story is the creation story of those who on the strength of close examination of the issue have come to the conclusion that the Big Bang does better than any of its competitors. The creation story of Genesis is the story that is told about the beginning because the storytellers (and here the reference is less to the redactors than to those who are behind the materials that the redactors used) are independently committed to monotheism. As such, the story's natural credentials are bogus. For monotheism is not a natural thing.[15]

Hysteron Proteron

This Greek phrase labels the fallacy of putting the later prior. If the creation story is informed by the monotheistic idea, the Bible would seem to be open to the charge of getting things back to front. There is, I maintain, no fallacy. The story is *not* what it seems.

The part of Genesis preceding the national story comprises three distinct phases: the creation; Eden; and the pre-history of men and women up to and including the Flood of Noah. The latter two are, in my coinage, anthropofocused. They expressly concern our kind. It would be a gain in thematic unity if the interest that is being worked out when the heavens and the earth, the animals and plants, the luminaries, are spoken of was in the same strong sense an interest in distinctively human reality.

The Bible is not a tight deductive system. Certainly, the cosmogonic agenda could be pursued separately from the special interest in humankind. The question is not however about possibilities. *Is* the first phase of the Bible more independent of the second and third phases than each of these is from the other? That is the question. To readers through the ages it has seemed that it is. Which, if explanation is sought, helps explain why the interpretation in the offing has not over the years been offered.

Beguiled by the compelling tale of disobedience in Eden, many readers do not see this phase as of a piece with the phase that follows, let alone appreciate how tight the unity is.

The post-expulsion story of the man and the woman is the story of making a go of it in a limitedly responsive world. The point is not that the pair must now, for the first time, exert themselves. To read the text as telling of easeful repose prior to the departure is to read it under the influence of an extra-biblical equation of Eden with Paradise. *Within* the Garden the needs of life do not dish themselves up while the dwellers loll about. The Garden is no Land of Cockaigne. Rather, outside Eden men and women must, in a technical sense, work. They must direct their energy to changing the world, to prodding responses that the world would not give of its own accord.[16]

The idea of work is given expression in the harsh phrase that God employs when just prior to expelling them from the Garden he curses the man and the woman: 'by the sweat of your face you shall eat bread' (3:19). Dramatizing the real-world conflict of farmers versus shepherds, the story of Cain and Abel gives flesh and fibre to the idea. Viewed in this perspective, Cain's '[a]m I my brother's keeper?' (4:9) immediately draws the negative answer. Once stakes are planted and plants are staked, steaks are produced in plants. That's just the way it is, so no one can have a legitimate beef.[17]

Directly the anthropogenic character of the Abel/Cain story is spotlighted – Abel's way of life is simpler than Cain's – the tale of Eden falls into line as telling of the yet simpler way that the textbooks label 'gathering.' If, conceptually speaking, work is criterial for genuinely *economic* existence, Eden qualifies as *pre*-economic.[18] To get by, the man and the woman have to exert themselves. That does not mean that they work. In contrast both to herders and to agriculturalists, the man and the woman do not – in Locke's phrase – *mix their labour* with the natural materials. They take. They do not make. So, we see, the salty exudation of their labours is *not* the sweat of the face that the Bible, showing them the door, foretells. Which accounts for the withholding of the phrase about secretions from the 'till[ing]' and keep[ing]' (2:15) that they are instructed to do in the Garden, activities that, the Bible writers will have known, cannot be performed without perspiration.[19] Tight thematic unity is thus achieved between the second phase and the third.[20] Both address ways in which men and women live as creatures in a world that doesn't magically meet their needs for food, shelter, and so on.

Given the unity, it's more than just reasonable to try to bring the earliest phase of the story on board too. Reading the opening in a *psychogenic* rather than *cosmogonic* manner does the job.

It is fairly uncontroversial to see Genesis 2 as telling of the kindergarten of humankind. It is equally uncontroversial to understand the exit from Eden as the coming-out exercises of men and women, their graduation, into what parents and teachers describe to their children and charges as 'the real world,' first at a rudimentary stage of economic and social existence that cleaves to the land, then in the city and the more diffuse international sphere. The narrative dynamic being what it is, it is therefore natural to look to Genesis 1 for the obstetric ward and nursery of humankind.

Natural it may be. Is Genesis 1 responsive? Two millennia of reading 'Let there be light' as the biblical correlate of whatever precipitated the Big Bang have built up a ton of resistance. Yet considered in themselves the words invite the anthropogenic construction. We say 'the light went on' or 'the light dawned' when we speak of achieving understanding. A bright yellow incandescent bulb is the iconic fixture. When the matter is approached from this angle and the sequel borne in mind, the biblical phrase comes over as signalling the advent of awareness – the specifically cognitive brand that outstrips the tropisms of plants and the four-F sentience of subhuman animals: flee–fight–feed–reproduce. The (non-visual) sense of 'seeing,' present in Hebrew too, gives the parallel. The light enables us to see, that is, to comprehend. Once that potential comes to be actual, things proceed apace. For no other creature does any such movement occur. All other creatures mark time in an eternal 'now.'

Robert Alter's recent translation of the Pentateuch[21] has drawn reactions ranging from 'Eureka' to 'Eheu.' The portion of the text that we are now examining, specifically the memorable conjunctive phrase 'tohu va'vohu' of Genesis 1:2, is a flashpoint of contestation – a light-shedding one for us.

Alter renders the Hebrew thus: 'welter and waste.'[22] The Authorized Version's 'waste and void' is, I think, superior, though I have no confidence that God's Secretaries, presented with my reasons, would accept the praise.

Both conjuncts of the phrase have verb roots. English 'to be in the dark about' and 'to be at sea about' capture the meaning of the root of 'tohu';[23] 'to stare vacantly' captures that of 'bohu.' (In the conjunctive form – 'va' means 'and' – the 'b' of 'bohu' softens to a 'v.') If we are attuned to these meanings, the sense of chaos that the conjunctive phrase imparts is one of confusion or bafflement. The attitude expressed by 'tohu' is not an attitude of awed amazement at what one encounters. It is an attitude of blank incomprehension. The stare is unfocused. Judging again by the psychological associations of the verb roots, we are being presented with a centre of awareness lacking a sense of what's up and what's down.[24] The subject of that awareness is, as the English vulgate has it, gormless. Or, to do some wordsmithying on a suaver English form, and with a tip of the hat to William Gaines, it wonders aimless like a clod.

'Confusion' has a pair of uses, one in application to consciousness-independent things (entropy is a measure of objective disorder), the other to states of consciousness. Think of the philosopher Descartes's 'unclarity and indistinctness.' Many words are thus Janus-faced. 'Understanding,' a central entry in the lexicon of cognitive psychology, is also English for what Aristotle calls 'substance,' substance being that which *stands under* the qualities available to sense. Part of a purely metaphysical/ontological analysis, this has nothing to do with the mind and its workings.[25]

'Tohu,' taken as describing confusion, works both ways. The transposition from the subject to the object is less easy when it comes to 'bohu.' *Its* extra-psychological use is not at all natural. What follows?

It's the interpreter's job to attend to the words. A miscue on the construal of a word here or a word there and the meaning of the whole might be lost. The fact is that the verses can be read as capturing a state of the subject who is trying to fathom the world, not a state of the world itself, and the fact is that 'bohu' resists being taken ontologically. Reading the verses psychologically, as this suggests we should, makes a profound difference. On the construal that has God imposing order, the world itself is initially chaotic. God's imposition of order is cosmofacient. On the psychological construal, at issue is the comprehension of the world, not its independent nature.

From this perspective I must take issue with Cynthia Ozick. In Ozick's effusion, Alter's translation is 'magically consonant' with the Hebrew. But how is 'welter and waste' more consonant with the original than 'waste and void,' which last, echoing the consonant 'v' of the Hebrew 'vohu,' has the additional merit of being literally more consonant? More to the point, these asseverations suggest a trumping version, viz., 'Waa! Waa!'[26] – the sonic emission of the newborn slapped into breath and life. In effect: 'In the beginning was the bawling.'

Along these lines a unitary reading of the whole is achieved. The availability of the reading establishes the present position as an option. The homogeneity bolsters the reading's claim to consideration. The text is not only being written *from* the human perspective. Too, it is exclusively *about* the human perspective. The babyhood of the world as depicted in Genesis 1 is the babyhood of the men and women born into the world. The Garden is their adolescent condition. Abraham explores nascent nationhood – a specific sort of distinctively human community. Joseph must live among the nations. And so forth. There is thus no conflict with scientific cosmology. The making of the physical world is not the Bible's issue. Puzzling *that* out is a job for the scientists.

That our awareness takes shape along a certain route does not oblige whatever it may be that we come to be aware of. Ontology is not anticipated, much less recapitulated, by developmental psychology. If

Genesis 1 is read as an account of developing awareness, what truth can it contain apart from such truth about the progress of consciousness as is accessible from the armchair?

In the absence of an answer, the interpretation could survive as an interpretation. The Bible's position, for telling us about things only *per accidens*, would reduce however to a curiosity. In the event, an answer is available. What we come to be aware of, that is, what is objectively there, is not always independent of our coming to be aware of it. Consider the matter from the standpoint of the anthropogenic story. Abel and Cain clash because real estate is a part of Cain's world alone. The problem does not lie in a deficiency in Abel's grasp, a cognitive deficit. The brothers' worlds are ontologically distinct. And Cain creates the real estate. It has its reality because of his activity.

Cain is a farmer. The farmer is an encloser. In the farmer's reality parcels of land, bordered with fence posts and girdled with barbed wire, count as (personal) property. In the pre-farming world, at least on this schematic story, the only property to speak of is that which can be taken with as one moves: chattel. The same goes, *mutatis mutandis*, for Abel vis-à-vis the gatherers of Eden. In the world of the gatherers, what is on offer for sustenance is no one's own. It is not common property, moveable or otherwise. It is not property at all.[27]

With respect to one sort of order, there is, we see, no gap between subjective and objective. This is the sort of order than falls under Giambattista Vico's dictum:

Verum et factum convertuntur

Translated: 'when something is (expressly, deliberately) made, its nature is understood.' In a wide range of cases, including the case of Abel's flock and the case of Cain's farm, this is correct. When men and women build a house, they understand the product because they make it. The dictum applies, that is, to artefacts. Breeders of animals also create what are in part artefacts. True, they do not create the genetic material from scratch. Neither however do house builders create the atomic components of the planks and the bricks that *they* use. To exploit what we've learned about the word 'understand': building a house, men and women understand it in both senses: they grasp its nature, and do so because they impart to it its substance.

It will be said that from the Bible's perspective the world, the natural world, is God's handiwork. This is so, I am sure, in a sense that goes well beyond what those who say it have in mind. God isn't just the creator of everything. The world of which Genesis speaks 'in the beginning' is nearly literally an artefact. Independently of any theology the world falls, from the standpoint of the composers of Holy Writ, in the category of the made rather than in the category of the found. Since the natural world is subsumed by the latter category it follows that Genesis's creation story is *not* about the natural world at all. The biblical narrative, we shall see, acknowledges this.

Let me do an inventory before the final push.

The earlier phases of Genesis have to be understood in the light of phases that come later. Since the very first textual phase, the primordial creation, is subordinate to the story of men and women, it does not compete with the (purely cosmogonic) views of Hubble, Hoyle, and Hawking. Monotheism is the central driver, in two ways. A geopolitical disaster that befell the members of the emerging monotheistic creed lies behind the production of the text as we know it, and determines the text's tone. More deeply, monotheism, which antedates the disaster, is at the heart of the conceptual contrast between the Bible and science.

Home and Garden

An objection from the secular quarter against the primeval creation story, when the story is taken as cosmogonic, is that purpose is imposed on what is essentially without purpose. 'The truth of the matter is that the separation of upper waters from lower waters results from natural processes and forces. The division did not occur because we needed the middle place for living our lives. Had it not occurred, *we* wouldn't be. Isn't the Bible straightforwardly at odds here with the truth? For isn't its creation story a story of the making of places for things whose needs are anticipated before they are brought into being – the heavens for the heavenly bodies, the sky for the flying objects, the dry land for the plants and the animals, the lower waters for the sea creatures?'

This objection, I say, is raised by those who see the primeval creation story as cosmogonic. But the story is *not* cosmogonic. What initially comes across as a poor analogy is in actuality an accurate model. The creation story doesn't just correspond to a story of the sort that would be told about the building of a house. It *is* the story of the building of a (kind of) house: an abode for men and women. Is a house, a habitation for men and women, constructed in accordance with a plan? Does it answer to a design? Is it adjusted (well or badly) to the needs of the eventual inhabitants? Yes on all counts. The distinction of roof (higher) from floor (lower) is deliberate. By contrast, the physical world, the world as it is in itself apart from the human presence, is isotropic. There is no up and there is no down.

The following experiment is most enlightening in this connection. That globe of the earth sitting in your study – take it and invert it in its stand. The howls of protest that this will elicit indicate that the globe is not a purely physical representation. It is a representation of the earth as people in the West regard the earth. Even those who live on the Antarctic side of the equator come to think, often resentfully, that North America and Europe are in the phrase's evaluative sense 'on the top.'

The roof of a house is to keep the elements out, the floor is to provide a level platform for furnishings and for going smoothly about one's business. By the same token, the light fixtures are installed for illumination: 'to,' as the Bible says, 'give light upon the earth' (1:15).

That the world is a suitable place for men and women, 'suitable' in the core biological sense that they can survive in it, is not true by design. Were there no niche into which we fit, we wouldn't *be*. That a house is a suitable place for men and women *is* by contrast the result of purpose. The house would not be but for the needs of men and women. It's because we exist that the house exists. It is fitted to us, not we to it.

In Genesis 2 the man and the woman are placed in a garden. Like houses, gardens are not natural parcels of the world. A cultivated place, a garden would not exist but for a cultivator. It results from, that is, is created by, working the ground and keeping it.

The text is telegraphing that the human world with which it is dealing is a distinctively human place, a place, then, in which the extra-human things have only such significance as is assigned to them in distinctively human terms: labour savers, furnishings, decorative fruit, knick-knacks, and so forth. Compatibly with what I said about reading back from the national story to the primeval one, here too we are to read back – from Genesis 2, in which the human world, that is, the Garden, is expressly extra-natural, to Genesis 1, where that at first sight seems not to be the case.

I will defend this fully two chapters hence. Let me now state, more generally, what the case is.

The Bible is for the most part not concerned with the natural world. Certainly, the nature encountered in Genesis isn't real nature. In stating that it isn't, I am not begging the question against those who see the Bible as holding a false, because anti-scientific, even Disney-like, view of rocks and stones and trees. The nature encountered in Genesis and through the bulk of Scripture is *deliberately* an instrument of God's for rewarding and disciplining humankind. Scanning the text, what do we find on the climatological side? Gentle mists at the world's gestation to ease the labour, zephyrs in Eden, Noah's genocidal deluge, healing winds, and covenantal rainbow, providential droughts in Canaan that compel the patriarchs to trek to Egypt. We find lean and abundant years in that alien land that assist Joseph's climb to eminence, plagues of thunder, hail and fire in Egypt to prod Pharaoh to let the Israelites go, and so on. The goings on in the heavens are relativized to men and women: *because* of them and *for* them. At no point is the extra-human world described as it is in itself.

A backdrop for our lives nature is not. To represent it as *mise-en-scène* is, in a patently objectionable way, anthropocentric. *The Bible writers know this full well.* In Genesis they gesture towards real nature. Doing so, they indicate that their interest lies elsewhere. The gesture, made in the story of the revivification of the world after the Flood, that is, the reprise of Genesis 1 and Genesis 2, consists in having the raven disappear over the horizon when Noah opens the hatch and lets it fly. The Bible is careful to indicate that the bird does not perish. '[I]t went to and fro until the waters were dried up from the earth' (8:6). Where then does it land? Though the text gives no direct answer, this much may safely be inferred from the contrast with the subsequent homing flights of the dove: the raven's place is not among men and women.

The world of Genesis is in effect climate-controlled. Only a human artefact like a house could have such a character, and Genesis's nature is just that: house-like. The *mise-en-scène* of Genesis is a house that God built – with the surroundings landscaped.

Living in the wilds poses many and serious difficulties for men and women. Only the adventurous willingly submit to roughing it. It does not however follow that living in a house is a picnic or idyll. The roof springs a leak. The floors sag. The pipes rust out and burst. The joists buckle. The wiring corrodes. The drain backs up. Uninvited guests knock at the door. But all this is usually because the controller is fiddling with the dials, because of slipshod construction and poor upkeep, because of loose-lipped ejaculations, no sooner emitted than regretted, about dropping by at any time.

Of that, precisely, Genesis tells: the looseness in the plan that causes trouble; the need to return to the drafting table and amend the blueprints. The natural world is not what requires improvement. In regard to the natural world God's initial response remains forever valid: 'It is good.' The problems lie in human and social engineering. The human world, that is, is what stands in need of redesign.

That, I say, is what Genesis tells. 'Isn't Genesis 1 fundamentally different in its teachings from Genesis 2?' My negative should by now be clear: the whole of the early part of Genesis is anthropofocused. Suitable readings of Genesis 1 have been supplied.[28] In a deepening of the negative, the links between Genesis 1 and Genesis 2 will be tackled from a variety of angles in the sequel. Let me end this chapter with a point drawn from the massive body of commentary on the Bible.

Rashi addresses a question that was asked by a certain Rabbi Isaac concerning the Bible's opening: Shouldn't the Torah have begun with Exodus 12? 'This month shall mark for you the beginning of months; it shall be the first month of the year for you' (2). Shouldn't the Torah have begun with Exodus 12 because the Torah is the charter of the Israelites, and Exodus 12 promulgates the first commandment to them? In instituting Tishrei as the first month, God is not a Pope Gregory, promulgating a calendar for all peoples. 'It shall be the first month of the year,' God is saying specifically to the Israelites, *'for you.* It shall be the beginning *for you.* Others may celebrate January if they wish.'

Rashi responds as follows. Had the Bible not commenced with Genesis 1, the other nations would have scoffed when the people of the Book cited the Book in justification of their territorial claims and ambitions. 'The world came to be independently of the deity who chose you. Your Scripture, at any rate, does not say otherwise. So your occupancy of the Promised Land is illegitimate. You are conquerers and usurpers.' But (concludes Rashi) since, as the Book says, the world as a whole is the product of God, it is God's prerogative to partition and apportion *ad libitum.*

Though in due course I will have something to say in defence of the chosenness of the Israelites, Rashi's specific needs I will not be able to meet. But implicit in my subordination of Genesis 1 to Genesis 2 is an answer to Rabbi Isaac that, though different from Rashi's answer, has *mutatis mutandis* the same general effect. Even what looks like world creation is part of the Bible's anthropofocus. To appreciate the significance of this, observe that a generalized form of the hostile remark that Rashi puts into the mouth of the antagonists of Israel is voiced nowadays by the science/philosophy constellation, the dominant post-Enlightenment creedal system, against any man or any woman who sees his or her basic condition in the world as captured in the Bible. Here, in an ecologist's phrasing, is the remark. 'Why should you think the world is created for you when the foundations were laid in a manner neutral as to your existence? Isn't Scripture anthropocentric, and false for being that? So isn't your conquest of the natural world usurpation?' One might indeed like to know how human reality fits into the natural realm. But the Bible does not directly take on that matter. Its focused concern is with human reality. The world that God creates in Genesis 1 is, that is, *'for you.'*

The Bible is however perfectly aware of extra-human nature. After a meta-interpretive excursus in the course of which several of the Bible's characteristic ethical views begin to emerge, that awareness and its implications, both crucial to the second set of questions set out at the outset, will be looked at.

3

An Ethical Compass

Two Narrative Features

Striking about Genesis, when the narrative is approached as a subject of literary analysis, is the repetition of plot lines. Frequently, the kinds of things that are portrayed as happening happen more than once. Not infrequently they happen more than twice.

Genesis 1 tells the story of creation. 'In the beginning when God created the heavens and the earth' (1). Genesis 2 reprises. 'In the day that the Lord made the earth and the heavens' (4). Genesis 4 reports on one line of humanity, the line of Cain, stemming from Adam and Eve. 'Now the man knew his wife Eve, and she conceived and bore Cain' (1). Genesis 5 tells of the alternative line of Seth, using a formulation that quotes God's creation, in the first chapter, of men and women. 'When Adam had lived one hundred thirty years, he became the father of a son in his likeness, according to his image, and named him Seth' (1). Cain and Abel, a pair of brothers, each sacrifices. 'Cain brought to the Lord an offering of the fruit of the ground, and Abel for his part brought of the firstlings of his flock' (4:3–4). The rain in the case of Noah (Genesis 7) is matched by the sulphureous downpour that incinerates Sodom and Gomorrah (Genesis 19). After the floodwaters subside, the world, a small part of it seeded with the few surviving germs, springs to life again (Genesis 8). Sodom and Gomorrah having been reduced to ashes, God (Genesis 19) offers a village, Zoar, as a place for Lot and his daughters, the sole remnant of the conflagration, to start over. Observe, also, the ghostly correspondence between Zoar and Eden as starting points. The Garden is a cultivated plot, an area of a size that a couple can tend. Zoar is a small cultivated area too. Furthermore, just as the first woman in Eden comes from the first man, so the (relevant) women available in Zoar, Lot's daughters, are of him. Famine gripping Canaan, each of the patriarchs makes for Egypt: Abraham in Genesis 12; Isaac, who gets no farther than Philistia, in Genesis 26; and Jacob, having sent ten of his sons ahead to procure food in Egypt, for 'the famine became severe throughout the world' (41:57), in Genesis 42. We have a thrice repeated story about a forefather's misrepresenting a wife as a sister, twice starring Abraham (Genesis 12 and 20), once with Isaac in the lead role (Genesis 26).

The fugue-like character of the story telling is difficult to miss. Even the reader who is only mildly attentive will pick it up.

It is well known that the Pentateuch's story lines are recycled in other scriptural works. Elijah's life is patterned on Moses's. The Gospels are full of borrowings. These salutes are ways of attaching authority. Repetition in Genesis of the sort that I have drawn attention to has nothing to do with authority. It is one of the ways in which the text gets its message across. In order to illustrate the feature's interpretive significance, let me enlarge on an early parallel.

Directly the anthropogenic character of the Abel/Cain story is spotlighted, the tale of Eden falls into line as telling too of a mode of economic existence, viz., the simple one usually labelled 'gathering.'

Or so I argued. If it is felt that the unity attributed to the narrative is willed onto it, the feeling is stilled by noting that Cain and the couple from Eden meet mirroring fates. The man and the woman are expelled from their abode. God 'drove [them] out' (3:24). Banished from the place that *he* had settled, Cain, a mere twelve verses later, is made into 'a wanderer on the earth' (4:12). We have, then, a pair of banishments, each triggered by a transgression.

Cain is a farmer. Like the idea of a desk-bound shepherd or the idea of a landlocked mariner, the idea of a nomadic man of the soil is paradoxical. That Cain, having been driven off his acreage, takes up residence in 'the land of Nod, east of Eden' (4:16) magnifies the paradox. God had ordained for Cain a life of wandering. But no sooner is Cain banished than he settles down, presumably to follow the plough once more. Has God relented? Is he more bark than bite? Once it is appreciated that 'Nod' is cognate with 'wandering' – 'Land of Nod' is prettily rendered in English as 'Wanderland' – the paradox vanishes. (A later writer might have had Cain drift as far as Rome.) The wandering is figurative. The Bible's point is that the viability of Cain's way of life is as yet up in the air – its viability as a way of sustaining the biological needs of those who live it and, more important, since the writers know that it is viable in the preceding sense (so is cannibalism), its viability as a way of life in which men and women can flourish. Cain is engaged in an *experiment* in living. Waiting on the findings of the experiment, God says to him (4:7): 'If you do well, will you not be accepted?' The experiment might come a cropper. Then again, the assay might hit pay dirt. God's assertion that the land 'will no longer yield to you its strength' (4:12) is not the announcement of a punishment to be meted out because of what Cain did to Abel. It addresses a more literal fact about farming. Cain will initially have believed that he, at last, can put down roots, reaping each harvest season what he sows at planting time. But movement, it turns out, is unavoidable in his way of life too, and movement for him proves much more difficult than it had been for the flock-following Abel, who had only to rise and wave his crook. Early workers of the soil soon enough discovered that intensive planting yields diminishing returns. They are unable to make a consistent go of it by cultivating the same plot of land, not unless they redouble the work on the plot. Like his parents, Cain too finds that the expenditure of sweat for bread increases. Who knows but that the increase will challenge the economic and/or social viability of his new way? Crippling expenditure on fertilizers and/or vast numbers of slaves might eventually be required. At this stage of the trial the jury is still out. Yet from the other side, the potential promise of Cain's departure from a less settled life supplies a different perspective on the departure from the Garden, a perspective within which leaving Eden is not the catastrophe that, whatever Milton himself thought, the opening pentameters of *Paradise Lost* bewail:

> Of Mans First Disobedience, and the Fruit
> Of that Forbidden Tree, whose mortal tast
> Brought Death into the World, and all our Woe,
> With loss of *Eden* . . .

Thus far the first of the two narrative features mentioned in the heading. As for the second, picking *it* up requires more sensitive antennae.

Close attention discloses that the narrative hangs the various episodes on a line that runs east to west, westwards being the direction that the text approves. For instance, while in the most important journey of his career Abraham travels from the lower Euphrates westwards, to Canaan, in the course of *his* decisive journey Lot, Abraham's double, moves in the reverse direction – eastwards towards the Jordan from grazing lands closer to the Mediterranean.

To be sure, compass directions themselves are ethically neutral. Compatibly with the Bible's delivering the same message, the story might have had Abraham squinting into the sun in the mornings. He might even have set his course north. So it's not just a matter of attending to the direction of movement when movement is part of the story. But once the obvious evaluations present in the narrative are noted (and a few are entirely obvious), eastward or westward movement cues the reader to the Bible's ethical line when that line is more obscure. Sometimes relevant here is a further parametric contrast, one which on the face of it is somewhat less neutral, ethically speaking. This is the contrast between chaos and order.

In a series of reprises of God's primordial activity, the protagonists almost to a man and a woman confront and struggle with chaos: Noah and the churning waters of the Flood; Abraham to liberate Lot in the dragnet of war that sweeps through the Jordan valley; Jacob contending with his wild brother Esau. The Bible disapproves of the totally chaotic. God's creativity in Genesis 1 is nothing if not anti-entropic. Despite condemning utter chaos the Bible does not however go to the other extreme and commend rigid order. God's intervention in Genesis 2 thaws a frozen, tightly ordered world. '[N]o herb of the field had yet sprung up – for the Lord God had not [yet] caused it to rain upon the earth' (2:5). The thumbs-up that the story gives to certain persons and certain callings and certain behaviours responds to their having a characteristic *ratio* of order to chaos. In the course of the narrative the proportion increases and decreases, along with the general direction of movement.

The narrative features are, each of them individually, interpretively significant. The two also mesh. The geographical dimension gives a ghostly line of latitude along which the story episodes are strung. Local reversals occur. But the direction of movement up until the destruction of Solomon's Temple and the exile to Babylon – a political version of the Flood and the event that brings the core scriptural story to a close – is with the sun. Most especially when they pair characters who are directly connected with each other – for example, Cain and Abel, Lot and Abraham, Jacob and Esau – the plot repetitions give a finer fix on the origin of the coordinate scheme. The origin, which I label *the {0}-position,* marks the cut between what the Bible evaluates from an ethical point of view in a positive way and that on which a negative verdict is returned. Being in negative territory amounts to falling below the lowest acceptable ratio of chaos to order. The narrative has in this regard that exploratory, even experimental character recently remarked. The impression is strong that the writers themselves are not clear in advance where the origin is located – that in fact, when they set it in a specific place they do so without full confidence that subsequent adjustment will not be needed. Abel's way (to offer one instance) is less orderly than Cain's. Yet it has a few attractive features. As the encounter depicted in Genesis 13 illustrates, when herders come near enough to lock horns, escalation of friction into active hostility can easily be averted by spatial separation. That does not however mean that judged in the round, Cain's more orderly way, with respect to which the movement of one's possessions is not possible, is inferior.

To firm up our grasp of the idea of an acceptable ratio of order to disorder, let us look more closely at several panels from the start of the national story in Genesis.

Critique of Pure Unity

After Solomon's Temple is destroyed the Jerusalemite elite are exiled to Babylon. The Tower of Babel, an imaginary construction, is inspired by the real-world ziggurats that scraped the Mesopotamian sky. Yet when one hears 'Tower of Babel' the strongest association is the verb 'babble,' not the land beside whose waters the exiles wept. This mix-up is no accident. 'Babel' has in its root the consonants of the Hebrew verb 'to mix up,' and the Bible exploits the identity. 'Therefore it is called Babel, because there the Lord confused ['balal'] the language of all the earth' (11:9).[1]

'Babel' in the biblical phrase 'Tower of Babel' puns on 'babble.' The place name is also of course Hebrew (for what we refer to as) 'Babylon.' As we might expect, the geopolitical label, which parses as 'bab-el,' has a meaning of its own. It means 'gate (bab) of god (el).'[2] Is the biblical story of the Tower making a point about Babylon? Or is 'Tower of Confusion' just a sophomoric play on words, like the one about the first Spanish explorers exclaiming '*Aca nada,*' viz., 'There's nothing here,' upon first spying Canada?

The form 'X–el' of which 'Babel' is an instance is sprinkled throughout Genesis. Here, from the story of Jacob, are three cases. The place where Jacob dreams of the ladder he names 'Bethel' (28:19), that is, 'house (= beth) of god.' Victorious in the wrestling match with the angel, Jacob is awarded the title 'Israel,' meaning 'one who has striven with god'

(32:28). The location of the match, where he had encountered God face to face, Jacob dubs 'Peniel' (30), that is, 'face of god.' The prominence of the form strongly implies that in speaking of a Tower of Babel those behind the text are doing more than just exploiting the sonic similarity with 'babble.' In the event, encoded in the quibble is a criticism of what the writers regard as an objectionable creedal possibility.

Abraham's departure from the lower Euphrates – the genesis of the national project – is described in the final verses of the same chapter that tells of the Tower. Is the thematically operative idea that Abraham is setting out on a *new* venture, in which case 'Babylon,' like 'Timbuktu,' is functionally equivalent to 'faraway place'? Or does Abraham's leaving *that* location carry a message? The editor of the Anchor Bible instalment on Genesis endorses the latter disjunct (xlviii).

> In Mesopotamia, the very tenets that stimulated the social growth of the country proved to be a source of weakness in its spiritual progress. The terrestrial state was non-autocratic because man took his cue from the gods; and in the celestial state no one god was a law unto himself, not even the head of the pantheon. All major decisions in heaven required approval by the corporate body of the gods. And since nothing was valid for all time, the upshot was chronic indecision in heaven and consequent insecurity on earth [about spiritual destiny].

In the Bible's telling, it is God who sows the linguistic confusion that chokes off the work of construction. '[O]ne language and the same words' (11:1) clucks the text disapprovingly of those who assemble at Shinar, exception taken to the unity of purpose they exhibit in coming together. Is it not therefore puzzling that the heavenly gate that the builders are trying to storm, the bab-el, opens onto a pantheon, the Babylonian pantheon, whose members themselves compose a squawkery? In a clear sense the terrestrial actors do *not* want 'to be like us,' as God had said after the man and the woman had eaten of the fruit of the tree of knowledge and while they still had access to the tree of life. Relative to Speiser's description of the life situation of the faithful in Babylon, the puzzlement dissipates. The believers wish to *overcome* the discord the pressure to lend an attentive ear to which makes them less effective livers. The reform they want requires abandoning the belief system that has this characteristic.[3] *Unfortunately for Speiser, the Tower episode we are considering is in the founding document of monotheism.* The men and women who adhere to biblical teachings are commanded to worship the Lord who is one. From the standpoint of monotheism an enterprise informed by the idea of *reducing discord on high* seems if anything to merit thunderous applause. Had God spoken the currently universal language mightn't he have exploited the similarity of the words 'babble' and 'Bible' to extol the builders? Isn't their construction a Tower of Bible? Yet God scuttles the enterprise. More puzzling still, God pulls the plug by *increasing discord down low*. Wasn't the discord the problem in the first place? Once we attend more closely than Speiser does to the thematically significant linkage of 'babble' and (the geopolitical label) 'Babylon,' God's call to Abraham to depart his native land starts to seem like a turn-tail response to an internal challenge, even an attempt to avoid a charge of patent violation by skipping the jurisdiction and setting up shop far enough away to avoid litigation.

Speiser characterizes the pre-monotheistic situation on high as motivationally relevant to the monotheistic démarche. But though it is hard to see how it could be otherwise, the fact is that in the narrative it is God himself who orchestrates the score of Babel cacophonously. If the biblical move towards monotheism were loose and separate from the Tower episode, the reader would not be faced here with a problem of reconciliation. However, the two issues share a single chapter, Genesis 11. To quote some famous words from outer space: 'Houston, we have a problem.'

Paying heed to what has been said about the workings of the text, we can bring the capsule home, acquitting God in the process of throwing out the monotheistic baby with Babylon.

The Bible is endorsing a path somewhere between unity and multiplicity. To give the model of tight community 'on [the] plain in the land of Shinar' (11:2), a heavenly seal of approval would by the Bible's lights be unwise: false to human nature (as it sees human nature) and, therefore, dangerous to human flourishing. With respect to the important idea of the brotherhood of men, aiming for a *complete* meeting of minds and hearts – 'one language and the same words' – is therefore aiming too high. The objection, then, is not that the Tower builders want to be God-like in their actions. ('God' here names the monotheistic deity.) Since, axiomatically to the Bible, we are all made in this deity's image and likeness, no fault could be found with that. Nor is it that they are trying to do something beyond their station, something supra-Godly. Rather, their striving does not acknowledge the mentioned God-likeness. The Bible in opting for the middle position is making a significant normative choice. The choice signals that the unity of monotheism is not totalitarian. It is not unanimity. The {0}-position is, then, located at a point where unity falls short of the maximum.

This, then, is why Abraham strikes out westwards in the narrative immediately after the story of the Tower. It's not because of Babylonian polytheism. It's because the reform of that creedal position that informs the Tower enterprise is deemed too flattening of diversity.[4]

Uncle and Nephew

Departing for Canaan, Abraham takes his nephew Lot with him. Although Abraham could not have travelled without an entourage, Lot, it emerges, isn't along just for the ride. True, the text telegraphs that Abraham will head the national caravan. Attention to Lot is nonetheless essential if we are fully to understand Abraham's patriarchal election. Take the episode at the dead centre of Lot's story. What transpires at Sodom puts on him a final stamp of disapproval. By that very fact it is indicated that Lot's end as an also-ran was no foregone conclusion.[5] Once again, through comparison and contrast the text is working to fix the origin of the ethical map.

Why should Abraham's nephew, who 'settled among the cities of the plain' (13:12),[6] be the first urbanite from the ranks of those associated with the birth of the nation? Abraham himself is removed from his native land by his father. At the same time and from the same place Terah draws Lot, left in the grandfather's care by the death of *his* father, Abraham's brother Haran. Assuming as we may that Lot is younger than his uncle by at least half a generation, it follows that Abraham's recollection of Ur is more vivid. Now Babylon, as the Bible sees it, is a culture of cities. Of Nimrod, the founder of Babylon, we are told that he 'built Nineveh, Rehobothir, Calah, and Resen between Nineveh and Calah; that is the great city' (Genesis 10:11–12). The string of urban centres calls to mind the crescent of seaboard from Boston to Washington, grazing livestock visible from the turnpikes only (if at all) through the haze. Abraham, then, emigrates from a part of the world where city dwelling is the norm. His shepherding thus constitutes a retreat from the complexity of the typical walks of life that he experenced in his formative years. Since the departure is not only *a quo*, from an extant way, but also *ad quem*, to a new way, it follows that the city is problematic for Abraham. On all that he turns his back. The Bible of course knows where things are headed. Written from there and beyond, the Bible knows that things are moving in the direction of the city – Jerusalem. Lot is therefore a fitting guinea pig for retesting the human potential of that way of life. A grandson of Terah, Lot has the pedigree. Since he has departed Ur younger than Abraham, the grid lines of urban existence are more lightly impressed on him. So he is not antecedently biased.

Anything that can be used for good can be used for bad too. Perhaps (this would be the Bible's undogmatic thought) the progeny of Nimrod put the city to uses that it wasn't designed to serve. It therefore makes sense to scope Lot out. Which explains why God's messengers, their visit to Abraham's tent done (18:22), continue on to Sodom (19:1). Indeed, in the teeth of negative intelligence about cities from back in Babylon, and despite nagging doubts about Lot that are reinforced at every turn, God goes out of his way to keep an open mind about the nephew's *modus vivendi*. But what Lot does at the very end of his biblical run reprises, though at the opposite extreme, the Tower story. And with that the valves of God's attention close shut.

The builders of the Tower showed lack of trust in God's promise to spare the earth a repeat holocaust. God's world they attempted to replace with a better. Just so, Lot too betrays limited faith in his saviour. Told to flee Sodom, *his* world, to avoid perishing, Lot is given specific instructions. '[D]o not look back or stop anywhere in the Plain; flee to the hills' (19:17). The instructions are problematic for him. Unless he is allowed to settle in an urban environment he will, he explains, die, sc., his way of life will expire. The city dweller requires a city. God takes the self-evident point and relents. 'I grant you this favour' (21). Does God reverse the negative judgment that caused a match to be put to Sodom? He does not. Though Lot is cleared to settle on the plain, the clearance is limited to the place that Lot himself had proposed. Why is Zoar acceptable but not Sodom? 'Zoar' is cognate with 'narrow' or 'small.' In suggesting Zoar to God as a substitute for Sodom, Lot himself had described it so. Among cities, it is, he had said, 'a little one' (20). Lot, then, is dimly aware that size is part of the problem.

God's agreement to give Lot's way another chance is, we see, hedged round. City dwelling is to be allowed only in a simpler form. Metropolis has proven to be beyond the pale. Perhaps Smallville is clear of its taint.

Zoar, then, is available. So isn't Lot saved? In the event, he authors his own downfall. The image of fire and brimstone pulsing in his head, Lot 'was afraid to stay [even] in Zoar' (30). Unable to conquer his dread *even though God himself had given the go-ahead*, Lot lights out for a cave in the hills. Goodbye, then, to his residual promise. He has retreated too far towards chaos and is now dead to the narrative. The problems posed by the urban environment notwithstanding, the cave – which certainly falls on the wrong side of {0} – is no solution. As far back as the primordial Garden, men and women are set apart from beasts and lairs.

If chaos were acceptable to God, or if the confrontation with it caused God a paralysing dread, there would not have been a creation. Though he has done this at the opposite extreme from the Tower builders, Lot has in effect shown a deep God-unlikeness.

Of Lot, we hear no more.[7] The city and the ethical problems that the city poses will have to be confronted along the line of Abraham. Otherwise, Abraham's story will end like Ishmael's and Esau's, in field and tent. Which explains why the narrative soon represents the patriarch (21:33) performing what for a tent dweller is an absurdity. Abraham plants a tamarisk tree – an organism requiring half a human lifetime to mature!

Again we see that with respect to the orientation of the story the doublets serve the twofold purpose of specifying what counts (by the Bible's lights) as positive movement and what as negative. Lot advances in form-of-life complexity. City dwelling is more complex than tent dwelling. But Lot's movement is a retreat, ethically. The angels, in visiting Lot, move eastwards from Abraham. They move in the generally regressive direction. Lot, in fleeing from Sodom to Zoar, moves westwards – *slightly* westwards! Observe that the text (13:10) previously had Lot passing *eastwards* through Zoar on his way to Sodom.

Off the Map

Up to and including the part of the national story brushed just above, Genesis is focused on the emergence into the world of men and women and on their early doings. In both world creation accounts God's activity is devoted to fashioning a habitable sphere *for* men and women. All the narrative effort is applied to determining the {0}-position in respect of *human* flourishing. The story of Noah leaves no doubt. It can scarcely have been an increase in depravity among the beasts that necessitated the global irrigation. The natural world serves only as *mise-en-scène* to the sentimental and social and moral education of men and women. The predominance of the judgment 'good' in Genesis 1 also points to the focus on the distinctively human. God can scarcely regard light as good in and of itself. For purposes of hiding, darkness is much to be preferred. The angel who wrestles with Jacob (to take one instance) fears the dawn. The judgment 'good' is relative to the function that the illumination serves. And the function is understood by reference to the culmination of the creation: humankind. Nor does the ominous-sounding introduction of 'bad' in the second panel of Genesis make, or signal, a fundamental change. The problem that the story of disobedience in and departure from Eden dramatizes is still a fundamentally human problem. But something is missing. Missing is a consideration of nature *qua* nature. I will now give a sense of this something. The Bible, I will in the process show, is quite aware of it.

A TV program of my youth, *Ben Casey*, commenced with the title character inscribing on a chalkboard the following symbols.

♂
♀
*
†
∞

Man. Woman. Birth. Death. Infinity. Genesis's agenda, nearly enough. The list might as a whole be titled 'Humankind.' The itemization is however incomplete. To a fuller tableau the general title 'World' can be affixed:

nature
humankind

The world of men and women, the world whose emergence is described in Genesis along with *their* creation, and indeed as the backdrop to it, doesn't exhaust the whole. The part housing non-human creatures is every bit as solid. Unlike Europe and North America, unlike Venus and Mars, these two worlds are not spatially distinct. The two are different ways of thinking about the selfsame physical whole that all of us share. One way is, to put it in the terms of religious typology, pagan; the other is theistic.

The Bible uses plot line repetitions to get its message across. The story of Noah, a double of the story of the primordial creation, itself contains a doublet: the flights of the birds. The repetition in this case is thematically revealing too. But in this case the repetition does not just raise issues about the location of the {0}-point. It indicates that the terms of assessment in the Bible are themselves of restricted applicability. The

Bible, that is, is underscoring that these terms do duty in respect of the Proverbist's four, not of his three.

The raven symbolizes the world understood in non-human, natural terms. Since these terms are non-human, spelling them out isn't easy. What's it like to be a raven? To answer the question, the Bible sometimes negates human terms, as with uncleanness; sometimes, as in the idea of darkness, it proceeds more metaphorically. The raven does not return to the ark, then, because its place is not among men and women.

After the raven vanishes over the horizon, a second bird is dispatched. The dove is sent aloft twice. The first time it wings back empty of beak; the second time, it returns bearing 'a freshly plucked olive leaf' (8:11). That the dove touches down on the first occasion with nothing in its hold highlights the fact that return is under the circumstances entirely possible. *So why not the raven?* That the dove passes twice makes it virtually impossible for the reader not to feel the spectral presence of a biblical Reveen suggesting this question into his or her head.

Had the dove retrieved the leaf on its first circuit the reader might have essayed the following naturalistic explanation on which the earlier bird's non-return is thematically inert. Not only are both creatures sent out; but also, they are sent out in a certain order. The raven was set loose when, the floodwaters being fuller, the chances of finding a landing strip were more remote. The raven had therefore to venture farther. Indeed, so far did it venture that it lost contact with the ark. Noah, inferring that this had occurred, proceeded to select a bird with a smaller compass and a less doughty character.

For reasons to be furnished in full in the next chapter, I do not grant that the bird of genus *Corvus* and the bird of genus *Columba* are both released to find San Salvador. The flight of the raven carries a different message. But even if a common mission is assumed, this treatment of the story won't fly. Independently of the assumption, it can be allowed that once the rains stop, drying is the trend. Since Noah is still at sea as to how far the waters have subsided, prudence dictates to him under the circumstances to select a similar or a more robust bird the second time. The selection of the weaker flier *invites* the same negative outcome, does it not? For all Noah knows, the percentage abatement of the water may be less than the percentage difference between the stamina of the birds. So the dove too may be lost. Noah is not of course John James Audubon. If, however, the explanation is backed up by pinning on the principal certain (false) beliefs, then the text turns sphyngian.

How would Noah have reacted to God's tocsin about the gathering storm had he believed that men were amphibian?

The contrast between the dove and the raven resists being treated like the contrast between Abel and Cain or the contrast between Abraham and Lot. Assuming, as we may, that the flights of the birds are thematically significant, we can conclude that more is at stake than an internal ethical or moral contrast.

Having indicated that the dark bird alights elsewhere, Genesis bids the raven adieu. But *Scripture* is not done with it. Scripture, we shall see, bids the bird *'À Dieu.'* True, we are never treated to a tour of Raven's Land. The Bible is however voluble enough to enable us to enlarge on the nature of the place, that is, the place of nature. The position is as just now stated: though men and women are represented in the Torah as creation's culmination, nature, independent nature beyond the rainbow that seals the covenant with humankind, is God's doing too. The gesture in Genesis is, then, in the direction of paganism.[8]

From the standpoint of the coordinate scheme, how is the matter disposed? It is not that Genesis doesn't travel back behind its {0}-position. Since the location of the origin is unclear, the Bible would be in constant danger of occasionally doing so even if it wished to avoid doing so, *and it does not wish*. But when venturing into that territory Genesis sticks all the while to human terms. When venturing into that territory Genesis is still investigating distinctively human reality. On the negative side of the {0}-position the narrative peoples the world with several characters close (too close for *its* liking) to nature but who stem from the same source as the refined types in whom a future is seen. Ishmael and Esau are more uncouth than their brothers. Ishmael, 'a wild ass of a man' (7:12), is said to be 'at odds' (ibid.) with all his kin. Esau is 'a skillful hunter, a man of the field' (25:27). Hunting and foraging, they have their being near to bedrock. They are, we might say, *naturals*. This, however, just accentuates the contrast. We are told what becomes of Esau and of Ishmael, of where their lives are lived and how. Of the raven? Silence.

The raven is entirely off this narrower map. It symbolizes a place to which the coordinate scheme has no application. Here and there the narrower map gestures towards the bird's habitat. It does so for instance in the cave on the hillside overlooking Zoar where Lot couples with his daughters; where the incest taboo, a hallmark of human culture, is removed and men and women revert to bestial status. Depravity is one thing. Of depravity the Bible is a connoisseur. Aside from the creation itself the most important act in the foundational chapters of Genesis is a transgression. Depravity is one thing. Beyond good and evil is another thing entirely, with which the Bible has the extremest difficulty. (Sexual relations between parents and their offspring are depraved in the human realm, but the corresponding thing in the subhuman realm is no more depraved than water's raining down onto and merging with *la mer* from which it vapourized earlier. So the cave overlooking Zoar is no more than a *gesture* towards that other place.) Yet to its credit and/or in an access of realism the Bible does not pretend that the area beyond good and evil doesn't exist, nor does it ignore the interface between that realm and the world of men and women.

4
Raven's Land

Flying the Coop

The rains have let up. Beneath the clearing skies the waters are beginning to recede. Noah seeks a place for the ark to berth and for the world, reseeded with its precious cargo, to be born again.

Noah's first postdiluvian act is to send a raven out over the waves. '[I]t went to and fro,' the Bible tells us, 'until the waters were dried up from the earth' (Genesis 8:7). Why doesn't the raven return to the vessel? Though Noah's annals conclude with no further mention of the bird, it does not perish. Its story *is* resumed later in Scripture – much later in fact. That the sequel is deferred until the ink has dried on most of the Tanakh is no accident. As will emerge, the place in creation where the raven comes to nest lies beyond the margins of the world that God, in the Torah, fashions for humankind. Its habitat is outside the borders of man's estate. The later inclusion of Raven's Land therefore concedes the incompleteness of the Bible's foundational story of the nature of things and of the place of men and women. The concession is deliberate. Otherwise, why mention the raven? But the later inclusion complements the core story. The story's stability is not thereby compromised. This is not to say that the inclusive account is self-evidently true, only that the position is no sitting duck. Indeed, the position is one from which philosophical instruction can still be taken.

Why mention the raven? The question isn't rhetorical. Could the raven's limelit quarter-hour not be a salute to extant stories of a watery holocaust with which the fashioners of the Bible were acquainted, notably the Gilgamesh Epic? Encounters with chapter-and-verse over the years have persuaded me that pretty much every textual element that functions to shape the biblical plot and keep it chugging along has thematic significance. Every such element is, that is, *thematically active*. So the one-way flight of the raven at 8:7 is an invitation.[1]

And There Was Evening and There Was Morning

Seven days pass, a full week of days, before Noah opens the hatch a second time to the dove. The duration is thematically significant. The first time the dove is sent out (this is described in the verse, verse 8, immediately following the single verse in which the whole story of the raven is told) is too soon. *Too soon for the dove!* It is sent out the first time into a world where the raven alone is at home. Only after the raven is a going concern does the creation in Genesis, the creation of the human world, begin. The world of the raven (to put it non-temporally) is a different kind of world.

This clear, we can extract theme from narrative particulars that at first sight seem subservient solely to plot. Not only are raven and dove (the birds) carriers of the thematic message. So are 'raven' and 'dove' (the words). Hebrew 'raven' perches on the same stem as Hebrew 'west' and 'evening.' The bird is black. The light dawns posterior to it. In that sense the raven pre-exists the opening of Genesis, the dawning of the human world. The raven is unclean. It is likened, that is, to the initial chaos, a mingling of elements that should be kept separate. The dove contrasts on all these scores, literal *and* figurative. White in colour, stereotypically so among the birds, *its* name is close to Hebrew for 'day.'[2] In folklore, the dove symbolizes brotherly amity. The raven stands apart from men and women.

Indubitably, a deliberate and systematic contrast. The dove is appropriate to signalling Creation Redux because of its unlikeness to the raven. The dove is sent out the second time *seven days* after its wild goose chase. The story of the Flood being a reprise of Genesis 1, the conjecture about the pre-existent character of the raven is thus sustained. Close attention to the text discloses that Noah does not dispatch the dove *because* the raven fails to return. The dove, the second bird that Noah sends out, is the first bird that Noah lets loose 'to see if the waters had subsided' (8:8). Why doesn't the raven return? *Its* world has nothing to do with the Flood. *Its* world is impervious to the waters. There is therefore no reason for the raven to come back. Why do the storytellers include the raven in Noah's floating menagerie in the first place? The bird is taken on board expressly by way of drawing attention to its difference from the dove, signalling thereby that the locus of concern is as it were the dovecote, not the wilderness.[3]

We now pay a visit to a biblical seminary where the teacher gives his charge a glimpse of that pre-existent place, the most extensive glimpse in Scripture. The student's card reads 'Job.'

In the genealogy given for their protagonist, those who take up the raven's tale in the Book of Job identify themselves as part of the tradition of the creators of Genesis, albeit displaced from its centre. A native son of Uz, Job is traced back to Abraham's brother Nahor. He too stems from the house of Terah.[4] The thematic connection between Abraham and Job parallels the blood relationship. The specific issue exercising those who take up the tale in the Book of Job is an issue that though gestured at in core Scripture is left undeveloped. Certainly, the generic issue that the Book of Job raises, viz., the *theodicy* issue, is one that Abraham had during his career wrestled with on more than one occasion. My thesis about Genesis, its anthropofocus, is verified by the relation of the answer Job gets from God to the answer that Abraham receives when, informed of the plan to incinerate Sodom and Gomorrah, he opens negotiations with his sponsor to temper the blow. The issue of justice between the Creator and Abraham is an issue, exclusively, of justice in the interpersonal sphere. Must courses of action be implemented that result in foreseeable harm coming to men and women who have done no wrong? God's lesson to Abraham (the person tipped as national patriarch) is that political imperatives sometimes unavoidably cause even the righteous to suffer. Good leaders strive to minimize collateral damage. Yet they keenly appreciate that political decision making cannot be predicated on its reduction to zero. Leaders whose otherwise successful choices leave the innocent unscathed are lucky. If their decisions are too narrowly based on the idea of passing over the houses of the blameless they cannot however be regarded as wise. The issue of justice between the creator and Abraham is, I said, an issue, exclusively, of justice in the human sphere. By contrast, the issue of God's justice in Job's case is *not* interpersonal. Job did *not* suffer due to the clash of nations or to civil strife. As to kin, sometimes the source of a man's troubles, we should all be so fortunate. No, the source of Job's suffering is different. Speaking from the whirlwind, God explains: it comes from (extra-human) nature. It originates outside Genesis's coordinate scheme; beyond the borders of the creation as Genesis presents it.

Here is a proportionality that capsules the matter.

Job : Abraham :: Raven : Dove

Not that *Job* himself is raven-like. Rather, the issue of the creation's justice that Job's case tries is the issue an appropriate emblem for which would be the pre-existent bird. Abraham contrasts with Job as problems of the sort encountered inside man's estate (e.g., amity-and-enmity, war-and-peace) contrast with problems that arise at the interface with the wilds (e.g., dearth-and-plenty, health-and-disease). Were the books of the Bible bound in illustrated covers, an appropriate illustration for Job would feature a raven perched on an oyster, the latter representing the (human) world in which we live.

What does the Book of Job teach? Here are two representative passages, the first 38:41, the second 38:25–27, both of them parts of God's answer from out the maelstrom:

> Who provides for the raven its prey,
> when its young ones cry to God,
> and wander about for lack of food?
>
> Who has cut a channel for the torrents of rain,
> and a way for the thunderbolt,
> to bring rain on a land where no one lives,
> on the desert, which is empty of human life,
> to satisfy the waste and desolate land,
> and to make the ground put forth grass?

Once we observe that the Torah's Weather Channel sends *completely moralized forecasts and reports* out over the waves, the force of these passages is clear. A list of climatological events has already been compiled: gentle mists at the world's gestation to ease the labour, zephyrs in Eden, Noah's genocidal inundation, healing winds, a covenantal rainbow, providential droughts in Canaan, plagues of thunder, hail and fire in Egypt. The unyielding earth is relativized to men and women, made (mere) backcloth for their toilsome lives. The passages from Job deny the relativization. But indifferent nature is God's handiwork too. If a person contracts cancer, then, assuming winner-take-all, either the malignancy is killed off or the bearer of the affliction succumbs. Victory for the one spells defeat for the other.[5] In such contests we people are homers. Unless God's *exclusive* interest is in us, that preference is however just a species of chauvinism – 'speciesism' it is unprepossessingly called in philosophical circles.

The story of Job is used to question the idea of belief-in-God in a world in which, short of subduing nature as parents do when they tame the wilds for their children, short of paving over the world as we know it or replacing it with a Buckminster Fuller dome, God cannot offer guarantees against winter and rough weather. Like Abraham, Job is singled out. 'Have you considered my servant Job?' God asks Satan. 'There is no one like him on the earth, a blameless and upright man who fears God and turns away from evil' (1:8).[6] But since nature is nature even in Job's world, the chosen-ness doesn't save him from the instrumentality personified in the figure of Satan. In effect:

Satan : Uz :: Serpent : Eden

'Where were you,' God thunders at Job, 'when I laid the foundations of the earth?' (38:4).[7] At first blush, this comes across as an epistemological question. 'Being in knowledge as puny as you are, who in the world are you to express reservations about my ways? What do *you* know?' When they presume to 'contend with the Almighty' (40:2), men and women are well advised to factor in the implications of their cognitive limitations. Yet the thundering has, has more basically even, ontological import.[8] 'You, a man, were not always part of creation, and in creation you are not alone.' That the world pre-existed our species is the less important of the conjuncts. Genesis itself represents men and women as arriving on the sixth day. The claim about having company is the more important. It is the claim that deviates from Genesis. 'Is the wild ox willing to serve you?' (39:9).[9] Who said that nature is merely a stage for your strutting and fretting?

If, *pace* Genesis's anti-pagan thrust, men and women were latecomers *for whom all of what preceded was not preparatory*, doesn't that void their existences of worth? If the parturition of men and women is improperly located in a place cultivated with them expressly in mind, what are the implications?

We need not decide whether the characterization of men and women as latecomers sucks the value out of their existences. A milder possibility is elliptical: more than one locus of value exists. That, however, is already problem enough for the Bible.

The deeper question is whether God's answer isn't an evasion from a theistic perspective. Needless to say, ravens and deserts don't got religion. What effectively is the difference between having God preside separately over extra-human nature and denying that God is omnicompetent and/or omnibenevolent? Cruel choices both for the devout! Before addressing the Bible's reaction, we must first improve our grasp of the pagan position.

Ornitheology

Was the communion that Abraham departed for the Promised Land pagan? That the charge of idolatry is levelled against its adherents indicates an affirmative. Abraham's departure is thus at least in part a leave-taking from pagan ways. The problem with the raven in the story of Noah offers oblique confirmation. So extreme is the Bible's minimization of the place of nature, and so unrealistic to the experience of men and women, that one must assume equal and opposite exaggeration.

Most amateurs of the literature here being addressed are more knowledgeable about Greek culture than they are in Mesopotamian, just as they are better versed in the pentameters of the English Bard than in the Hellenic one's hexameters. Following Abraham as he treks to Canaan, but keeping due on '[t]o the Propontic and the Hellespont' when he turns south, let me therefore shift the discussion to the Aegean basin. The swap of cultures will enable us quickly to see why the abandonment of the raven, theistic evasion or no, is crucial to the biblical agenda.

Male deities associated in the way of identity with nature dominate the Olympian pantheon: Zeus is the emperor of the air; Poseidon's moods account for the calm seas and their distempers; Hades presides over the nether region's misty exudations. Yet in this frame the meteorological, marine, and geological happenings are morally neutral. The Olympian gods proceed heedless of the men and women whose lives they affect.

With the picturesque anthropomorphizing neutralized, this is a not unrealistic picture. Investing the weather with psychology (let alone with moral significance) falsifies it. True, in Homer's epics the gods interact regularly with creatures of flesh and blood. But only readers whose *Weltanschauung* is Walt-*anschauung* will swallow whole the dramatization of, say, Pluto. When Homer depicts a god taking the side of a human actor, this partisanship, the reflective will appreciate, can be captured by a figurative form like 'The sun smiled upon me,' or 'The currents ran favourable to my course.' (Since the sun and the waters are always doing *something* to men and women, the regularity of interaction reflects the reality.) Homer's men and women are struggling to define themselves and make a go of their lives in the face of an engulfing nature that does not care. Nature is as indifferent, as self-absorbed if you will, as the gods. The similarity is no accident. The rains in season may mean a bountiful harvest. That meaning is however to *us*. Nature in short is neither benign nor malign. It does not care, and not because it is uncaring. It plays no favourites, though not because it is even-handed. It is entirely in itself. Wallace Stevens ('A Room on a Garden') puts it well:

Order, the law of hopes and rakes,
May be perceived in windy quakes
And squalls.

The gardener searches earth and sky
The truth in nature to espy
In vain.

He well might find that eager balm
In lilies' stately-statued calm;
But then

He might well find it in this fret
Of lilies rusted, rotting, wet
with rain.

The Torah cannot comfortably incorporate such a view. If the world described in the Torah were not by design our oyster, we would have to look elsewhere for the foundational creation story of the West. True, outside Eden, toil and sweat are the daily portion. The pearls strung at intervals on the thread of life – our successes, our good times, the offspring that light our days, and so on – congeal around pieces of grit. The Genesis story does not however treat the irritants as natural. If the oyster is more flophouse than five-star hotel, we – Genesis says – have no one to blame but ourselves.

Since a great deal of bad arrives from outside the human realm, should it really be so hard for Genesis to have it worming its way in from that quarter? A walker in the woods felled by a trunk is just as dead as a walker on the city streets cut down by a drunk. Nor would introducing bad from the quite different sector of being upset the Bible's applecart of distinctively human depravity. (Cain's sin in regard to Abel would not be mitigated by his indicating that the latter's sheep had succumbed in the past to foot-and-mouth.) Yet while the problem, as a dramatic one, is child's play for writers as able as the Bible's, it is, as a philosophical problem, tough going. In Job, extra-human nature is represented, along lines that *we* readily understand, as a place where God is on holiday. In nature, God dons Bermudas, slips on the flip-flops, and heads for La Finca to hang out with Papa Hemingway (41:1, 5):

> Can you draw out Leviathan with a fishhook,
> or press down its tongue with a cord?
>
> Will you play with it as with a bird,
> or will you put it on leash for your girls?

If at the gate of the Temple that God has instructed us to construct for him is frequently found suspended a sign – 'Gone Fishing' – how can there be any certitude in the human realm? God can declare himself a holiday and head for the wilds whenever the getting and spending is too much with him – whenever, in fact, he wishes.[10]

The core part of the Bible does not ignore such matters. As the struggle to leash *our* bird, the raven, has shown, the issue is confronted obliquely. Let us take a last look at the very first chapters of Genesis to see what more, prior to the story of Noah, is pertinently said.[11]

An air of contentment wafts over Genesis 1. At each step of creation, God delivers the verdict 'good.' The judgment is not a moral one. The idea is that each thing that is brought into being does its proper job. More than just consistent with friction, the truth of this also probably *presupposes* friction, functions usually being exercised by some X 'on' or 'with respect to' some Y that puts up resistance. Waters, seeking their level, encroach upon dry parts; and dry parts for their part keep waters at bay. When wet and dry each does its thing, a rough equilibrium results. Advancing waves throw sand onto the beach. Retreating, they scour the sand back. Similarly, to make another round of the ward, should penicillin check the spread of bacteria, that too is 'good.' But a fundamental change occurs once men and women are spirited onto the scene. These do not have a function as do water and dry land. These stand in a skewed relationship to the world into which they are injected. They are by nature misfits.

The text marks the skew in a variety of ways. '[D]ominion' (1:26) over the whole is bestowed upon men and women. Men and women are understood not to be in balance with nature in anything like the way that the various parts of nature are in reciprocal balance. We can just as accurately say that the flowers make use of the bees for pollination as say that the bees make use of the flowers for food (our preference for the second description is anthropomorphic). But no one save as a grim joke would say that the forest that is being clear-cut is making use of the fellers. In human terms (to approach the difference from another angle) we say that an infant mortality rate of 25 per cent is 100 per cent failure, not 75 per cent success. Also, men and women are given a blessing. The blessing is needed because men and women don't have a natural, 'hard-wired' way of proceeding. Recall the distinction between the Proverbist's three and his four. In cases of the latter sort alone would the use of the plural, 'ways,' be appropriate. If you can go this way or that way, you need a blessing. 'Lots of luck.' So while it is true that the Genesis 1 account of our advent is more 'natural' than the Genesis 2 account, the 'un-naturalness' of our 'nature' is still marked. Hopes flickering in a reader of the Bible's first chapter of an eventual rapprochement between the natural and the human are dealt a more serious blow by Genesis 2, where the binary 'good and bad' predominates.

Is rapprochement possible on the basis of Genesis 1 alone? If it is, then perhaps naturalists – on the political side animal rights activists and environmentalists, on the philosophical side deep ecologists and Benthamites for whom the capacity to feel pain is the morally relevant common denominator – could make limited positive use of Scripture, and those committed to the Bible would not have to turn their backs on nature.[12] I am doubtful. What does God's judgment 'good' mean? Is it, even though not a moral judgment, a value judgment? It is hard to see how outside the theistic frame the affirmative could be defended. Take the determination of function. Apart from saying that the function of X is to be X and to do as X does, what more can be said? The term 'natural' is not univocal. Sometimes it means 'that which happens most often.' In this sense, hurricanes and earthquakes are unnatural. In another sense, such storms and rumblings are perfectly natural: unusual but not miraculous. *This* would seem to be the sense appropriate to God's judgment. If so, dreadful and catastrophic things (by human standards) are quite natural, and hence 'good.'

The world could be a place of, by *our* lights, only catastrophic events. As the disease example shows, every interaction can be seen as catastrophic for some party. Casting our gaze beyond the parties directly involved, even in symbiotic cases we invariably find something that answers to 'catastrophe.' Consider the tickbird that rides the rhinoceros and pecks food from the pachyderm's skin. The animal gets cleaned of ticks. The bird has a meal. The two live symbiotically. But what about those insects that infest the beast? *They* perish.[13] So either God's judgment 'good' is a value judgment, or else 'good' is void of discriminatory force. If the latter, *whatever* God had seen would have qualified. In the words of the Buick commercial: 'It's all good.' Since 'good' is certainly not empty, we must agree that Genesis 1 is beyond naturalism. The relativization to the human condition is deep and inexpungeable.[14]

Ich-theology or Ichthyology?

Our next port of call is Raven's Land, there to inspect the anti-biblical value position, the anti-theistic cultural *ensemble*, that is (supposedly) rooted in nature. Two elements are central to the position: *autochthony* and *contingency*. Of these I hold a pair of things, the first as a matter of straight analysis, the second as a matter of normative politics. On the analytic side: the labels for the elements are ambiguous just as is 'good' in Genesis 1, and the value position based on them that advertises itself as 'natural' trades on the ambiguity. It is one thing to liken oneself, analogically, to the raven. It is quite another thing to assert, in a straight comparison, a resemblance or similarity to the raven. A position can be founded on the morally active side of the double meaning. Such a position is indeed out there in the world of positions. But I hold, now in a morally engaged mode, that the position, whose major appeal lies in its allegedly 'natural' basis, is problematic. 'Problematic' is euphemistic. The position is dangerous, even pernicious.

Although neither of the two elements is itself value laden, the first, autochthony, gets linked with the normative notion of belonging or proprietorship (to be from elsewhere diminishes one's claims), the second, contingency, with the normative notion of accident or chance (what is had or gained accidentally is not deserved). In Raven's Land, *qua* cultural *topos* rather than natural place, we find autochthony and contingency illicitly transformed into their value-laden counterparts. They are, to speak the current lingo, frankenvalues.

The rejection of autochthony is the very beginning of the Bible's story of humankind. Three characters, all with starring roles, enact the message of separation. The (cultural, sc., human) life of Adam, the archetypal chthonian of the Western tradition, is lived outside Eden, the primordial womb and nursery. The world, in Genesis 2, springs into life when God sprinkles water onto it. Just so, Abraham's cue is God's beckoning call to depart the land in which he first saw the light and was acculturated. Whatever historical migration Abraham's movement tracks, the underlying idea is, again, that human beings are only loosely rooted in this soil or that humus. Like Abraham, God too hits the road. He departs Babylon, *his* native land.

Kangaroos are at home in Australia. Lions stalk the African veldt. Maple trees are native to North America. Clouds populate the sky and the planets wheel in *their* orbits. In none of this is there anything to fault. What happens when we extend the idea of being native to men and women?

From the standpoint of the biblical conceptualization, men and women are the very opposite of autochthons. A shade tree won't survive in a desert clime, and a cactus will rot in the tropical rainforest. By contrast, men and women, carrying their environment, the human environment, with them, can live anywhere. Some day the term 'cosmonaut' might come to apply literally to more than a few ex-Soviets.

The idea of home for men and women thus differs from the idea as it applies to beasts. We know about the migration of the tern from one region of midnight sun to its antipode; about the journey of salmon from mid-ocean to the stream they left as fingerlings, there to spawn and die. Powerful images, these, of place and belonging. Images only, though. The tern is no less at home south of the equator than north of it; the salmon's habitat is the whole comprising ocean and river and stream. Like tern and salmon, men and women often expend great quantities of energy to get back to where they were before. But when men and women return, and this does not occur after forcible displacement, it is nostalgia. Of nostalgia we hear from the Bible at the end of Genesis 3: terrifying guards are stationed at the gates of Eden to bar the way back. No place is off *our* flight path. *We* are never fish out of water. *Our* home is where we make it. We leave our parents' abode, as they left theirs, and as our children will ours. We all leave the place of our nativity. For good and for ill, that – according to the biblical story – is our condition.[15]

To put it thus makes it sound, erroneously, as if the rooted way would be better. Louis Menand pinpoints the seductive power of the emotion that nourishes the mistaken thought about roots.[16]

> We think of nostalgia as an emotion that grows with age, but, like most emotions, it is keenest when we are young. Is there any nostalgia more

> powerful than the feelings of a third grader revisiting his or her classroom? Those tiny chairs, the old paste jars, the cubbies where we stuffed our extra sweaters – we want to climb back into that world, but we're third graders now, much too large. We've fallen off the carrousel. Although 'youth' is supposed to mean an enthusiasm for change, young people don't want change any more than anyone else does, and possibly less. What they secretly want is what Holden wants: they want the world to be like the Museum of Natural History, with everything frozen exactly the way it was the first day they encountered it.
>
> A great deal of 'youth culture' – that is, the stuff that young people actually consume, as opposed to the stuff that older people consume (like 'Lord of the Flies') in order to learn about youth – plays to this feeling of loss. You go to a dance where a new pop song is playing, and for the rest of your life hearing that song triggers the same emotion. It comes on the radio, and you think, That's when things were truly fine. You want to hear it again and again. You have become addicted.

For the sake of being fully human, one must kick the habit. The result of remaining hooked? A witches' brew of inwardness, collective thinking, and xenophobia, a cauldron seething with fabricated grievances and trumped-up resentments. The death star of this constellation for our times is anti-Semitism: the Jews vilified as rootless internationalists, vagabonds and wanderers, their passport money to which borders are porous. As history ought by now to have taught, racial nostalgia and purity of stock belong to a very dangerous suite of ideas indeed.[17]

The 'logic' of cultural autochthony is featured by what might aptly be labelled 'the principle of natural conversion.'

A belongs to B; so, B belongs to A.

The Aboriginals belong to the land; the land is their *element*. Ergo, the land belongs to the Aboriginals; the land is *their* element. The conversion might work for animals and plants. The cactus and the desert, the Douglas fir and the rainforest, really do belong to each other. When it comes to men and women the conversion fails.

Like any piece of illogic this piece has the capacity to generate problematic entailments. Here, from recent events, is an illustration of the kind of havoc that adherence to the principle can wreak.

In 1996 human skeletal remains dated nine thousand years past and typed as Caucasian by the standard scientific tests were unearthed in

Washington State.[18] The Aboriginals of the region, repeating the mantra that white men, interlopers and exploiters, arrived with Columbus and that they alone are native, claimed the bones ancestral and demanded their repatriation for ritual interment.

The moral claims of Aboriginals are perfectly comprehensible apart from such mythic deposits and metaphysical infusions. That men and women constitute a species native to nowhere does not mean that all claims to ownership of a particular area or to rights over its contents are of equal merit. The early colonizers concluded treaties with the Aboriginals. When the provisions no longer suited them, the relative newcomers proceeded in many instances cynically to violate their solemn undertakings. The issue of redress and compensation is difficult. Those who have benefited cannot justifiably condone the colonizers' forked-tongued duplicities. Some response to the negatively affected is required.

I've used unfriendly language to describe the 'natural' position. In *Out of Africa* Isak Dinesen sympathetically evokes the 'deeper' idea of belonging.[19]

> The Natives have, far less than the white people, the sense of risks in life. Sometimes on a Safari, or on the farm, in a moment of extreme tension, I have met the eyes of my Native companions, and have felt that we were at a great distance from one another, and that they were wondering at my apprehension of our risk. It made me reflect that perhaps they were, in life itself, within their own element, such as we can never be, like fishes in deep water which for the life of them cannot understand our fear of drowning.

This isn't at all clear. Similes are by nature unstable. Waxing explicitly theological (19–20), Dinesen just makes matters worse:

> This assurance, this art of swimming, they had, I thought, because they had preserved a knowledge that was lost to us by our first parents; Africa, amongst the continents, will teach it to you: that God and the Devil are one, the majesty coeternal, not two uncreated but one uncreated, and the Natives neither confounded the persons nor divided the substance.

No difference between good and bad? A truth is present here that the Bible dimly recognizes in holding back 'bad' in Genesis 1. Nature is beneath good-and-bad. *Pace* Dinesen, 'beneath good-and-bad' is not however synonymous with 'a mixture.' And, as I have indicated, the waters are muddied when men and women are added. Dinesen is getting theology out of ichthyology.

So much for autochthony. As for contingency, the lines of division are less sharp, since what is said is not just plain false. The idea behind contingency is that the disposition of things in the world, and specifically our presence in the world, is not preordained. For obvious reasons, the Bible cannot say this straight. The Book of Job, which amends the core biblical story, does more than just exhibit sensitivity to the point. In a slightly oblique manner it actually *asserts* the point. Given that our condition is accidental, what follows? Given that we are the products of chance, what view should we take of ourselves?

Using the idiom as it is usually used, I spoke of the world of Genesis as our oyster. Bill Reid's sculptural rendering of the anthropogenic myth of the Haida of the Pacific Northwest, *The Raven and the First Man*, depicts men and women emerging from a bivalve's shell that the trickster figure of the mythical world view has pried open out of sheer curiosity.[20] Quite different, this, than Michelangelo's God fingering Adam into life. Needless to say, the representation of our presence as answering to no transcendent intention or plan is one that *my* readers are more than likely to endorse.

The proposition that our presence here is not necessary is not a proposition that I would dispute. More to the point, I do not think that the Bible disputes the proposition. The story of Genesis 1 is the story of a maker who finds that the creation does *not* answer dutifully to his creative efforts. Time after time God is obliged to go back and try again. But the biblical view obviously does not infer 'our self-image should be one that stresses that our existence is just a matter of chance' from 'our presence here is accidental.'

Here also there is a questionable logic. From 'our presence is not necessary' is conjured 'we should not raise ourselves up.' The Bible is typically misunderstood in regard to the idea of elevation. Having been made in God's image and likeness, we are enjoined to perform an *imitatio Dei*. Such performance can look from a distance like prideful self-aggrandizement. But the situation of men and women outside Eden is the same as the situation of God with respect to creation as a whole. When we leave the Garden our *imitatio* has to reflect the fact that God's road to creating a habitable world wasn't strewn with thornless roses. Where's the self-aggrandizement in that?

At the start of this chapter I reported that, seeking a place for the ark to berth and for the lifeless world to be born again, Noah sends a raven out over the waves. In point of fact the world outside the ark isn't completely lifeless. One class of God's creatures survives. Are we supposed to think its members sinless? Our course would then be clear. Be schooled by the fish! The fact is that the Bible takes some encrypted steps to supply an informative negative answer to this linkage of morality with ichthyology. Of the organisms that God creates in Genesis 1 only two classes get a blessing: men and women (28); and fish (22). What parallel could the writers have in mind? In contrast to the other things that God made, men and women lack a function. Not designed for a purpose, they follow no set pattern in their behaviour. They can move every which way. (They have 'ways,' not just 'a way.') So they need a blessing.[21] In regard to motion, the same is, topologically speaking, *literally* true of fish. In their watery medium, they move up and down, backwards and forwards, left and right, diagonally too. (What might 'flounder' be in biblical Hebrew?) By contrast, the luminaries, as if on a set of tracks, follow a fixed course. The same goes for land animals, since dry land lacks the z-axis. The message is clear, and the message is not that fish need a blessing. The message, if I may switch species, is that it's the later bird, not the early one, that gets the worm.

Xenophanes Answered

The raven is Genesis's emblem for honest-to-goodness nature. By having the bird vanish beyond the rainbow the Bible is indicating that the biblical agenda *in principio* does not include nature as an independent item for discussion. But the raven, though gone, is not forgotten. Its story is picked up again at several points in Scripture. It is brushed in the story of the prophet Elijah, and the Book of Job fledges it out fully. Job thus fills in the gap in Genesis; does so *deliberately*, I would say. Reincorporating real nature into the creation, Job traces a few central implications of the fact that the world was in some aspect not made for men and women. Let me quote again God's rhetorical question to Job (38:41):

> Who provides for the raven its prey,
> when its young ones cry to God
> and wander about for lack of food?

Just so, the raven provides for Elijah when, having delivered a harsh message to Ahab, the prophet hightails it to the safety of the wilderness east of the Jordan. (See 1 Kings 17:4–6.) Not only, then, is the creation a habitation for men and women. Also, its subhuman inhabitants are more of the zoo or the terrarium or the aviary or the aquarium than of the wilds. This is not how the text puts it. It has the man naming the animals, a point that reflects, in a more rarefied way, what I said about mixing labour and about Vico.

The contrast that the writers know, between real nature, nature as it is in itself, and the human-relativized nature of Genesis, nature for us, draws out the Bible's answer to a question that the secular are itching to press. 'I will never again,' God had stated, 'curse the ground because of humankind' (9:21). What about the Black Death of fourteenth-century Europe, the tsunami of 2004, the AIDS epidemic ravaging Africa, and so much more? If the devout were to point to the phrase 'every living creature' (ibid.) and say that the first and second were geographically local, while the third, though global, was affecting only one sector of living things, the appropriate response would be scorn. The correct answer to the secular is that God undertook not to use nature as a punishment. About natural catastrophes God promised nothing. (In and of themselves, natural catastrophes are in any case not catastrophic. They too would draw the 'good' of Genesis 1.) Nature, God said, would not be unleashed to discipline men and women for their moral transgressions and failings. No claim was made that nature would not do its own thing, inevitably on occasion with devastating effects from the human point of view. Indeed, had God claimed that he would see to it that nature not do its own thing, what could that have meant anyway?[22]

Proponents of the Documentary Hypothesis do not have to penetrate far into Scripture for confirmation of cutting and pasting. The two creation stories, the first in Genesis 1, the second in Genesis 2, are evidence enough. Further to the claim that DH's truth is neutral on the Bible's interpretability, let me show how the chapters cooperate with respect to the present issue. Specifically, the later chapter, which tells the more human, biographical-type story, is conceptually prior to the earlier. That Genesis 1 cannot fully be understood without retroactivating elements of Genesis 2 means that what appears at first sight to be a 'natural' treatment of human reality, a treatment under the head of the Proverbist's three, is not that at all.

Genesis 1 distinguishes men and women in a pair of ways from the rest of creation. The immediately more accessible one finds men and women, and men and women alone, described as 'having dominion' (1:28).[23]

No appeal is made to anatomy. None to physiology. What men and women *do* is alluded to. Isn't the behavioural way of drawing the distinction problematic? Birds use twigs retrieved here and there to fashion nests. Beavers build dams with branches from the trees they fell. Each of them, in its restricted sphere, dominates. Restricted domination, is that not domination still? Even if, ignoring the parasites that dine on us, in and out, we were to agree that men and women can be separated effectively from the rest as non-dominated dominators, by itself that would not do the trick. A finite, non-circular chain must have a last member.

The same problem affects the harshest scriptural expression of our domineering character, in Genesis 9:2. After the Flood of Noah, God asserts: 'The fear and dread of [men and women] shall rest on every animal of the earth, and on every bird of the air, on everything that creeps on the ground, and on all the fish of the sea.' What however about the obvious fact that many animals dread other animals?

We dominate all. Everything dreads us. How, *uniquely and not just more extensively*, are men and women dominators? How, *apart from only in its externals*, is what the nest-building birds do to nurture their young different than what is done by men and women who build nurseries for *theirs*? How, *otherwise than merely over a broader range*, are we feared? How – to put it concretely – does the deer caught by the wolf differ from the wolf snared on a trap line?

The second manner in which Genesis 1 distinguishes men and women points towards answers to these questions. Among the creatures, only men and women are fashioned 'in [God's] image, according to [his] likeness' (1:26).

If the Bible told us no more about God, this would be unhelpful. Given God's extra-physical status, it would be *dangerously* unhelpful, ostensibly planting one of our feet beyond the physical world. The text *is* however more forthcoming about how men and women resemble God. The information supplied removes the danger posed by the spectre of an ontological gulf with common knowledge and science.

One thing that the text is saying is the following thing. Just as God stands outside the whole of the creation and exercises supremacy over it, so men and women stand outside the rest of the creation and have over it a large measure of control. Though they are parts of the world that God brought into being, men and women are external to the rest *in that respect* in which God is, in the biblical representation, outside the creation *as a whole*.

The 'likeness' claim, then, isn't separate from the 'domination' claim. And the latter is an informative claim.

The mentioned danger is removed. But we are not safely home yet. *What*, in the case of men and women, does the outsideness or externality to the rest consist in? *How* is it special to men and women? *What* is the mentioned respect? *How* is it unique to our kind?

The (non-human) constituents of nature are organically interlinked. The wolf and the deer require each other, as do the bee and the flower, the marsh and the beaver, in a way that nothing requires and is required by human beings. Unlike the nest weaving and dam building of the birds and the beavers, unlike the predating of wolves, characteristically human exchanges with nature are not system-like. Judgments about the characteristic doings of men and women in relation to nature are made otherwise than from the standpoint of the whole. In a manner that gives the lie to the casual assertion that we 'share' the world with the other creatures (which implies that they share it with us), men and women stand apart from the whole. Put it like this. In the sense that deer benefit from being predated upon by wolves, the natural world does not benefit from human activities of shepherding, farming, and city building.[24]

This expands and clarifies what I understand the Bible's attribution to men and women of God-likeness to mean. What, over and above that enigmatic simile, is the textual basis for the attribution?

God *made* the man and the woman. God *commanded the waters to bring forth* the fish and *commanded the grasses* to grass. The basis is present in the contrast between these two.

Let us survey the verbs used in the Genesis 1 story of the coming-into-being of things. According to chapter-and-verse, the earth, commanded by God to do so, 'brought forth vegetation' (12), the waters '[brought] forth swarms of living creatures' (20), and (once again) the earth '[brought] forth living creatures of every kind' (24). In the case of humankind, the form 'bring forth' isn't used. The verbs employed are 'make' (26) and (three times) 'create' (27). What attracts attention is that God does not create vegetation, marine animals, and terrestrial ones. God commands the waters and the earth to do so.

The evolutionary story explains neither the brute existence of the physical world nor the physical laws that govern its goings on. Evolutionary theory's explanatory reach extends only as far as the changes and the increasing complexity within one specific sector of the physical realm, the biological sector. Judging from the passages quoted, the Bible is consistent with the evolutionary story. In the Genesis 1 narrative, from which I have quoted the essentials, God does not micromanage the organizational changes. He establishes the physical and nomological preconditions and then what happens happens. Excluding the arrival of human beings, the story unfolds in a fashion that is consistent with Darwin.

What then is the Bible saying when it describes the earth as 'bringing forth' vegetation and likewise the waters' marine creatures? What is the Bible saying when it says these things rather than saying – what it has the vocabulary to say – that God creates the plants, the sea dwellers, and the land animals? The animals and the plants are complex patternings of the matter and energy of the world, and the increase in organized complexity comes about in a natural way. A plastic version of what the language of 'bringing forth' purports is one of those remarkable M.C. Escher drawings in which disorder on the left slowly resolves into order on the right. The point is that what comes to be is part of a wider churning. So far, so good. God and Darwin are both berthed on the *Beagle*.

What difference does the verb 'make' mark? Only in Genesis 2 does the difference emerge with clarity. Genesis 1 describes the origin of mankind, the species. In Genesis 2, God, who is a particular, breathes life into the original of the group among whose members we each of us are numbered. He whom God's breath inspires, referred to as 'the man' (2:7), is a particular. It is of course a simple matter of logic that without a member of a species coming to be neither can the species come to be. But in speaking of the origin of a species, *Cervidae* for example, it does not matter which deer wins out. In Genesis 2 it is by contrast very much *this* member, the man, who is first. The story is his story.[25]

In Genesis 2 the human enterprise starts with a particular man and a particular woman. The 'likeness' and 'dominion' claims of Genesis 1 do not make full sense until the level of particulars is reached. It is not then the case that the animals of Genesis 1 have dominion, albeit limited dominion, of the same general sort that is ascribed to us. Such is the system-like character of subhuman nature that conceptual distortion attends the singling out of animals necessary for judgments of domination to be formulated. This does not mean that it is empty verbiage to say (as we do) that the lion stands atop the food chain. There might be a good internal reason for seating the lion at the head of the table. But on whatever basis judgments are made about who or what does best, if such claims are not to mislead us the chain as a whole must be taken into consideration, not just several of its links. Don't microbes dine out on the lion's carcass? So isn't the chain a circular one lacking a top? The lion, in sum, is the king of the beasts only in a borrowed sense of 'king.'

Genesis 1 betrays not the slightest sense that the creation of humankind brings into being a species whose members are immortal. Created is one more among the myriad biological kinds. The life that God breathes into the man whom he creates in Genesis 2, the life that is communicated to the woman, is the life of a particular. This explains why the issue of mortality isn't broached until Genesis 2. It's not that for being limited in the capacity to think, and/or for lacking the concept of mortality, subhuman creatures are not distressed by the idea of the inevitable end that awaits. Rather, being part of the system, the death of any one of them does not mean what the death of a particular man or of a particular woman means. While the particularity of each man and of each woman is *original,* the particularity of subhuman creatures is derivative. (I remind the reader that non-human animals do not figure in the Genesis 2 creation story.) Even if subhuman creatures had full control of the concept of death, then, assuming that they do not make the mistake about themselves that projecting from our case we make about them, their transit from biological entrance to organic exit would not be punctuated by night terrors. From the biblical perspective a stoical attitude is in other words ontologically appropriate only for subhuman organisms. That God calls upon the man to name the animals is, once again, crucial here. It's not just that the man is invited to participate, as a parent might include a child in baking cookies. It's that the world of men and women is not the natural world. Just as they think of the sky as up and of the ocean as down, men and women, projecting from their own case, think of animals in non-system terms.

The claim of dominion and the claim of God-likeness in Genesis 1 make full sense only if the compartment of being comprising men and women is more strongly distinguished from the rest of creation than merely in terms of its constituents. When on the afternoon of the sixth day God creates humankind he does not *alienate* dominion from, say, lionkind and reassign it to men and women. If the world of the first five-and-a-half days has a topmost member, that member is on top only in an internal and relative sense: above the others. Men and women are distinguished more strongly. The distinction emerges explicitly in Genesis 2, where our coming to be in the world is described not as the creation of the kind to which we belong but as the creation of each of us individually. Since, in Genesis 1, an external and non-relative distinction between men and women and the rest is certainly intended, it follows that a backward influence is being exerted.[26] Genesis 2 is closer than Genesis 1 to the biblical centre. Conceptually, the Bible begins more nearly with its second creation story than with its first.[27]

What does this have to do with the contrast between anthropocentric and anthropofocused? It was stated in chapter 2 that a biography of Nobody is just as possible as a biography of Napoleon. For failing to make clear that not just anything is grist for biography, the statement, it will now be appreciated, can mislead. 'Biography' and 'story' are not synonyms. One could write the story of a (subhuman) animal. Its biography could not be written. Biographies are of particulars.[28] So though the Bible is focused on and provides a biography of men and women, they are not being singled out arbitrarily or raised up when from some objective standpoint the pre-eminence is sheer chauvinism. If science finds this problematic, so much the worse for science.

The insight about the particularity of men and women that emerges through the Bible's anthropofocal treatment is a very fruitful insight. Its fruits will be harvested in chapter 10. Here, I will content myself with two connected points.

The deer that is brought down by a wolf does not fail to benefit. So I stated in a recent footnote. Isn't it just a matter of perspective? Had it the capacity to plead its case might the deer not return the compliment to men and women? That is what Xenophanes, pleading in its stead, said. If a cow were to produce a scripture, *its* bovinities would, he said, have horns and udders. They would denounce the lupine depradations.

Xenophanes is saying that the religions to which we adhere are anthropomorphic. He means thereby to deflate our eschatologies. But it's not just that cows produce whey, not a Way. Rather, cows are not particulars. They are parts of a system. They are individuals, no more.[29] That being the case, a vaccinocentric religion makes no sense. To take a clearer example, and play turnabout with Xenophanes's flattening mockery, it would be as if the tire of a car, accorded cognitivity, declared its god to have treads. Unless it were deluded the tire would know that relative to the power that is it is just a cog.

This may seem a debating point. The second point does not. Banishing the man and the woman from Eden, God says: 'out of [the ground] you were taken; you are dust, and to dust you shall return' (3:19). Don't animals also return to dust? What did *they* do to deserve such a fate? Where did *they* go astray? The answer is that they do not *return to* dust. *Qua* parts of the organized whole they *never leave it*. They remain within the system even when they die in the organic sense. For this reason again, though changing mounts, a horse-centred religion is, *pace* Xenophanes, a nonsense, and not because there never was among the maned quadrupeds an Equinas.

Tractatus Corvo-Politicus

Monotheism sits at the centre of Genesis. The Bible through its stress on this theological – ism conveys its commitment to the normative significance of the ontological idea of human particularity. The specifically creedal content of monotheism – one God and the exclusive worship of him – lies atop, and is separable from, the point of philosophical anthropology. A key to the thinking here is the story of the Tower of Babel.

The Tower story follows the story of Noah and precedes the annals of Abraham. Given the episode's placing, one expects that it will have something to do with both, even constitute a hinge. The connection, though genuine, turns out however to be quite convoluted – indirect though straightforward in regard to the story of Noah, direct though complex in regard to the annals of Abraham.

What motivates the Tower? Since the construction follows the Flood, *this* reason suggests itself: insurance against a future deluge. Yet there is no textual sign that fear of a second world-inundation is the driver. Had they wished to assuage worries about a repeat watery holocaust would the Tower builders not have chosen a mountaintop or highland plateau? In the event the site selected is a location not much above sea level: the 'plain in the land of Shinar' (11:2).

The Tower builders' words are these: 'let us make a name for ourselves' (11:4). English usage inclines the reader to see them as seeking renown. But putting one's name in lights does not constitute a reasonable response to a worry about a future inundation. True, by putting one's name in lights one in a non-personal sense survives one's death: after one departs one is remembered. Since, metaphorically speaking, the higher the lights are placed the better, a tower is a good narrative choice. Again, however, the aim of attracting attention by making an impact is most readily understood as a response to brute mortality. It isn't death that one cheats by gaining celebrity through one's deeds. A dead celebrity is every bit as dead as a dead nobody. It is oblivion that one cheats – being forgotten after one exits. What's that got to do with the Flood?

The Tower builders speak of 'making a name.' Genesis contains much name giving, the bulk of it having nothing do with fame. This looks, then, like a promising avenue to follow.

Naming begins no later than five verses into Genesis. 'God called the light Day, and the darkness he called Night.' After the Tower story ends, Abraham too is given a name by God. Whatever (else) the Tower builders are attempting to achieve, this much at least is therefore clear: their activity constitutes the assumption of a godly function.

Acts of naming in Genesis 1 link closely to God's world creating.[30] Albeit on a lesser scale, men and women create worlds too. Planting fence posts and stringing wire, Cain makes the distinctive world that he inhabits. Cain is also the first city builder. In this capacity he gives a name. He calls the city after his son Enoch (4:17), an action about which the text is, at that juncture, morally neutral.[31] Nor should we forget that God enlists the man to name the animals. So from the biblical perspective there is nothing necessarily usurpatory about assuming the name-giving function. Made in God's image and likeness, we are indeed *supposed* to perform the *imitatio Dei*, for example, by exercising dominion. What, then, is wrong with *this* effort? The right answer in my view, though an answer that requires a lot of clarification, is that the effort is an attempt to put human reality on a basis that does not respect what God has done.

'Put on a basis disrespectful of what God has done' sounds of pride and self-inflation. But, again, a thumbs down is not always the Bible's judgment on those who deviate (or attempt to deviate) from God's model. After initial misgivings many parents are *delighted* when a child strikes out into what for them personally is the unknown. Among parents not a few *encourage* offspring to spring off. It is indeed possible to see God, figured in this phase as a parent, offering encouragement (albeit with profound regret about the implications for them) to the first man and woman. Though they violate a solemn imperative, God at the deepest level does not disapprove of what the two do.[32] So we are still at sea as to what it is about *this* effort that marks it from the biblical standpoint rather as a case of categorically blameworthy overreaching than of potentially admirable gumption. How does what God accomplishes constitute a basis for justifiably criticizing the Tower builders?

The details bear out that the Tower builders' project is to start as near *ex nihilo* as possible. The enterprisers set to work 'upon a plain' (11:2).

Why of all places such a place? A plain, featureless, is a dry version of the chaos that God confronted in the beginning. It is as it should be, then, that the builders do not take from nature what they use on the construction site. They do not chop down trees and collect boulders. They *manufacture* their building materials. The text is explicit: 'they had brick for stone' (11:3).

To the maximal degree that their incapacity to create or destroy matter allows, the builders act in an autonomous and self-contained manner. They are setting out to make a world *by* themselves and *for* themselves. Which is what the text had said. '[M]ake a name for ourselves.' Not just 'make a name.'

But, again, how far does this take us? To efforts that deviate from what God had wrought or that overstep the bounds that God has marked out the Bible does not object *per se*. So great is God's unhappiness with his own handiwork that on one occasion he looses the contained waters and goes back virtually to square one. God had indeed explained to Cain (4:7): 'If you do well, will you not be accepted?' 'If yours proves to be a way of life that enables men and women to prosper,' God is saying, 'it will get the thumbs up, and we shall wave goodbye to the ways to which it puts paid.' Doesn't God *expressly* bar the path back to Eden? And truly, the odd moment of nostalgia apart, who among us thinks back with anything besides relief to the hand-to-mouth existence of the gatherers, the rough paths of the shepherds?[33]

Were we driven to conclude that God blows his top about the construction from jealousy, we would have reason for suspecting some printer's devil of having hacked the narrative and spliced in the story of the Tower. If so, we would be within our rights to expurgate the mischief. Would we feel a gap if the national phase commenced immediately after the Flood and the genealogy? The point has got therefore to be more specific. The point has got to be that something is wrong with the Tower builders' reprise of the creation.

Might the idea be that by making a name *for themselves*, the Tower builders will forget God? This does sound quite ambitious. It sounds problematic too. But, putting aside the difficulty that to speak of the Tower builders 'forgetting' seems groundless when the text never represents them as exhibiting awareness, the proposal, left unelaborated, just swings us round in a circle. After the floodwaters subsided God began afresh, trying to improve on his first attempt. If the world that the builders aim to create *is* a better one, why *not* close the book on the past?

The next phase is monotheism. Having so far come up empty, we might expect to find in the story starring Abraham the basis for saying that the world created by the Tower builders is not better.

Reconsider the following puzzle. The Bible puns on 'Babel.' 'Therefore it was called Babel, because there the Lord confused ['balal'] the language of all the earth' (11:9.) As a result of the (perhaps accidental) link with the verb 'to babble,' the pun is available to English speakers. The babble at Babel is God's doing. By Berlitzing the construction site God puts a stop to the enterprise. But isn't monotheism itself a rejection of a cacophony?[34] Shouldn't God *approve* of what the Tower builders are up to?

The Tower story precedes the story of Abraham. When the matter is considered from the later perspective the questions arise again. God enjoins Abraham to depart Babylon, invites him to follow a single voice, because of the caterwaul of polytheism. Shouldn't the builders therefore be lauded? In their unity of purpose are they not purposing to blaze the trail that God in his one-ness travels immediately afterwards? If so, God is (sc., those behind the monotheistic démarche are) taking credit for inventing what the Tower builders had already roughed out on their drafting board. Indeed, the effort of the builders seems the more heroic. *They* stand and fight.

On the reasonable assumption that the story of the Tower is offered by way of sharpening, through contrast, the positive teachings of Genesis, it may be inferred that God and the Tower builders stand for different sorts of harmony. In the light of what we have seen of Raven's Land, and attentive to the Tower builders' assertion that they want to 'make a name for [them]selves,' we can now untie the preceding knots.

The monitory point of the story of the Tower is capsuled in the following proportionality:

Tower story : story of Abraham :: Genesis 1 : Genesis 2

The left-hand item of each pair is the story of a collective; the right hand item, of a particular. Coming from the Tower builders, 'we,' 'us,' and 'our' are effectively singular. 'The whole earth had one language and the same words' (11:1). It isn't democratic-type consensus that underlies the enterprise on the plain in Shinar – a meeting of disparate minds. Presented is what amounts to a group mind and a group will.[35] Abraham's act of nation building, like God's act of world creating, is by contrast the work of one person. 'Let us,' say the Tower builders, 'build ourselves a city.' 'Go from your country' says God to Abraham, 'to the land that I will show you.' The shift from plural to singular pronouns corresponds to the shift from the creation of humankind in Genesis 1 to the creation of the man in Genesis 2.

The world that the Tower builders are trying to build – 'a city, and a tower' (11:4) – is a social version of the world of Genesis 1. To be properly answered, the question of good-and-bad for a species requires that the entire system be taken into account. Just so, the question of good-and-bad in *this* world is a question about the whole. It therefore has a different logic than does the question of good-and-bad for particular men and particular women. The latter question is about each man and each woman separately. The whole it addresses only distributively. Would the death of this or that worker on the Tower site be bad? Not if the effort is seen as tightly collective. Think of a bald tire on a car. Its removal and replacement is certainly no bad thing for the car. And it's impossible to say with a straight face that it's bad for the tire. If a *bona fide* biological model is wanted, consider the beehive. 'All of the death in the city of the bees had been scheduled, provided for, tens of millions of years ago; each death as it occurred was translated, efficiently and immediately, into more life for the hive.'[36]

At the foundation of the Bible's normative position is a point of philosophical anthropology: men and women are particulars. Receptive though the Bible is to alterations in God's original plan, the brakes must therefore be slammed on the Tower enterprise. Attempted on that plain in the land of Shinar is nothing short of reversion, on the social and political plane, to an ontological level from which the biblical deity's full likeness is absent, since on that level nothing that God created is inspired with his breath. Retreating from Genesis 2 (the particular) to Genesis 1 (the species, the system), the Tower builders are indeed inattentive to the deity who presides over the story as a whole. This inattention goes beyond mere back turning or apostasy. Like Raven's Land, the world of the Tower builders stands in an unclear relation to the line of latitude along which the Bible's story of men and women is told. Theirs is a different kind of world.

I spoke a few pages ago of the way that men and women, projecting from their own case, mistakenly think of animals in non-system terms. That meant: 'men and women, projecting from their view of themselves, each one, as a separate individual, a particular, &c.' The Tower story explores the representation by men and women of men and women in the image of the animals, that is, as essentially parts of a system. The story is in fine a critical exploration of attempts to align social and political structure with biology. The Tower builders are so to speak the social and political wing of the Party of the Raven.

Consistently with the Genesis 2 account of human nature, the Bible objects to forms of social and political organization that submerge the particularity of men and women in a wider whole, be the whole species or be it system. The Bible's position on what is good and bad for men and women, liberal in its look and democratic in its trend, is thus a corollary of the view of human particularity. The theological expression of this ontological position is monotheism.

Qua operating in the conceptual field of Genesis 1, the Tower enterprise *is* inconsistent with monotheism. Which is what one would have predicted given that the objective is to return to Go. The act of creation that makes the Bible the book that it is is God's creation, in Genesis 2, of particular humans – the man and the woman. The Flood of Noah dramatizes a felt need to reconfigure some of the internal arrangements of the world that the descendants of the man and the woman inhabit. About each of the changes one could quarrel. But the Tower builders are not part of the (ongoing) debate. They are out to remake the world, not to reconfigure it. They are out to remake the world in a fashion that is consistent with their not being inspired with the monotheistic deity's – God's – breath of life.

The story of the Tower immediately follows the story of the Flood. The difficulty of linking the two thematically occasioned a large fraction of our head scratching in past pages. We were worrying our scalps for good reason. The Tower is *not* a direct response to the Flood, the Flood being in the field of force of Genesis 2. (The story of Noah is absent from the proportionality.) But the return of the world to chaos in that watery holocaust provides a suitable narrative location for the story *qua* story of a new (kind of) beginning, one that, because of the conceptual affinity for Genesis 1, constitutes a negative double of the story of Abraham that immediately follows. The Tower story tells us how the world of men and women as social and political creatures would have looked if, *per impossibile*, Genesis 1 had not been subordinated to Genesis 2.

The serpent had said to the man and the woman that they would not die. The Tower builders make the same promise – to themselves. And though it is a promise that would be kept in their world, it, like the serpent's, is deceptive. If we conceptualize ourselves at the basic level as elements in a collective, the idea of personal death has no more dominion. But according to Genesis the price for deposing death is the loss of what makes each one of us what he or she is.

I referred early on to Homer. Let me close with another Hellene, the single most powerful Greek thinker, and one of the most powerful thinkers ever. This thinker, by express contrast with the humanistic epic poet, is a Tower builder with a vengeance.

Here, in a telling passage from the *Republic* (406d–407a), Plato is discussing the life of a typical denizen of his ideal city, a carpenter:

> When a carpenter is ill, he asks his doctor to give him an emetic or a purge to expel the trouble, or to rid him of it by cautery or the knife. But if he is advised to take a long course of treatment, to keep his head wrapped up, and all that sort of thing, he soon replies that he has not time to be ill and it is not worth his while to live in that way, thinking of nothing but his illness and neglecting his proper work. And so he bids good-bye to that kind of doctor and goes back to his ordinary way of life. Then he either regains his health and lives to go about his proper business, or, if his body is not equal to the strain, gets rid of all his troubles by dying.

The carpenter is, in effect, a tire with consciousness. When the tire is worn out, it is unemotionally chucked. When the carpenter is worn out, he unemotionally tosses himself on the scrap heap. Alternatively: the carpenter conceives his life very much in the way that a subhuman animal, had it the capacity to do the conceiving, would, in Darwinian terms, conceive *its*.

Plato has been tagged 'the Greek Moses.' From this perspective, he is the Greek Pharaoh. Since Plato's political thought, like the Bible's, is anchored in philosophical anthropology, it is no less than one expects to find that the particular is analysed away in Platonic metaphysics.

5
The Reformation

A Reformed Scripture

In the Bible's story, God does *not* get the world going *ex nihilo* by saying. So I said. Even the many for whom the opposite goes without saying will say that the Bible itself doesn't get going *ex nihilo*. The Bible is part of a global ferment that historians of culture bottle as *The Axial Period* or *The Axial Age*. The span of years so labelled saw the beginnings of Hinduism, Confucianism, Buddhism, Taoism, Zoroastrianism, Bible-based Judaism, and Greek culture as we know it. Developments of the same general sort occurred in the Americas too. In rough concurrence, men and women round the world came up with a range of ways, more general than the ways that had hitherto been used, of thinking about themselves, their place, their destinies, duties, and so on, and they began to produce, sometimes in literary form, sometimes in brick and stone, a bunch of disparate torahs that each expressed a different one of the ways.[1]

Judging by influence down the ages, the Bible's core constitutes the major Western explosion in the conceptual fireworks display that lit up the two centuries or so in either direction pivoting on 600 BCE. Consistently with the Bible's position as part of the pyrotechnics, and in an imaginative extension of the psychogenic reading of Genesis 1, the tohu and bohu can be construed as a very unfriendly swipe at an extant belief system dissatisfaction with which motivated those responsible for the text to take up their writing implements; or, as referring to a smorgasbord of belief systems each of which the reconfigurers regarded as hard to swallow. Either way, more waste than void.

No matter how the beginning is taken, the fact is that the Bible is a *reformed* document. It is reformed in a pair of senses, one formal, the other substantive.

To say that the Bible is reformed in the formal sense is to say that from the standpoint of the narrative the shift in ways of thinking that lies behind the text has been completed. Accordingly, one can only specify what the writers oppose by applying 'not' to what they endorse. Readers of the Bible are therefore like the children of parents, immigrants to the New World, who keep mum in their presence about the Old Country. In the parental accents and comportment foreignness is detected about whose nature the offspring are left to conjecture. The contrast here, a self-explanatory one, is between *reformed* and *reforming*.

The assertion in regard to some document that it is reformed as opposed to reforming is silent about content. All it says is that the advocates of what the document propounds have rejected something else, something about whose character only faint traces are detectable in the finished product.[2]

Characterizing the Bible as reformed in the non-formal or substantive sense *is* making a claim about its doctrines and teachings. *Reformed* stands opposed here to *unreformed*. The labours to date have indicated that being reformed has to do with shifting men and women from the periphery to a central position in the value system. In this sense of 'reform,' the process of reform corresponds therefore to what occurred during the movement known, with a capital 'r,' as the Reformation.

We have in our hands a text that resembles the Bible in substance – it is reformed rather than unreformed – but that differs from it in the formal respect – it is reforming rather than reformed. Like the Bible, this text, also Axial, enjoyed near-scriptural status in its culture. The *Iliad* (the text in question) tracks a change in how men and women think of themselves – how, more precisely, they position themselves in the world. The *Iliad* in fact constitutes a dramatic narration of such a change. The change is a partial version of the very change that had been completed before the Bible writers set to work. On Homer's stage, what from the standpoint of the biblical story is a *fait accompli* unfolds before our eyes. The classical tragedian Aeschylus, who was in a position to know, said of those of his craft that they processed slices from the banquet table of Homer. Elaborating the culinary metaphor, we can say that Homer's epics are the kitchen to the dining hall that is the

Bible. The *Iliad* and the *Odyssey* show the preparation of a repast of the sort that the Bible serves up in a finished form.

In cultural time, the Bible therefore begins further along than the *Iliad*. This, I stress, is not a historical judgment. Culturally speaking, the Bible could in principle be later than a document hot off the presses. In point of historical fact the Pentateuch could not however postdate anything produced after about 500 BCE. Just so, older in years than the young fogy in the three-piece, the aged hippy who smokes the plant he suits up in is more youthful in spirit. Speaking purely chronologically, the materials out of which the post-*Hurban* redactors stitched the Bible together almost certainly, as literary pieces, predate the *Iliad*.

From the fact that the Bible *starts* later in cultural time than the Homeric epic it cannot be inferred that in cultural time the Bible is *as a whole* later. From *its* starting point to *its* end the Bible could traverse ground all of which is covered in the twenty-four books of the *Iliad*. It could. But it doesn't. Culturally speaking, the Bible ends later too. The Bible has so to speak a dessert course while the *Iliad* goes post-prandial immediately after the meat and potatoes. This means that the change that the Bible regards as completed is not quite done by the end of the *Iliad*. In the substantive sense of 'reform,' the *Iliad* ends *in medias res*.

Why not say that the epic ends exactly where it should end? Why measure the *Iliad* by a text – indeed a culturally alien text – that does something else, especially when applying the yardstick delivers a hiding? Who says that Homer is interested in reform? You live several doors down the block from me. Do you complete a journey that I cut short when I turn at *my* walkway? The answer, programmatic at this stage, is two-pronged. First, the fact is that the culture for which Homer was so central did not view the *Iliad* as self-contained.[3] The epic came shrink-wrapped with the *Odyssey*, which takes up where the *Iliad* leaves off – takes up thematically, not just in story line. Second, in developing a frankly reformed view classical Greek culture also used Homer as a launching platform. Recall Aeschylus's paean. I venture that the classical artists understood Homer at least as well as we do.

The lines of connection between the *Iliad* and the Bible will now be sketched. A main aim of this chapter is to clarify what it means to say that the *Iliad*, *because* it is reforming, is more revealing than the Bible on matters central to both. In contrasting three and four, the Proverbist draws attention to the distinctiveness of men's and women's ways. The reference (made entirely explicit in the Book of Proverbs as a whole) is to the wide range of personal and social relations within the

Proverbist's culture. The *Iliad*, being a reform*ing* text, goes beyond a consideration of a single culture. In the process of extracting the *Iliad*'s content, we will also get a line on the specific view of men and women, the reformed view, that the Bible advances and endorses.

The Bible as Reform*ed* as Opposed to Reform*ing*

Here is how the NRSV renders the opening of Genesis 1:1. 'In the beginning when God created.' The Hebrew consists of three words. Translating word by word, and keeping to the word order of the original, we have: 'In-the-beginning-when (first word) created (second word) God (third word).' The Hebrew of the part preceding 'God' is the following:

בראשית ברא

The first three letters of 'in the beginning when' and of 'created' are identical. The first three letters of the former, corresponding to the b and r and a of our alphabet, make up the latter in its entirety.[4]

Jumping ahead now to Genesis 12, the beginning of the Bible's national phase, we find precisely the same feature in the two opening words. God, employing the imperatival form, says to Abraham, 'Lekh Lekha.' Again in the original:

לך לך

The two words are orthographically identical. Cole Porter's song title 'Begin the Beguine' prettily simulates the lilt of the first Hebrew phrase. Archaic English's 'Get thee going' approximates the second, capturing its content too. 'Hie thee hence' is not half bad. In both 1:1 and 12:1 the idea is that the movement or change is self-initiated, along the lines of an Aristotelian self-mover. Genesis 1:11 furnishes confirmation. The writers go out of their way to grow the verb completions from the corresponding verb roots. The grass grasses. The fruit trees fructify. The germinating things germinate. The NRSV captures only one of these, and that one it captures less clearly (though more idiomatically) than I have: 'fruit trees bear fruit.' The use of (as it is called) the cognate accusative in the mentioned verse indicates that the object is to be regarded as inseparable from the activity – as, to play upon the bottom of a W.B. Yeats poem, the dance is inseparable from the dancing.

Neither of the Hebrew phrases set off above is a cognate accusative. The one presents an adverbial phrase and a verb; the other, an imperative and the pronoun for the individual to whom it is addressed. Still, the reverberations with the cognate accusatives in Genesis 1:11 bear witness to writerly intentions. The linguistic facts accord with my claim that the Bible is, in the formal sense, reformed. Its starting points, of the world as a whole and of the national enterprise, are represented as absolute. The world starts up from scratch. Abraham gets himself going.[5]

There being no Genesis 0, nothing textual precedes the primordial 'In the beginning.' Though the national genesis begins verbally in an echoing manner, *it* comes quite a way along in the life of the world. Also, the story thereof gestures in its contents towards the process through which the nation came into being. Here, then, we do find elements of a reforming text.

Abraham's departure, the beginning of the Bible's story of the Israelites, is an earthbound reflection of God's departure. What happens on high is – to put it from the secular angle – an upwards reflection of what transpires below.[6] Let's take a closer look at the earthly goings on, and then let's see what we can scare out of the neighbouring bushes that helps with the heavenly happenings.

The textual spur for this search is the fact that Abraham's father departs too. Terah's leaving is described at the close of Genesis 11 in what looks like a coda that, in content, has an affinity for Genesis 12. There seems to be a break in verse 26 of chapter 11. Up to that verse, each named person in the line of Shem is said to have had 'other sons and daughters,' but only one child, a male, is named. Here, for the first time, a person in the genealogical chain, that person being Terah, is ascribed a number of offspring all of whom are named. Verses 27 to 30 are even more out of character, mentioning women, speaking of the location of a person's death, and alluding to a wife's barrenness. Going considerably beyond a cold sketch of a family tree, this describes the knots on the trunk and the disposition and viability of the seeds.

Central for us is the inconsistency between Terah's taking 'his son . . . from Ur of the Chaldeans' in verse 31, the penultimate verse of Genesis 11, and God's call coming to Abraham in his birthplace in the first verse of Genesis 12. The fact that Abraham is already beyond the borders of his native land prior to Genesis 12 appears to ascribe to God a deficit of knowledge in entreating him to 'Go from your country' (1). The problem reappears at the end of chapter 12's verse 4. Abraham is said to depart 'from Haran.' How could he have heeded a call in Babylon, the call of verse 1, when he is situated several days' journey from the lower Euphrates? Very likely, texts from different sources are being put together. Indeed, scholars committed to the Documentary

Hypothesis always assign 11:31 and the part just quoted from 12:4 to a different source than 12:1. It would not however have taken a mangle for the redactors to smooth out the wrinkles. The call to Abraham could have come in Haran. Terah could have been Saul to Abraham's David. The fact that the redactors present things as they do I take as an invitation to interpretation.

I linked God's departure with Abraham's. What of the fact that Terah leaves before God calls? How would the text have been compromised had Abraham taken off, as Terah did, independently of his father? Haran, where Terah halts his caravan, is halfway along the route that Abraham follows from the lower Euphrates to the Jordan. Later, forswearing marital union with Canaanites, Abraham and then Isaac seek spouses back in Haran for their sons. Abraham dispatches an emissary there from Canaan to find a 'kindred' (24:4) mate for Isaac. Sent by Isaac, Jacob himself treks to Haran in quest of a partner. Though a reason therefore exists inside the narrative for having Terah settle part way to the Promised Land, this by itself does nothing to explain why he should have left before God invests in his son. Later, Joseph, as a settler in Egypt, precedes Jacob. So had Terah left later it would not have been a unique case of a son's preceding a father. As to purity of stock, did anything prevent the patriarchs from finding consanguineous mates back in Babylon or nearer its borders?

Terah lit out for greener pastures without having felt a divine tap on the shoulder. Any number of social, personal, or economic reasons might have got the motor running. Perhaps Terah's hitting the road is a wink to the effect that Abraham too departs for earthly reasons. It is hard to see why overcoming dissatisfaction with life conditions in Babylon required acceptance of one god. Even if the acceptance of a single deity *is* loosely indicated by the character of those life conditions, can't sense be made of a non-theistic system having the desired feature? On this reading, the fact that Terah is senior and Abraham junior is a structural match of God's seniority over Abraham. We look at the doublet, and draw a moral for the dominant story from the recessive one. Another possibility: just as Abraham's departure was not without precedent, neither was God's. Discounting the *ex post facto* reason set out above, viz., to provide a pool of suitable mates, we are in the case of Terah reduced to guessing. Might Terah's departure signal that some cultural movement of a monotheistic tenor had occurred outside the core of the group from which Israel would come?[7] Terah goes roughly halfway to the Promised Land. The link between Terah and Abraham would thus resemble slightly the later relation between Abraham and Lot. Abraham, after all, serves as a surrogate father for his nephew, whose own father had expired in Babylon prior to the exodus. This, then, would be another of the myriad doublets.

Terah goes halfway with Abraham. Lot too, in his *pas de deux* with the patriarch, is also dropped en route, after the fiery fiasco at Sodom and Gomorrah. Both, then, serve as middle terms.

Bringer of Light

Abraham is moving westwards. So are we. We shall travel a good deal farther in that direction of the compass than he does, all the way to the Pillars of Hercules, even slightly beyond. To gather momentum for exiting the Bible's orbit, let me leave the text itself and address myself directly to God's departure.

Although the departure isn't part of the narrative, the biblical story contains a few words and lines that call up a pertinent parallel from Greece.

The genealogy of Noah in Genesis 10 takes the reader on a busman's tour of the known world. Each of Noah's three sons – Ham, Shem, and Japheth – is associated with a geographical region. Javan, the fourth son of Japheth, has a close connection to the more northerly part of the eastern Mediterranean. Mentioned in verse 4 are the Island of Rhodes ('Rodanim'), Larnaka on Cyprus ('Kittim'), and, a bit more conjecturally, Crete ('Tarshish'). In fact, the linkage with what we know as 'Greece' is explicitly forged by the very name 'Javan.' Visibly, it is a version of 'Ionia.'[8]

The point towards which I am working concerns not 'Javan' but 'Japheth.' Hellenic in origin too, 'Japheth' is a transliteration of 'Iapetos.' (Sounded in Hebrew, 'Japheth' is 'Yaphet.' Like 'Yavan,' the latter is phonetically closer to the Greek.) Who bears the name? In Greek myth, Iapetos is the father of none other than Prometheus!

Return now to God. God gives light to the world. God has a special link to men and women. He is on their side. God, evidently, bears a family resemblance to Prometheus. The resemblance supplies a springboard for my conjecture.

Prometheus is a minor Titan, the Titans being the generation of Greek deities sandwiched between the lumbering first-generation deities, personifications of the rudimentary and large-scale order emerging from the original chaos, and the rather carefree members of the airier Olympian pantheon. In one version of the Prometheus myth, Prometheus himself creates man from clay and then proceeds to instruct him in the management of fire. Prometheus, a rebel against the gods, bringer of civilization to humankind, helps men and women emancipate themselves from both the regularities and the caprices of the natural world and to take one thread from the skein of fate out of the spinning hands of Clotho.

Once the *mutata* are *mutanda*, all of this echoes my story of the first instalment of God's lost autobiography, *Passage from Babylon*. From the standpoint of the Bible, the departure is towards something new and, by the Bible's lights, unprecedented. It is also a departure from something old, with which strong enough dissatisfaction was felt to cause bags to have been packed and tickets to have been purchased. Might there not be a parallel between God's leave-taking from Babylon, as here imagined, and the exit of the man and the woman from Eden? The man and the woman in the Garden act so as to cast off God's yoke. God acts to cast off the yoke of *his* father's (or: fathers') way. Through what they transgressively do the man and the woman thus move towards an autonomy that is God-like; they *extend* the *imitatio Dei* that their root character in the creation mandates.

The formal issue of reform was addressed at the outset. In the process, the substantive one came to be addressed too. The Bible is tight-lipped about what is being sloughed off. The few telltale signs, eked out with the Greek parallel, provide some data. The filling in also tells us more specifically what the reform means.

Greek myth is a complex organ. It is not out of synchrony with the general trend thereof that the civilization of Greece is a departure from the gods, which suggests why Prometheus serves well as an emblem of the substantive shift. He, one foot above, in the Olympian air, one below, in the elemental muck, is betwixt and between: *meteôros*. The manner has been identified in which the Greeks of the historically real or imaginary time that Homer is describing tended to see themselves *vis-à-vis* the universe. Their fragility and evanescence struck them as a compelling reason for divine indifference. I quoted the words of the Trojan fighter Glaucus. Here, from Book 21 of the *Iliad*, are the near identical words of one of the chief Olympian gods, Apollo [527–530].

> God of the earthquake – you'd think me hardly sane
> if I fought with you for the sake of wretched mortals . . .
> like leaves, no sooner flourishing, full of the sun's fire,
> feeding on earth's gifts, than they waste away and die.

Perfect harmony (though total discord) between heaven and earth! 'So,' the wretched mortals would ask, and ask rhetorically, 'why, except perhaps for sport, would the power who created everything, the master of the universe, attend to a veritable nonentity?' We want to see how they came to a more Davidic position.

Think of the charter myth of Athens, sculpted onto the frieze of the Periclean Parthenon: Athena supplicates to be patron god of Athens; and she does so by offering a bribe. Recall also the choice facing Achilles: divine matrilineage or human patrilineage. These signposts towards answers we shall take direction from anon.

One further anticipatory point. Prometheus's actions are heroic. What he does he does against overwhelming odds and at great personal cost. Establishing civilization, if one focuses on the transition from savagery, is also a colossal task. God, in the first chapters of Genesis, does heroic work too. Though in many ways mixed, the success of God still contrasts with the fate of Prometheus. Fire, the control of fire, was delivered to men and women. The deliverer had to pay dearly for the donation. Prometheus having taken their side, his life, lived now on their side, becomes a daily struggle with nature.[9] On reflection, did God enjoy success? The other belief systems (to avert attention from straight geopolitics) seem to have made God's life, the life of God's people, a hardship.

Prometheus is a hero. The lyrics of a Tina Turner song capture the biblical position: 'we don't need another hero.' Several episodes in chapter-and-verse encode the negativity. One, to be looked at later, concerns Lamech, father of Noah. In this episode the self-styled hero is deliciously, though in my view somewhat unfairly, mocked. 'Big hero!' The other, having to do with the genealogy of Ham, is more in the way of historical anthropology than of poetic send-up.

Tina Turner sings that *another hero* is superfluous. The lyrics might be taken to imply the need for at least one. That is the Bible's view. God himself is that hero. God wrestles with chaos and, on a larger scale than Prometheus, creates a world hospitable to men and women. Thereafter, heroic activity is insolent. An example, again, is the construction of the Tower, an attempt to outdo God. The mockers of Lamech represent him as attempting the same. And the same is true for the offspring of Ham. Consistently with the present line, the Bible's point is not that heroism is the exclusive prerogative of God. The point is that the world is from the biblical perspective a place for men and women to pursue their human-sized activities. In a post-agricultural society, in civil society, heroism even as an ideal of conduct (let alone as a norm) is out of place, even positively dangerous. It belongs to minstrelsy and poesy.

That the Bible is beyond heroism also explains why its treatment of human reality is too narrow to supply a full perspective. It explains why the Bible is not, while the *Iliad* is, reform*ing*.

The Proverbist alludes to 'the way' in which men and women comport themselves. This he contrasts with 'the way' of each of the myriad other sorts of things. The former alone, says the Proverbist, is closed to understanding. The significance of the contrast has been explained. No matter how complicated they are, extra-human things have, each of them, one way and one way alone. They are strictly law-governed. No blessing is given them in Genesis 1 because none is needed. But the Proverbist's point needs to be extended. In addition to the many and varied differences between people, there are as well differences between *peoples*. Think of how a culture of heroes differs from a culture comprised of citizens who live private lives and who are only occasionally gripped by a concern for transcendence. The modes of behaviour that the Proverbist has in view are not cross-cultural ways. They are ways within a fairly stable mode of communal existence.

To be sure, plenty in the monocultural social sphere engenders bewilderment. Gender differences. Differences in gentility. Generational differences. But beyond, there is more. When cultures clash, we also see 'the ways' of men and women. This is not the difference between Mars and Venus, as the conjunctive phrase is currently used. It is more the difference between Mars (the planet) and Venus (the other planet). In this respect, the Bible, *qua* charter document of our sense of ourselves, is too much focused on a single culture.

Our interpretive wrestle with the Tower of Babel story imparts a sense of this. On the dominant reading, the story is a kind of aversion therapy. Given that Abraham departs Babylon immediately after the episode, a cross-cultural contrast is hinted at too. Let me now pick the point up in terms not of Babylon and Jerusalem, but of Athens and Jerusalem.

Let's Make a Deal

In the beginning of the national story, God promises greatness to Abraham in return for fealty:

> I will make of you a great nation, and I will bless you, and make your name great, so that you will be a blessing. (12:2)

Achilles, at the start of the *Iliad*, has unsheathed his sword. He is about to run Agamemnon through. Streaking from the skies, Athena stops him. The god gets the inaction going (for the *Iliad* is the story of Achilles's inaction) by promising threefold compensation for mastering the murderous impulse:

> And I tell you this – and I *know* it is the truth –
> one day glittering gifts will lie before you,
> three times over to pay for all this outrage.
> Hold back now. Obey us both. [1:248–251][10]

'Step right up! Gifts galore! Triple your money!' It certainly sounds in both cases like an offer that can't be refused. But cast ahead to the sequels of the two stories. Achilles gets killed. Abraham's progeny end up exiled in Babylon, as far from the Promised Land as up to then they ever were. Nor are these denouements in the future from the standpoint of those responsible for the texts. Though it occurs on the far side of the *Iliad*'s final full stop, Achilles's death during the struggle at Troy is telegraphed within the epic. 'Hard on the heels of Hector's death,' Thetis tells her son, 'your death must come at once' [18:112–113]. Similarly, the Bible is put together after *its* people's catastrophe. Is the talk of pay-offs a bad joke? Not at all. National greatness, promised in both cases, need not consist in military might and commercial power. It can consist in making a significant and lasting ethical or conceptual contribution. In both cases the promises were kept.[11]

What was written might have been written with *literal* greatness in mind. Prospective crowing is no rarity. The position here is that whatever the original inspiration and inflection, the message mutates in the course of being worked into, respectively, the Bible and the *Iliad*.

Beneath these similarities there is however a difference, a crucial one for this study. It is the modal difference between a reformed and a reforming scripture.

The Olympian pantheon consists of deities who resemble men and women. Behind their backs, you might refer to your irascible grandfather as 'Poseidon,' to your coquettish aunt as 'Aphrodite.' But the similarity is only skin-deep. Although, on the biblical side, God is figured much less anthropomorphically (it is hard to imagine a family member being called 'Yahweh' even in Proust's Bloch family, where such jests are meat and drink), at a subcutaneous level the biblical deity *is* very like men and women. This difference associates with a host of related differences. The domain of the Greek deities (to mention a difference that has already been explored) is nature. The natural world is an expression of *their* natures. The Greek deities certainly have an impact on the world that is man's estate (the rain and snow fall on the Easter Parade, not only in mid-ocean). Still, they do not preside over it. By contrast, God of the Bible does preside over that world. He controls natural forces rather than expresses *his* nature through them. To put the difference with maximum generality: the deity of the Bible is on the side of men and women; the gods of Olympus pursue an independent agenda. They are almost by definition fair-weather friends.

This difference implies that of Athena's call to Achilles and God's call to Abraham, the former is the more radical. The former is of unlike to unlike, the latter, of like to like.[12]

Athena departs Olympus. God departs Babylon. The two movements are parallel. The background to God's departure is however only a very recessive part of the biblical story. The Bible is reformed. Because it is reformed, it is less informative. Because it is reformed, the tracks in the sand are hidden.

The Bible's David and Michelangelo's

In the Bible men and women start out at the centre of the value system. They do not get shifted to that location from the periphery. More than just reformed, the Bible is in fact *unabashedly* reformed. The men and women situated at the centre are not in the least idealized. Their centrality is that of creatures with flaws and shortcomings: men and women, warts and all. David, I stated earlier, is an earthly correlate of God, even the model for God in nearly a biographical sense. In putting the story together the writers and redactors drew their inspiration for the representation of God from what they believed of David. (The writers of some of the materials might have been personally acquainted with the man. Others will have relied on legends.) I will now supply a sample of the evidence of the tight link. A true likeness of David is, we shall see, very unlike Michelangelo's image of perfection. For all his greatness David is a human being with flaws and shortcomings. David's greatness would in fact be diminished if the blemishes were airbrushed out. Were David more perfect, he would be less perfect.[13]

Saul is represented as a king given to an Israel that had rejected God (1 Samuel 8:7). David, Saul's replacement, is God's preferred representative. Samuel, as we therefore expect, shows none of the reluctance to anoint the son of Jesse that he exhibited in installing the son of Kish. David's career follows the right trajectory. Shepherding precedes his political activity. In this David also corresponds to the patriarchs of Genesis and, on the conjectural biography that I gave earlier, to God who departs the highly urbanized Babylon.[14] The activity in the public sphere proper commences with the defeat of Goliath. This corresponds to the chaos control and chaos management that mark God's original work in Genesis. Just as God causes Dagon the Philistine idol to fall over and lose its head (1 Samuel 5:4), so David removes the Philistine champion Goliath's head (1 Samuel 17:51). David asks leave to build God's house, as a result of which offer God promises to build *his* house – that is, to guarantee David's lineage (2 Samuel 7).[15] As a corollary, one may note that David's actual abode is described as built of the same material that Solomon later uses to construct the Temple, and that in both cases Hiram, the same Tyrean neighbour (2 Samuel 5:11), contributes the cedar. The description of David as 'ruddy' (1 Samuel 17:42) recalls Adam, so named because of the red clay of which his body was fashioned, and inspired, first among us, with God's breath of life. To Nabal God does what David does to Uriah. In the plea that Abigail (Nabal's wife) makes to David to spare her husband (1 Samuel 25:26ff), the dizzying interchange of the appellations 'lord' (for David) and 'Lord' (for God) invites the running of the two together. Throughout his career, David is associated in a singularly intimate and not always wholesome way with the Ark of the Covenant, wherein the Tablets of the Law repose. One episode finds David dancing before the Ark as it is transported into the city, where it is to find a permanent home. His wife, Michal, Saul's daughter, chides him for what she sees as unseemly frivolity. Her words (2 Samuel 6:20) imply that David in fact cavorts in the buff. This, if so, is highly reminiscent of the way God and nakedness are linked in the Bible.

A broader point serves as a buttress. A core concern in the Bible is human chaos and its control. The decisive political expression of chaos in the Hebrew Scriptures is the split of the United Kingdom after the death of Solomon. David, however, is the agent responsible for the unification of the loosely federated tribes. It is he who solders them into a political entity in the institutional sense, just as God made them, in a more basic national sense, into a people. David's is not the only case, then, in which an act of unification gives a less than perfect result.

David slays the Philistine champion Goliath, the personified threat to Israel's national integrity, and God tames the forces of mayhem that challenge cosmic unity. But David's state disintegrated. The hopes of the

Israelites, hopes that the various covenants expressed in legalese and that the Scriptures periodically confirmed and ratified, were dashed. While the redactors' use of the early material about David was, we see, child's play, since David's political efforts corresponded well to the positive, development-of-monotheism thematic, even casual reading finds that the problematic aspects mount ominously as the story unfolds. We are getting here the more negative, fragility-of-unity thematic. David's behaviour, examined closely, is powered not only by godliness as this is so far understood: confronting the problems and overcoming. An internally unruly element, libido, is also a driver. I mentioned David's treatment of Uriah. The episode is crucial. The issue of David's eventual marriage to Bathsheba is Solomon. Not only does David covet another's wife and commit adultery and murder in acting out the desire, he also lies about his lying about. With palpable disgust, the Proverbist spoke of an adulteress who 'eats, and wipes her mouth, and says, "I have done no wrong."' David could easily have sat for the portrait.

David vanquished Goliath. The threat had to be removed in order that the Israelite entity be able to flourish. More basically, David has to control the Goliath, the chaos, within. He has to keep himself under control. If we see David as a mirror of God, the change this makes is evident. The chaos is not external to God. So far as libido goes, the linkage between Israel and God is often figured along the lines of a tempestuous conjugal union.

The Decalogue, on the moral side, is a set of directives that David systematically violates. On the more devotional side, God could, so far as David goes, state the commandments in the optative mood rather than imperativally. David is God's man implicitly and throughout.

In the mode of a recent best-seller, *The Bible Code*, let me end with a piece of conspiratorial analysis about the all-time best-seller.

Genealogical lists pepper the Bible. One of these lists, an especially tangled one, sets out the line of Esau. Genesis 36 presents to us a gorse of a family tree, a phantasmagoric mess of names. A sense of the surreal quality is easily imparted.

The conjugal connections reported in Genesis 36 conflict with the details of the running story of Esau and Jacob. While Elon the Hittite is here described as the sire of Esau's wife Adah, 26:34 calls the female issue of Elon whom Esau weds 'Basemath.' Similarly, Mahalath, presented at 28:9 as the daughter of Ishmael and sister of Nebaioth, reappears at 36:3 in the guise of, once again, Basemath. I'm reminded of a joke about a man who as he walks along the street thinks that he spies a long lost friend coming towards him. 'Johnny,' he exclaims, grabbing the man's lapels, 'it's been ages. You're looking great. When we last hung together you were going to pot. Now you're in fighting trim. I see you've also ditched the spectacles. And that mop of hair looks so natural. Not at all like a weave . . .' 'Hold on,' interjects the other, 'I'm not Johnny.' 'Fantastic, you've even changed your name!' The genealogy tosses in a sex change too, and then, for good measure, issues a new passport. Anah, first introduced to us as the daughter of Zibeon the Hivite, is encountered later, in verse 20, as a male sibling of the same Zibeon, and later yet, in verse 29, as a Horite. The gender bending suggests an extension of the joke. 'I'm not Johnny, I'm Johanna.' 'Fantastic. How about a date?'

The tohu bohu suits the wildness of the first of the line, Esau. At the end of the list is appended a list of 'kings who reigned in the land of Edom, before any king reigned over the Israelites' (31). The attentive reader will certainly do a double-take. 'Kings of Israel? The Israelite monarchy is centuries off.' Apparently, the writers are going well out of their way to make a point.

A resonance is set up between the Edomite kings and the Israelite ones. This is a sketchy doublet. That being so, one among the Edomite names stands out, 'Shaul,' that is (as we know the name in translation), 'Saul.' Saul was the first king of the Israelites. This Saul's predecessors are Hadad and Samlah.

'Samlah,' in Hebrew, is:

שמלה

The name consists of the same letters as 'Solomon.'

שלמה

If a reader of the original misses the connection, the writers are not to blame. The text thus contains verbatim the name of the first king of Israel and a transparent anagram of the name of the third of the inaugural trio of monarchs.[16] This leaves 'Hadad.' With 'Saul' and 'Solomon' priming expectations, one cannot but register in 'Hadad' a *soupçon* of 'David.' To generate the constituents of 'David' from 'Hadad,' one need only move one letter along in the alphabet from the Hebrew ה (phonetic value: h).[17] What happens, now, if we do the same as we just did with respect to all the consonants of 'Hadad'? The letter ו (phonetic value: v) follows ה, which comes after ד (phonetic value: d). The resulting letters – הוה – make up, nearly enough, the standard appellation for God – 'Jehovah' in the usual rendering. This would explain why 'Hadad' comes before 'Saul.'

I present this for what it is worth. No more, perhaps, than the more extravagant conceits of *The Bible Code*. Given the Edomite lists, and the utterly anachronistic mention of the Israelite monarchy, one is however compelled to search for some pattern. This is such a pattern. One, too, that supports the linkage of David with God, a linkage for which the narrative supplies extensive independent grounds. That the Israelite kings should be embedded in the enumeration of Edomite monarchs confirms that the normative side of the Bible's position is deeply sensitive to the internal wildness of the human animal. Accordingly, a statue of David more in keeping with the Bible's portrayal would be less decorous than Michelangelo's marmoreal ideal. This, I would say, indicates that the reformed character of the Bible is (by our measures of realism) quite realistic to human reality. God and man, the latter represented by David, are indeed each other's image and likeness.

The general line taken in this discussion on the motivation of the biblical text was set out in chapter 2. Even if the treatment of the names is dismissed as fanciful, the anachronistic mention of the Israelite monarchy dovetails with what was said about that impetus. Those post-exilic redactors who configured the text are exploiting materials to explain the catastrophe.

Was what was done remarkable from the standpoint of those who did it? It's hard to say. The redactors did what they did under the creedal and political and intellectual and emotional pressures exerted at the time. Just so, many a decorated veteran, disclaiming any special gift of heroism, claims to have acted with grace under fire just because the circumstances demanded. Nonetheless, from our standpoint what those who produced the text did is remarkable to the nth power. The major scriptural work of the West is reformed from the start. A mirror of what the secular among us see when we look in the mirror, it presents a quite modern picture of men and women and their condition. Organized Western religion has been playing catch-up for several thousand years. A large sector of organized Western religion has still to close the gap, even shows no desire to.

Before God made a man, heroes trod the earth – creatures like we men and women but whose footprint was larger than ours. They did not live in a cultivated garden, and they never were children. They lived in a much harsher world. They lived among gods who were not like them. Their world was not unlike Raven's Land. Let us visit their world, the pre-reformed world of the *Iliad*.

Westwards Homer!

6
Contemplating the Bust of Homer

A Philosophical Text

Is there a connection between the walled city of the *Iliad* and the Bronze Age settlement in the region of the Hellespont? Does the mayhem that fills the epic, the local inhabitants and their allies pitted against a confederation of cultural cousins from over the Aegean, relate to contemporary bloodshed in those parts? What – to echo the blunt Tertullian – has Homer's Ilium to do with Troy? On the circumstantial evidence, it is unreasonable to deny real-world bases to the events that Homer depicts. Why shouldn't happenings of which the poet heard tell have been an inspiration? Yet allowing that Heinrich Schliemann's search for Priam's Treasure was not a search for the Golden Fleece scarcely decides how the *Iliad* is to be taken.

To judge by an excited telegram from Mycenae – 'I have gazed,' Schliemann cabled the King of Greece, 'upon the face of Agamemnon' – we may imagine that three years earlier, in 1876, thinking that he had unearthed Priam's city (and some of its treasure) on the western edge of Asia Minor, the archaeologist had gone considerably beyond a Teutonic 'Eureka.' The Turkish hamlet of Hissarlik, where Schliemann applied spade and sieve, is situated at the Aegean opening to the Sea of Marmara, whose waters connect through the Strait of Borporus with the Black Sea. Among the experts not a few opine that it was a precipitous rise in the Black Sea's level, caused by the sudden removal of a blockage in what thereafter became the Strait, that deposited the recollective sediment for the Bible's Noah and his Flood. As the crow flies, the two conjectural real-world bases are thus alongside each other. Though their proximity is entirely coincidental, a few similarities instructive with regard to the *Iliad*'s character emerge if we consider the Greek text alongside the Hebrew one.

Genesis's second creation story locates the verdant abode that God planted for the originals of our kind at the headwaters of four rivers. The Tigris and the Euphrates, more Stygian today than Elysian, appear nightly on TV. The Gihon and the Pishon flow from the fancy. Why a map that mixes two parts fact with equal parts fiction? At the same time as they signal that the story is not to be relegated to the plane of mere entertainment, Scripture's plotters are indicating the futility of mounting an expedition to find the birthplace and nursery of the species.[1]

A similar buoy bobs in the *Iliad* to steer the reader away from the straight matter-of-factual course.

Troy too has rivers, though only half as many. The main river, the Scamander (the other is the Simois), Homer describes [22:177–187] as in one place along its channel springing both hot and cold. A welcome natural feature? Certainly. But an implausible one. Some might take the fact that Homer sees fit to remark the feature as attesting to (his belief in) its reality. In the fashion of a Herodotus, Homer is noting a curiosity of which he heard tell, thereby adding verisimilitude to his tale. It's not however the reference itself that I am signalizing. It's the context. Why in the course of narrating Hector's harrowing death should Homer mention the cheery detail that the double-spring serves the housewives of Troy as an open-air laundromat? Like Raymond Chandler's 'tarantula on a piece of angel food cake,' the juxtaposition of washday and deathday cannot fail to raise an eyebrow, even send a chill down the spine. As we shall eventually be in a position to appreciate, the natural plumbing is apt to what Troy signifies for Homer. Troy is for Homer, as Eden is for the Bible writers, less specific place than representative of a kind of place.

What *are* we to make of the *Iliad*? The epic comprises claims whose truth-status approaches the truth-status of assertions of a conceptual nature. To put it ontologically: the epic does not tell of things and the contingent things that befall them – the province of chronicler and historian. Homer's text has to do with essences, not with facts. Aristotle's proposition in the *Poetics* about the difference between poetry and history is valid of Homer's poetry. Poetry 'is something more philosophic . . . than history, since its statements are of the nature rather of universals, whereas those of history are singulars' (1451b5–7). To be sure, Homer's looks very little like a work of philosophy. But since a much later Greek figure, Plato, has shaped our expectations in the matter of philosophical form, that's not surprising. The fact is, though, that too much of the epic appears haphazard and gratuitous unless the work is so understood.

Neither Fact nor Fancy

M.I. Finley, most vigorously among classicists of recent vintage, argues that the world of Homer's epics taps into and is redolent of a way of life that once was – the way of life, he says, in tenth-century BCE Greece.[2] Not, according to Finley, that Homer is holding up a sociological rear-view mirror to the bygone ethos. The proposition is only that the conduct of the characters reflects what Homer believes to have been the case some centuries prior.

Whether Homer is drawing on something real is ultimately for empirical research to decide. Even if the source materials turn out to be as Finley says, those interested in an earlier phase of Greek life must still, for the following reason, approach the epics circumspectly.

Homer is rarely placed before the eighth century. Many experts date the epics as late as the seventh. Intending thereby to support his position, Finley states that 'neither the *Iliad* nor the *Odyssey* was essentially contemporary [sc., contemporary with Homer] in outlook' (30). It is however fallacious to move from the premise that Homer draws on an ethos that precedes his time to the conclusion that he is committed to the faithful rendering thereof, and the very fact that Finley situates the way of life hundreds of years before Homer lived further erodes confidence in the quality of the inference. If, *à la* Thomas Malory, Homer were ladling out nostalgia to the target clientele, his repast would have been consumed, as it unquestionably was not consumed, as junk food. At *Republic* 606d-e, Plato, no fan of the poet, has Socrates refer to the many in his own day, mid to late fifth century, who 'praise Homer and say that he's the poet who educated Greece, that it's worth taking up his works in order to learn how to manage and educate people, and that one should arrange one's whole life in accordance with his teachings.' If the reception of Homer is anything to go by, the poet is seasoning the ingredients that he uses to issues and concerns that are at the very least contemporary with his creative activity.

With another defender of Homer's historicity my disagreement is, because sharper, more productive. In a book that enjoyed a considerable vogue in its day, *The Origin of Consciousness in the Breakdown of the Bicameral Mind,* Julian Jaynes asserts: 'The *Iliad* is *not* imaginative creative literature and hence not a matter for literary discussion' (1976, 76). What is Jaynes's basis for the position that Homer's writings tell it like it was?[3]

Jaynes recruits the *Iliad* in defence of a startling thesis about the nature of (higher) consciousness: as recently as a few thousand years ago men and women were not conscious beings. Not that men and women of the time had no *mental* lives. Rather, the self-communing inner voice that each of us takes as the manifest form of his or her consciousness they referred to an external (albeit non-physical) source.

The human characters of the *Iliad* continually hear voices that other human characters, even those standing right beside them, do not (and cannot) pick up, voices that the hearers assign to sources that are external to their own minds but that are not physically locatable. So far as the plotting of the epic goes, the voices are those of the Olympian gods. Since Homer never describes the human characters simply as thinking – either they are conversing aloud or else they are communing silently with their geniuses – Jaynes boldly declares that '[t]here is in general no consciousness [in our sense] in the *Iliad*' (69).[4]

The contacts between the gods and the humans as Homer presents them constitute for Jaynes a vital trove of data. Nothing of comparable volume and age is available in the literary arena, and plastic materials – sculpture, pottery, jewellery, and so no – are by nature tougher on the interpretive nutcracker. No wonder Jaynes is so anxious to keep Homer's descriptions of the mental life of the human characters from the clutches of the literary types.

While granting literary analysts ownership over other sectors of the epic, one can with full consistency maintain that the transactions between men and gods set down in the *Iliad* exemplify a real-world conception of the topography of mental space. Jaynes does not however exploit this point of logic to portion out dominion. It is readily understood why he would think twice about doing so, even though the flattening that attends the undivided treatment produces an impression of vast hyperbole. Suppose Jaynes were to grant that the metrical structure of speech is a presentational feature alone. That would provoke the question why the transactions with the gods, which strike us as of purely literary significance too, aren't also treated presentationally. When a god's voice issues a command to a human actor or offers a piece of advice, why is that not just a way of saying that the actor is super-motivated or hyper-hesitant? But Jaynes avoids the charge of begging the question only at the price of implausibility. Certainly, he does not believe that a military stenographer at Troy would have set down hexameters.

Precisely because he is so committed to Homer's historicity, Jaynes makes a claim that leads into the heart of my discussion, which is why I have devoted a few paragraphs to his view.

Jaynes (77) fields the following objection: 'The siege [of Troy] lasts ten years, an absolutely impossible duration given the problems of supply on both sides.' In effect: the *Iliad* is not plotted realistically. Jaynes's response? The work was altered in the course of transmission.

That the work was altered we know to be true. When *Jaynes* speaks of changes, he means that in the course of the material's transmission changes were made that violated Homer's representational conventions.

Pace Jaynes, the *Iliad*'s representation of the conflict's duration can be rationalized regardless of whether Homer's narrative conventions are realistic. The factually incredible duration of the struggle around Troy is no departure from verisimilitude, no movement into caricature and fantasy. Homer is not making a point about the war. His point is about the *concept* of war. The ascription of a factually incredible length is a move to the level of essences. What Homer writes amounts to saying: 'I am talking not just about a war among wars. My topic is *war itself.*' Doesn't a latter-day conceptual analyst indicate that he or she is making a point about meanings by using italics or by inserting quotation marks? Are these conventions deviations from realism?[5]

Worlds Apart

Readers of the *Iliad* join the fray as the ninth year bleeds into the tenth. In using this numbering Homer is drawing upon mythic deposits. The vault of Greek lore contains materials telling of Achilles's fall towards the end of a decade's fighting. Interested in those of Achilles's actions that ensure his death, Homer plots accordingly. But I do not say that Homer's plotting is a pious bow to the mythic patrimony. To the contrary. Homer selects from and actively weaves his narrative through the myth about Achilles's demise because it serves his decidedly nonmythic purpose. Indeed, Homer's very interest in Achilles – the main character of the *Iliad* – has, we shall see, a myth-busting thrust.

Are the numbers nine (and its iterations) and ten (and its powers) significant? Some numbers are characteristically applied to periods or quantities when these are regarded as internally complete or as a way of representing them as self-contained. The move beyond such numbers is therefore felt as a rupture of integrity or a disturbance of equilibrium, not to mention, given the human gestation period in months, a new birth. That the longest-lived of the Bible's mortals, Methuselah, expires at nine hundred sixty-nine years of age gestures at a ceiling for a human life: one thousand effectively counts as immortality, and life without end is not for men and women. The biblical narrative takes a ride on the shift from 999 to 1000.[6] A case more directly relevant finds Hesiod (*Theogony,* 722–725) making use of nine and ten in a manner resonant with the length of the Trojan War:

> A bronze anvil falling from the sky would travel
> nine days and nine nights to reach earth on the tenth day
> and a bronze anvil falling from the earth would need
> nine days and nine nights to reach Tartaros on the tenth day.

Tartaros is a world away from the earth; the earth a world away from the heavens. The places in each of the pairings are of fundamentally different sorts, the members of each pairing a twain that may meet at the horizon but never overlap.

For evidence of the significance of nine and ten one needn't exit the *Iliad*. Apollo, accepting the prayer of his priest Chryses, turns his bow against the Greek forces. 'Nine days the arrows of god swept through the army. / On the tenth Achilles called all ranks to muster' [1:61–62]. Launched by Zeus himself as a portent of the eventual Trojan defeat, a snake glides up a tree and gulps down a brood of sparrows. '[E]ight they were all told/and the mother made the ninth' [2:369–370]. Hephaestus reports living in hiding from gods and mortals for '[n]ine years' [18:468]. After feuding for 'nine whole days' [24:131] over the disposition of Hector's corpse, the gods reach consensus only on the tenth. Achilles tries to console Priam when he comes to retrieve the body. Priam should, Achilles says, turn his thoughts from the grievous losses he has suffered by recalling that Niobe, her children slaughtered, turned her thoughts to food after nine days of mourning had elapsed – 'on the tenth [day]' [24:720].

This (and there is a good deal more of the same) hints at what Homer is on about. The expanse of stone and stubble encircling Troy is a world away from the world to which the Greeks will go – if they do not exit the place on a pyre. It's not a question of map miles and calendar years. Ships cannot sail an infinite distance; men and women can't ceaselessly pursue an activity. Homer's point is about the nature of the world that the men and women at Troy inhabit, especially the men on the Greek side. The world of the warriors is a different kind of world. As Odysseus puts it [14:104–107]:

> us,
> the men whom Zeus decrees, from youth to old age,
> must wind down our brutal wars to the bitter end
> until we drop and die, down to the last man.

'For such a war as we are fighting,' Odysseus is saying, 'death is the sole end. The world is a battlefield. On a battlefield we are born and on the battlefield we pass our lives. We leave only when we breathe our last.' This, then, is not a humanly declared war. We are part of it simply by being in a world over which the gods preside.

Further support for the construal of the Trojan battlefield as the Greeks' world, all of it, is gained by further harrying Jaynes's lines. The war is entering its tenth year. Yet surveying the enemy ranks from Troy's ramparts Priam asks Helen to identify for him the Greek leaders. Come again? Ten years have elapsed and the Trojan king is still ignorant of his main antagonists? To be sure, Homer needs to identify the prominent Greeks for his audience. But has he not *already* done so in Book 1? Some years prior an embassy, headed by one of the Greeks whom Helen identifies, Odysseus, had been dispatched to retrieve her. The diplomatic mission is mentioned in Book 3 [247ff]. Antenor, who fills out Helen's descriptions, reports that *he* hosted the ambassadors [250]. Is Antenor not a senior counsellor to Priam? How much artistry would it have taken to rewrite the scene on the ramparts so as to lower the eyebrows? Consider too that, judging from the description of the gathering of the armies in Book 2, it is as if no one has yet died when the action starts. How does this square with nine years of armed combat, 'the corpse fires burn[ing] on, night and day, no end in sight' [1:60]?

Warriors and Soldiers

Lots of questions. A good place to begin moving towards answers is with a distinction between 'soldier' and 'warrior.' The difference is elicited by observing that Clausewitz's classic statement does not apply to the Trojan War. 'War,' quoth the Prussian theoretician of war, 'is the continuation of politics by other, sc., violent, means.' Whatever Clausewitz meant (the meaning is much contested), the statement makes sense to us. Peace and war go together. As we see it, fighters of wars are, therefore, soldiers. Had geopolitical relations been less frictional, or had certain political ends been achievable without the sounding of bugles and the drumming of drums, their civilian existences would not have been disrupted.

The Greeks at Troy are not soldiers. They are warriors, war being for them the normal condition. Always under arms, their whole field of operation is battlefield. The Trojan War cannot therefore be subsumed under our concept of a war. Of peace the Greeks at Troy are innocent. For them, the following equation balances:

Life = War

The Greeks of the epic regard life as in essence a struggle with an implacable foe, and regard it, moreover, as a struggle from which they cannot emerge the victors.

If life by its very nature is a struggle, the foe cannot be an armed hoplite opposite. Through life one cannot get without living. But many reach the end never having buckled on armour. Nor can the murderous opponent be an occasional thing like plague. The lucky among us live healthy lives and wear down and out with age. For its truth the equation of life and war requires an unavoidable and relentless enemy, an enemy that each and every person faces, and faces without let-up, simply by virtue of being. It is easy to identify that enemy: death. From the battle with death a person cannot go AWOL. To this battle conscientious objection cannot be declared. The battle with death is waged every second of every minute of every day. It is moreover a winner-take-all contest from which the flesh-and-blood combatant inevitably exits on the losing end.

For individuals to whom the Homeric label 'warrior' adheres (and this includes all the Greek individuals), the flanking terms of 'Life = War' equate. The Trojan War is not a kind of war. It is a kind of *life*. Homer's depiction of war captures how a whole culture regards life. Life is understood as a perpetual struggle that the living beings must lose, a struggle that necessarily ends in their defeat. Words and phrases like 'must,' 'necessarily,' 'in essence,' identify the point as philosophical in nature.

We have still to explain why Homer's Greeks view their lives this way. Though Glaucus's assertion resonates with us, we do not think or act like a Diomedes or an Ajax. Glaucus's words could be inserted right into, say, Ecclesiastes (the lines are 1:4).

> A generation goes, and a generation comes,
> but the earth remains forever

And Apollo could have intoned Ecclesiastes 2:22–23:

> What do mortals get from all the toil and strain with which they toil under the sun? For all their days are full of pain, and their work is a vexation; even at night their minds do not rest.

Or Job 14:1–2:

> Man that is born of woman hath but a short time to live, and is full of misery. He cometh up, and is cut down, like a flower; he fleeth as it were a shadow, and never continueth in one stay.

But we side with David.

Once we know what we are looking at, the plot line oddities in the *Iliad* that agitate Jaynes – the length of the war, the absence of supply lines and of reserves from the rear, and so on – fall smartly into place. So far as the Greeks are concerned, life is war. To leave the war is to leave life. Not having come from elsewhere, the warriors therefore have nowhere to return to.[7] By joining the action as it enters its tenth year, Homer fills our field of vision with the fray. However far into the distance we look we see nothing but warriors, bivouacs, combat, and so forth. In its compass the scene resembles one of those vast canvasses of Brueghel's that picture myriad men and women engaged in the myriad activities that men and women engage in. Only on Homer's pages a single activity alone is, on the Greek side, represented. Homer's stage management is a way of dramatically capturing the equation 'Life = War.' Had he been able to do so without affecting the story's plausibility Homer would have made contact with the mayhem in the hundredth year.

Assume the equation and you gain illumination about the *dramatis personae* on the Greek side. Only able-bodied adult males are present and accounted for. Agreed, no one would expect to encounter in the ranks a child, or a woman, or an aged man.[8] But once this homogeneity of actors is connected to the length of the campaign, something deeper emerges. If life is figured, in plot terms, as war, then the livers must be warriors. Since the metaphor is (literal) war, it is as it should be that the characters are all males of fighting age in fighting trim. The fact that the Trojan side includes women, children, elderly people too, confirms the point. For the equation, as we shall see, does not balance for the Trojans.

Priam's exchange with Helen about the Greek principals, at first sight marking the king as past it or the poem as pastiche, is entirely apt relative to the equation. You had a morning meal yesterday. The day before you ate one too. Here you are, then, about to tuck into your toast and coffee. What sense would it make for me to press you as follows? 'Have you forgotten? You had breakfast yesterday. And the day before yesterday. Yet you breakfast again? Get a life!' The activities that keep us alive are activities that we have to repeat. Our not remembering them from day to day is no symptom of amnesia.

Not that the idea of beating swords into ploughshares would baffle Homer. The dynamic of the epic is *from* war *to* peace, and the writing is being done on the peace side. But the movement from the *Iliad* through the home going of the *Odyssey* is not *back to* peace; it is a movement to a different understanding of life.

The defining characteristics of the warrior view are set out systematically in the next section. This section, intended to establish 'Life = War' as *the* constituting equation of the world view of the Greeks at Troy, or at any rate to show how clarifying the equation is of the epic, may be concluded with a point about the *casus belli* of the hostilities, a point that supplies near-decisive confirmation.

Herodotus makes much the same mistake about the cause of Homer's war as Jaynes makes about its length. Herodotus's cast of mind being historical, it is not surprising to find him explaining, in commonsensical terms, why the description of the war must, even discounting the gods, be fictional. (What Jaynes says cannot so readily be extenuated. The thesis about consciousness, which lacks prior credibility, drives his reading.) The Trojans, Herodotus says (*Histories* 2:120), would unquestionably have handed Helen back soon after the Thracian siege engineers had emplaced their fearsome catapults. As an even harder-headed historian sees it, Thersites, the cynic of *Iliad* Book 1, hits the jackpot. According to Thucydides (*The Peloponnesian War* 1.9) Agamemnon was in it for the money.

If we take the epic straight, as a story of conflict, it's impossible to disagree. So acutely do the Trojans fear the consequences of the action – almost all of them repeatedly give voice to foreboding – that the return of Helen would have been estimated as a trifle. Achilles later refers to the enterprise as 'insane.' But he means something different. His, in the sense explained, is a conceptual claim.

The question virtually poses itself. Why, just because the woman was taken away, would the Greeks have left their homes, made the perilous journey over the sea, and encamped at Troy for ten years, not knowing whether a further decade under arms, perhaps even more, did not await (in the [lucky?] event that they survived)? It's not that what Paris did is no reason at all for reacting. It's that the Greeks' reaction is massively disproportionate. The fighters are under no illusions about the likelihood of seeing their loved ones again. In the hand-to-hand combat that day after day takes place, the chances of surviving are slim to none, and as the saying goes, slim just left town.

One might think to answer the question by saying that Homer, out to rub our noses in the horrors of war, has to get the action going, and calls for the purpose upon the mythic cause. In effect, the *casus belli* is just a plot catalyst. But consider: if Life = War, it follows that *casus belli* = *casus vitae*. 'What brings the war about?' converts, if so, to 'What precipitates life?' There is of course life's biological causation. Impregnation, fertilization, meiosis, and so on do not however explain life in the way that the need for *Lebensraum* or for access to deep water ports explains war. Had Homer supplied a cause/explanation of the usual geopolitical type, that would have shrunk and localized the embroilment. The conflict would be understood to take place against the background of the kind of life in respect of which space for a growing population or suitable harbours to conduct trade might be needed. Nothing insane about that, despite the inevitable material and human costs. This, however, is precisely what Homer is concerned to bracket off. So he supplies a war whose cause is massively out of balance with the suffering, the pain, the mayhem. The point, again, is conceptual, not factual. Fortuitously perhaps, the cause in this case is not much different than the cause of each of our lives: the way of a man with a woman.

It's not that Homer's war is (either in Jaynes's sense or in Herodotus's and Thucydides's sense) a fictional war. Homer is not describing a war at all. He is describing a cultural ensemble, a way of life in which life is figured as, primarily, a terminal struggle. The *Iliad* is at core a dramatic rendering of the incipient shift from one conceptualization of human reality to another.

War, What Is it Good For?

Here is a structured sketch of the warriors' value system:

For the warrior, Life = War

If to live is to be at war, then a living person is *eo ipso* a warrior.

The second term of the equation is not to be understood literally. But while to see life as war is to see life as difficult, there is more to it:

> The warrior sees life as a war that he or she must lose. The end, unavoidably, is the grave.

Aren't we also conscious of our mortality, so acutely conscious that we require a dose of laughing gas to look it square in the eye? 'Life,' we say, 'is a near death experience.' 'Life,' we say, 'is a short story.' 'Life's a bitch' – our bumper stickers declare – 'and then you die.' Life is 'a sexually transmitted disease,' wrote R.D. Laing, 'with a terminal prognosis.' Forgoing the nitrous oxide, Denmark's third most famous son adds an immortal entry to the list. 'Fear and trembling, a sickness unto death.'

Consciousness that birth delivers a death sentence, that the carriageway is a dead end, that no one gets out of life alive, is however consistent with not accepting the equation. Acceptance also means denial that life has intrinsic worth:

> Because of the inevitability of death, the warrior denies that life is valuable for its own sake.

The negative valorization of life beats at the heart of the warrior ethos. Thus Glaucus's use of the leaf metaphor in describing his condition. This is precisely what Achilles is questioning.

Axiomatic to the warrior view is the denial of intrinsic worth to life. But if the ethos construes life as a losing battle, why do those who buy into it bother to engage? Why do they not open their veins or drink hemlock or leap from the nearest cliff? Isn't nihilism the unavoidable result? It isn't. Though the warrior denies that life has intrinsic worth, the warrior does not *ipso facto* rate life worthless. Nor does the warrior say that nothing has value in and of itself:

The warrior holds that life is valuable
as an instrument for achieving what is valuable
for its own sake.

The warrior uses his or her life as a tool for gaining – for trying to gain – what is of intrinsic worth. What might that be?

For the warrior, survival or lastingness
has intrinsic worth.

The survival for which the warrior strives isn't personal survival. Literal immortality belongs only to the gods. It is for survival in memory that the warriors do their thing. This lastingness – a simulacrum of what the gods alone have – is achieved by performing glorious deeds, being seen to do so, and, as a consequence of drawing the attention and gaining the awed admiration of others, being sung.

Confronting what he perceives as his certain end, Hector makes a statement that captures well the thinking [22:359–362]:

let me die –
but not without struggle, not without glory, no,
in some great clash of arms that even men to come
will hear of down the years!

The words to Edwin Starr's Vietnam-era pop anthem, 'War,' from which the heading of this section comes, make for a nice summation and contrast. Here are several lines, slightly edited:

War
What is it good for?
Absolutely nothing!
It ain't nothing but a heartbreaker,
Friend only to the undertaker.
It's an enemy to all mankind,
The point of war blows my mind.
War has caused unrest

Within the younger generation
Induction then destruction.
Who wants to die?
War
What is it good for?
Absolutely nothing!

The warriors don't see it this way. For them, war (sc., life) is a valuable commodity. It has worth as an instrument or tool for achieving that which is of paramount value: godlikeness. Fraught as (mortal) life is with sorrow and pain, not one of them would choose to live for the sake of living, any more than you or I would choose struggle for struggle's sake. Just so, when *we*, sick at heart, bare our breasts to the scalpel, it is in the hope of gaining the good health that we rate intrinsically valuable. Not that the warriors want to die. In this regard they differ in no wise from our soldiers. But for them, in contrast to the men and women of our armed forces, the War = Life equation balances. Life is worthwhile because of what it supplies an opportunity to achieve. So each of them is, as a matter of core value, prepared to lose his life, since considered in and by itself it is second best.

Plainly, this position differs from the biblical one. Those who are in the gravitational field of the equation do not think of the world as their establishment. Neither was it established for them, nor do they find it hospitable. It is as it should be, then, that the habitations on the Greek side are to their occupants what suburban dwellings are not to theirs: places belonging to the main activity in which they engage. On the Greek side, everything, including women, is part and parcel of the trouble and strife.

Applications

Fully to understand the view we have to add to the mix the attitude that a consciousness of a nature indifferent to their joys and sorrows inspires in the warriors, an engulfing nature that, in the game for all the marbles into which we are all willy-nilly delivered as players at birth, invariably leaves us with only a marble slab. Nature, irresistibly powerful, elicits a response of awe. Though the sense of being overwhelmed would motivate some men and women to seek an inconspicuous corner, the warriors react differently. Each of them it motivates to stride into action and to strive on the field of action to duplicate nature's power to the highest degree that a mortal can. Each of them it motivates to live his or her life to the full – to the full, that is, as he or she understands plenitude. Taking their cue from Zeus, Apollo, Poseidon, who personify aspects of nature's power, the main characters of the *Iliad* are thus occupied in treating those with whom they come into contact as energetically as is possible for a mortal.[9] Emulating the lightning bolt and the searing sun, the tidal wave and the typhoon, a warrior tries to immobilize or to knock over or to sweep away everything in his path.

As parts of nature, all men and women exemplify (some of) the power of the supra-human (natural) forces. It is however *as* exemplifiers of (some of) that power that the warriors perceive themselves and others. Inevitably, some among them possess (some of) that power in greater measure than do others. Often, some stand out from *all* the others in this regard, possessing (some of) that power in a degree unusual for a mortal. Helen's extraordinary beauty verges on divine. Paris, to put it indelicately, is a supreme swordsman. Not just a great fighter among fighters, Ajax scours the field of opponents. For the warriors to perceive themselves in terms of the power that they possess is, obviously, for them to perceive themselves in terms of the use of that power. And so it is. The warriors use the power that they possess as nature itself does, heedless of the effects on others. They no more lacerate themselves about injuring an opponent than a rainstorm sheds tears over a drowned field. Nor, any more than does the waterlogged meadow, do they feel resentful or bear grudges when they find themselves on the receiving end. Their hearts are, as Homer often says, of iron.

This makes good sense. *We* can even make sense of it, though only in limited spheres. The movie stars and élite athletes among us are *our* demigods. The King. The Great One. The Chairman of the Board. The Divine. The Boss. It is therefore as it should be that the 'private' lives of such persons are parts of their overall roles. Business also lends itself well to being figured along the lines of the Trojan War. Once bankruptcy is aligned, functionally, with death – you die when the margin call comes that you cannot meet – life on Wall Street or in The City corresponds pretty much across its whole range to life around the walls of the city of Troy.

The case of Diomedes, to which Book 5 of the *Iliad* is given over, casts intense illumination here. The son of Tydeus and Deipyle fights the Olympians, sc., the less limited powers, and prevails. Not only does he inflict damage on Aphrodite (who, as Zeus scolds, doesn't belong on the battlefield), he even manages to injure Ares! Scholars have maintained that Diomedes's display of virtuosity, his *aristeia*, is spliced into the action. Book 5, they say, is a spur line in the narrative. It *is* past doubt that like the Bible the text as we possess it comprises diverse elements from different sources. But in the force field of a system that valorizes most the gods and their status the representation of Diomedes as Hillary to Olympus's Everest is not a bad idea to float, to counteract the thought that this whole business of god-approximation is nonsense on sky-high stilts, gnats and elephants. Nor should one forget that Athena, in Book 21, god-handles these same two Olympians, so that what Diomedes accomplishes with her encouragement could be a case of fighting fire with fire.

The warriors try to approximate in their actions the power of nature. It is not for self-expression's sake that they exert themselves. For such a sake their prodigies could just as well have been performed out of the sight of men's and women's eyes. For the same reason that he stands in awe of the surrounding forces, the warrior expects fellow warriors to stand in awe of him. Gained by eliciting the drop-jawed response is survival. Not personal survival. Remembered for his deeds, the warrior, like those who make an entry into Guinness, survives *in memory*.

To casual readers, the list of combatants that takes up nearly half of Book 2 is like a transcription from a phone directory (not of course the Yellow Pages). As in the case of Diomedes, scholars have detected a heavy editorial hand. In fact, in Book 2 as in Book 5 an important thematic point is made. In one of a few first-person interpositions into the narrative, the poet laments the fact that he can only sing of the leaders [2:577–582]:

> The mass of troops I could never tally, never name,
> not even if I had ten tongues and ten mouths,
> a tireless voice and the heart inside me bronze,
> never unless you Muses of Olympus, daughters of Zeus
> whose shield is rolling thunder, sing, sing in memory
> all who gathered under Troy.

'Sing in memory.' The idea of an unknown soldier, of fighting anonymously, would have struck the warriors as a nonsense. Which indicates that the fighting is not ignited by causes of the sort for which we take up arms.

The idea that to be alive is to battle thus gives expression to a heightened sense of life's fragility, a sense that informs the realism of Glaucus and the hostility of Apollo. How could something so flimsy and evanescent, something that the surrounding world dwarfs and ultimately crushes, something invariably accompanied with so much sorrow and pain, be of primary value? That is the warriors' deepest question – a question that is for them rhetorical. Yet the warriors do not react by throwing in the towel. Since losing is understood to be a foregone conclusion, the warriors, if their fighting isn't meaningless thrashing about, have therefore to fight with the objective of gaining something of greater worth than life itself. For Homer's warriors, that greater thing, the thing that has more basic – indeed primary – value, is, once more, survival. Survival is valuable for its own sake.

The contrast between the warrior culture and ours is clear. *We* assign *intrinsic* value to life. The warriors regard their individual lives only as *instruments* for achieving that simulacrum of what in its primary form is the prerogative of the gods.

Through their doings the warriors are thus performing what in the culture is an *imitatio deorum.* They hope thereby to achieve (and are regarded by their fellows as capable of achieving) the nearest thing possible for them to what is had by the gods *qua* gods: immortality.[10]

This, then, is the kernel of the position. The warriors' motivation is explained. It isn't death that the warriors fear most. With death they can live. What quakes the warrior's gut is the thought that when he or she departs it will be to the world as if he or she has never lived. Most of all, the warrior fears erasure. The warrior also fears *negative* memorialization. Helen says so much [6:422–426]:

> whore that I am,
> and this blind mad Paris. Oh the two of us!
> Zeus planted a killing doom within us both,
> and even for generations still unborn
> we will live in song.

Live on in memory, she means, for ill. Live on in infamy.

Lest all this seem to turn the Greek fighters into intellectuals, it is worth adding that the value system is linked to and serves the needs of the society. The achievement of the warriors' objective requires that they impress their fellows. Their fellows are impressed precisely by actions that advance the communal cause. The same goes for Wall Street and The City. The activity of risk-takers benefits the economy. If all the players in the market purchased low-interest bearing instruments or socked most of their money away under the mattress, the economy would stagnate. Yet the risk-takers, out to enrich themselves, could care less about the commonweal.

This is an apt place to field an objection that is sure to be made. Early in the action, Agamemnon administers a test to his fighters. He declares that the war is lost [2:161–165]:

> Our work drags on, unfinished as always, hopeless –
> the labour of war that brought us here to Troy.
> So come, follow my orders. All obey me now.
> Cut and run! Sail home to the fatherland we love!
> We'll never take the broad streets of Troy.

Far from resisting departure in the name of glory, the men race for the ships. Patently, the Achaeans here do not satisfy my definition of 'warrior.'

The answer to the objection has two parts. The first part, whose textual basis is the fact that the test is administered to the rank and file, not to the major figures, is that the values of a culture are only absorbed *in part* by some. It is Odysseus, fully committed to the values, who halts the retreat. The scene contrasts directly with a later one, two books on, in which Agamemnon, critical of Odysseus's comportment at the front, accuses him [4:398–404] of holding back:

> First you are, when you hear of feasts from me,
> when Achaeans set out banquets for their chiefs.
> Then you're happy enough to down the roast meats
> and cups of honeyed, mellow wine – all you can drink.
> But now you'd gladly watch ten troops of Achaeans
> beat you to this feast,
> First to fight with the ruthless bronze before you!

But in this case it is explained to Agamemnon that there is more than one way to skin a cat. What looks to him like Falstaffian behaviour is nothing of the kind. The second part of the answer is deeper. No rounded treatment of human existence can ignore the very basic resistance to dissolution. This self-preservative tendency is not cultural. It is instinctual. Rousseau ascribes *amour de soi* (as he calls it) to all creatures.

The fighters' race for the ships is an acknowledgment of the visceral or organic recoil. By parity, imagine that the ascetics in a culture of fasting are given a holiday: 'All obey me now. Cut and eat to your hearts' content.' The race to the groaning board that will result does not show that the erstwhile self-deniers only feigned commitment to the values that find expression in abstinence. 'Voluntary self-denial' is not inconsistent.

Returning now to the warrior ethos: the case of Ajax is most revealing. Homer makes as clear as he can that Ajax, even more than Achilles, is soldered to the equation. He even at one point ascribes to Ajax the specific fighting capacity for which Achilles is known: 'no one alive could run down men in flight like him' [14:609]. Ajax is the exemplar *par excellence* of the warrior ethos. After Achilles is killed, Ajax does not inherit the armour. Devastated, as *qua quintessential* warrior he should be, he takes his own life. (The suicide is mentioned in the *Odyssey*. Ajax falls on the sword that Hector had given him after their inconclusive one-on-one.) The sad fate that Ajax meets he meets on account of his inability to dissociate from this identity. The world of the warrior is (=) the battlefield. The life of the warrior is (=) battle.

Ajax's case asymptotically approaches proof that in thinking thematically of the *Iliad* we are not to think of the warriors as having taken up arms and assembled at Troy. Otherwise, no proper sense would attach to the denial that Ajax can return. Why should Achilles's gear go to Odysseus? In a postwar world, Life ≠ Battle. Warriors, superannuated, are unsuitable types to inherit. A version the story therefore is of the biblical episode in which the Odysseus-like Jacob procures his father's blessing, a seal of his suitability to carry on the paternal program, his suitability over the very Ajax-like Esau, who as firstborn has a presumptive entitlement. I stress: *presumptive entitlement*. The world has however changed. It is no longer safe to presume. Ajax is yesterday's man. Wild with the sense of having been disgraced, Ajax ends his own life. That is the fate he meets.[11]

The translation of the *Iliad* from which I am quoting contains a revealing slip in this regard. A related confusion affects the scholarly essay that introduces the edition.

Here is Robert Fagles's rendering of some of the words that Agamemnon spits at Achilles during the set-to in Book 1 [211–213].

> What if you are a great soldier? That's just a gift of god.
> Go home with your ships and comrades, lord it over
> your Myrmidons!

Fagles enlists the noun 'soldier.' The term is the wrong *nom de guerre.* Soldiers are civilians who through enlistment or conscription take up arms when diplomacy hits the wall, 'war war' often being the only recourse when, as Churchill inimitably rhymed, 'jaw jaw' no longer avails. For soldiers, that is, war is a deviation from, a disruption of, peace. At the cessation of hostilities, the survivors from the ranks resume normal lives. (I refer to the soldiers among us. Enslavement was in earlier times a predictable consequence of ending up with a pulse on the losing side.) Where warriors are concerned the case differs utterly. For warriors, Life = War. It's more than just this, that peace is not for a warrior the normal condition. Peace for the warrior is not a condition at all. Warriors live, breathe, and eat war. Like the warrior Karna in the Indian epic *Mahabharata* they are born with their boots on. Peace does not hang in their conceptual wardrobe.

Does the problem of translation signal a problem of interpretation? It could be that a poetic motive underlies Fagles's selection of what after all is in English a near synonym for a word that today has come to have a more poetic feel than 'soldier.' With regard to Bernard Knox, we cannot be so relaxed. Knox's introduction to Fagles's translation acknowledges the influence of Simone Weil's essay *L'Iliade ou le Poème de la Force.* Weil's words come out of her experience in mid-twentieth-century Europe. But to liken the Trojan War as Knox does (38) to what transpired on 'the beaches of the 1944 Normandy landing,' and to say as Knox says (29) that Homer is capturing this feature of 'the human condition,' that 'we are . . . lovers and victims of the will to violence,' is to shoot wide of the mark. The warrior view is a response to life, specifically to mortality. Knox elides unavoidable struggle with avoidable violence.

The Ladder

Through their actions the warriors are performing, or trying to perform, what qualifies in their thinking as an *imitatio deorum.* Since, in the Bible, men and women are made in God's image and likeness, and since, in the Bible, God is a standard-setting model, the two texts can seem to be advancing one view. On closer inspection, the cases turn out however to be incommensurate. The warriors, the reforming of whose value system the *Iliad* is tracking, measure themselves against, and try to measure up to, what they are unlike. The Bible's men and women imitate what they are like. The warriors, their armour removed for good, have to secrete a new self-image. How the change is made in the

Iliad is the next substantive item of business. For now, let me draw the preceding contrast in a punchy way.

In a touching lament over a friend recently departed at an early age, the journalist and essayist Adam Gopnik imagines the following rah-rah speech for a group of boys who make up a touch football team that the friend had coached.[12]

> We're here to separate the men from the boys, and then we're going to separate the warriors from the men. And then we're going to separate the heroes from the warriors – and then we're going to separate the legends from the heroes. And then, at last, we're going to separate the gods from the legends.

Presented to us here is a ladder of levels:

GODS
LEGENDS
HEROES
WARRIORS
MEN
BOYS

Movement is possible in either direction. Depending on the anchorage of the value system and the location of the players, either the move upwards or the move downwards can be accounted positive.

The movement of the fighters is in the upwards direction. As the culture with which they identify mandates, they do their utmost to raise themselves to as high a level as they can – to within hailing distance of the gods. Aphrodite says it of Diomedes: '*he'd* fight Father Zeus!' [5:408]. To dramatize the cultural shift Homer has his protagonist do a *volte face.* The fleetest of runners puts off his divinity and takes on board his fleetingness – does the last, I mean, without endorsing the nihilist view that life is valueless, or coming to accept the flattening, absurdist view that, in the words of Albert Camus's anti-hero Meursault, '*çela m'est égal.*' Achilles, that is, fights Zeus & Co. too. But unlike Diomedes, *he* does not take the gods on to make a name for himself. He fights them in defence of anonymity.

The remarkable thing, then, is that the Bible, at least in the major parts here focused upon, is reform*ed.* In a clear sense, its cast is anti-religious. I just now wrote, figuratively, of a ladder. In Genesis 28, Jacob has a dream of a literal one:

> And he dreamed there was a ladder set up on the earth, the top of it reaching to heaven; and the angels of God were ascending and descending on it. (12)

God's messengers are negotiating the stairway that links earth and heaven.[13] What is their direction of movement on its rungs? Up and Down. Theologically, wouldn't Down and Up be more natural? 'No one has ascended into heaven except the one who descended from heaven' (John 3:13). Jesus, expression of the godhead, delivers the news from on high. The text we are looking at has a different centre than the Gospels. It is humanology, not theology. This is the kernel of what Jacob means when, in a shock of realization, he calls the place 'awesome' (17). Which we might more accurately render 'awful.'[14] He hadn't known that the place of God was down on earth, among stones that play so large a part in his, Jacob's, life. And so 'he took the stone that he had put under his head [for a pillow] and set it up for a pillar and poured oil on top of it. He called the place Bethel [= house of God]' (18–19). Here, then, *he* will stand.

This is remarkable. How did it occur? I can only conjecture about its causes. Later we shall look at the difference from the inside.

David Copperfield on the Carmel

Here, from the later scriptural story of Elijah, is a more revealing case of angels going up and only afterwards going down. Elijah's activities as a man of God find many reflections in the ministry of Samuel. Elijah's gathering on the Carmel cannot fail to recall to attentive minds an earlier gathering at Mizpah (1 Samuel 7) just prior to which the Israelites had been prevailed upon to 'put away the Baals and the Astartes' (4). At Mizpah, Samuel oversees the sacrifice of 'a whole burnt offering to the Lord' (9). The Philistine enemy, poised for an attack on the newly resolved people, are then routed with God's help: 'the Lord thundered with a mighty voice that day against the Philistines and threw them into confusion; and they were routed before Israel' (10). Also worth reading into the record is Samuel's giving of a sign to the Israelites of God's power. At harvest time, when the weather is usually clement,

'Samuel called upon the Lord, and the Lord sent thunder and rain that day' (1 Samuel 12:18).

By the time of Elijah, during the Israelite reign of Ahab, the backsliding of the people has gone much further. While Samuel sacrifices *after* the people had returned to the fold, in Elijah's case the offering's acceptance is required in order to draw the renegades back from Baal. In a reversal of the attitude that the children of Israel displayed at Mount Sinai, they have to be shown before they will do.

Declaring himself the only prophet of the Lord left, Elijah calls to the Israelites on Mount Carmel. 'How long will you go limping with two different opinions?' (1 Kings 18:21) He proceeds (ibid.): 'If the Lord is God, follow him; but if Baal, then follow him.' The prophets of Baal, four hundred fifty in number, are challenged to a winner-take-all competition. The episode is highly dramatic. Elijah lays out the ground rules:

> Let two bulls be given to us; let them choose one bull for themselves, cut it in pieces, and lay it on the wood, but put no fire to it; I will prepare the other bull and lay it on the wood, but put no fire to it. Then you call on the name of your god and I will call on the name of the Lord; the god who answers by fire is indeed God. (23–4)

Speak of cutting the bull! The text goes on to jeer at the acolytes of Baal. They limp about their altar; they call on the name of Baal from morning until noon; they immolate themselves with swords and lances, raving on until the time of the oblation. To what effect? In words worth setting off, since we shall hear them again, we are told:

> there was no voice, no answer, and no response. (29)

Elijah mocks them: 'either [your god] is meditating, or he has wandered away, or he is on a journey' (27).

Elijah knows that no answer will come. Whence his assurance? The only explanation, I think, is a conviction (a conviction shared by us) that *nothing* of the sort will work. The belief system that he is ridiculing is a lot of Baal-oney. Later in the story, on the run from Jezebel, whom the performance doesn't fool, Elijah is portrayed as questioning God's protection. '[H]e was afraid; he got up and fled for his life' (1 Kings 19:3). How sharp the contrast between the bravado on the mountain and the despondency that sends him into the wilderness. The text manages to suggest that Elijah's confidence on the Carmel is not confidence in God, which would know no bounds, but self-confidence, which can wax and wane.

Self-confidence by itself has no power to light fires. How (it will therefore be asked) could Elijah have been so sure that *he* would win the contest?

The game – whose rules, I repeat, are established by the captain of God's team – is rigged. The text tells us that Elijah 'repaired' the altar of the Lord (30). 'Repaired' can literally be rendered as 'doctored.'[15] Elijah does not just say 'Let There Be Fire' and piously await ignition. His pitch is reminiscent of the carnival barker's come-on, his stagy comportment very like the flimflam of a professional prestidigitator. Elijah works the crowd: 'Come closer to me' (ibid.). The attendant preparations are numbing. Elijah shifts stones about like a master of the shell game. He arranges the scenery in a fashion that conjures up the image of a Las Vegas headliner. All the while his confederates – despite the suggestion created by Elijah's words that his band has one man, he has an entourage – are beavering away downstage, filling trenches surrounding the sacrificial altar with (so the text says) 'water.' The hint, carried in the line 'the fire of the Lord . . . even licked up the water that was in the trench' (38), is that the confederates use a combustible liquid. ('Water' could be a generic word meaning 'liquid.' At my parents' table, where Yiddish ruled when guests were present, 'vasser,' whose English equivalent was 'ginger ale,' functioned as a term for all carbonated soft drinks.) When heated, water boils and steams. Oil, feeding the flames, has tongues of flame.[16]

Speculating on such particulars is of course silly. The tale is not reportage. What moral do the writers wish to impart? Crucial is the theophany – or, more precisely, anti-theophany – on Horeb. God says to Elijah: 'Go out and stand on the mountain before the Lord, for the Lord is about to pass by' (19:11).

> Now there was a great wind, so strong that it was splitting mountains and breaking rocks in pieces before the Lord, but the Lord was not in the wind; and after the wind an earthquake, but the Lord was not in the earthquake; and after the earthquake a fire, but the Lord was not in the fire; and after the fire a sound of sheer silence. (11–12)

The Lord's response to Elijah is mute, like that of Baal to *its* followers: 'there was no voice, no answer, and no response.' Immediately, in a departure from precedent, Elijah anoints his own successor, Elisha.

Looked at independently of the rest, the experience on Horeb might reasonably be seen as dramatizing the fact that God does not appear on demand. The wider story gives the lie to this perception. Recur to the sacrifices atop the Carmel. The prophets of Baal resemble the deity of Genesis. 'Let there be fire!' In their case fire does not however come. Elijah's 'method,' as I have described it, is to lend God a hand. Like the first natural philosophers in Greece, who came several centuries later, he exploits a knowledge of natural processes.[17] He also has a public person's sound grasp of crowd psychology. Fire emerges not magically, but causally, albeit in a manner that the assembled are made to regard as magical. (Observe that Elijah works on both sides of the Proverbist's line between three and four.) How could this not reflect back on creation?

Samuel had also experienced noise in the clouds. At Mizpah, 'the Lord thundered with a mighty voice' (1 Samuel 7:10). And by supplication Samuel brought the rain in harvest time. Does not Elijah also bring the rain? He does. The difference from Samuel is however more evident than the similarity:

> Elijah went to the top of Carmel; there he bowed himself down upon the earth and put his face between his knees. He said to his servant, 'Go up now, and look toward the sea.' He went up and looked, and said, 'There is nothing.' Then he said, 'Go again seven times.' At the seventh time he said, 'Look, a little cloud no bigger than a person's hand is rising out of the sea.' . . . In a little while the heavens grew black with clouds and wind; there was a heavy rain. (1 Kings 18:42–45)

Even in more arid climes the rain will eventually come. I daresay that meteorologists would not be the butt of jokes if a predictive track record of one out of seven were satisfactory.

What is the point of winning over the renegade Israelites in this deceptive manner? In Elijah's career is found no basis for characterizing him as an Israelite Elmer Gantry, forging fire for personal profit, nothing likening him to the artisans of Hiero. The Prophet is trying to convert the Israelites to the truth (as he sees it) about their condition. Believing as he does in its relevance to human flourishing, he is committed to the belief system. Like a politician with a manifesto rather too technical for the average voter to take in; like a doctor administering a pill that is too bitter to be swallowed without sugar coating; Elijah has however to resort to guile. The hoopla is directed to the undecided Israelites more than against the Baalites. Elijah is trying to romance the balky bride to the Lord's altar. Having got there, it will remain open whether the Israelites will take the vows, or whether, having taken them, they will take them seriously. God himself had learned that faith that miracles secure is loosely secured.

Prefatorily, I likened the religious content of the Bible to training wheels. Elijah's performance confirms the simile, heretical though it sounds. It is only appropriate, then, that Elijah (2 Kings 2:11) departs the earth in a chariot of fire.

'Aniconicism' refers to the Decalogue's prohibition on graven images. One acute Bible reader[18] says of this sort of scene that it takes iconicism to its logical conclusion. There is human reality. There is physical reality. That is all there is. The prohibition on imaging God is a warning against living a fantasy life. 'You are on your own.'

Though the message certainly is a tough one, plenty of choice is left as to what kind of life to live. Who says that subscribers to the warrior ethos are indulging in fantasy? Unlike the idea of squaring the circle, the idea of making a lasting impact is intelligible. So is the idea of making the impact by emulating the forces that impress us powerfully. Could the ideas, as elements of a value system, survive if cut loose from the hyperbolic claim that the immortality aspired to is a version of that which the gods literally have? I do not see on the face of it why it would be boxing the compass to say that they could. So aniconicism does not designate the Bible's normative stance, down to earth though it may be, as correct. In our terms: the aniconicist point is made within the confines of, and is to be understood in the terms of, the reformed view.

A Critique of Metaphysics on the Mountain

In the dramatic confrontation on the Carmel, Elijah engages in subterfuge. Beneath the performance lies a point of deepest principle. God does not respond to Elijah's call. Why not? The reason is simple. God – 'sheer silence' – does not exist. Does that not mean that the Bible's claim that men and women are inspired with God's breath is itself nothing but hot air? It doesn't, though it does mean that the claim is figuratively encoding the underlying verity. To penetrate to the point of principle, note that that there is a clear sense in which (leaving aside the question of existence) God *could* respond. God is the kind of entity capable of responding. God is a person. Just as men and women can respond to one another (though for a variety of reasons they might not, and frequently do not), God can too. Informing Elijah's mockery of the prophets of Baal is the proposition that a god of their sort cannot answer. A god of their sort is an expression of (subhuman) nature, and (subhuman) nature does not understand. The Bible's attack on idol worship often seems unfair, an attack on a caricature. Those who are mocked in the Bible for bowing down before sticks and stones do not however worship the graven objects. They worship what those objects represent.[19] The caricature is, then, not conceptually unfair, since what is represented is like the representation. The activities of the prophets of Baal are, in effect, in principle futile. Baal can no more respond than a stone can.

But *are* the efforts futile? Nature *can* be made to respond. True, sheep-like calling of 'Baal' and acts of self-immolation are pretty poor ways of getting the world to smile on one's endeavours. If the sower is to reap, it is best to curry favour with the rain god by doing the rain dance in the rainy reason. Who knows (especially when not much is known) but that such an act might be causally linked with the desired result? If dancing was followed by rain in the past, perhaps (it is not stupid to assume) it will work in the present. Causal links are after all very intricate. (That is not to approve the sacrifice of Iphigenia on the off-chance that the winds might pick up.) Some who interact with nature – those we call 'scientists' – are very good at figuring out how to get a response. Seeding the clouds with silver nitrate is, I am told, a more effective way of getting rain onto the crops than is the dance. Happily, the point of the encounter on the Carmel is not to say that science is ineffective. If an updated Elijah were trying to wean us off reliance on science, I at any rate would stick with the Baalites; or, moving from the altar to the laboratory, with Baal-lite. The point of the episode is that 'response' in the case of the Baalites is metaphorical. We find the same metaphor in Bacon's talk of 'interrogating' nature. True, it's a long road from the Tishbite to Sir Francis. But it's not a long way, either in space or in time, from Elijah to the proto-philosophers of Greece. The Baalites are proto-scientists. Their attitude to the world is an early form of the scientific attitude. They hold a Thales-type view. As they see it, human reality is just part of physical reality: we can ultimately understand the response of a person to a beseeching in the same way as we understand the reaction of a cloud to the seeding. The problem is that the reaction of the cloud, as we may describe it, is not of the cloud alone. It is of the wider meteorological system, a system that includes a vaporous thickening. To see the human case along such lines is to lose the particular person.

The metaphysical battle is joined. Is the particularity of men and women irreducible? Do we need a special ontological category to rationalize the distinctively human world? Are we men and women, each of us, inspired with an extra-natural breath of life? Elijah is taking the biblical view: 'yes' to all the questions. The monotheistic deity's assertion of his nature, 'I am that I am,' is for Elijah an assertion of the principle of particular existence. Since God is a hitherto unknown deity, this is (in the Kantian sense) an *original* principle, unavailable to worshippers of the 'other gods.' A few paragraphs back I wrote: 'Elijah is trying to convert the Israelites to the truth (as he sees it) about their condition. Believing as he does in its relevance to human flourishing, he is committed to the belief system.' The conversion is from Elijah's viewpoint (this is of course the Bible's viewpoint) a conversion to a correct self-understanding. It is in that sense that it bears on human flourishing. For all we know, the Baalites might be happier than the followers of God. That's an empirical issue. As the Bible sees it, they do not however understand themselves. The Carmel is the Bible's Academy, Elijah's encounter, a bloody symposium in which self-knowledge is taught.

What then of the sacrament of sacrifice? We encountered sacrifice in the story of Cain and Abel. But the sacrament functions in the story merely as a narrative device. So far as Cain and Abel are concerned, the activity comes from nowhere, and I am sure we as readers are not supposed to ask 'Why are they doing it?' The question is: why are the storytellers making use of it? The answer is easy. The activity is used by the storytellers as a litmus test. They are giving their assessment, in a graphic way, of the acceptability of the simpler and of the more complex way of life. (The judgment that is delivered, I might just say, is fence sitting.)

So much for Cain and Abel. Their story is not a scriptural basis for sacrifice. Nonetheless, the practice is in fact a central cultic activity among the chosen. In the days when the Temple was standing, sacrifice was indeed the main mode of communal religious expression. In this frame it is not a narrative device. What are we to make of it? Here is a very short answer.

Some maintain, entirely reasonably, that a guiding intention behind the promulgation and enforcement of God-ascribed ordinances on the Israelites is to bind the members of the communion through a set of common practices that set them apart from outsiders. If so, the character of the practices does not matter. What counts is the effect. The Athenians attended the amphitheatre at festival time. The Israelites went up to Jerusalem thrice yearly. Still, why this practice, which is so closely associated with the opposition? Maimonides, who feels strongly the conflict between sacrifice and the basic principles of the creed, is very helpful in answering. Sensitive apostles of change do well to bear in mind that old habits die hard. The practice, Maimonides argues,[20] is a sop to the Israelites. Having become inured to the practice during their lengthy period in Egypt, the Israelites were loath to abandon it once they achieved a land of their own.[21] The control of sacrifice in the inner books of the Pentateuch, the proscription of it as an element of private worship, offers confirmation. The intention is to gut the practice of what idolaters derive from it. By keeping the activity public and by surrounding it with numbing conditions, the potential danger that it poses is held in check. An outright ban would have turned it into forbidden fruit. We know very well where that can lead.

7
Nobodies

Frost Points

Archetypically, Ajax lives and breathes within the field of the defining equation of the pre-reformed view that the *Iliad* dramatizes. 'Call up the joy of war!' bellows the quintessential fighter [15:557]. Unsuited though they are to the man's plainspoken manner, the preceding polysyllables suit the man. The Platonic Form of white is white, wholly white, and nothing but white. A yellow streak, however slight, it does not abide. Ajax is very like a particularized Platonic Form. Pure warrior, he repels all that associates with peace. Subtract strife, trouble, and their accompaniments from the RHS of 'Life = War,' and the LHS reduces to zero. Ajax has therefore to die fully armed, snuffing out his own life if no external antagonist is a match.

Ajax's suicide carries a deep thematic meaning. The meaning is encoded by means of a literary characteristic that I call a *Frost Point*. Paradigmatic is the closing couplet of Robert Frost's 'Stopping by Woods on a Snowy Evening.' Here is the poem's final stanza.

The woods are lovely, dark, and deep,
But I have promises to keep,
And miles to go before I sleep,
And miles to go before I sleep.

In a purely phonetic sense, a word is its own perfect match. But English prosody has 'moon' rhyming with 'June,' not with itself. Primed for a rhyme, the English poetic ear tends to register disappointment should the same word that terminates the relevant earlier line be sounded a second time. Consider in this regard a couplet from T.S. Eliot's 'Prufrock' – a deliberate disruption of rhyme, the inner repetitions stumbling the forward movement in a verbal simulation of J. Alfred's existential paralysis:

> The yellow fog that rubs its back upon window-panes
> The yellow smoke that rubs its muzzle on the window-panes

In respect of 'Stopping,' however, the ear does not protest. That what would usually be a prosodic scruple is disarmed confirms that in crossing from the poem's penultimate line to its identical closer the reader detects, subliminally, a change. Frost's first 'And miles to go before I sleep' refers to the distance of the field from home. Voiced by the night traveller is the mundane need to bring the day's activities to a close and to take some rest. The second 'And miles to go before I sleep' has an eschatological reference – to death, the last end, the ultimate resting place. The change that occurs is a change of state, like the sublimation of atmospheric moisture as rime that occurs at the frost point.

The phenomenon isn't unique to poetry. A mimetically marvelous shift of much the same weather/whither variety to which Frost gives expression ends James Joyce's 'The Dead.'[1]

> [S]now was general all over Ireland. It was falling on every part of the dark central plain, on the treeless hills, falling softly upon the Bog of Allen and, farther westward, softly falling into the dark mutinous Shannon waves. It was falling, too, upon every part of the lonely churchyard on the hill where Michael Furey lay buried. It lay thickly drifted on the crooked crosses and headstones, on the spears of the little gate, on the barren thorns. [Gabriel Conroy's] soul swooned slowly as he heard the snow falling faintly through the universe and faintly falling, like the descent of their last end, upon all the living and the dead.

Ajax's auto-vacation of the field is the end of a giant who cannot live with a belittlement that has been visited upon him. Too, it dramatizes the axiomatic status of 'Life = War' in the ethos of the *Iliad*'s Greeks. Ajax's non-reception of the armour amounts to a stripping off of his *raison d'être*. Once the equation no longer balances, once regime change has been effected, Ajax is a misfit. Like an irrational number among the naturals, he has no place.

Helen, on the ramparts, singles Ajax out. She also identifies Odysseus. Ajax and Odysseus serve in several respects as reciprocal foils. Where a comparison-and-contrast is intended, our feelings go out to Ajax. On a more cerebral level Odysseus is the one whom we find appealing. Consider the poignant encounter between Odysseus and Ajax during Odysseus's visit to Hades. Odysseus extends a hand and speaks consolation for the disposition of the panoply [11:643–644]:

So I cried out but Ajax answered not a word.
He stalked off toward Erebus, into the dark . . .

Even after his race is run Ajax will not let bygones be bygones. He *cannot* be consoled. The race of those he typifies is at an end, and he remains of them.

The epic that bears his name tells of Odysseus's travels and travails after the Trojan War is ended. Once Life ≠ War, what is man? Odysseus's extended sojourn in Wanderland addresses that question. As befits the wily tactician, the journey pursues the answer in exciting and ingenious ways.

Here's Mud in Your Eye!

The case of Odysseus is twice removed from Ajax's case. One episode in the *Odyssey* brings out the difference in a manner that is as forceful as it is economical. During his stay on the island of the Cyclopes this hero quite literally becomes Nobody. But *his* nothingness does not equate to Ajax's. Subtract Ajax's 0 from Odysseus's 0, and you get a positive remainder.

Here's the story, from Book 9. Trapped in a cave whose mouth is stopped with a slab of rock that the men so far spared from the man-eating Cyclops's maw cannot budge, Odysseus, playing for time, plies the monocular (the cave is the Cyclops's abode) with the potent wine that he had procured during his travels from Maron, a priest of Apollo. The monster, to whom the wine is Crème de Tête, bargains for more [398–400]:

a hearty helping!
And tell me your name now, quickly,
so I can hand my guest a gift to warm *his* heart.

Odysseus complies. After the Cyclops drops in a drunken stupor Odysseus sets to work implementing the escape plan that he had concocted when he signed off on the deal. He puts out the drunken Polyphemus's eye with a pointed and fire-hardened staff. Awakening in agony, the monster sets up a wail to wake the dead. Roused by the racket, neighbouring Cyclopes arrive on the scene [450–453]:

> What, Polyphemus, what in the world's the trouble?
> Roaring out in the godsent night to rob us of our sleep.
> Surely no one's rustling your flocks against your will –
> surely no one's trying to kill you now by fraud or force!

In answer [454–455], Polyphemus refers to his immolator with the *nom de guerre* that Odysseus had given, viz., 'Nobody':

> '*Nobody*, friends' – Polyphemus bellowed back from his cave –
> 'Nobody's killing me now by fraud and not by force!'

To which the Cyclopes react [456–460]:

> 'If you're alone,' his friends boomed back at once –
> 'and nobody's trying to overpower you now – look,
> it must be a plague sent here by mighty Zeus
> and there's no escape from *that*.
> You'd better pray to your father, Lord Poseidon.'

Satisfied that foul play isn't afoot the Cyclopes withdraw, leaving Odysseus and his men with a blind jailer who cannot count on the help even of the one-eyed.

What's in a name? Nothing short of salvation. Any other name, and Odysseus's hash would have been settled.

Pleasing as the story is, sticklers might swipe at Homer's artistry. Despite what Homer wants us to believe, Odysseus's ingenuity – 'my great cunning stroke' [462] as the man himself calls it in an access of self-congratulation – isn't his salvation. How could he have known when he gave the name that Polyphemus's neighbours would pose *that* question? Had they simply shouldered aside the boulder, the jig would have been up. Had they asked 'What is causing you such distress?' 'Nobody' would have availed him nothing. Plan of escape? Odysseus is saved by dumb luck. The post-classical Greek critic of Homer, Zoilos, might well have had a go.[2]

Indicating that 'Nobody' is a Frost Point parries the thrust, pouring in the process much light on the poem as a whole. Granted, Odysseus could only have guessed what the neighbouring Cyclopes would say. If the name served to spring the captives, no more, that *would* be a weakness. But the name does thematic duty too. Once the clang of arms subsides Odysseus is no longer what he was. Too, what he will become is yet to be determined. He has leagues to go but does not know where he will sleep. (Contrast Virgil's epic: Aeneas is on a clear mission, which makes the *Aeneid* less philosophical.) The journey is a version of a search for a new equilibrium. Odysseus passes from one surreal *Lebensort* to the next. At the most general level Odysseus stands apart from being this or being that. His journey is a higher-order reflection, in journey-mode, on being this and being that. Odysseus's slow mutation is a dramatization of the non-algorithmic transformation of (a conceptualization of) life. 'Non-algorithmic.' If the transformation spooled out formulaically, no real displacement, no qualitative change, would occur. Working through the journey, we understand better the meaning of the destination. We also understand the dangers of not thinking philosophically. Homer might be going too far in implying that the monocular, non-stereoscopic, way of thinking is that of the brute.[3] Still, shaking our heads at a lot of what passes for thinking in our day, we understand what he means.

Meanwhile, back at the story . . . Although they are now able to hide from Polyphemus and need not fear the other man-eaters, Odysseus and his men are not out of the cave yet. During the ensuing sleepless night Odysseus proceeds with the escape plan. At the approach of rosy-fingered dawn the others are trussed up on the undersides of the monster's woolly sheep. The party then slips through Polyphemus's fingers when he rolls the stone aside and, after a quick palpation of each of the animals, sends the flock to graze. Hastening back to their ship (though not without some gratuitous taunting of the Cyclops by an irrepressible Odysseus), the voyagers resume the hazard-laden journey.

Odysseus eventually makes landfall at Ithaca. He has undergone myriad changes since he set sail a score of years earlier. Clad in tatters, he passes unidentified except by two. Outside the palace, a four-legged version of a beggar, Odysseus's abandoned and tick-infested dog Argos, recognizes him [17:330–331]:

> . . . the moment he sensed Odysseus standing by
> he thumped his tail, nuzzling low, and his ears dropped

It is doubly right that the dog should be the first. Through the long years of battle and wandering Odysseus's appearance has altered much. Dogs, in contrast to men and women, aren't however put off the scent by weathered skin and crow's feet. On a deeper, thematically active level, it is right too. Odysseus is as yet a Nobody. His mutations are unlike those of Proteus, in respect of whom the appearance/reality distinction applies. Typical human mutation does not affect the dog's relationship to the master. It is not the underlying reality that the hound recognizes. Canine identification works on the level of existence rather than of character. To his valet, so the saying goes, even the most eminent person is no hero. Even a Nobody is all the world to a pet.

The second identification occurs within the palace's precincts. Remembering a scar on his body [19:447–448] –

> that old wound
> made years ago by a boar's white tusk

– Eurycleia, the nurse of Odysseus's youth, puts 2 and 2 together and computes the odd man's identity. True, Eurycleia picks Odysseus out in a mediated way. But the fact that she tended him before he became the Odysseus of Homer's epics carries the same message. She picks him out on the basis of an external mark, not on the basis of what he is or is not.

Odysseus must leave off wandering and take up his position in the world. Shakespeare's *Tempest* is called to mind here, as is Abraham's trek from the banks of the southern Euphrates, and later that of the Israelites from Egypt, to the Promised Land, both described in a book roughly coeval with the Homeric epics.

Odysseus is not the central figure either in the *Iliad* or for us. The difference between Odysseus and Achilles reveals a lot about the two Homeric epics. It would not have done for the *Iliad*'s maker to employ an Odysseus-like figure as the vector of reform, even though, had he done so, we would have followed a single character through an extended journey – an attractive prospect for an artist. One reason for this is carried in the story of the encounter with Polyphemus. It can be extracted from the business about names.

A double change is played on the Greek that our translation gives as 'Nobody.'[4] Though Odysseus's calling card says 'Nobody,' he has something to sell.

In Greek, both 'ou-' and 'me-' operate as negating prefixes, like 'un-' and 'dis-' and 'ne-' in English. 'Outis' (which therefore has roughly the sense of 'no this') is exchanged in the story with 'Metis.' The latter handle is ambiguous. It also (and primarily) means 'ingenious.' So the name Odysseus chooses signalizes his imaginative flexibility, and does so in an imaginatively flexible way. In addition to being Nobody (which saves him from the neighbours who come calling), Odysseus is also Wily (which saves him from Polyphemus). In this duplicity he contrasts markedly with Ajax. Homer is evidently at pains to hammer home the difference. The ramparts scene we have looked at, and the encounter in the underworld. The wrestling match between Ajax and Odysseus during the funeral games for Patroclus is another episode in which the two are paired. After considerable sparring the match is declared a draw. Odysseus holds his own because he 'never misse[s] a trick' [23:806]. As one expects, Ajax uses brute strength.

The story of Odysseus's escape from the Cyclops is ingenious. Once the thematic side is appreciated, the reader's pleasure doubles. Shifting from War to Peace is not however a matter of wiliness. The change, to couch it in military terms, is strategic, not tactical.[5]

Athena comes down to stop Achilles. She would not have had such an effect in the case of Odysseus or been so much needed. The tactician's head is teeming with ideas. A master of obliquity, he has likely canvassed lots of angles. Who knows but that he has already mused upon the idea that Athena represents? Quite apart from such constraints as the mythic background placed on Homer, to have cast Odysseus in the lead role would have been a poor artistic choice.

Achilles is the central figure for us. It's also the case that though Achilles does not remind us of Forrest Gump as does Ajax, he, like Ajax, is far from being reflective or cerebral. This is thematically important too. For the shift must not only be sudden and unprepared. It must also not be too cold-bloodedly intellectualistic. That, if I may say so, would be putting Descartes before the hearse.

Achilles's Tent

A revealing parallel exists between Homer, on my description of his enterprise, and Descartes, 'the father,' as he is known, 'of modern philosophy.' Homer's Achilles aligns with *the meditator* – the speaker of Descartes's *Meditations,* the reforming scripture of modern philosophy. The parallel's reality further sustains the characterization of Homer as a pre-Socratic philosopher.

Some scholars supply real-world coordinates for the stove-heated room in which the meditator executes the intellectual prophylaxis. On the basis of Descartes's autobiographical remarks in the *Discourse on Method,* they situate it at Ulm in Bavaria. As with the Homeric Achilles, so too however with the Cartesian meditator. Whatever its inspiration, the *poêle* is not a place that one can visit on a day tour. It is a philosophical place – a place not of action and the thought that goes into it, but of reflection on action and the thought that goes into *it*.

The *Iliad* contains a correlate of the meditator's stove-heated chamber. Tents are part of the furniture of war/life. After the confrontation with Agamemnon, *Achilles's tent* is not however the place to which the warrior returns each evening to recharge the batteries. It is in a more radical way *hors de combat.* When, having stalked off the field after the confrontation with Agamemnon, Achilles unbuckles his armour, he isn't doing what he did the previous evening and the evening before that. He is divesting himself of his identity as one who subscribes to the warrior ethos. Similarly, we are told in the *Meditations* that the meditator has unplugged from the current of everyday activity. *This* withdrawal isn't the kicking back of a person in front of the hearth after a hard day's work. The meditator, too, is in a more radical way withdrawn from the world.[6]

What happens in both the *poêle* and the tent is philosophical reflection – more aggressive in the first. The essential features of a way of thinking are identified (the descriptive part) and subjected to pressure (the critical part). The tent and the *poêle* are physically represented headspaces. In both, the temperature is dialled up. The concepts begin to run into one another. The mental condition is dreamlike.

'Headspace' resonates multiply with the action of the *Iliad.* In Book 1, Athena grabs Achilles by the hair. Athena herself is known in Greek myth as the deity sprung from Zeus's head. In Book 5, Homer makes reference to the unusual parturition. Ares explicitly mentions the chief Olympian's having been delivered of her 'from your own head' [1018]. It will facilitate our discussion of the parallel between Achilles and Descartes to bring Athena on board.

The meditator recognizes that in the past he had gone astray, epistemically speaking. He had accepted many falsehoods and uncertainties, and not only through inattention, gullibility, and suchlike local and temporary lapses. As any reasonable person does, he had relied on his senses and his reason. That is, his belief-forming standards were adhered to, responsibly so we are to suppose. The meditator comes to see the standards themselves as wanting. *Mutatis mutandis*, Athena's intervention prevents Achilles from continuing to act as per the dictates of the ambient ethical system. (The parallel with Abraham does not need to be laboured.) In the course of *his* journey of reform, Descartes's meditator also, in a literal sense, becomes a no-body. He puts off his physical body, not just his armour.

The value attached to positive memorialization requires Achilles to draw a sword against Agamemnon. If Briseis is removed without a fight, Achilles will go down as the guy whose girl was taken away while he fidgeted. Even vanishing without a trace rates higher for a mortal than the negative commemoration. The doublet with the background story of Menelaus and Helen is obvious. The taking away of Helen being the *casus belli*, that *casus*, obviously, is being interrogated.

Athena restrains Achilles from acting as the imperatives of the ethical system dictate, the imperatives that he has *qua* member of the culture absorbed. Why Athena? The question has two parts. Why *a* higher being? And why *this* higher being? Relevant to the latter, it is significant that Athena's intervention in regard to Achilles is overdetermined. The overdetermination, to be rationalized later, is conveyed in Athena's explanation to Achilles that she comes in Hera's name as well as in her own.

If Achilles listens, he will, Athena says [1:248–251], be multiply recompensed. We have listened to this claim before:

> And I tell you this – and I *know* it is the truth –
> one day glittering gifts will lie before you,
> three times over to pay for all this outrage.
> Hold back now. Obey us both.

Given that Achilles dies, one might treat this as a cruel joke. However, the fact is that the Achilles of the epic bests the gods; but, by contrast with Diomedes in Book 5, who actually injures Ares, the god of war, *he* does not get the upper hand in the warrior way.

This illustrates wonderfully how inherited mythic materials are retooled in the *Iliad*. Athena's words are naturally read as a promise of martial victory and the attendant plunder and renown. Homer's subject is something else entirely. To identify that something, I now redeem the promise concerning the myth behind the Trojan War.

'None of woman born shall harm . . .'

I mentioned the nuptials of Thetis and Peleus. If the bride and groom are joined in love, the mutual affection is a bonus. Significantly to the theme, the marriage is brokered. It serves the purpose of the broker.

The Olympians frequently take their pleasure with mortal creatures. Usually, their behaviour when they do this is shocking. But a solemnized union between ichor and blood, a *ratification* of a boundary violation, is more than shocking. It is monstrous. The myth reports that to Zeus, who fell in love with the goddess, it was foretold that Thetis would bear a son greater than him. Remembering how *he* had overthrown *his* father (I will sketch the story presently), Zeus does not want history to repeat itself. He therefore arranges the affiancing of Thetis to Peleus, a flesh-and-blood king. Zeus thus sanctions, indeed makes, a monstrous match to save himself. Knowing that those with only one deathless parent have a date with the reaper, Zeus is convinced that he is out of harm's way. The gene for mortality being strictly dominant, the fruit of Thetis's loins poses no threat to his sovereignty.

Homer inherits the myth. On the level of plot, the part of the myth concerning the apple explains the line-up of the gods in the *Iliad*, Aphrodite with the Trojans, Hera and Athena against. But Homer is also exploiting the part about Zeus's matchmaking. The account in *Theogony* has the internecine struggle terminating. Power is stabilized on high in the third, Olympian, generation, Zeus at the helm. Look more closely now at what Zeus was told about Thetis's issue. The oracle, as Zeus understood it, prognosticated his ouster by *a son whom he would sire upon Thetis*. The oracle had simply spoken however of *a son*. Zeus fixes the bond because he believes that he cannot be bested by a mere mortal. He brings Thetis and Peleus together to disarm fate. To the possibility that Thetis would deliver a male child in that union he gives no thought. *Giving the myth an imaginative twist, Homer, in the Iliad, tells the story of Thetis's male child, the mortal Achilles, besting Zeus.* Achilles does not do this by force. Rather, he becomes the focus of a different, human, value system. The centre of value is shifted downwards, from the all-powerful, the everlasting, to *terra firma*, there to contend with all the vicissitudes on their own terms.[7]

Diomedes bests the gods too. *His* (literal) victory is the reverse of the (figurative) victory of the other. Diomedes raises himself. Achilles lowers himself. Achilles does not however abase himself. Nor is Achilles lowered by the gods.

Achilles is the *legitimate* offspring of a monstrous union. This hybrid status makes him the appropriate vehicle of the change. For what is the change? Achilles comes to regard his finite and fragile life as more than just a tool for an *imitatio deorum*. He thus rejects the equation 'Life = War.' He does so, for the view that life has intrinsic value is – or, better, is consistent with – the view that one can, even in a limited span, flourish. *Pace* Simone Weil, it is not then the case that '[t]he true hero, the true subject, the center of the *Iliad*, is force, force as man's instrument, force as man's master, force before which human flesh shrinks back.'[8] The true hero is Achilles, he of the vulnerable heel, who takes his own mortality on board. Weil, making the same mistake that Zeus makes, focuses exclusively on the epic's unreformed content.

Hero-to-Zero

Let me zoom in on Achilles's shift. The shift sees the hero, in the old sense, reducing to a zero, and then, at the zero point, locating something, like the Cartesian *cogito*, on which to build. That something, I might say, inspires an 'Eheu.'

Back in his tent, fuming from Agamemnon's insult and full of self-loathing, Achilles now has negative thoughts about the value system. Free of the immediate pressures of the culture to dust off the armour and wade into the fray, he, like Descartes's meditator, is calling the old certainties into question. '[H]av[ing] expressly rid my mind of all worries and arranged for myself a clear stretch of free time . . . at last I will devote myself sincerely and without reservation to the general demolition of all my opinions.'[9] Like Descartes's meditator, though in rather a more emotional way, Achilles is in some sort of cognitive turmoil: unclarity and indistinctness. The sentiments he expresses when the ambassadors come calling verbalize the rumblings.

To make his point effectively Achilles cannot just say: 'I value my life for its own sake.' Because the culture attaches instrumental value alone to life, and because Achilles is understood when he speaks to speak Warriorese, the quoted words would come across as gibberish. When Achilles does in fact intone words embodying that meaning [9:385–388] –

One and the same lot for the man who hangs back
and the man who battles hard. The same honor waits
for the coward and the brave. They both go down to Death,
the fighter who shirks, the one who works to exhaustion . . .

– the emissaries are 'struck dumb' [9:523]. 'A stunned silence seized them all' [524]. 'What is it,' we imagine each of them scratching his head, 'that the man wants? He's got to want more booty from Agamemnon to compensate for what was appropriated. Yet that too he spurns.'[10]

Like Polyphemus, the ambassadors are monocular. Polyphemus takes 'Outis' in only one way, as a name. *They* take Achilles's words in terms of the semantics of their lexicon.[11]

Achilles had prefigured the point. A bit earlier, referring to 'this insane voyage' [9:443], he had asked: 'why did he muster an army, lead us here, / that son of Atreus?' [410–411]. What is insane about the voyage? Life = War. Is life insane? The point is not the one that we initially make, the one that Herodotus makes, viz., that the taking of Helen is completely disproportionate. The point is a philosophical one. What is regarded as the core value is actually worthless.

Encountering Achilles during the visit to Hades, Odysseus speaks the following soothing words [11:547–558]:

'. . . Achilles,
there's not a man in the world more blest than you –
there never has been, never will be one.
Time was, when you were alive, we Argives
honoured you as a god. And now down here, I see,
you lord it over the dead in all your power.
So grieve no more at dying, great Achilles.'

I reassured the ghost, but he broke out, protesting,
'No winning words about death to *me*, shining Odysseus!
By god, I'd rather slave on earth for another man –
some dirt-poor tenant farmer who scrapes to keep alive –
than rule down here over all the breathless dead.'

Again, Achilles can scarcely expect the ambassadors to nod sympathetically. Not that they disagree. Rather, they do not comprehend. Their response can only be perplexed bewilderment.

Athena intervenes. That *a god* intervenes is the epic's way of stamping a seal of approval on the incipient change. Not only is Achilles the son *of* an immortal, one to whom the idea of immortality as the ultimate value therefore makes even genetic sense; too, his swerve from that value assignment is powered *by* an immortal. As to why the latter should be Athena, recall that in Hesiod's telling the gray-eyed daughter of Zeus is the instrument of stopping the generational struggle on high.

Athena, in Book 1, had said to Achilles: 'Obey us both.' The plural reference is to Hera as well as to herself. Why the double determination? Athena is no Olympian dogsbody, gofering for Hera. There is a compelling reason, internal to the war, for Achilles's staying his sword. With Agamemnon dead, the campaign would collapse. Since Hera and Athena line up, mythically, on the Greek side, they *would* have an interest in Agamemnon's not being skewered. So Achilles should obey Hera. But what Athena says indicates that obeying *her* does not have the same significance. To obey her is to put off the accoutrements of the warrior for keeps.

Why *Athena*?

When Homer was a cultural staple for the Greeks, Athens was the golden arches. Aside from the citizenry, the body of consumers consisted of those who trekked to the *polis* for the Panathenaia, the festival a central element of which was the public performance of the epics. Whatever their domicile, the attendees were steeped in lore about Athena. The mere mention of the goddess would have set a carillon of associative bells pealing. Let me draw out a few mythic facts explanatory of her pertinence to the *Iliad*.

Hesiod wrote the book on the genesis of the gods: the *Theogony*. We are told therein of three generations of higher beings: the first-generation nature deities, the Titans, the Olympians. The transition from generation to generation finds Athena playing a crucial (though passive) role. Here is a precis.

Ouranos, the first of the dominant male gods, is threatened by Kronos, the chief Titan. Kronos in turn is challenged by Zeus, the leading Olympian. Intent on maintaining power, the senior god proceeds in each case to neutralize would-be usurpers. Ouranos does so by blocking the entry of the children into the world. This he accomplishes by stuffing them back into his wife Gaia's womb as soon as they emerge.

'Unborn,' Ouranos thinks, recalling to us Macbeth, 'they pose no danger.' After Gaia's counterplot succeeds (wielding 'a huge sickle' [162] that Ouranos had fashioned, Kronos, strategically situated, emasculates Ouranos when the father comes to lie with her), Kronos, having gained ascendancy, contrives to prevent *his* issue from issuing. Going to school on his father's failure, he swallows each newborn immediately upon parturition. Notwithstanding the thinking outside the box, the cycle is not so easily brought to a halt. Taking *her* cue from Gaia, Rhea, Kronos's wife, swaddles a stone when the next child is born and tricks Kronos into believing that he is engorging Zeus. The Olympian, saved, is able eventually to 'drive [Kronos] out of his rule, and become king of the immortals' (491).[12] When he does, he finally stops the cycle. Rather than swallowing his offspring after they issue, he, in an anticipation of a dialectical synthesis, swallows his pregnant wife Metis; and, as the part of the myth that has worked its way into the language has it, Athena, the product of their coupling, eventually springs forth fully armed from his head.[13]

A straightforward point of this jaw-dropping story is that underpinning the internecine friction on high is the immortality of the gods. One of a series of jokes contrasting the two types has it that the British leave without saying goodbye while the Yiddish say goodbye without leaving. Unlike any of us poor sods, the gods do not say goodbye *and* they do not leave. Come into being they do. Once around, they are however around for good. And for ill. So succession as in the human sphere is not on. Doubtless, King Lear was foolish to divide his United Kingdom before the ground admitted him. While dressing British, he would have been better advised to think Yiddish. But since Lear is no god, there would eventually have been a transition no matter how he dressed and regardless of what he thought.

There is more to the story. I will return to what Zeus does in the following chapters. The present point, the point about Athena, is that with her devious birth the struggle on high stops. Stability is achieved in the third, Olympian, generation. Athena is thus linked to the end of strife.[14]

Moving to Homer, we find Athena playing precisely the same role. The event that precipitates the action of the *Iliad* (inaction, rather, since the story is of Achilles's absence from the battlefield) occurs, as it should, *in principio*. In Book 1 Agamemnon expropriates the girl Briseis, Achilles's prize of battle. At this stage, Achilles stands squarely within the warrior society. He craves the good regard of his fellows. Kudos and kleos are needed to achieve that for which a warrior lives:

immortality = survival in the public memory. Agamemnon, Achilles feels, has tarnished his lustre. His comrades, Achilles fears, will ridicule him as the man whose girl was snatched away while he sat on his hands. His fear is not paranoid. Hadn't Menelaus set sail for Troy, ten thousand oarsmen plowing his wake, to expunge the indignity of Helen's removal and to cancel the attendant shame? If the Spartan king had remained in the Peloponnesus, his confederates would have laughed at him. (In taking the girl away, Agamemnon is acting irrationally from the standpoint of the campaign. Still, what he does isn't arbitrary and/ or self-serving. His supremacy requires that he remove Achilles's trophy. He would lose face if he pulled rank on some minor confederate or vassal. So Agamemnon's actions too are rationalized in the frame of the warrior ethos.) Since the ultimate value attaches to leaving a permanent and positive mark, that is, to overcoming (personal) mortality, Achilles feels himself diminished. His initial reaction is to kill Agamemnon – a course of action that makes perfect sense in the context of the culture, no less sense than the Trojan War itself. Poised to draw his sword and lunge, he is however restrained by Athena. This remarkable intervention from on high is the beginning of his ethical change.

Athena streaks down to prevent Achilles from responding homicidally to Agamemnon's slight. The disarming of Achilles has at least three meanings. Athena sides with the Greeks. Should Achilles run Agamemnon through, that would imperil the Greek cause. So she is motivated to step in. Also, now on the level of theme rather than just of plot, Athena's intervention gives dramatic expression to the quantum leap that is occurring. A cultural change does not come about formulaically. By no means fated to happen, such a change is beholden to all manner of contingencies. The persons who change, also, must divest themselves of the identities that they acquired in and through the environment of their acculturation. Lastly, and most importantly, the fact that *Athena* makes the move is significant. What Athena does Ares could not have done. Hera could not have stood in for the grey-eyed god. Aphrodite would have been utterly miscast as hair-puller. Athena is not just one more god. She has a special role in the Olympian pantheon, not just a distinctive one.

At the end of *Iliad* Book 4, Athena is referred to as 'third-born of the gods' [597]. The name becomes resonant when, soon after, in Book 5, Ares, whom the mortal Diomedes has injured, complains about Zeus's preference for Athena, having just mentioned the fact that 'you gave her birth' [1017]. Homer is echoing the story set out in detail in

Hesiod's *Theogony* – the story, outlined a few paragraphs back, that tells of the termination of strife on high, Zeus at the controls. (Signally, Zeus is nearby [864] denominated 'son of [K]ronos.') In generational terms, *Zeus* is the third born. Could Athena's staying the decapitating sword in Achilles's hands *deliberately* invert what happened with scalpel and ruler among the earliest gods?[15]

The ending of strife among the higher powers is, from where we stand, Hesiod's story. Did Homer draw on Hesiod as a source? Did the two exploit independent material? As the case may be, Homer's application of the myth of Thetis and Peleus brings his view into line with Hesiod's. In both cases gods are cast out. Both poets are describing the process of reform.

In the *Odyssey*, the protagonist pays a visit to Hades. There he encounters both Ajax and Achilles. Achilles through his words and Ajax through his actions each gives expression to what he perceives himself to have lost – Ajax his immortal life, Achilles his mortal one.

Arms and the Man

Achilles eventually resumes the battlefield. Not, however, as a warrior. The new shield, on which is engraved a new map of the world, signals the shift of identity. Even apart from that sign (which, as I shall explain, tells of less than a completed shift) we can readily appreciate that before us is a changed man. The description [19:427–435] sets Achilles sharply apart from the others:

> The glory of armour lit the skies and the whole earth laughed,
> rippling under the glitter of bronze, thunder resounding
> under trampling feet of armies. And in their midst
> the brilliant Achilles began to arm for battle . . .
> A sound of grinding came from the fighter's teeth,
> his eyes blazed forth in searing points of fire,
> unbearable grief came surging through his heart
> and now, bursting with rage against the men of Troy,
> he donned Hephaestus's gifts . . .

The death of Patroclus is what now impels Achilles. Warriors do not however act to avenge confederates. *They* act to achieve immortality (perhaps avenging confederates as a by-product). In seeking out Hector,

Achilles, teeth grinding, eyes ablaze, heart-sick, cares not a whit about the regard of others.

In the *Iliad* we get, incipiently, a move from the self-regarding ethical view – one that accords, to the degree that fact and value can be said to accord, with the idea of the gods as self-absorbed – to an other-regarding one. This, as *we* see it, is a shift from non-moral thinking ('I would not have this done to me, but you are fortunate if I don't do it to you') to moral thinking ('I ought not do to others what I would not have done to me'). For being less formal or abstract than Kant's, Homer's basis for the shift, now to be extracted, is in some ways more illuminating. More than it resembles Kant's, Homer's engineering resembles the manner in which John Rawls, enlisting the veil of ignorance, defends his idea of liberal justice. But as in regard to Kant so in regard to Rawls, Homer's basis, though imaginative, is also less imaginary and more concrete. The Hellenic bard comes close to accomplishing the feat of turning the Harvard philosopher's counterfactuals into indicatives! I might also observe that Homer's basis, by contrast with the Bible's basis, or perhaps non-basis, at which we glanced when considering David's question, is thoroughly non-theological.

In the course of his musings in the tent Achilles shifts towards attaching value to finite, limited life. Why should anyone take that shift as more than a personal choice? Even had the ambassadors understood his words – 'One and the same lot for the man who hangs back and the man who battles hard. They both go down to Death' – they could still justifiably have complained that what emanates from his mouth expresses no more than one person's valuing his own finite life. Just so, a man or woman may decide to keep the promises that he or she makes. 'I have given my word. I will do as I undertook to do.' In and of itself, that decision scarcely sustains 'One must keep one's promises.' Others may take a more self-interested view. How then does Achilles's shift get generalized beyond Achilles himself? What is it that makes Achilles's shoes shoes in which all of us walk?

The key to the answer is the relationship in the narrative between three components: Achilles, Patroclus, Achilles's suit of armour. In the course of the action, both characters wear the suit (the correlate in the epic of the shoes just mentioned).

When Hector kills Patroclus, who is wearing Achilles's gear, this to Achilles is a concrete vision of his, Achilles's, losing his life. (Patroclus was sent out in Achilles's armour with the idea that the Trojans should think that Achilles himself had resumed the field.) But he, Achilles, lives on.

To have a vision of one's own demise is no small thing. One can easily imagine oneself on the funeral pyre as the brand is applied. Plainly though, for a person to imagine his or her death in this way falls short of *experiencing* it in the relevant sense, viz., the sense that would supply a firm basis for judgments. In seeing Patroclus, dressed in *his* armour, cut down, Achilles gets closer to having the latter experience. He sees what is happening through his own eyes ('It is as me that Patroclus is killed; the death is in a sense my death') and also through the eyes of another ('I, who am seeing the killing, am not killed').

The double-sidedness of the scene, the mirroring without a mirror, is significant. From the ambassadors' perspective Achilles's valuing his life for its own sake falls in the sphere of the self-regarding. The ambassadors would take the same view of Achilles's grief at the loss of Patroclus. As they see it, that loss is primarily if not solely Achilles's loss. Consoling words, should they be spoken, would not be spoken because *they* feel what he feels. However, the configuring of the death of Patroclus, which Achilles regards as an evil, as Achilles's own death, takes, or supplies a basis for taking, the evaluative response beyond the self-regarding. It's not (to give voice to the relevant thought from Achilles's mouth) that the loss of *my life* is an evil; it's that the loss of *life*, mine or anyone else's, is an evil.

In the warrior context the valuing of one's own life in a fashion that acted to brake one's aggression on the field of battle would be accounted cowardice. But Achilles values Patroclus's life too. To the degree that the latter evaluation is based on close friendship it too would fall within the sphere of the self-regarding.[16] Losing a friend is painful. Without inconsistency, one laments less the passing of a stranger. The death of Patroclus, as Homer handles it, is not however entirely the death of another. The armour identifies the man as Achilles. This is Patroclus's life seen by Achilles as his own. So the life is at one and the same time both his and not his. Through that merger he procures an understanding of how Patroclus might value his, Patroclus's, life. This is not a selfish valuing of life. We treat others as we treat ourselves; and we do so appreciating that they are no different than – that is, are identical with – ourselves. This is a generalization. More than just a generalization, in Homer's representation of Achilles it is a concrete generalization.

A vague echo of Rawls's updated Kantianism may be registered. The veil of ignorance is Rawls's imaginary device for getting a person to consider things less parochially by cogitatively abstracting the person from his or her situated position. Achilles's experience is not however counterfactual. At any rate, describing it that way does Homer a considerable injustice. Homer's dramatization presents us with an Achilles who at one and the same time is in his own shoes and is displaced from those shoes.

The closing panel of the *Iliad*, the meeting between Achilles and Priam, is crucial to the former's transformation. Before explaining how Achilles's response to the Trojan king draws upon what the death of Patroclus means to him, I want first to exploit the scene for a more critical purpose.

The warrior ethos is a viable one. If ever it was realized, the ethos did not have to change. The gods might have remained supreme. Homer in his depiction of Achilles shows us how much such a change is a result of contingencies: bad weather, an insult, a vague rumbling, a ruse. As to the nature of the change, we can get a formal sense by reference to the oft-mentioned glass of water. One and the same object some see as half full, others, as half empty. Consider the feature of life that informs the defining equation of the warrior ethos. Life is so flimsy, so short-lived, that it cannot be valuable for its own sake. That is the overarching thought. A slight shift of perspective and everything looks different. A slight shift and 'There is so little of life that it can't be valuable in itself' transmutes to 'There is so little. How precious it is.' The point is that Achilles's shift is not based on the introduction of anything hitherto unknown. It is the same overall conceptual ensemble, only with the signs of value reversed. Figure for the warrior, the value attached to immortality, becomes ground for Achilles; ground, finitude as limitation, figure. In becoming human, the figure becomes grounded.

The *ethos* into which Achilles was born, with value calibrated to the extra-human, could have survived. And, for all we know, it could return. There is, then, a position in Homer on changes like Achilles's. Such changes do not follow a formula. They belong to the realm of the perplexing.[17]

One More Nobody

Who, in a book at the centre of the Western canon, matches the following description? To gain a benefit that would otherwise be withheld, this person misidentifies himself by using an alias. Special food procured from a third party having been served, contributing to the lowering of the benefactor's guard, our man, taking advantage of the latter's reliance on the sense of touch, dons a disguise of animal hides to prevent his cover from being blown. Fearing the reaction from the various parties whom the deception affects, he flees the scene soon after the objective is secured, journeying onwards on a none too smooth spousal quest.

Who is this person? Given what precedes, the expected response is: 'Odysseus.' But the description was framed with one eye on the third of the three biblical patriarchs. The relevant part of Jacob's story is told in Genesis 27–29.

Jacob, a second son, is angling for the paternal blessing – the birthright, by traditional usage, of the eldest. After assuming Esau's name, and having softened Isaac up with a meal of savoury meats that his mother Rebekah had dressed and made ready, Jacob, exploiting his father's dimness of vision, tops off the ruse by dressing up his exposed parts with the skins of kids. Fearing the short-sighted father's anger and the hirsute brother's vengeance when the fleecing comes to light, he then takes it on the lam, departing for Haran, there, after a number of unanticipated reversals, to win Rachel, his heart's desire.

Two men, two central figures in two central texts of the West, pass themselves off as something they are not. Two men, in fact, whose given names are semantically related, both bespeaking flexibility or, less neutrally, deviousness.[18] Failing their acts of impersonation they would not have become what they are for us – and not merely in the trivial sense that *their* stories would have followed different courses. If Jacob's ruse comes a cropper God's promise of national longevity passes through (and very likely ends at) Esau. If Odysseus perishes, the ravening suitors inherit *his* patrimony. Would the world be a better place had the uncouth man of appetite prevailed? had Greek ingenuity, with its power to transform the environment, been snuffed out?[19] Some might say so. But no one would say that the world would be the same. *Our* stories would have followed different courses.

Since only Odysseus passes himself off as 'Nobody,' some might deem the parallel forced. Jacob's career does however contain an episode that in this very particular resembles what takes place in the cave. The episode is no minor one. In it, Jacob gets the name 'Israel.'

The patriarchs are intensely interested in the deity from whom the call comes, the deity who issues and then several times reaffirms the pledge to magnify the Israelites. After all, the geopolitical undertaking apart, insight into the nature of the deity is, given the likeness between God and humans, insight into their own natures. The interest in knowing the deity is, then, an interest in self-knowledge. Jacob wrestles with an angel. After the angel asks for *his* name, and characteristically offers the antagonist a new one, 'Israel, for you have striven with God and with humans' (Genesis 32:28), Jacob plays turnabout. '"Please tell me *your* name"' (29). Along what have come to be regarded as stereotypical Jewish lines, Jacob's request is answered with a question. '"Why is it that you ask my name?"' (ibid.) The angel chooses to remain anonymous.

Or does he? The angel's question could be interpreted so as to dovetail with the message of the dream of a ladder: 'Why do you have to ask my name? You already know it.' The answer that Jacob knows he does not like. He is struggling to wrest an answer more to his liking. This would explain why the angel does not want to be seen by the light of day: Jacob would have to confront himself too directly, which, in view of his patriarchal burden, might make matters too difficult for him.[20] The story, then, is another instalment of aniconicism.

In one respect Jacob's encounter with the angel resembles Achilles's with Athena. In another respect the encounters differ. The similarity and unlikeness trace to that basic contrast between the *Iliad* and the Bible: the epic is reform*ing*, Scripture is reform*ed*. Achilles recognizes Athena. Meaning: Athena is a fixture of the culture. But the Athena whom Achilles recognizes is really foreign to him *qua* warrior. In stopping Achilles from using his sword Athena is taking the first step towards beating the weapon into a ploughshare. Meaning: Athena is initiating a process that will ring a cultural change. Jacob *should* recognize the angel. But so heavy is the weight of the reformed view – the view that, as Moses later puts it, the answer is not in the heavens, it is in us – that he does not. Jacob comes away limping from the tussle. Recall here the dream of the ladder at Bethel. The ladder is set up on earth, not lowered from heaven. Because of the rocky and uneven human terrain on which its feet are planted, one imagines that the ladder too is less than steady. In effect, the blessing that Jacob receives is also, in a sense, a curse. Isaac, a strong father shielding him and making his arrangements, does not have Jacob's problems. The world as Isaac experiences it is in this respect rather Edenic, Isaac himself rather like the Garden-dwellers.[21] Jacob walks the world alone. So too does God, as I see him, walk the world alone.

I alluded to Moses's valediction. Here is what Moses says to the Israelites as he, in the more demotic view, is about to ascend (Deuteronomy 30:11–14):

> Surely this commandment that I am commanding you today is not too hard for you, nor is it too far away. It is not in heaven, that you should say, 'Who will go up to heaven for us, and get it for us so that we may hear it and observe it?' Neither is it beyond the sea, that you should say, 'Who will cross to the other side of the sea for us, and get it for us that we may hear it and observe it?' No, the word is very near to you; it is in your mouth and in your heart for you to observe.

Moses is represented in the Bible as a stammerer. Not only is the neutral phrase 'slow of speech and slow of tongue' (Exodus 4:10) applied, but so also the less clinical 'uncircumcised of lips' (6:12, 30). The person among persons of whom it can most truly be said that God's word 'is in your mouth' cannot speak fluently! We need not bother with the idea that Moses really was like that, an idea that calls to mind Michelangelo's sculpture, itself due to a speech impediment, of a horned Moses. (The Hebrew for 'ray [of light]' is the same as that for 'horn [of an animal].') Could it be that the ascription of lingual lameness is the work of the priestly class, eager to establish that *extra ecclesiam nulla salus*?[22] Aaron, Moses's brother, is the first of the priestly line, the first cohen. That Aaron speaks for him in the court of the Pharaoh might be entered as corroboration. On my view, Moses's stammer accords however with the basic thrust of Scripture; Aaron's fluency is a problematic idealization. God speaks to Moses 'mouth to mouth' (Numbers 12:8). Moses stammers, then, because God stammers. The stammer is rather like Jacob's limp. God limps too. That is what Jacob learns at Peniel, where this element of God-likeness is transferred to him.[23] Another Cohen, the poet and pop music icon Leonard Cohen, brilliantly captures God's orolingual condition, as I understand the Bible to depict it, in the poem 'The Window':

> . . . the Holy One dreams of a letter
> Dreams of a letter's death
> Oh bless the continuous stutter
> Of the word being made into flesh

Can the transcendent viewpoint, the viewpoint of traditional religion, be defended? Perhaps it can. Yet even if God-is-dead declarers are right on this score, the following can be said in criticism of the Super Obituarist among them. At least so far as the parts of Scripture here being addressed, the biblical view is a view of men and women being Nobodies from the standpoint of the universe, and making something of their condition and estate despite that. That what is made of their condition and estate differs from what Nietzsche endorses suggests that quite a few suppressed premises inform *his* reasoning.

Before *we* leave the dust of Troy behind, I propose to sift that other dust that we only leave temporarily behind. 'Dust thou art.'

8
The Birth of Death

The Elohiad

The second of the epics attributed to Homer resembles the second of the books attributed to Moses. Like Exodus, the *Odyssey* is the telling of a journey of return.

For a tale to loop back to its point of origin is nothing unusual. The Bible identifies the prolific mother of such trajectories. '[O]ut of [the ground] you were taken; you are dust, and to dust you shall return' (Genesis 3:19). But the resemblance between the mentioned works goes beyond congruency. In the *Odyssey* as in Exodus the returnees, Odysseus and the Children of Israel, meet temptations to abandon the home-going and confront obstacles to concluding the trek. In the one story as in the other the protagonists complete the circuit with an altered grasp both of the place that they departed long years earlier and also of their own situation.

The typical consumer of the central exhibits of the Western canon would justifiably feel insulted if the presenter of these likenesses paused here to await a 'Eureka.' Still, the conjoint mention of the two literary second instalments stimulates a question that such a consumer has probably not asked. Does any Greek text of comparable antiquity stand to the *Odyssey* in the thematic way that Genesis, the curtain raiser of the Torah, stands to *its* sequel?

Although Hesiod's *Theogony*, like Genesis, starts with 'each thing as it first came into being' (115), it soon emerges that *this* α differs substantially from the א. True to its name, the *Theogony* takes for its subject the origin of divinity. Genesis, by contrast, caters primarily to an *anthropogenic* wonder. We men and women, what are *we*? Where do *we* come from? What is *our* place? It is in the frame of the answers to these questions that the Israelites' journey of return fits. The *Theogony*, for failing to address itself to how we came to be delivered onto the scene, does not then appear to be connected to Odysseus's homegoing.

Genesis is (at least on the surface) a cosmogony and an anthropogeny, not a theogony; Hesiod's work, the reverse. But should we not *expect* as intricate a depiction as the *Theogony* gives of the birth of the gods and of the manner in which the relations between them fall out to reflect how the world's flesh-and-blood dwellers, who are doing the depicting, think of *their own* comings and goings? Living in the world over which the deathless beings are conceived to preside, a world in which they themselves are conceived to play only bit parts, how could the world's flesh-and-blood dwellers turn oblivious of their own precariousness when they set themselves to the task of doing the depicting? By the same token, a self-reflective account such as Genesis's of the birth of men and women is likely to be informative about how those who supply it think of the wider world into which they are born and in which they must make their way. While seekers after a Genesis for the *Odyssey* would therefore be hasty to scratch Hesiod's work from the running just on the ground that it pulls towards the theogonic, I believe that another Hellenic horse, precisely the one suggested by the alignment of the *Odyssey* with Exodus, has the inside track.

Had I asked after a Hellenic stable mate for Genesis not having trotted in the *Odyssey*/Exodus resemblance, odds are the *Iliad* would not have come to mind. If at all anthropogenic, Hesiod's work, I just now said, is anthropogenic only in a recessive way. The recessiveness I advanced as working against the *Theogony*'s placement alongside Genesis. The designation of the *Iliad* as the more suitable partner thus generates a commitment: locate in the epic a story of human beginnings comparable to the one in Holy Writ. That, with reference to one important aspect, I shall do. As to why the *Iliad*'s anthropogeny is so elusive, my conjecture is that the *biblical* story of mankind's creation is culturally so dominant as virtually to hard-wire the expectation that any such story will have an obstetrical cast.

Homer, then, is my Greek Moses; Moses, my Israelite Homer. The parallel, illuminating on both sides, illuminates some of the most vexed issues – and not just issues of scholarly interpretation.

Mortality and Eden

The Bible addresses the mortality that is so basic to how we men and women in the West think of ourselves. Eastwards, to Eden, we therefore look to see the dawning of our self-conception as here today, gone tomorrow.

On the massively influential Christian decoding of the story, chapter-and-verse relates the *avoidable* loss of immortality, the tragedy of which 'one greater Man' will ultimately redeem. The phrase just quoted is from the first pentameters of Milton's *Paradise Lost*. John Donne, Milton's slight senior, expresses the same thought.[1] In Holy Sonnet 9 Donne glosses the Pentateuch's story by referring to

> that tree,
> Whose fruit threw death on else immortal us

I proceed by confirming a trinity of claims that severally conflict with this, *the standard view* of the Bible's position on mortality. The three combine to banish all doubt that whoever is behind Genesis doesn't regard our mortality as a cicatrix.

Whatever 'good and evil' purports, to gain a grasp thereof the man and the woman had to eat of the fruit of the tree designated 'knowledge of good and evil.' At the start of their story the pair thus suffer from some manner of epistemic deficit. The second tree goes by the label 'life.' Accordingly, to acquire what it offers – identified clearly in 3:23 as unending life – they had to bite into *its* fruit. Prior to eating, the condition of the man and the woman is therefore as indeterminate relative to life without end as it is in respect of what answers to 'knowledge of good and evil.' That being the case, no credence attaches to the claim that because of what the man and the woman do they are stripped of an immortality that *antecedently* was theirs. The fruit of the forbidden tree (or the act of tasting of it) does not therefore '[bring] death into the world.' That is the first claim.

The second claim is that the logic of the standard view entails banishment for Adam and Eve no matter what. Suppose that the originals of mankind had eaten of the permitted tree. Unless the food ingested (or the act of ingestion) reprogrammed them to apathy about the other tree, would not the reason for expulsion still apply? In 3:22, the verse lately alluded to, God, referring to the fact that the man has partaken of the prohibited fruit, observes:

> See, the man has become like one of us, knowing good and evil; and now, he might reach out his hand and take also from the tree of life, and eat, and live forever.

Members of the English poets' party hold that 'both knowledgeable and everlasting' converts with 'exactly like one of us.'[2] It may be inferred that the quoted words continue to have application in the scenario that reverses the biblical menu. Unless the man and the woman, having eaten of the tree of life, are distanced from the Garden, the danger remains that they will consume of the other tree, thereby becoming 'exactly like one of us.' The serpent certainly doesn't stand for a serpent. Does it dramatize a fairly widespread outside temptation? Or perhaps a built-in tendency of psychic make-up? Combining the two, Milton takes the serpent to represent a standing inner urge to respond to an external attraction. If so, first eating of the tree of life would have done nothing to neutralize the danger.

The third claim is that *pace* the standard view God does *not* categorically disapprove of the actions of the man and the woman. The idea of ultimate restoration to a paradisiacal state through the intermediacy of that 'greater Man' is, therefore, tendentious, the very portrayal of Eden as Paradise, problematic. It *would* be difficult to understand how God could approve the unnecessary loss of *that* state, much less its loss through sin.

Further to this difficulty consider the point that the expulsion, though it follows the disobedience, lags it by quite a bit. Immediately God discovers that the man and the woman have eaten of the knowledge tree he curses the curse of a hard and terminating life. 'By the sweat of your face you shall eat bread until you return to the ground, for out of it you were taken; you are dust, and to dust you shall return' (19). Yet the driving out occurs only after the claim about 'being [in knowledge] like us' is voiced. Nor is there a lag here only in that several verses are interposed between curse and exit. God states *a reason* for the departure that seems extraneous to the background of the malediction itself.

What position *does* the text take in the matter of human mortality? With the help of the point about the delayed exit we can reach the position by pressing on a *prima facie* problem in the first of my claims.

If the fruit of the tree of life confers immortality, it cannot be correct to ascribe life without end to the man and the woman as they first appear. Mortality and immortality being, in logic, contradictories, doesn't it follow that the man and the woman are mortal? Regardless of whether it follows, the straight assertion of mortality violates the sense of the text: prior to eating the question of long-livedness, like the fruit of the tree of life, is still pending. I tried to remain true to this sense in writing: 'Prior to eating, the condition of the man and the woman is therefore as indeterminate relative to life without end as it is in respect of what answers to "knowledge of good and evil."' To say 'as indeterminate relative to' is to remain indeterminate on what the indeterminacy comes to. What the indeterminacy comes to, however, is precisely what needs to be determined.

Return to the apparent disconnect between God's threat and the outcome. '[I]n the day that you eat of [the tree of knowledge] you shall die' (2:17). So God says, in what seem to be no uncertain terms. You eat, it'll be your last supper. Yet though they eat the man and the woman do not die. The serpent had said 'You will not die' [3:4]. Did the serpent speak true? Only sophistically. On the day that they eat, the man and the woman gain *cognizance* of their mortality. In telling the man and the woman that on that day they will die, God is not issuing a threat. In a monitory tone he is simply telling it like it is: they will then acquire knowledge of their condition, and that will be a bitter pill to swallow. Which, on anyone's reading, is what happens. The death sentence is death sentience.

The construal is multiply attractive. Agreed: to lack clear awareness of one's standing *vis-à-vis* the line that divides being from nothingness is not to *think oneself* immortal. Still, to lack such awareness is to be free of the panic-creating presentiment, the fear and trembling, that before many turns of the sun life is to be extinguished. Also, the resolution knocks out the unhappy thought that the sheer fact of miscreancy triggers God's ire. God is not saying just that by eating (and hence disobeying) the two will put themselves under sentence of death, which sentence he will then carry out. Act is internally linked to result: their eating is their dying. Finally, the fact that death does not instantly follow eating leaves the brow unfurrowed. God does not think better of his malediction and grudgingly dole out a few years more of sweaty toil. *From the start, the claim was a psychological one.*

The internality of link holds for the other curses of Genesis – which adds collateral confirmation. The curse of Ham we shall touch on below. The curse of Cain has already been interpreted along these same lines. It's not that Cain's having killed Abel results in his banishment to Nod, the way that a villain's stealing from the vault results, when he or she gets caught, in a stint up the river. Rather, the killing puts Cain into a condition of ethical disorientation. Having shattered a tried and tested form of life, Cain is *ipso facto* in Wanderland. Just so, going to the moon does not cause one to be in an airless environment. The moon's atmospheric condition is unaffected by the travel. Being on the moon is being in a vacuum. Airless is how it is on the moon.

We depart the early panel of Genesis appreciating that the biblical issue of mortality is not biological. The world of (subhuman) animals is full of death. Still, in a non-biological sense deathless is precisely what the world of animals is. In a poem titled 'The Animals' Edwin Muir penetrates the apparent paradox:

> . . . these have never trod
> Twice the familiar track,
> Never never turned back
> Into the memoried day.
> All is new and near
> In the unchanging Here

Birth is the ultimate Whence, death the ultimate Whither. But when you dwell in the eternal Now and tread the unchanging Here, you aren't coming and you aren't going. In your regard death cannot puff itself up with pride. For you non-existence is non-existent.

Prior to the dawning of their consciousness of themselves as temporal, the mortality/immortality duality is, in the biblical story, inapplicable to men and women. Acquiring that self-awareness is not however the only way for a defining sense of oneself as mortal to come to be had; a cognitive grasp of one's temporality is only a necessary condition for a conscious and finite subject to conceive himself or herself as human. Here, the Greek side, which proceeds in anthropological terms rather than in the terms of developmental psychology, is theoretically and conceptually more helpful. On the Greek side sense is made of the idea of immortality with respect to men and women who are not cognitively immature. Accordingly, sense is made of the idea in a fashion that indicates that Adam and Eve do have something to lose other than their ignorance. Their 'adult' or 'knowing' condition is their no longer having access to a cultural option, an option every bit as adult or knowing as theirs and in the frame of which death is not what it is for the Bible's inheritors.

Trojan Fields

Embedded among the warriors, we have done an extended tour of duty on the stony expanse between the walls of Troy and the water where the Greek ships ride anchor. The locale seems a world away from the lush garden that God plants 'in Eden, in the east' (2:8). Conceptually speaking, the *champs de mars* where the action of the *Iliad* takes place, and the *champs elysées* where the core of Genesis is situated, are, however, adjacent.

'What could be more remote from God's little acre than a corpse-strewn battlefield?' The reader's incredulity will very likely turn querulous once he or she hears that it is as I see it on the field of battle that the awakening to mortality occurs.

No one could seriously assert that the warriors are oblivious of their short-livedness. The battlefield is drenched with blood, and the warriors are never depicted as sleepwalking into the long night. But the very ambiguity that attaches to 'the man and the woman become mortal in Eden' infects 'the warriors become mortal on the fields of Troy.' On the strength of the preceding, can we not dimly appreciate the aptness of 'the killing fields of Eden'? God speaks a sentence of death to the man and the woman whom he installs in the Garden. Eat, and they die. Since the execution of a death sentence produces a killing, Eden is, it follows, a killing field; and since, in Eden, *the whole of mankind is killed*, an even more genocidal killing field it is than the battlefield outside Troy. The Garden is left at the end of the story to the creatures of the fifth and the first part of the sixth day. Obviously, though, the biblical case differs here from the Homeric one. Whatever meaning attaches to the idea that the warriors do not think of themselves as mortal, it cannot be this, that they have no sense of the past, the present, and the future.

Having closely surveyed the stony expanse surrounding Troy, we can present the essentials of the case in a summary fashion. It's a matter of rearranging the living and dying room furniture.

Although the warriors have sailed the seas and marched overland to muster at Troy, Homer is not playing the field of battle off against the home front. The *casus belli* attests that the warriors are incorrectly seen as pacific beings temporarily under arms. The purloining of Helen *we* regard as entirely disproportionate to the war. The warriors don't see it that way. They have assembled in great numbers to avenge the slight, and many will breathe their last in the protracted campaign. Who would do that on a lark? For the Greeks, Life = War. Identifying themselves on the most basic level as warriors, they would not therefore wish to get out of Ares's path. When life itself is what transpires there, vacating the *champs de mars* amounts to withdrawing from life.

Obviously, then, the biblical God's warning – 'in the day that you eat of it you shall die' – would leave the warriors unmoved. Death is not for them the prime evil. Yet neither are the warriors like the man and the woman in Eden prior to eating of the tree of knowledge. *They* are not innocent of the world or confused about it.

The equation 'Life = Strife' makes sense only in the context of a conception of the world as a field governed by extra-human forces over which men and women exercise no control but which decisively impact their affairs. That conception is figuratively expressed in the epic by the place of men and women *vis-à-vis* the gods who go about their business heedless of the terrestrials for whom their self-absorbed decisions have life-and-death consequences. The Greek pantheon is, at its core, anthropomorphized paganism. Zeus is the sky god; Poseidon, the god of the sea. Etc. A city such as Troy is by contrast a distinctively human world. Appreciating this enables us better to understand both what makes Hector appear Hamlet-like and also that Priam's palace is not *au fond* a Trojan Elsinore. Hector knows all about the warriors' code of honour. He recognizes that he cannot at the end of the day refuse to face Achilles. But fear of death is not at all what keeps Hector back. He is committed also to other values: wife, children, hearth. The honouring of these values points in the direction of his not fighting a fight wherein his doom is sealed. For Achilles, the time is out of joint. For Hector, the ethical duties are disjoint.

The following episode from Book 7 of the *Iliad* offers confirmation that Troy, the locale of settled and non-combative life, stands in a skewed relation to the world of the warriors.

The destruction of their fleet would spell catastrophe for the Greeks. They have therefore thrown up a protective earthen rampart. This has Poseidon boiling and frothing. The earthwork is so massive that, he grumbles to Zeus [523–524], subsequent generations

> will forget those ramparts I and Apollo
> reared for Troy in the old days –

Initially dumbfounded by his brother's reaction to what the Greeks have done, Zeus quickly recovers composure and thunders [527–8]:

> Unbelievable! God of the earthquake,
> you with your massive power, why are you moaning so?

One gargle and spit on Poseidon's part and the rampart will dissolve like a child's castle of sand before a breaker. The sky god's mockery captures what we think, and the spectacle of a sputtering and kelp-covered Poseidon raises a chuckle. But if a human artefact causes such unease, why a mound of dirt? Shouldn't the sight of a city like Troy itself precipitate apoplexy? Describing Hector's return to Troy in Book 6, Homer had limned its magnificence [288–294]:

> And soon
> [Hector] came to Priam's palace, that magnificent structure
> built wide with porches and colonnades of polished stone.
> And deep within its walls were fifty sleeping chambers
> masoned in smooth, lustrous ashlar, linked in a line
> where the sons of Priam slept beside their wedded wives,
> and facing these, opening out across the inner courtyard,
> lay the twelve sleeping chambers of Priam's daughters,
> masoned and roofed in lustrous shlar, linked in a line
> where the sons-in-law of Priam slept beside their wives.

Why indeed bemoan so crude a thing as the rampart? The reason is that the idea of living at peace is peripheral at this stage to the conceptualization. Even the female deities, many later representative of what we see as more civilized values, line up in the *Iliad* for or against the combatants as do the testosterone-driven nature gods Zeus, Apollo, Ares, Poseidon.[3]

An extra-Homeric tradition concerning *the* classical Greek metropolis conveys the message more clearly. The story, frozen on the Parthenon's frieze, has Poseidon and Athena vying for status as the city's patron deity. Each offers the citizens a gift. As the city's name indicates, Athena's, an olive tree, wins out over Poseidon's, a salt spring. 'Choose me,' begs Athena. 'No, choose me,' Poseidon implores. Since when do the immortals compete for the favour of men and women? Did not Poseidon, in grousing about the Achaean rampart, bewail the omission of offerings in the reverse direction? A god's supplicating to a mortal seems unseemly until we appreciate that in the city the gods reside as aliens.

Taking the epic's measure requires acknowledgment of the equation. Even as acute an observer of the classical scene as Bernard Williams can write that Homer is *anxious* to remind us throughout the action of the *Iliad* that 'the Trojan War [is] not the whole world.'[4] This is not the case – not, at any rate, in the way that Williams means. The Greek home front is mentioned for a simple narrative reason. Since the Greek warriors do not grow on trees rooted in the soil around Troy, a rounded depiction cannot avoid making reference to their identities as sons, fathers, husbandmen, and so forth. The post-bellum movement of the warriors may be to the home and the city. (Once Troy has fallen, Odysseus sets sail towards Penelope and Ithaca.) Yet to understand the *Iliad* aright, the happenings after arms are downed must not be understood as a movement *back to* the peaceful environment. In the conceptual system of the *Iliad*, that environment, as a locus of value, and hence as a live possibility for human existence, has yet to be born.[5]

The Greek fighters don't grow on trees rooted in the soil around Troy. We have however visited a place whose inhabitants do, as it were, grow on trees. In Eden, Adam is autochthonous; fashioned of the locale's red marl. Eve is propagated from the arch-autochthon by a fleshly version of plant-cutting. But, of course, the biblical view does not make the home front a background. At this stage the pair have no elsewhere. *Their* authochthony, though nowhere in Homer's plotting, cuts through to the poet's real position on the Greek warriors. The fields around Troy constitute their whole world. The Greek warriors, at this stage, have no elsewhere. As Odysseus was quoted to say, *Zeus* has decreed the embroilment, in which we, 'from youth to old age,' are fated to fight 'until we drop and die, down to the last man.' The Trojan War is Life. Troy and its environs are the world entire.

To Ajax and Achilles, war's toils are as water to fish. Achilles's withdrawal from the action is not due to his having sprouted lungs. Rather, Agamemnon has fouled the water. Ajax's suicide is no rejection of the martial life. The leave-taking is *for him* an appropriate exit from a world in which Odyssean guile and diplomacy, for which he is not cut out, are slowly superseding swords and javelins and arrows.

Yet while war equals life for Achilles *qua* warrior, the shift to a different equation is dramatized via a shift in his *qua*-tion. Achilles's shift is monumental. *His* change, the epic's centre, foreshadows the cultural quake that, independently of Hades's distempers, is rumbling. The object, to get the fleetest of runners to lace on his own fleetingness, is no easy matter. Despite the deathlessness of she who bore him, Achilles is not an immortal. Something of the character of the first man and the first woman in the Garden does however attach to him. In Book 24, what we see, with the god Hermes conducting the proceedings, is Achilles's deathday – in the broadly epistemic/conceptual sense. The Bible had spoken of this day. It is the day on which the Garden-dwellers partake of the fruit of the tree of knowledge (Genesis 2:17):

> in the day that you eat of it you shall die.

Our primary objective is to draw out the parallels between the *Iliad* and Genesis on the matter of mortality. Let me set out what we need of the position of the warriors for the purpose.

On the warriors' conceptualization intrinsic value does not attach to individual life. Only something more lasting than so fragile and evanescent a quantity could have intrinsic value – 'lasting value,' as we ourselves say. What could that be? Some monument that survives their passing; some mark impressed on the public memory. To achieve such a thing they must comport themselves in whichever ways in their culture draw the accolades, thereby ensuring, to the degree that the efforts of men can ensure, that when they depart it will not be as if they had never been. Each of their lives is thus assigned a restrictedly instrumental worth: it is the occasion for achieving lasting status in the public memory. The latter, more permanent than life, is what is valorized as primary.

Achilles is sorely aggrieved. His honour has been smirched. It is not the removal of Briseis *per se* that irks. Agitating Achilles is the thought that he will be thought of while he lives and go down afterwards as the man whose trophy was lifted. Some have likened Achilles to a child who throws a tantrum over a lost rattle. But isn't his position exactly like Menelaus's? To characterize his response as juvenile is to imply that the Trojan War is a schoolyard brawl over the class cutie, which implication only stands a chance of being sustained from a vantage point outside the culture. In the *Odyssey*, Achilles, speaking of Agamemnon's fate, not his own, makes the inside position completely clear [24:32–36]:

> If only you had died your death in the full flush
> of the glory you had mastered – died on Trojan soil!
> Then all united Achaea would have raised your tomb
> and you'd have won your son great fame for years to come.
> Not so. You were fated to die a wretched death.

What happens to Achilles in the course of the *Iliad* is a transformation: the warrior enters the chrysalis of reflection and emerges partially reformed as a human being. Achilles starts to think of individual life along lines that are second nature to us – as valuable for its own sake.

Here is the crucial passage from Book 24 (I will analyse it in the coming chapter). Achilles raises Priam from the hard ground to a higher level [24:609–614]:

Come, please, sit down on this chair here . . .
Let us put our griefs to rest in our own hearts,
rake them up no more, raw as we are with mourning.
What good's to be won from tears that chill the spirit?
So the immortals spun our lives that we, we wretched men,
live on to bear such torments – the gods live free of sorrows.

Unlike the childlike dwellers in Eden, blissfully oblivious that their allotment of days dwindles, of their mortality the warriors – as Glaucus's speech about leaves and leaving makes clear – are fully cognizant, intensely so. They just discount it. 'Discount' does not mean 'ignore' or 'make light of.' Rather, the warriors do not attach to their biological mortality the significance that we do. They do not, for instance, struggle to preserve their lives. Here, finally, after Achilles's interior odyssey, the short-livedness is taken on board, as it is, at a much earlier stage in the biblical narrative, with the eating from the tree of knowledge.

The warriors, in sum, are in the state of the man and the woman prior to the expulsion. But with one vital difference. The warriors *have* tasted of the tree of life. They live for eternity. Achilles, in the *Iliad,* nibbles from a tree of the same species as the Bible's tree of knowledge of good and evil. Having done this, he must then regurgitate and spit out what as a warrior he had thitherto been nourished on. Just as with milk and meat in the Bible, taking these two foods together violates a dietary prohibition of the culture.[6]

Zeus, pregnant with Athena, has a splitting headache. Ending the parturitional pangs the birth of Athena marks a cultural advance in the heavens: the ongoing strife has ended. Given the background myth, the image of Achilles suffering in his tent from stomach upset supplies a nicely balancing indisposition.

The parallel is before us. Achilles, representing a shift in the culture, is reborn from the Trojan battleground as a human being, albeit one who has not quite been carried to term. He is reborn, just as Athena is reborn, more the child of his father than the issue of his mother. It is entirely appropriate that when the epic ends Achilles's days are, in a completely new sense, numbered. The man and the woman depart Eden in human form too. But where the Bible treats the shift genetically, in the mode of developmental psychology, and hence implies that anyone who fails to undergo it is retarded, the *Iliad* does so anthropologically, as a shift from one cultural ensemble to another. The difference makes the *Iliad* the more informative.

Our discussion of the Bible's technique affords useful terminology for encapsulating the difference. The Bible locates everything along the axis of a single, one-dimensional, coordinate scheme. What varies in its explorations of the reality of men and women is the location of the origin of the scheme. The Bible can express doubts about the location of {0} – the cut between good and bad – but cannot however locate it simultaneously in two places. Since different cultural ensembles have different value systems, we really need several such schemes, layered like the floors in a high-rise. Achilles's shift in the *Iliad* is not along, not even a lot further along, the dimension of warrior options. Nor is it a leap to culture from Raven's Land, which lies beyond good-and-evil. It is a leap from one storey to another.

Conceptually speaking, shipping out from the battlefield of Troy is not a *return* to peaceful life. No more is it that than is the leave-taking of the man and the woman from the Garden a *reversion* to hardship. The Greeks who inherited and saved Homer probably estimated the city, the *topos* of postwar existence, too high. Given the steep ascent of their *polis* from the days of Solon and Pisistratus to the Golden Age of Pericles, the exuberance might be forgiven. Whatever prospects for human flourishing the *polis* offered, the locale was however no Eden.

The new location of life, the location to which the culture is moving and in the frame of which the warrior's equation no longer has application, will be examined in the next chapter.

Having aligned the *Iliad* with the early chapters of Genesis, and the *Odyssey* with the Israelites' trek that begins in Exodus, a successor question naturally arises. What would a *Homeric* sequel to Exodus be? The biblical sequel finds Moses promulgating laws for the Israelites. That does not seem to be what Homer has in mind for *his* protagonist. Since his protagonist represents the advancing culture, it does not seem to be what he has in mind, period. That, I mean, is not the sense that is imparted in the *Odyssey*.

Taking his cue from the seer Tiresias's prophecy to Odysseus that he would die far from his home, Tennyson, in the poem 'Ulysses,' vouchsafes a sense of the thing. Tennyson's idea is that Odysseus, unlike Moses, could not stomach the life of a lawgiver. So there would have been no sequel with a counterpart in the Bible. The Bible has in it no adventurers, and in this regard too the Bible's reformed position restricts its scope to a small part of the cultural spectrum.

Having returned to Ithaca and taken up his political position, Tennyson's Odysseus is restive:

> Matched with an aged wife, I mete and dole
> Unequal laws unto a savage race.

He goes on:

> I am become a name;
> For always roaming with a hungry heart

Tennyson's Odysseus becomes his name, understood as per *our* lexicon. Life is an odyssey; he, a ceaseless voyager. He will not be bound to political assemblies and courts of law. But this does not amount to backsliding on the *Iliad*'s cultural advance. Odysseus wants to test life to the full for the sake of living it to the full, not for the sake of leaving a mark. As Tiresias tells it, Odysseus will expire of old age far from anyone who knows who he is – that is, in the anonymity the very thought of which chills the warriors at Troy to the marrow.

Reform Completed

Take the biblical text as it comes and the banishment from Eden appears necessary to prevent the man and the woman from gaining eternal life. The text (3:22–23) says that having eaten of the tree of knowledge the man and the woman have 'become like one of us' – that is, god-like in their knowledge – and hence must be prevented from eating of the tree of life. Since God quickly decides to 'sen[d them] forth from the garden' it would seem that mortality does not come with the eating of the tree of knowledge. Yet the curse connected with that tree (3:17–19) included the pretty unequivocal 'to dust you shall return.'

Not a few scholars represent the problem as an unintended by-product of the way the text was quilted. The temptation story does not mention the tree of life. The fact that it does not, they contend, relieves the tension between 3:19, which brings the story to a close, and the banishment stated by 3:23. Such a resolution merits consideration. But it should be accepted only *faute de mieux*. Someone attached the verses in this manner. That someone might have had a thematic motive for not marking the splice. An interpretive possibility here, from the Bible's direction, consists in taking 'they have become like one of us' literally: for having acquired knowledge of good and evil the man and the woman are *in every respect that counts* God-like. Not only are they in possession of the kind of consciousness unexemplified in the subhuman world. As well, the new awareness of temporality, and hence of mortality, reflects the divine condition. God too is in other words limited: above the natural, but not beyond. (This limitedness certainly applies to the creating deity, who proceeds by trial and error.) The point, then, would be a quasi-logical one: banishment from the Garden is essential since the combination of knowledge and eternal life is a round square.

The language of logical inconsistency is not the Bible's. Something a bit softer is suggested by a Roman classic. Petronius's *Satyricon* tells of a sibyl to whom the god Apollo gifted eternal life. Eternal youth to match wasn't however part of the package. Schoolboys, on an outing to Cumae, view her, suspended in an ampoule, shrunken with age. What, they ask, does she want? 'Respondebat illa, αποθανειν θελω.' 'I want to die.'

It is not far from how I am here interpreting the biblical message to say that eternity is intolerable if time is real and has its usual ravaging effects.[7]

A couple of scriptural signs attest the interpretation. The first concerns the serpent. Why of all the creatures such a creature? The biblical serpent is a deceiver. Knowledge is not the subject matter of its wiles. It deceives about death and mortality. Distinctively among animals serpents in a clear sense do precisely that. Like the trees of Philip Larkin's poem 'Trees,' they have the 'yearly trick of looking new.' Shedding its skin, the reptile annually recovers its youthful appearance.[8] So it is quite plausible to construe the temptation of the serpent, which in the NRSV's rendering Eve calls 'trickery,' in terms of the idea that eternal youth would be good and would be achievable by knowledge. Petronius's schoolboys learn a more accurate lesson from a non-molter: wizened, liver-spotted. And, I am saying, the Bible might well, in its distinctive terms, be doing a Petronius rather than a Peter.

The second sign is a late biblical book in which the sense of time and of time's passage is near unendurable. Bemoaning fugitive youth and sapped vitality, and doing so in terms that were they not so grim would tickle the funny bone ('the grasshopper drags itself along' [12:5]), Ecclesiastes winds down with this penultimate tag line: 'Fear God, and keep his commandments; for that is the whole duty of everyone' (13). In view of what has come before, the line sounds magnificently inconsequent. But if God is seen to suffer from the same difficulty, then his example constitutes a model for emulation. There he lies, in a double-vault, the Holy of Holies in the Temple in Jerusalem, having when time was young applied his vitality to make a world in which we might do well. If we do less than keep his commandments, his judgment, as the final sentence of the book says, will indeed be upon us. One may walk painfully on three in the evening and be laid out supine at night, 'sans teeth, sans eyes, sans taste, sans everything.' No help for that. To take these facts as justification for limping in the morning or for lying at noon is however to misunderstand, and to live in such ways is to fail at life. In the words of Ecclesiastes (3:1–2): 'there is . . . a time for every matter under heaven: a time to be born, and a time to die.' Make good use of the in-between time.

Anthropotheogony: Hesiod and the Bible

So much for the Bible's theogony – a story of God's coming down to the earth that he creates. I turn now to the anthropogenic element in Hesiod. Here, my cue is one of the central texts of classical Greece, Sophocles's *Oedipus the King*. The issue can be introduced by melding the poetic voice of Edwin Muir with the despondent rasp of the Cuman sibyl.

The sibyl specializes in prophecy: knowledge of the future. Muir makes clear that a sense of time – of past, of change, of the future to come – is needed for world-awareness of the human level. Otherwise, awareness is in the eternal Now. Oedipus is a middle term between the two. And that is his error.

Oedipus is in a key respect very like the man and the woman in the Garden. They have acquired knowledge of their condition, though without fully understanding the acquisition. (Had they had full understanding, there would have been no danger of their eating of the fruit of the tree of life.) Oedipus too is a knower. He has solved the riddle of the Sphinx, a riddle that encodes the question: What is man? The form of the riddle is significant. It speaks of the temporality of men and women: crawling on all fours at one time, walking on two at another time, and at a yet later time limping with a stick. So do animals come and change and go. But men and women know about their entrances and mutations and exits. Oedipus does not however understand the answer that he himself has given to the Sphinx. His knowledge, he thinks, is salvific. How, specifically, is he wrong? His *life* exemplifies the error. He is at once Jocasta's child and Jocasta's husband. His position as son collides with his position as husband. A father is the husband of the mother and begetter of the child. Oedipus is a monster of a man. His monstrosity consists in living in the eternal Now while having a full temporality. The roles that Oedipus simultaneously fills collapse differences that time normally separates – that should be kept apart. The man is a temporal version of the Sphinx itself, the latter being a spatial monster, a tectonic clash of head of a woman, wings of an eagle, hind parts of a lion.

This seems far from the world of the *Theogony*. Arguably, however, the conflict of the generations among the gods is a time-unlimited version of the conflict that Oedipus exemplifies in his person.

According to the Delphic Oracle, Oedipus is a threat to Laius. Just so, the chief male deity of each generation of gods is threatened by his offspring. Ouranos, the first of the dominant male gods, is threatened by Kronos, the chief second-generation god. The Titan is in turn under threat from Zeus, the leading Olympian, and Zeus, when he comes to be in control, from *his* offspring. Laius attempted to scotch the danger by infanticide. Striving to maintain power, the senior god proceeds along similar lines to neutralize the usurpers. The full story, told in chapter 7, ends with Athena springing from Zeus's head.

The story parallels that of Oedipus in the fact of a challenge to the father. The father will be vanquished should the son get the chance. While the mother's complicity with the son in each of the first two generations has no direct resonance in Sophocles, might the idea of such an *entente* not be taken to contain the suggestion that the son would replace the father *vis-à-vis* the mother? As the case may be, important in Hesiod's telling is the very idea of an ongoing cycle of internecine violence in the godly sphere, and the description of how it is brought to a halt.

Why should the problem have arisen in the first place? For the most part, fathers naturally give way to sons. Willy-nilly, time will see to that. Here, however, the father is *immortal*. For an immortal, natural succession is a non-starter. Given the presence of competitors, an unceasing power struggle is in the cards. The mother is however in a different position. The filial bias has its source in her nature, producer of offspring, rather than in some objection to the husband's. As Ouranos's behaviour attests, the male deity's interest in sex is recreative, not creative. What does Zeus do? He takes some of the mother into himself. He brakes the cycle by swallowing the tail. The various elements are present in him simultaneously.

How, in non-figurative terms, does this way of proceeding do the trick? Zeus performs an *imitatio Dei*. God of the Bible makes a break from the pantheon of Babylon and founds a monotheistic faith. Zeus's is a proto-shift from the unruliness that is a standing feature of a belief system comprising a multiplicity of deities towards the tighter order characteristic of monotheism. No story of God's departure from the lower Euphrates is found in the Bible. But within the core language of biblical monotheism traces of an exodus from that Egypt may be detected. Consider the biblical use of the plural in referring to God. The name 'Elohim' is syntactically non-singular; and 'we' is frequently employed when the deity speaks *in propria persona*. Indeed, the *Shema*, the chief avowal of faith within the biblical communion, reads as easily as an assertion of divine unity as it does to declare divine uniqueness. 'Hear O Israel, the Lord is our God, the Lord is one' (Deuteronomy 6:4). The Lord is One. That is, the Lord is not a congeries.

Order in the realm of the eternal is – has to be – space-like. Power is sprinkled among the elements. Though the relative placing of the constellation's elements may shift as time passes, the elements neither come nor go. In the realm of the mortal, the disposition of power has, more basically, to be time-like.

Oedipus's fatedness mirrors Zeus's. Zeus's mode of stopping the cycle accords fully with the former's. Ouranos and Kronos, by contrast, try, as Laius tries, to disarm fate. In their cases, fate proves too robust. Zeus responds more flexibly to the predicament. Fate can have its way, he reckons, and so can he. In the exemplary instance of Athena, Zeus makes his progeny part of himself. He has become at once father, husband, mother. The mother had mythically made common cause with the son in the previous generations. Having assumed the role of mother, Zeus is out of harm's way.

Oedipus's monstrous condition corresponds: he is an unholy union of child and father. His bringing the cycle to a halt in this way won't however work as the corresponding thing does for Zeus. Oedipus is a finite being. He will be replaced willy-nilly. Also, he can only become father, son, and so on, at one and the same time by incest and parricide. The incest is a grotesque version of the itself grotesque reinsertion of the sons into the mother's womb; the self-immolation, the blinding, a grotesque version of the itself grotesque castration. These last we take in stride, and not merely because the events described are mythical. The immortal beings, by that very fact, are inscrutable to us.

This furnishes a fresh perspective on Genesis 3:23. Perhaps eating of the tree of life will make the men and the women god-*like*, putting a *disproportionate* number of grains of sand into their lifeglass – more than is good for them. God outlasts Methuselah, the longest lived of men and women in the Bible. God is larger however than men and women. The number of years that he has is proportionate to his nature. For men and women to live as long as God, to 'be like us,' would be tantamount to their living forever. What is wrong with that? A world without death as we know it lacks proper succession. The generations in such a world would clash as do the continental plates, Pelion atop Ossa, none giving way, a nauseating assemblage like the Sphinx.

In fact, the Bible does allow men to dwell alongside their fathers and grandfathers and great-grandfathers in the way that Ouranos and Kronos live on with Zeus, viz., in the Now. The Bible has Abraham and Isaac and Jacob all joining their fathers: in death – timeless and capacious enough to accommodate any number.

I have argued for similarities between the Greek scriptures and the Hebrew. Can't we dimly discern in the story of Isaac's sacrifice a distant cousin of the generational war played out in Hesiod and a Sophoclean judgment on Oedipus's monstrosity? God has covenanted with Abraham. As his part of the bargain, God will make Abraham a great nation. Yet God asks Abraham to sacrifice his only son. Illogical from the human standpoint, since the promise cannot be fulfilled if Isaac, issueless, is dead, this makes perfect sense from the standpoint of immortal divinity. Ouranos would have eliminated Kronos, and Kronos in turn done Zeus in, each for the greatness of *his* generation. Being immortal, they could still have achieved. It also makes sense from the Oedipal standpoint. Oedipus, having married his mother, has become his own father. God has not asked Abraham to commit suicide. Accordingly, were the patriarch like Oedipus the commandment to kill the son could, for a logical reason, be resisted without disobeying. But God of the Bible relents, as his incipiently human nature requires. In staying Abraham's knife, God is ratifying our human sense of the temporality of existence by acknowledging his own temporal status.

Which means – to couch it in the formulation of *Paradise Lost* – *God's* bringing death into the world.

9
Becoming Political

The Shield of Achilles

Homer's scene in the *Iliad* resembles in its compass one of those vast canvasses of Brueghel's picturing myriad men and women engaged in the myriad activities that engage men and women. But on the Greek side the epic's pages represent one activity and one activity alone. No matter how far into the distance we look we see only warriors, bivouacs, combat, and so forth. Homer's plotting is a way of dramatically capturing the equation 'Life = War.' Had Homer been able to do so without affecting the story's plausibility, he would have made contact with the mayhem in the hundredth year.

The preceding lines, transcribed with a few changes from chapter 6, contain the basis for the claim that the *Iliad* is pre-reformed. There may seem to be a couple of horseflies in the ointment.

The events at Troy are events at *Troy*. Encircled by massive walls, Troy is not part of the battlefield. In his conduct and thinking the central character on the Trojan side exemplifies something that lies outside the warrior's theatre of activity, hence something that *qua* locus of value is at odds with the warrior way. When Hector is first mentioned in the epic, in Book 1, it is as 'man-killing Hector' [1:285]. The epic's final phrase makes reference to him – 'breaker of horses' [24:944]. Had the first mention occurred in the opening line Homer might have been thought to be driving at something. As it is, we may just have two of a very large number of epithets of the sort that pepper the epic. Still, the contrast between the uncontrolled use of force (killer) and its control (tamer) is significant to the epic's dynamic and will loom large in the sequel. The Greeks repair to their tents at night. Hector can return to his city and his family. Book 6 finds him doing so. Plainly, the two returns differ markedly in character. The Greeks are not returning home. Since in passing through the Scaean Gate Hector is exiting the battlefield, would it not however be natural to say that *Achilles*'s change is in Hector's direction? Aren't those who take up Achilles's legacy going home to their cities and their families? If so, the change that the epic tracks would not be a change to a hitherto non-existent condition. To put it from a different angle: Ajax's death is a dramatic representation of the end of the warrior way. Isn't the death of Hector the death, too, of a way – one, however, that was *not* permanently extinguished along with him but that Odysseus, reunited at journey's end with Penelope, resumes? Doesn't the trio of the happy ending, Odysseus, Penelope, and Telemachus, balance the doomed threesome of Hector, Andromache, and Astyanax? Why speak then of the text as reform*ing*? Don't the dramatics just explore a number of available options? If so, doesn't Athena's intervention in Book 1 come down to stopping a man from following his otherwise overmastering impulses? While it can be fascinating to examine a person in the grip of powerful drives, who but an innocent of worldly affairs would find in this anything conceptually revolutionary?

That, in a hail of questions, is the first difficulty. The following related thought might independently have occurred to the reader. 'Achilles has been dealt with extensively. That is as it should be. Deservedly, the spotlight has also picked out Odysseus and Ajax, Helen, Priam, Agamemnon, Diomedes, and a few others. Hector, the epic's second-largest character, has not however been allotted space at all proportional to his role. So isn't the *Iliad* as discussed in these pages a *Hamlet* without, say, Laertes?'

The second difficulty concerns the shield that at Thetis's urging Hephaestus smiths for Achilles to replace the one that Hector had stripped from Patroclus. The shield (like the rest of the panoply) is matchlessly crafted – as befits the divine Cellini. The detailed description in Book 9 seems to unbalance the equation 'Life = War.'

Though the first difficulty cannot peremptorily be waved off, its force is easily overestimated. If Achilles is seen as (monumentally) obdurate, the ambassadors' bafflement when he spurns their entreaties fails to make proper sense. The idea of resistance to duty the ambassadors understand perfectly. Consider how the Greek fighters react to Agamemnon's test in Book 2: Odysseus has to bring all his carrot-and-stick talents to bear to return them to the lines. The case of Achilles cannot fit this form.

So far, let's call it a draw. A closer look at the shield will break the tie and shift 'exaggerated' over towards 'mistaken.'

Here, from *Iliad* 18:565–654, are about half the elements depicted on the shield: the earth, the sky, the sea, the blazing sun, the moon, the constellations; two noble cities, weddings and wedding feasts, young men dancing; flautists and harpists playing, a thronged marketplace, a dispute about the blood-price of a murdered kinsman and a judge to decide between the parties; a siege, an army split about how the battle is to be waged, shepherds surrounded and butchered; a fallow field with a crew of ploughmen; a king's estate, harvesters labouring to bring in the crop, heralds announcing a harvest feast, attendant women pouring out provender.

The following comment about Hephaestus's handiwork, expressing a view that is fairly typical among classicists, would if correct pose a problem for the present reading. '[T]he images on the [new] shield are related to one another and arranged into a coherent description of human reality – including the reality of war.'[1]

Even when I scour the text, what the classicist quoted claims to see eludes me. '[T]he Ocean River's mighty power girdling / round the utmost rim of the welded indestructible shield' [708–709] apart, where in the multi-page description are the marks of careful placement – positional phrases like 'near the boss,' 'at the bottom edge,' 'where the strap attaches'? Severally, the individual elements are coherently described. But the combination is a hodgepodge. The shield is *not* a coherent arrangement; it is a *congeries*. Were one to undertake to transpose the words into a plastic form, one would have to decide for oneself how to arrange. No two would decide in the same way.

The epic movement is from a world in which Life = War to one in which the equation is out of balance. All the elements are there for the choosing. The choice of the right-hand term for the successor equation – a choice, Homer makes clear as soon as he moves from the description of the natural backdrop to the human sphere, for 'mortal men' [573] – has yet however to be made. By setting out the various scenes higgledy-piggledy, not by adhering to a pattern, Homer gets the point across. In the fashion of latter-day aleatoric artists, Homer might have drawn the elements from a bunch of papyrus strips tossed into an amphora. Jackson Pollock–like, he spatters the elements onto the shield's surface.

An earlier point helps hammer this home. War, on the Clausewitz statement, is a violent extension of politics. The definition fits our understanding of war well (obviously, it informs the quoted classicist's thinking). But when Life = War there is nothing for war to extend. In representing strife, the shield represents soldiers under arms, not warriors, a soldier being a civilian pressed into temporary military service after diplomacy has hit the wall. The Achilles of *Iliad* Book 1 could not have been accoutered in such a piece of armour. His return to the field is the return of a changed man.

The guest list in chapter 4 of *The Great Gatsby* supplies a nice parallel of the replacement shield. The catalogue of those in attendance is beautifully done. Here is a portion, proportionately quite a bit less of the whole than the portion that I transcribed from the description of the shield:

> From East Egg . . . came the Chester Beckers and the Leeches, and a man named Bunsen, whom I knew at Yale, and Doctor Webster Civet, who was drowned last summer in Maine. And the Hornbeams and the Willie Voltaires, and a whole clan named Blackbuck, who always gathered in a corner and flipped up their noses like goats at whosoever came near. And the Ismays and the Chrysties (or rather Hubert Auerbach and Mr. Chrystie's wife), and Edgar Beaver, whose hair, they say, turned cotton-white one winter afternoon for no good reason at all.

The list is a mishmash. *That is Fitzgerald's point*. What's happened to social order? Anyone and everyone comes to Gatsby's parties, including many who haven't been invited. When the music's over, one of the guests, Klipspringer, even takes up shadowy residence in Gatsby's mansion.[2]

Think of a menu on which appetizers, soups, desserts, main courses, and beverages are not assigned to different sections. In just such a fashion the shield presents the gamut of life activities. The scene depicted on the shield has no clear centre. Accordingly, no stable order can be discerned. Lacking a focus in relation to which the various elements align, the shield is an anti-artistic work of art. The Grandma Moses quality is a testament to Homer's artistry. The artlessness serves his thematic message.

Before Hephaestus is commissioned Achilles considers borrowing Ajax's shield. Why *doesn't* Achilles do that? Ajax, we are informed, is off at the front. Lurking here is a Frost Point. On the level of plot Ajax's distance means that Achilles, if he is to stride out onto the battlefield, will need to find other armour. But the unavailability of Ajax's shield has thematic significance too. *That* shield is inappropriate for the altered Achilles. It comes from the front. Achilles could not appropriately have borrowed from Ajax even if Ajax had been resting in his tent a stone's throw away. There is no rear for Ajax, and certainly no home front. Ajax is always at the front.

To sum up: just as Achilles is in a transitional state, so is the world-representation on the shield. These are two sides of a single coin.

Recurring to the *Odyssey* strengthens the point. If the shield presented 'a coherent description,' Odysseus's wandering would also fail to make proper sense. Rather than an Outis, he would simply be a man negotiating an obstacle course back to that coherent world.

Another list we've discussed, the Edomite list of Genesis 36, resonates with the new shield. In the biblical instance, the wildness of the genealogy matches that of the originator. Had a God who was like Esau created the world, what would that world have been like? In the case of the *Iliad* the centreless character of the shield matches the 'Nobody' status of Achilles after his *volte face*. What will be the boss-value on the shield in the post-warrior system?

In discussing the *Weltanschauung* of the Greeks at Troy I underscored the fact that everything is part of the furniture of war. No women are present, no children. This, I then said, is just a way of dramatizing life as a struggle that those possessed of life must lose. Obviously, though, life does involve the other activities too. How do the two things square? The shield, with its spatter of elements, supplies the key to answering.

Hector's Elliptical Value System

The shield represents the central elements of life: women, children, workers, judges, fighters, civilians at odds, and so on. A value system is a conceptualization with a centre and an orientation. Not everything has value; and not everything that has value is of equal value. A value system rates certain things, certain forms of conduct, certain objectives, over others. Some things, modes of conduct, and objectives are relegated to an area of indifference. In their regard, you are at liberty to do what you will.

That is a key to Hector. The Trojan's value system assigns worth to things that fall in the warriors' area of indifference. Not only is Hector a fighter reaching for eternity, he is also a son, a father, a brother, a husband, with the this-worldly duties and concerns appertaining thereunto. In Book 5 [559–560] the Trojan ally Sarpedon says this to Hector:

> Beware the toils of war . . .
> the mesh of the huge dragnet sweeping up the world.

Directed at a Greek warrior, this would not make sense. For such a one, there is no relief from war. The dragnet is the world. But Hector is different. He knows of more than strife.

A Greek warrior unbuckles armour only to recharge the battery. Resting is part of the normal activity. No fighter can fight non-stop. *Hector*, removing his armour, presents a quite other face to the world. The warriors fight for recognition. Hector, in his warrior guise, is unknown to his son. Only after Hector lifts the ridged helmet does the child recognize him. Not the memorializing recognition of shock and awe, *this* is the child's happy and affectionate recognition of a parent.

Hector's son does not recognize him. The allusion is to the scene in Book 6 that describes Hector's return to city and family. The pertinent passage [556–566] comes immediately after Hector has quite tenderly voiced justified fears for Andromache, his wife, and for Astyanax, their child, should he meet defeat:

> In the same breath, shining Hector reached down
> for his son – but the boy recoiled,
> cringing against his nurse's full breast,
> screaming out at the sight of his own father,
> terrified by the flashing bronze, the horsehair crest,
> the great ridge of the helmet nodding, bristling terror –
> as it struck his eyes. And his loving father laughed,
> his mother laughed as well, and glorious Hector,
> quickly lifting the helmet from his head,
> set it down on the ground, fiery in the sunlight,
> and raising his son he kissed him, tossed him in his arms

Hector is a warrior. Also, he is a family man. His value system is bifocal. The domestic focus is absent on the Greek side, though the Greeks certainly have families and live domestic lives, to which they now and again allude. It's just that these, for the Greeks, fall in the area of indifference with respect to what is valuable, like, for us, the order in which one puts on one's shoes.

It can now be better appreciated that despite what may have been the reality of Bronze Age warfare Homer would have been unwise to surround the Greeks with an entourage. That would have smudged the contrast. The point is that the Greeks are, and are fully, warriors from the value standpoint. Their shields present to the world only one motif.

Defending his thesis about consciousness, Julian Jaynes entered the following piece of Homeric evidence: no character in the *Iliad* ever speaks to himself or herself. The epic in fact contains two soliloquies, the one Agenor's, in Book 21, the other Hector's, in Book 22. It is as it should be that Trojans speak them both. The Trojans have a place outside the battlefield – an inner place, then – where positive value resides. Since 'Life = War' does not balance completely on the Trojan side of the line, two voices are therefore lodged inside the breast of the Trojan paragon. For the Greeks, by contrast, the only questioning that can be done of the value system is philosophical in nature.

What of the difficulty with which the chapter began? Isn't the second focus of Hector's value system, the family and city, that to which the Greek world is gravitating? The answer is given by noting that *Hector's* concern on the non-warrior side is exclusively for kith and kin. This is not to say that he is indifferent to the city's fate. About Troy he is *deeply* concerned. The point is that the two concerns really are one. *Troy is not a political entity*. An *oikos* in structure, not a *polis*, Troy is in effect a giant household. Hector the dweller in Troy is just a magnification of Hector the family man. Though more than a warrior, Hector is less than a citizen. I wrote earlier that Hector, on a brief furlough, returns to his city and his family. 'City and family' is in Hector's case pleonastic. His city is (=) his (extended) family.

If Ajax's death represents the end of the warrior way, what does Hector's death, which is a high dramatic point in the *Iliad*, represent? Look again at the description of Troy in Book 6 [288–297]:

> And soon
> [Hector] came to Priam's palace, that magnificent structure
> built wide with porches and colonnades of polished stone.
> And deep within its walls were fifty sleeping chambers
> masoned in smooth, lustrous ashlar, linked in a line
> where the sons of Priam slept with their wedded wives,
> and facing these, opening onto the inner courtyards
> lay the twelve sleeping chambers of Priam's daughters,
> masoned and roofed in lustrous ashlar, linked in a line
> where the sons-in-law of Priam slept beside their wives.

The palace, which represents Troy, has a somewhat oriental character. At any rate, its family orientation is stressed. Occupying the palace is an extended family of astonishing size. This supplies the answer. Hector's death represents the end of a communal way that is family-based and/or that has the structure of a family.

Let the foregoing lines not be misunderstood. The epic is in no position to write *finis* to the non-warrior way that Hector represents, especially if it dates from fairly far back in the archaic period. In fact, even if at the time at which the epic was written *warriors* had long since been turned into resource people for grade school history classes and become fixtures for days of remembrance, the writers would not even have been able justifiably to wave a permanent goodbye to the warrior ethos. The point that is being made is only this. On Homer's portrayal, Greek culture is moving beyond the communal ethos that Troy embodies. It is moving to something new and unprecedented – new and unprecedented for Greek culture. Otherwise put: the epic is advancing a view of social and anthropological movement on which the tribal condition, like the warrior ethos, is giving way.

These last paragraphs supply a different perspective on the first difficulty. The *Iliad*'s main change is, in a figurative sense, the death of Achilles. The epic also gives us, explicitly, the death of Hector. The first death is, thematically, the passing of a way, the warrior way. Since Hector and Achilles are close counterparts, one therefore expects that the death of the Trojan will be more than just the sad end of a noble man. To read the *Iliad* as if it bounces around between available options is thus to read it in a manner that makes it less philosophical, and that also, more importantly for present probative purposes, is insensitive to the carefully wrought structure.

Knox, in his Introduction to the *Iliad*, states (30): 'The first city we hear of in Greek literature is Troy.' We see, then, that this is misleading. In a sense that is conceptually crucial, especially in Greece, Troy is not a city at all. Its orientation is biological, not political.[3]

The distinction here between two forms of communal existence, the non-political and the political, is important for what follows. An anticipatory word is needed about the defining characteristics of the city *qua* theatre of political activity.

A city as a collection of people living in proximity differs from a family. The individuals who come together in the city do not have connections to one another of the sort that knit husbands to wives, that tie parents to children, and that link siblings. Accordingly, the interpersonal duties and obligations of the city dwellers differ in kind from the obligations of parents to children, brothers to brothers, and so forth. In the city, the inhabitants are citizens primarily. They stand in family relations only *per accidens*. Thus the scruples concerning nepotism in the public sphere: a mixing in of the familial where it does not belong. Political existence is communal existence of men and women who, *qua* politically linked, stand in no other relevant (basic) relation than that of common citizenship. They do not come together within the city limits because they are citizens. Living within the limits is what *makes* them citizens. Living together politically thus requires regulations and laws and institutions that adjust the interactions of otherwise unrelated individuals, since these cannot be expected to care about one another as parents and siblings do. Just as Troy is not a political entity, so the warriors do not live political lives. They also, though in a slightly different sense, are uncaring about the effects upon others of what they do. (They do care about how yet others think about the effects on others of what they do.) All the players know the rules of the game. No one feels resentment for what occurs, even when what occurs is injury and death.[4]

Hector certainly is noble: deeply attentive to the welfare of those dear to him. Still, in the sense of 'moral' that is brought out by Achilles's dawning appreciation of the intrinsic value of life generally, Hector is not moral. Hector's burning concern is with his family. So large is his family, taking in so many beyond the nuclear unit, that the concern has a moral look. That is, the impression of general equality of interest and treatment is illusory. When Hector unstraps his armour in Book 6, he does so to resume his *domestic* identity. He sees things from the standpoint of a husband and a father and a brother and a son. Neither is he wrestling with his self-understanding, nor is he questioning the values for which he acts. Hector is no Hellenic meditator.

The reader who keeps tabs on an author's 'I will do's' may have begun to wonder whether *this* author has forgotten the Scamander with its double spring. I claimed that the bizarre juxtaposition of the river's hot-and-cold running water with Hector's death wasn't just an accident. Troy itself is configured as a giant household or *oikos*. In effect, all Trojans are family members; that's how they think of one another. Hector's death is a death for the family. Thus the appropriateness of the outdoor, industrial-sized, Whirlpool, quite different from the one branded 'Charybdis' that Odysseus, who inherits the cultural enterprise from Achilles, must navigate to leave the dust of Troy behind.[5]

To appreciate the epic's internal dynamic, it has, in fine, to be understood that the two foci of value for Hector, though different, share a characteristic. As a warrior, Hector strives for a god-like status. Primary value is outside the individual man or woman. As a father and a husband and a brother and a son, Hector is concerned for the ongoing life of the family. (Observe that the odd character of Troy matches the odd character of the Trojan War itself. Just as Homer's treatment of the Greek side is a way of dramatizing the equation 'Life = War,' so the manner of Troy's characterization is Homer's way of indicating that we are speaking not of a city in our sense but of a family.) Again, primary value is outside. In both cases, that is, the individual is subordinate to what counts most. The warrior subordination might be called 'vertical,' the familial one, 'horizontal.' In neither case is mortality the final resting place. In both cases value is calibrated to something transcendent of the individual man or woman.

Achilles and Priam

The discussion of the *Iliad* can now be concluded. The poignant meeting between Priam and Achilles, described in Book 24, rounds off the epic's thematic content.

Priam has stolen to Achilles's tent, and on bended knee begs for the return of the body of his son. Achilles raises Priam from the ground [24:609–614].

> Come, please, sit down on this chair here . . .
> Let us put our griefs to rest in our own hearts,
> rake them up no more, raw as we are with mourning.
> What good's to be won from tears that chill the spirit?
> So the immortals spun our lives that we, we wretched men,
> live on to bear such torments – the gods live free of sorrows.

'*We* wretched men.' Achilles, the half-divine, includes himself. He casts his lot in with the fully human, fragile, vulnerable, suffering men and women. Significantly, touched by Priam, Achilles remembers his father, Peleus, not his mother, Thetis. He focuses straight ahead, on his mortal parent, not upwards, on the immortal one.

Priam (now) and Achilles (now), wretched humans, are not just clods of clay; nor do they stride about godlike. They are in-between creatures. And so, Achilles, sensitive to that status, would have them sit together part way between the earth and the heaven, neither prideful nor abject.

Priam is Hector's father; Achilles, his killer. The one originated Hector's life, the other terminated it. Our focus in the scene is directed tightly on our mortal span, with void before and void after. Priam, suspending the honour code (as Trojan king he would sooner die than humble himself before the enemy), and Achilles, momentarily setting it aside too, shift in the direction of a recognition of a common humanity. They grieve about, and hence set apart, what happens between birth and death, not what happens before or transpires afterwards. The scene is brilliantly wrought. The mortal span has become the figure to the ground of engulfing eternity, a reversal of the arrangement on the battlefield, where eternity is the figure to the ground of our short span of life.

That Priam reaches Achilles's tent with a god's assistance is, then, thematically significant. In Book 24 Homer does with Hermes what he does with Hephaestus in Book 18 and with Athena in Book 1. In the first case, as in the other two, the god's presence signals a change of ethos.

On the level of plot, Hermes's role is straightforward. The decision has been taken in the cloud-shrouded conclave: Hector's body is to be repatriated. To spirit Priam across no man's land to Achilles's tent in the heart of enemy territory, Hermes is pressed into service. Hermes, the gods' messenger, is just doing his job. As I indicated in the previous chapter, that job goes beyond accompanying the traveller from A to B. It is accompanying the traveller on a journey that is especially difficult. Since Hermes's role in Greek myth as chief psychopomp is, on the evidence, post-Homeric, it would, despite Hermes's appearance in a limited form of this capacity in Book 24 of the *Odyssey*, be courting anachronism to say that Homer is exploiting the role here – that by conscripting Hermes he is signalling a movement from one view of life to another. Still, the use of Hermes in the *Odyssey* to get the souls of the suitors to Hades does at least confirm that Homer associates the god with *especially* monumental transitions. On the level of theme, Hermes, then, is pressed into service by way of indicating that what is occurring between Priam and Achilles, that what transpires in the scene as a whole, is out of the ordinary. In what manner out of the ordinary? It's not just that a Trojan, let alone an elderly one, cannot easily get to the tent 'so none will see him' [24:400]. Nor is it just that Priam, in going to beg for the return of the body, is tarnishing his crown. (Hecuba expresses to Priam precisely the fear that Achilles will show 'no respect for your rights' [24:246] as a king.) For it is in the first instance at least as a grief-stricken father, not as a king, that Priam confronts Achilles. The point, rather, is that in moving into Achilles's tent we are moving into a place in which the value assignments are detached from those either in Troy or on the battlefield.[6]

The body is returned. In Book 1 Chryseis is given back to *her* father, a priest of Apollo. The return occurs under the sign of the divine. Apollo responds to Chryses's prayer. In Book 24 Hector's body is returned because his father beseeches. Achilles responds to the man's anguish. The return occurs under the sign of the human. *This* has nothing to do with Hermes, nothing to do with the divine. A passage from the very end of Euripides's *Hippolytus* is revealing here. Hippolytus is near death. The goddess Artemis, excessive worship of whom led him to this pass, departs the scene: 'Farewell, I must not look upon the dead. My eye must not be polluted by the last gaspings for breath.' A *defining* moment of human existence is outside the gods' scope.

The scene is compelling. We are moved by the pair who meet in the tent. The two recognize each other in a way quite different from the one way recognition for which the warrior acts. Nor is the mutual recognition familial in character. *That* kind of recognition is acculturated very early on. But what is this middle position? Is it sustainable as a position, or is it just a momentary and unstable thing – an aberration? What are its implications for the (conceptual) future?

We are touched by the scene because, among other things, life for us, as fragile and compromised as it is, has intrinsic value. That valorization is however still in the future from the standpoint of the epic, so we must move cautiously. A shift has been made away from the warrior view. In this regard the *Iliad* is reform*ing*. But the shift, though decisive, is only slight. It's not that now life is regarded as valuable because, like gold, there is so little of it. In fact, it's not at all clear if at this juncture *anything* is recognized as inherently valuable. The two who come together in the tent are partners in suffering. Are men and women to be valued because their lives are attended by so much pain? One doesn't have to be a Nietzsche to question such an assignment. Mutual pity is not necessarily to be despised as a basis for partnership. It can in fact work well, as mutual fear can sustain peaceful relations among neighbours between whom no love is lost. Indeed, few bonds are as close as the bond of grief, few communities as deep as the community of sorrow. The solidarity of the rich, a solidarity against the loss of the material things that are individually possessed, is unlikely to survive the loss. If anything, it is likely to transmute into a bitterness that corrodes unity. All this is true. But the worthless as worthwhile?

'What are human beings that you are mindful of them, mortals that you care for them?' At the heart of the Bible's answer to David's question lies what Genesis describes as the likeness between God and creatures such as we. This is ultimately a way of saying that human beings assign a special worth to themselves. The fact that the self-valuing receives a divine imprimatur in the Bible cannot be taken as it comes. But it is not a mere flourish. The 'Approved' indicates that the worth attached is positive. In the encounter between Priam and Achilles, the two recognize each other – do so apart from, and indeed even despite, what *their* gods think. The fact that the mutual recognition is accomplished in the frame of pain and suffering marks a fundamental difference in inflection between the Greek case and the biblical one. Since the new mutual valuing is based in commiseration, the Greeks are still a distance from having a positive view of the individual man and woman. The traverse of the distance we shall soon address.

The New Focus

Taps has been sounded on the *Iliad*. Hector is buried. Achilles's life clock is into injury time, his heel awaiting the arrow from Paris's quiver. He is, to quote again the poet Edwin Muir, 'a corpse with streaming hair.'[7] What next? Looking forward to the tragedians of classical Greece, we find material for answering.

In form, the interpretive problem here resembles the problem of determining the nature of the Bible from what we gather about the condition, creedal, personal, political, of those who fashioned it. What stands to post-Homeric culture as the destruction of the Temple stands to biblical culture? In this chapter, whose title telegraphs my answer, I blueprint what I see the situation to be, and conclude by examining parallels over on the Jerusalem side. The next chapter will supply a full defence.

The *post*-Homeric culture was not just *post*-Homer. To a large extent it was also *propter*-Homer. But something was added that Homer did not provide. The *Iliad* ends *in medias res*. The *Odyssey*, though it does not disappoint our sense of what qualifies as a proper ending, is also inconclusive. Despite (or perhaps because of) the high excitement sustained throughout, the reader must feel dissatisfied that it should close in a marital embrace. And then to sleep. All *that* for *this*?[8]

As I see it, the view of men and women as wretched creatures, a view that a warrior like Glaucus and the reforming Achilles both state, remains a given. The fundamental change that Homer dramatizes through Achilles, the shift of the centre of value down the ladder whose top rung the gods occupy, is also not reversed. Given these two entailments from Homer, what can we gather about the thinking of the classical period?

Here's the short answer. The shift in the value system away from the gods does not find in human reality enough to constitute a centre that can hold. Odysseus remains restive. Achilles has thrown in his lot with wretchedness. Still, something new did occur. The period prior to the flowering of classical culture saw the emergence of Athens. It saw the emergence of the *polis*.

The situation in Greece is thus a kind of reversal of the lie of the land in the biblical arena. The emergence of Athens was the decisive event in the former; the destruction of Jerusalem, in the latter. This difference is inseparable from another difference – the crucial one. The biblical context had no problem with value located in the human. That is axiomatic to the Bible *qua* reformed scripture. The problem was to defend the reform. Given what had occurred, the reform, whatever its original inspiration, began to look like Pollyanna-ish dreaming. In the Greek context, where the reform had not occurred, a different problem needed to be confronted. A new value had to be located. That value was the *polis*.

The new focus is thus a move back in the unreformed direction. Just as nature engulfs the individual, so does the *polis*. Both pre-exist and survive the individual's demise. Seeking for something beyond the fleeting existence of the fragile individual, one might easily light upon the sturdier city. The city and the gods are functionally quite similar. The glorification of the city will take the place of the glorification of the gods.

In the coming chapter I shall look at how the dramatists of classical Greece viewed the shift. Their response was critical. They advocated for something very like biblical reform. At any rate, they warned against the tendency to slide back.

The Biblical Log's Jam

The explanation of the movement in Greek culture has a biblical echo. The Greek movement puts the *polis* in the place from which the gods were displaced. In the biblical context the movement to the city is regarded as problematic from the standpoint of God. Prior to discussing the conceptual content of the movement on the biblical side I want to draw attention to a problem of continuity that affects its narrative because the Bible is reformed. The problem arises in the case of the two most prominent city fathers, Cain prior to the Flood, Ham after. This, like the case of mortality, is another case, then, in which the Greek side illuminates the biblical one.

The first mention of the city in the Bible comes with Cain. Agrarian life has replaced the more nomadic shepherding. Cain, that is, has killed Abel. The city is just a stone's throw away:

> Cain knew his wife, and she conceived and bore Enoch; and he built a city, and named it Enoch after his son Enoch. (4:17)

The city, that is, is the product of man. For that reason it is built in the Land of Nod, the Land of Wandering; a place where the distinction between good and bad is blurred. Nod is a geographical version of Achilles's new shield.

Immediately Cain – Citizen Cain, then – leaves the scene, a genealogy is set out. Issue issue, and issue issue, in quick succession: Enoch, Irad, Mehujael, Methushael, Lamech. About Cain's great-great-great-grandson we are given quite a bit of information. Lamech's two wives are named, their sons mentioned and walks of life described. Why the special interest?

Relative to God's plan Lamech is a throwback. He wishes to return to what his great-great-great-grandfather was, an avenger of a slight. Lamech thus exhibits historical amnesia. (Perhaps this is why he is situated so far up the family tree. Cain's son will certainly not have lost touch with the meaning of Cain's experience. *He* will have lived its consequences.) Plainly, on the moral side the Bible sees Lamech as a dinosaur, and warns against looking to him as a model, as a Greek confronting danger might have been encouraged to emulate Achilles or, when in a bind, to look to Odysseus for inspiration. It is fair to issue the warning. Time dulls the memory. But the laughter that the Bible directs at Lamech is malicious and self-serving.

Lamech took two wives (Genesis 4:19). A speech of his, its poetic character typographically marked in our biblical texts, is then reported (23-24):

Lamech said to his wives:
'Adah and Zillah, hear my voice;
you wives of Lamech, listen to what I say:
I have killed a man for wounding me,
a young man for striking me.
If Cain is avenged sevenfold, truly Lamech
seventy-sevenfold.'

Given the heightened diction and the formal tone, it is odd that Lamech delivers the speech to the distaff side. 'To his valet,' says the old saw, 'no man is a hero.' What goes for the batman goes double for the bat-adam. This, at any rate, is the Bible's judgment, presenting to us from Eve on a series of independently minded daughters of men who as often as not take matters in hand when their spouses exhibit (as they frequently do) wavering resolve and limpness of purpose. So it is significant that Lamech clucks his defiance euphuistically before Adah and Zillah. From a Homeric point of view Lamech is a walking oxymoron: a man who affects the hero in the domestic environment, far from the 'war where men win glory' [14:190]. Bombastic fellow that he is, Lamech is just parrotting formulae that have filtered through from afar; perhaps from the mouth of a rhapsode heard declaiming of days of yore when men were men. One imagines his wives sniggering behind his back as he struts about festooned with ribbons and listing under the weight of his decorations. The contrast with Hector's poignant visit home could not be sharper. Here's my sense of an appropriate response from Lamech's reviewing stand.

Seventy-seven fold hero Lamech;
hear *our* voices.
Here's the mop.
Make yourself useful.
And take off that ridiculous helmet. You're scaring the cat.[9]

God had threatened sevenfold punishment in the case of Cain. Lamech arrogates to himself an elevenfold multiplier. Lamech is thus represented as swollen with pride. Also, he grasps wrongly what God had said about the consequences awaiting those who would dare to harm Cain. As Lamech sees him, God after the death of Abel is seething with anger. God is like Achilles after Patroclus is slain, Achilles who in his rage, taking sevenfold revenge and then adding fivefold more to make an even dozen, proceeds to butcher 'twelve brave sons of the proud Trojans' during the funeral games for his friend. Yet God's threat of seven-for-one is not carried out, and the sense of the text is that no such response was literally intended. Consider here *our* schedule of criminal punishments. The very point is for the thought of being punished according to the schedule to work as a deterrent. To have the effect, the costs must seem to would-be perpetrators to outweigh the gains that the contemplated villainy is regarded as promising. That is what God is about. He is trying *to prevent* the Abelites from meting out rough justice to the Cainites. The price to be paid for not restraining themsleves, he is saying, will beggar whatever short-term satisfactions they derive. They will stoke the fires of vengeance. Not that Cain should get off scot-free. Quickly, God offers something else, something unprecedented and in fact epochal in the annals of crime and punishment. God offers what in instituting the Areopagus Athena in Aeschylus's *Oresteia* offers – an objective system of justice interposed between the transgressors and their victims.[10]

From the standpoint of how the Bible sees things, Lamech, we see, is labouring under more than one misunderstanding. The several misunderstandings, as the Bible depicts them, are instructive. But *is* Lamech guilty on all the counts? The city is a late development. In the Greek case, the warrior way precedes it. Whether this is what actually happened is a question for science. Still, an armchair anthropologist would likely excogitate exactly such a scenario. Why then ridicule Lamech? Meeting Ajax, the throwback, in Hades, Odysseus speaks consoling words, gently explaining that there was no alternative.

The problem is that the Bible's world is domesticated, tamed, from the very start. The Bible's world therefore has no place for heroism. So Lamech is treated as less than an anachronism. He is treated as a joke. Be the real-world anthropology as it may, is it not literally true that cities are hacked out of nature through the channelling of force to a constructive purpose and defended against human incursion by the organized use of force? Once the imagery is cashed, is the Greek story of the first city father, Cadmus, who slew the dragon of Ares and sowed its teeth – that is, who ended war and domesticated raw force – not perfectly reasonable? And the reverse movement could occur too. The dragon – shades of Jurassic Park – could stir and come to life again.

What goes for the line of Cain also goes for the line of Noah. When I introduced Lamech, I referred to Ham. Lamech and Ham are counterparts. Cain is the first city father. Ham is the progenitor, after the

Flood, of the chief builder of cities: Nimrod. Ham stands to Noah, then, as Lamech does to Cain. In both cases, the background idea is that the values that motivate men and women at an early stage, values of the kind that inspire the warriors of the *Iliad* to act as they do, are overtaken. The successor values channel the energies to the new, postwar task of city building. One part of this is smooth sailing. If cities are to be built, capacities that are applied in a destructive way, capacities for killing, have to be redirected to taming. The other part is controversial. Prior to being redirected, the powers and capacities are those exploited in the heroic way. The Bible limps a bit here with the two different opinions. Its anthropological story and its cultural one sort poorly. Cain is a farmer. The rise of the city is linked, anthropologically, with settled, agrarian life. That, I mean, is what armchair anthropologists would say. But even though the linkage is smooth sailing, the figure of the hero is still introduced into the biblical story. It is introduced through Lamech, who comes along later than the city. Again, the Bible's point is that Lamech is a throwback. He is not a throwback to the shepherd. He is a throwback to the warrior. Since the text had never dealt with the warrior way – Genesis's story of mankind begins after warriors are already history – this creates an anthropological logjam. A similar point applies in the case of Ham. As Ham's story unfolds, we find among his progeny the major city builder Nimrod. Prior to his acts of urban construction, Nimrod was *not* a farmer. He was 'a mighty hunter before the Lord' (10:9). That the Bible is having a bit of trouble is hinted by what follows immediately: 'a mighty hunter before the Lord; therefore it is said, "Like Nimrod a mighty hunter before the Lord"' (ibid.). The text is quoting some standard epithet. The idea is not coming directly from the quoters.[11] All this we are advantageously placed to understand. The Bible, *qua* reformed, is beyond the heroic. In the heroic system, the centre of value is outside the human. To acknowledge the heroic without changing its human focus, the Bible must as a consequence introduce it later. Lamech is, as a result, a degraded hero.

The Problem of the City on the Side of the Bible

Ham views his father's nakedness and is cursed. '[L]owest of slaves shall he be to his brothers' (9:25). The word 'slave' fires up the imagination. But as the mention of their construction of 'the great city' (10:12) indicates, far from turning up in manacles and leg-irons Ham's progeny emerge in vast urban conglomerations. What then might the malediction mean? Why should Ham's viewing his father's unclothed body have provoked it? Let me take the questions in reverse order.

After the Flood, Noah is the new Adam. From his loins the whole of the human world will spring. To view him naked is, then, to view a basic principle of being. Exposure to the principle has equipped Ham with the wherewithal to become an alternative world-maker, a creative potentiality that his line proceeds to actualize. What he has acquired belongs to the same family as what was not too long ago referred to as 'the secret of the atom,' and even more recently, in the unravelling of DNA and the decoding of the genome, as 'the secret of life.'

Some might regard the knowledge that Ham acquired as a blessing. The Bible does not. The Bible is sponsoring the normative position that C.S. Lewis very pithily expresses in the caution against 'tak[ing] the thread of life out of the hand of Clotho.'[12] Whatever view is endorsed, the curse's content still needs to be explained.

How is city dwelling linked to slavery? There are two sides to this, both elicited only partially in the text. No picture is painted of the offspring of Ham bound and shackled. The enslavement has, that absence correctly suggests, to be construed figuratively.

The intent of the curse is not the grinding subjection that the translation immediately conjures up. The intent is *service*. Ham serves his brethren in the way the waiter ('server') or the butler ('servant') does, or the telephone technician ('serviceman') or gas jockey ('service station attendant'). He is, as we say, *a wage slave*. Ham caters for the needs that arise for his brothers in the new, civilized situation that his line brings about – for blenders, computers, the martini, the Porsche. Ham is Inigo Jones. He is Georges Eugène Haussman. De Lesseps. He is Henry Ford. He is Ray Kroc. Hugo Boss. Ermenegildo Zegna. Stephen Jobs. An illustrious line indeed!

The sense in which Ham is 'lowest' is clear. He works down here, in the human realm. Even vending securities or polishing diamonds atop the loftiest urban tower, he is lowest. The city dweller serves man, not God.

Among the descendants of Ham I listed the entrepreneur who parlayed McDonald's into the largest restaurant chain the world has yet seen. It is consistent with the Bible's wit to observe in this regard that Ham is a burgher. The inclusion of Haussmann, the city planner who laid out Paris, makes for a yet more intricate piece of verbal humour. The very name is an onomastic distillation of the route that the Bible is tracing and morally annotating. 'Georges' speaks of a man of the land, 'Eugène' of an improvement to the species, and 'Haussmann' of a domestic, urban type. 'Georges Eugène Haussmann'? A progressive movement from the land to the town. As it happens, recognition of what is very likely a corruption in the text makes the mention of Haussmann even more fitting. Among the cities listed as the products of Ham is Rehobothir. The word 'rehobothir' means 'city streets.' The original source from which the text derives might have stated that Nimrod, the Hamite who founded Nineveh, was responsible for its urban grid, which, as archaeological reconstructions of relevant Babylonian sites confirm, was impressive. Perhaps a city named 'Streetsville' actually existed. Either way, Nimrod was a Haussmann.

In the preceding sense, the progeny of Ham are cursed. They are cursed in a second sense too. Not only do Canaan & Co. serve others alongside whom they dwell in the city. Also, they are in *servitude* to the city. The structures of the city, that is, play a large role in determining their lives. Think of the night shift. How is it possible to work from midnight to eight, when mammals with perceptual powers like ours get their shut-eye? With its electrically lit climate-controlled buildings, the city eliminates God's distinction between the solar and the lunar dominions. To be sure, this is not necessarily a bad thing. It *is* however a significant change. And (this being the Bible's position) the change, which the city makes possible, is problematic from the standpoint of human flourishing. Bad may preponderate in it over good. The city may lie east of Eden. The song's refrain comes across here as an appropriate Frost Point. 'Working nine-to-five, what a way to make a living.'

Leviathan

On the side of Athens and on the side of Jerusalem too, the city is regarded as problematic. As in the case of the issue of death and mortality, and for the same general reason too, the Greek side here is the more revealing, supplying a diachronic perspective that straddles several cultural ensembles. The Bible does not give much insight into the specifics of political life, both because it does not start with a cultural ensemble like the (pre-political) warrior one, and also because it does not distinguish clearly between family (the children of Israel) and polity (the Israelites). The Greek materials are very articulate here, and very analytical. Let me close with a closer look at the biblical case.

Sodom is the biblical version of the Thebes of the classical Greek tragedians. We shall investigate the dysfunctionality of Thebes in the coming chapter. What problem does the story of Lot identify? The name 'Sodom' suggests sexual depravity. The story does involve the male inhabitants of the city attempting to violate God's messengers, who are gendered as males. But why should the city be especially linked with the mentioned practices? What is that amusing saying about what goes on out back in the Australian outback? 'Where the men are men and the sheep are nervous.' There being no obvious link, let us not bleat the standard homophobic line.

The messengers who come to scope out Sodom have just concluded their visit to Abraham. The visits clearly constitute a doublet. A pair of questions are pertinent to probing the doublet. Why does the Bible bother with Lot? Part of the answer was given in an earlier discussion of uncle and nephew. It is not clear whether cities are acceptable. There is some urgency in knowing, since the times they are a'changing. Abraham, a tent dweller, is far from the city. *Lot* has settled in a city. So why not take a look? The second question is this. What are the relevant differences between the two visits? An answer emerges if we examine how the messengers are hosted in Abraham's tent and in Lot's house.

When the messengers arrive, Abraham (18:6)

> hastened into the tent to Sarah, and said 'Make ready three measures of choice flour, knead it, and make cakes.'

The description is echoed when the messengers arrive at Lot's house (19:3):

> he made them a feast, and baked unleavened bread . . .

The echo is incomplete. In Lot's house, only Lot does the grinding, the kneading, and the baking.

Just as the story of Noah is narrated so that the reader will wonder what becomes of the raven, this episode is formulated to stimulate the question: Where is Lot's wife? Later, as the city is going up in flames, the woman looks over her shoulder and forthwith becomes a pillar of salt. The reader is again provoked to ask: At what is she turning to look? Usually, it is explained that the backwards glance dramatizes an inability to detach from what needs to be left behind – a common enough problem in human affairs. The claim that Lot's wife is too firmly lashed to the mast, and hence goes down with the ship, is certainly part of what the text has in mind. But the answer is less than adequate. For one thing, the Bible does not invariably object to backward movement. The man and the woman get no standing ovation when they leave the Garden. Cain is criticized for moving past the simpler ways of his brethren. The biblical narrative is thickly thematized. Details almost always have a thematic significance. So, for another thing, the answer is too general. The text contains details that it ignores, specifically the detail about Lot's single-handed hospitality.

The text is voluble enough to enable the reader to give a specific answer. Lot's wife does not participate because when the guests arrive she isn't at home. Where is she? Explicitude is unnecessary. Spelling her whereabouts out would even be a negative, for homing in on too narrow a problem. Where *could* she be? She could be daubing numbers at the local bingo hall. Doubtless, to some the razing of a gaming place is ground for lamentation. Different horses, they say, for different courses. The odd sexual encounter apart, the texts we are looking at are rather thin on the need for men and women to have a little fun in life. I dare to say, though, that *this* woman's looking back suggests an extramarital affair – a tryst with a gigolo. The Bible's point, then, is that the family unit is disrupted in the city. Why in the city? It's no mystery. One is confronted in the city, as one is not in the tent, with myriad interpersonal and social options. When one lives cheek-by-jowl with strangers, the number of available permutations and combinations increases exponentially. The homophobic inflexion, I would therefore say, is no more than an especially charged way of making the point about the dissolutive forces of the city upon the nuclear structures that are regarded as central to social stability. 'The modern city . . . is the locus classicus of incompatible realities. Lives that have no business mingling with one another sit side by side on the omnibus. And so long as that's all, they pass in the night, jostling on Tube stations, raising their hats in some hotel corridor, it's not so bad. But if they meet! It's uranium and plutonium, each makes the other decompose, boom.'[13] Homosexuality *per se* is inessential to the story. For conveying the point, a bibulous session of bingo is as appropriate as (though narratively less effective than) an adulterous boink. In fine: men and women, made for falling, are apt in town to fall sooner rather than later.

This again marks the Bible, at least in this phase, as less advanced than the Greek side. The city is recognized to be not like the family. That, however, is seen as a ground for criticism. Which is perhaps not surprising given the tribal experience of the Bible's people.[14]

It is not surprising, then, and it even offers confirmation, that in the sequel of Lot's story God reluctantly accepts Zoar as a new place to settle. What is highly likely in the way of objectionable conduct in impersonal Megalopolis is less likely in Miniapolis. A village, a hamlet, where everybody knows your name, is apt to have a more family-friendly character.

Both on the Greek side and on the biblical one, the advent of the political animal is conceptualized as a problem. The Greek side is much more acute in its delineation of what politics is all about. It is more acute because it starts from a position in which individual life counts for less, and hence is less clear about what in the city constitutes a problem. Those who addressed the new development have much to say that is still worth hearing. But for the Greeks as for those behind the Bible the problem is that the city begins to live a life of its own. The *zoon politikon* becomes the city, rather than the citizen. The city becomes the value that replaces the heaven-high ones that have been superseded. The reforming tendency is nipped in the bud.

10
Love Stories

Founders and Keepers

Imagine that *Macbeth, Hamlet,* and *Lear* were known to us only via allusions and references. Cognizant of Shakespeare's power through *Othello, Romeo and Juliet, The Tempest,* and the rest, we would think ourselves much the poorer for never having laid eyes on Thane, Prince, and King. Just so, a loss is keenly felt at oblivion's having spirited off of all but a handful of the tragedies of Aeschylus, Sophocles, and Euripides.

Of the three hundred plays and more that the classical trinity authored, about a tenth grace our shelves. Among the survivors (most of which belong to the tragic genre) the largest proportion, a substantial ratio, addresses the situation of men and women newly installed as political actors in the new world of political action. Some tackle difficulties that had been confronted as the *polis* took shape. Others look at problems found to affect the conduct of city life. Yet others flag dangers to political existence, including the danger of backsliding, that the authors regarded as probable and/or thought worth warning against.

While we know of the writings of many of Plato's reflective contemporaries only by hearsay, his have come down to us intact because formative Christianity found the cosmology of Neoplatonism, taken symbolically, receptive to its miraculous history. Could it be that the fifth century BCE dramas in our possession made it through the gauntlet of years specifically because of a later interest in their political content? We have no basis for such a judgment. What the historical record reveals about the civic role of the classical theatre independently suggests a contemporary preoccupation with the *polis.* Whether or not the remnants are fully representative of the bolt, this much is still true. In applying themselves to the new mode of communal existence, the playwrights were picking up, culturally and conceptually, where Homer had left off. Let's go back to *their* starting point in this regard and proceed from there.

In the *Bacchae,* Euripides hitches a ride on the myth of the founding of Thebes, the venue of (and even indeed a sort of character in) many of the tragic plays.[1] The myth, featuring Cadmus as founder, reveals much about the nature of the city, that is, the nature of political life. Relevantly to present interests, the myth's conceptual content is encoded in the following telegram about the first political king in Greece: *Cadmus slew the dragon and sowed its teeth, which sprung up as armed men.*

Mythologese translates easily into Vernacular. The dragon is not just one more fearsome monster from the mythological bestiary, selected at random for valiant Cadmus to ride out and lance. It is the Dragon of Ares, the god of war. For life at peace to begin, the dragon must be brought down.

So much for Cadmus the saurian slayer. What about Cadmus the DDS? Decoding the image of pulling teeth is also not like pulling teeth. Unless they hit the road as adventurers or vagabonds or head for their correlate of Appalachia, once peace breaks out demobilized warriors must turn into law-abiding citizens. The operative terms here are 'turn into' and 'law-abiding.' War is conflict between various groups. War is *violent* conflict, unnatural death, a normal outcome. The city comprises a single group, a community of men and women living at peace, but whose members frequently enough quarrel over this and that. To prevent the friction of the constant shoulder rubbing from igniting war-like kindling, the city requires a fire department. That is what the sowing of the teeth symbolizes. The sown men – cultivated parts of the dragon – symbolize the institutions and functionaries of internal peace-keeping and peace-making: police, courts, prisons, and so forth. Jesse 'The Body' Ventura becomes Governor of Minnesota. The Terminator, Arnold Schwarzenegger, takes the helm in California.

Genesis's treatment of the origin of the city parallels the myth of Cadmus.[2] An act of violence lies behind the creation, as the Bible tells it, of the first such habitation. Also, the divine intervention after Cain's fratricide is a proto-police action – Cain's mugshot is taken and posted throughout the territory – to deter the victims (in this case the party of Abel) from administering rough justice against their malefactors. In the Bible's story, God is cast as the sown man of the piece.[3]

As treatments of the advent of the city, the story of Cain and the myth of Cadmus are Buda and Pest. In the representation of Cadmus as *sowing* the dragon's teeth is dimly discernible the linkage of farming with the city that is at the very centre of the biblical story.[4] And Cain's fratricide faintly echoes the blood-spilling violence of the reptile. As for the second, the post-deluvian, biblical story of city founding, we find more of the same. Though he is spliced into the action anachronistically, that is, later than sheepdogs and oxen, *qua* mighty hunter Nimrod, who *mutatis mutandis* reprises the part of Cain,[5] specializes in the very sort of activity an exercise of which gives Cadmus his mythic significance.

At what Genesis (4:17) says about the birth of the city we have already looked:

> Cain knew his wife, and she conceived and bore Enoch; and he built a city, and named it Enoch after his son Enoch.

Cain and Abel are the issue of Adam. Enoch comes from the seed of Cain. The city, Enoch, originates in the intensive working of the ground. Settled life supplants the nomadic way of gatherer and herder; the city springs up only when the farmer puts down roots.

In Hebrew, 'Enoch' is the same series of letters as 'education.' 'Enoch' belongs then to the Thesaurian entry that includes 'culture.'[6] In effect, Cain's city is called 'Cultured Place,' aptly so given that Cain works the cultivator. True, norms and standards apply on the Trojan battlefield too. The battlefield is not Raven's Land, where the only surprises are statistical. Nonetheless, the differential application of 'culture' to the city makes good sense. The salient feature of this culture, political culture, and the main reason for restricting 'civilized' to it, is that men and women, as a condition of living together in the distinctively political way, arrogate the exclusive use of coercive force against any of their number to the institutions mentioned earlier. Unlike their erstwhile selves, they do not take matters into their own hands.

Three Features

Another Greek political myth, one that addresses the city as a going concern, has at its centre the as-yet-unincorporated settlement in Attica that eventually rose to world-historical prominence. The myth, which invites the title 'How Athens Got Its Name,' was set out in chapter 8. In the following respect, the myth corresponds in content to the story of

Cain, in which a name giving to an urban newborn also figures. 'Enoch' means 'civilized.' Just so, Greek lore associates Athena with the termination of strife, and hence links to the same idea of being civilized.

The myth is revealing both about how the inhabitants of the *polis,* Athens especially, view their life's locale, and also about their self-image as inhabitants. Revealed are the constitutive norms of the characteristically political form of communal existence, as distinct, say, from monastic existence, or domestic life, or cohabitation in a frat house.

The myth's thematically active features are three. Athena *asks* for entry. Athena asks for entry *from the citizenry*. Athena asks for entry from the citizenry *on the basis of something useful to the city dwellers.*

Athena *asks* for entry.[7] In a reversal of the intervention at the start of the *Iliad,* Athena tugs her own forelock. Judging from the epic, it's entirely out of character for a god to supplicate. In this case the bowing and scraping makes sense. The *polis* is carved out of and cut off from nature. Human hands do the cutting and carving. This is not to deny that the gods sometimes enter man's estate uninvited. Just ask the inhabitants of Banda Aceh and New Orleans, to both of which Poseidon recently paid an unwelcome visit.[8] Certainly, the gods can wreak havoc in the city. The point is that the gods have to be naturalized as a condition of taking up residence. As soon as they gain admittance, they are served a restraining order: they must trickle in conduits and pipes, flow through vents and ducts, and cycle along conductive wires, taking their marching orders from the civil engineers. The prohibition is clear: 'No wild behaviour tolerated.' A far cry, this, from being given the keys to the city.[9]

Athena asks for entry *from the citizenry*. No one of them can decide whether to lower the drawbridge and raise the portcullis or to lower the portcullis and raise the bridge. The city is configured neither as a collective with a natural hierarchical character like a family, nor as a structure like an army or corporation that typically involves a non-natural pyramid. Each of the city-dwellers has a say.

Athena asks for entry *on the basis of something useful to the city dwellers.* Neither Athena nor Poseidon offers transcendence of mortal troubles. Nor are the gifts just ornaments or baubles, bribes designed to romance the citizenry into declaring him or her the fairest. It's vegetable oil and washing liquid. Had *he* been a candidate, Zeus might have offered lightning in a bottle: the incandescent bulb.

The three features lie perfectly along the arc of our discussion. To live among the gods is to live in the field of 'Life = War.' The city is beyond the equation's range. To live where the two sides balance is to live in a way that, in contrast to the way of the gods, is not self-absorbed. The actors must take account of one another other than as means to achieve their (selfish) ends. And the city, *qua* outside of nature, tames the natural elements.

Egalitarianism

The features I describe as 'defining characteristics' and 'constitutive norms.' So much of what we call politics being non-egalitarian, one might query the *bona fides* of the second of the three.

At the time of the flowering of drama and art and architecture, Athens was, or at any rate was well on the way to being, democratic. Here's a Western Union of what transpired.

After several decades of coups and depositions, Cleisthenes, as the fifth century wound down, implemented reforms to dissolve the faction that had made Athenian life so turbulent since Pisistratus's day. Not that Pisistratus, a three-time tyrant, played an entirely negative role in the formation of the Attic city that is for us the emblem of ancient Greece. Though Pisistratus drew his power from his own people, the Hill people, favouring them over the people of the Plain and the people of the Shore, a larger, pan-Hellenic, vision informed the mandate that he took upon himself to carry out. Pisistratus began to raise his country town to the central position on the national and international stages that it would before very long occupy. The cultural happenings that became so important to Athens, the Dionysia and the Panathenaic Festival, trace back to Pisistratus's reorganization of what must have been freelance expressive enterprises. The first city-sponsored tragic contest was staged during the last phase of his rule – in 534 BCE. Such nonpartisanship as Pisistratus imposed and maintained by his personal force Cleisthenes institutionalized, laying a groundwork of structure and practice sturdy enough to withstand the dissolutive effects of special interests even during times when no strong hand gripped the levers of control.

H.D.F. Kitto capsules Cleisthenes's politicking. 'Cleisthenes,' Kitto writes, presenting to us a man who could have taught Elbridge Gerry a thing or two,[10]

> dealt with th[e] danger [of powerful noble families pursuing their partisan interests] by inventing a preposterous paper-constitution which in

> fact worked perfectly. He created ten brand-new 'tribes' – all provided with ancestors – each composed of a roughly equal number of 'demes' (or 'parishes'), but not contiguous: that was the whole point. Cleisthenes divided Attica roughly into three areas: city, inland, coast: each of these new 'tribes' contained 'parishes' from each of these three divisions: each therefore was a cross-section of the whole population, and when it met to conduct its business its natural meeting-place was Athens – which of itself helped to unite the polis. Then since each tribe would contain farmers and hill-men, artisans and traders from Athens and the Piraeus, and men who lived in boats, local and family loyalties could do little in the election of archons: they could find expression only in the open Assembly, where they could be recognised for what they were.

The fact that the 'preposterous' arrangement 'worked perfectly' attests a *ravenous* appetite for radical change in civic affairs. Cleisthenes would otherwise have had insurrection on his hands.

The democratic form thereof is a *rara avis* in the *terra* of governance. Putting into practice a broadly based management of communal affairs, the Athenians, surveying the years of turmoil, might easily have felt as we do when having thitherto thought of gravitational attraction in terms of bedsprings we come to see the matter on the model of the rubber sheet. Having up to then transposed structures that they knew – the family, the fighting force – onto the city, they might have emitted a collective 'Eureka,' pluming themselves for at long last actualizing the true potential of postwar communal existence. Can equality be defended as a political norm? As the case may be, it is not therefore surprising that the tragic plays, which belong to Athens as musical comedy does to New York, explore problems that arise from pressure on the egalitarianism that, in the playwrights' own experience, strikingly informs their politics. Sometimes the problem has to do with imbalances that remain, or are perceived to remain, in the new mode of life. For Euripides, who often comes across like a lobbyist from the women's quarters, gender inequality is a standing preoccupation. Sometimes, the pressure against equality exerted from a totalitarian direction is explored. That is what we have in *Antigone*.

'Totalitarian' is not self-explanatory. Once the term's meaning in the context of the drama is figured out, the deeper significance of the egalitarian element will emerge. Relevantly to the normative status of equality, it will emerge that it's as much a general question about human nature as it is a political question about how to arrange communal lives.

Pluralism or Individualism?

The *Iliad* goes beyond depicting the horrors of martial conflict. In the sense of 'philosophy' explained in chapter 6, Homer's poem is philosophical. The same goes for Sophocles's Theban dramas, on which I focus my discussion of the theatre of politics. In *Antigone,* which the present chapter will put under the microscope, Sophocles transcends reflective normative politics and descends into the depths of anthropological ontology.

Two issues of totalitarianism may be distinguished. One is axiological: How many basic values are there? Here, totalitarianism stands opposed to pluralism. The totalitarian is a value-monist. The other issue is ontological: What is the basic unit of action? Here, totalitarianism faces off against individualism. The totalitarian is a collectivist. In *Antigone,* Sophocles, in my view, is primarily concerned with the latter.[11]

Plotwise, Sophocles's story locks two characters in a dispute to the death about values, duties, and actions. Creon, king of Thebes, bans the burial of Polynices. A traitor to the city, Creon insists, cannot be so honoured. Antigone maintains that she is obliged to administer the rites: Polynices was her brother, and a person's political misbehaviour, even serious misbehaviour as in this case, does not dilute his or her blood ties. The stage at the end is strewn with corpses. Walled up in a tomb for having sprinkled earth on Polynices's body, Antigone hangs herself. Dead too, in both cases also by their own hands, are Creon's son Haemon and his wife Eurydice. Yet while Sophocles slants our sympathies towards Antigone, he does strive for a bit of balance. Creon is stubborn. Antigone too wants no compromises. This is not, then, a conflict of strong-willed individuals who may be more or less appealing. The immovable object and the irresistible force each represent something deeper.

The bulk of interpreters say that Antigone advocates for family values. A sizeable minority see her as religiously motivated. In point of fact, the text can be called as a witness for both sides. Rationalizing her course of action, Antigone asserts not only that Polynices is kin [55, 581] but also that the gods want the same rites for all the dead [88, 504]. Since a clear choice between the familial and the devotional would not have affected what interpreters of the two persuasions understand to be the play's major conflict, it has to seem to them a blot on Sophocles's artistry that the wobble is not eliminated. This difficulty (a difficulty for those who see *Antigone* as arguing the pluralist case) is only compounded once it is observed that though Antigone offers both reasons for her deed, she hedges the second – no one, she asserts, knows what the gods want ('who on earth can say . . .?' [586]) – and contradicts the first. She states [995–1004]:

> Never, I tell you.
> if I had been the mother of children
> or if my husband died, exposed and rotting –
> I'd never have taken this ordeal upon myself,
> never defied our people's will. What law,
> you ask, do I satisfy with what I say?
> A husband dead, there might have been another.
> A child by another too, if I had lost the first.
> But mother and father both lost in the halls of Death,
> no brother could ever spring to light again.

How do these words square with the claim that Polynices must be buried because his blood is œ-type?

The baffling speech is a scholarly crux. It would not be an exaggeration to say that interpreters, in their dealings with the speech, show their interpretive colours. On the speech I, too, will plant my standard.

To sharpen our sense of intractability, consider Jean-Pierre Vernant's construal of the play's major conflict:[12]

> The conflict between Antigone and Creon . . . is not an opposition between pure religion, represented by [Antigone], and total irreligion, represented by Creon, or between a religious spirit and a political one. Rather, it is between two different types of religious feeling: One is a family religion, purely private and confined to a small circle of close relatives . . . centered around the domestic hearth and the cult of the dead; the other is a public religion in which the tutelary gods of the city eventually become confused with the supreme value of the State.

If Sophocles were exploring this conflict, it's hard to see why *Creon's* stand should not be approved. Given the losses that she has suffered, Antigone, one expects, is dressed in weeds. Are we to believe her to be a Theban Goth, black the normal habit? Well, that is Vernant's position. But the position – Sophocles is advocating for the cult of the dead[13] – must confront more than my incredulity. Vernant's distinction between varieties of religious belief is supposed to de-baffle Antigone's speech. It does nothing of the kind. A religion 'centered around the domestic hearth' that distinguishes a brother from a child is, I daresay, a religion not readily comprehended. More furrows assail the brow if it is added that such a creed rates the child below the sibling. As lately observed, Antigone in any case raises a general epistemological doubt about religion.

Hard-pressed to come up with a reading that does not treat the words on the page as apparatus for a trapeze act, quite a few interpreters opine that the text as we have it is corrupt, the speech spurious. Others, wary of grasping *this* nettle, contend (what comes at the end of the day to much the same) that Sophocles is not in complete control.

Taking the text as it certainly seems to come, Knox, who proposes to preserve the play *and* to defend the playwright, opens by declaring that Antigone advocates for family values. 'In all her arguments [Antigone] speaks . . . as if no unit larger than the family existed' (44). But no sooner does Knox reach the problematic speech – 'a spectacular betrayal of that fanatical loyalty to blood relationship' (46) – than he does a shuffle. Signalizing an allusion to 'the tormented . . . crimes of the house of Oedipus' (48), he now avers that Antigone stands for 'one particular family, her own, the doomed, incestuous, accursed house of Oedipus' (49).

On this reading, when Antigone speaks of the duty to bury her brother, 'brother' does *not* mean just 'male blood relation with same parents.' When she says [520–522]

> if I had allowed
> my own mother's son to rot, an unburied corpse –
> that would have been an agony!

we are not to infer that she is acting on the principle that would require any child to administer the final rites to the mother's other offspring. The ability thus gained to take what comes from her mouth straight comes at a high cost. To follow Knox is to commit to swallowing whole Antigone's claim that had Oedipus and Jocasta still been alive she would have consigned Polynices's body to the vultures. This is exactly like saying that only a father with two faithless daughters and a dutiful Cordelia could learn from *King Lear*. Could the message in *Antigone*'s case depend to that extent on the protagonist's family particulars, as if Sophocles were an early incarnation of Jerry Springer? 'Women who love the men who kill their husbands.' In the event, Knox's last word is a betrayal of his oath of interpretive loyalty to Antigone's specific situation. 'Antigone discovers that her deepest motives were purely personal' (ibid.). 'Personal' here means 'to herself,' not 'to her own (peculiar, monstrous and doomed) family.'

Though Knox's reading is unsatisfactory, the idea of a purely personal commitment does link with the play's opposition to totalitarianism. For the unit of opposition to the totality is the individual person. I shall take up the matter two sections hence. More immediately instructive, albeit in a negative way, are a couple of questionable features of Knox's approach. Both a problem of commission and a problem of omission are present.

The classical playwrights always draw their story lines and characters from bygone lore. The instructions for submissions to the competitive festivals must have run something like this. 'Take a traditional tale or myth, make an extract, toss Tiresias into the plot, season to contemporary taste, bring to the boil.' As the recipe also indicates, the dramatists use the story lines and characters for their present-centred purposes, as Shakespeare uses English history for his. They *recycle* what the tradition entails. Knox's assumption that the myth of Oedipus, in its original form, is thematically significant to *Antigone* is therefore hard to grant. Anyway, Knox obviously has Sophocles's *Oedipus the King* in mind. But this *isn't* the original myth. It is a Sophoclean reworking.[14] Given how the playwrights were constrained, it follows that an interpreter has to justify the interpretive use of an inherited story. To do that, he or she must first say what the story means. To even the most cursory peruser of the scholarly literature, it quickly becomes plain that the myth of Oedipus isn't anywhere near as plain as 'Cadmus and the Dragon.'[15] It is quite within the bounds of possibility that some intellectual types in Athens lamented Cleisthenes's disruption of the patrician families; though this is more in the spirit of a Burkean like Pindar than even of Aeschylus, who is closer to the scene of reformist action than Sophocles, and farther from the post-reform Pericles, with whom Sophocles was on friendly terms. There might be a point to likening those families to the family of Oedipus, which lost its control, though what the incest and the fatedness could have to do with current affairs is anyone's guess. There might be a point. To determine whether there *is* a point, the interpreter has however to interpret the myth. Knox fills his mouth with water. In any event, isn't the myth of Cadmus more prominent in the play than the myth of Oedipus? Why not use *that* myth to interpret the play? It would not be at all unreasonable to see

Antigone, in sprinkling earth on Polynices, as implanting what Creon regards as a carious fang. Certainly, Creon is convinced that the infection of sedition will spread unless scavengers carry the traitor off. Since the tragedians drew so heavily on Homer, why not contrast Creon with Achilles? The one refuses the foe's burial by a sister until it's too late. The other undergoes a change of heart and permits the interment to ease a father's pain.

The last point but one locates the problem of omission. Knox pays scant attention to the character of Creon's city. Witness the credibility-defying leap from (in effect) 'Antigone opposes Creon' to '*Antigone* is critical of democratic Athens.' May Antigone not be giving defensive expression to some feature of Athenian political life that makes good a problem affecting Creon's *very undemocratic* Thebes? Isn't the presumptively proper move from 'Creon objects to what Antigone does' to '*Antigone* rebuts Creon's objections'? As I observed, like Sodom in the Bible Thebes in Greek drama is a dysfunctional place, a place from which one learns by negative example.[16]

Creon and Antigone do not contrast as a person who sees the city as paramount and a person who regards a non-civic obligation as categorically imperative. A person filling either of these bills would normally be aware that diverse duties exist; and aware, consequently, of the need to compromise and/or accommodate. But I anticipate full agreement that the following imaginary speeches, which would under the circumstances make excellent sense, jar with the spirit of the play. Creon: 'I grant that because Polynices is your brother you have a duty to perform the obsequies. Don't forget that he is a nephew of mine too. Just try to understand my position.' Antigone: 'I grant that Polynices was a traitor. However, as you say, he's my brother. As you also say, he is your sister's son too. Avert your gaze and I will sprinkle earth on him quietly, with no fanfare. My conscience will give me no peace otherwise. Yours might also before too long torment you too.'

The Dragon of Peace

A threat to the city, *qua* place in which men and women are for the first time able to live their lives with the reasonable expectation that they will expire of old age, is no laughing matter. We surround our cities with dikes to divert the flow of rising rivers and criss-cross them with storm sewers so that the buildings will not be swamped by run-off. Against extremes of temperature we insulate. Lightning rods stand at attention on our roofs as safeguards against the fate of Semele. We keep Zeus and Boreas and Poseidon out or at bay.

In the Ode to Man (as it is called), the chorus sings of the mastery that men and women have achieved over nature [382–385]:

> . . . the oldest of the gods [sc., Gaia] he wears away –
> the Earth, the immortal, the inexhaustible –
> as his plows go back and forth, year in, year out
> with the breed of stallions turning up the furrows.

One line distils the point [391]: '[Man] conquers all, taming with his techniques.'

Though all this, albeit somewhat hyperbolic, is true, it is irrelevant. *Walls* encircle the Thebes of Antigone. Walls are not dikes; Polynices is not Poseidon. The walls are to repulse human attack. Before us is a contest of (political) succession and legitimacy. Moreover, the son of Oedipus has a claim on the crown of Thebes. Does anyone doubt that Polynices would have been better contented had Creon stolen under cover of darkness out of Dodge? Certainly, had Polynices succeeded by force of arms, he would not have proceeded to reduce Thebes to rubble.

The chorus, earlier on, had made mention of the Dragon of Ares [138, 154]. The action of the drama occurs, however, more than four generations beyond Cadmus. The threat that has been repulsed in this instance is a straight political threat. Clausewitz's slogan, as I have taken it, applies. Polynices does not, that is, threaten a return to a world in which Life = War.

Failure to distinguish natural and political threat can easily cause havoc in thinking about the city. The story of the boy with his finger in the dike is just a story. Protecting the city against the forces of nature necessitates a communal effort – the sort required to construct the dike in the first place. Also, since nature never goes fishing and since the exterminating angel is always trolling, the defence of the city against flood and pestilence necessitates ceaseless vigilance. But political threat is different. The internal arrangements in the city are designed to adjust the relations between individuals in a manner satisfactory to all concerned. They are designed to obviate the need to remain on the alert about what those whom we meet might do. '[T]he ship of state,' Creon declares [180], mixing up the two, 'is safe.' He speaks (ibid.) of '[t]he gods who rocked her.' Thebes was not threatened by natural seas. The gods did not rock her. Distinctively human forces rocked her.

What is true of the city in face of nature is not the same as what is true of the city in face of human threat. Creon's Thebes is improperly conceptualized. Creon's Thebes is like the Sphinx that had prevented Thebes from flourishing until Oedipus solved its riddle. It is an assemblage of different ways of thinking that should be kept apart. Creon, that is, is himself of the breed of the Sphinx, preventing the state from flourishing.

Previously, war was the harrow that raked the world. A juggernaut of peace now rolls over the terrain: Creon's tyrannical *polis*. The one threatens everyone. The other threatens its own.

The broad point here has been prepared for in the preceding chapter. The shift from the *terminus a quo*, the warrior view, to the *terminus ad quem*, the human one, does not go smoothly. The god-sized values attached to the extra-human come to be annexed to the city. God-sized values. The idea is resonant.

The Speech

Antigone does not just set the city as the paramount value against the individual. If that were the point of opposition, the two main characters could, grudgingly, agree to disagree. The contrast, a deeper one, is between the submersion of the individual and the autonomy of the individual. This is first and foremost an issue of ontology, not an axiological one. And (as we shall see) it affects the language, so that the two main characters, though vocalizing the same words, are saying different things. To accept the individual is not *ipso facto* to grant that any value attaches to the individual. That's a separate matter. Not to recognize that the individual exists is however to foreclose on the very possibility of value's reposing there. We are looking, then, at what philosophers call a *presupposition* of a certain way of thinking and acting, an underlying condition the satisfaction of which makes that way of thinking and acting possible.

Creon exaggerates. He does not, I stress, exaggerate in his own terms. With regard to those terms he is perfectly consistent. Rather, he exaggerates from the standpoint of what the play presents as the truth. In order to determine what Creon's terms are, let's look at what he says.

When Ismene stresses that Antigone is Haemon's betrothed – 'What? You'd kill your own son's bride?' [641] – Creon responds that his son could take another wife. 'Absolutely: there are other fields for him to plow' [642]. Confronted with Haemon's reservations about the edict, Creon responds. 'Don't flatter me with Father – you woman's slave' [848]. 'For speaking against me,' he is saying, 'you are no son of mine.'

Up until the last two lines of her speech Antigone agrees with Creon. Yes, says Antigone, a replacement spouse is possible. 'A husband dead, there might have been another.' Yes, she proceeds, echoing Creon once more, another child is possible. 'A child by another too, if I had lost the first.' Then, without missing a beat, she denies, what Creon certainly would not deny, that there could be another brother. '[N]o brother could ever spring to light again.' It is more than just presumptively reasonable to see the playwright as intending the theatregoer to attend to the partial overlap. Once we register the echo the specifics of Oedipus's family situation drop out as thematically otiose. Antigone is making a claim about what is replaceable and what isn't.[17] There is, she is saying, an important distinction between the two. She is using her own family tree to make that distinction. But the distinction itself, not the biological unit, is what matters.

Before taking up the business of the replaceable and the irreplaceable, let me rehearse the meta-dramatic issue. Assuming the genuineness of Antigone's speech, is Sophocles in complete control?

Sophocles formulates the case in terms of brothers and husbands and parents and children. That he would do so when he has something non-familial in mind suggests an infirm grip. And that, if we follow Knox, is the conclusion to which we are driven. The highlighting in preceding paragraphs puts me in a position to get the playwright whose work is considered the pinnacle of Greek tragedy off the hook. Creon speaks in terms of the family – wives, sons, mothers. The dramatic axis of the play being the clash between Antigone and Creon, Sophocles has a strong artistic reason for giving Antigone the same vocabulary. I would not say that Creon's claims are more baffling than Antigone's. But I would say that they aren't less baffling. *And Creon's claims precede Antigone's!* Again, it is presumptively reasonable to assume that in order to understand Antigone's speech one must pay concerted attention to what Creon says and to how he says it. After developing a biblical parallel to clarify Creon's words, I will offer another reason why Sophocles writes as he does, one that enables us to respond to the question about control with a virtually unqualified affirmative.

Creon's words are, I said, not less baffling than Antigone's. This is a minority view. Most interpreters, seeing Creon as a hothead, find his speeches easy sledding. By formulating the conciliatory speeches two sections back, I took steps to illustrate that approaching Creon in this way rings false. The approach implies that Creon knew the truth all along, only, from apoplexy at being defied, lost perspective. I will now furnish the wherewithal for interpreting Creon in a fashion that preserves the dialectic link between his claims and Antigone's speech. This will elicit what position Antigone represents.

Genesis 2

Antigone and Creon, exchanging words, speak past each other. Theirs is a (futile) conversation between an imaginary Thebes and a real, though idealized Athens, two places that, conceptually speaking, are not commensurate. What do Jerusalem and Athens have to say to each other about this matter? A reciprocally revealing parallel exists between Sophocles's play and the anthropogenic phase of the Bible. The relevant material, on the biblical side, is found in the second creation story – the story of Adam and Eve. The relevant material is the whole of Genesis 2,[18] and the opening of Genesis 3 up to the transgression. For ease of reference, I will speak of this expanse of text as 'Genesis 2.'

From a conceptual point of view the world described in Genesis 2 is a fascinating place. In more than just a physical sense it falls between the world of Genesis 1 and the world of Genesis 3. Genesis 2 is where, so to speak, the particular (the unit of action) emerges from the individual. That I maintain is what *Antigone* is about. What Antigone does in the play is Sophocles's dramatization of the emergence of the agent. It's a version, then, transposed into the political context, of the emergence of the first man and the first woman into (what the Bible figures as) their full role in the world. I observed in passing that *Antigone* is dense with death. Antigone's transgression brings about her death. Her death is the first of a series within the play. Haemon is the next domino to fall. Eurydice follows. Death, too, has a major role in the move beyond Genesis 2. The links, we shall see, are deep-going.[19]

In Genesis 1 a single word of evaluation is used: 'good.' Whatever God sees is so characterized. The negative counterpart 'bad' is first encountered in verse 9 of Genesis 2, where the tree of knowledge is spoken of. Although it is mentioned in Genesis 2, 'bad' does not however come into play until Genesis 3.[20]

Bad is present as a possibility in Genesis 2. What is the relevant difference from Genesis 1, where it's all good? Genesis 1 tells a story that is (more) consistent with Darwin. The creative activity, for instance, concerns species, not individual things. That, in part, explains Genesis 1's monopolarity of value: in Raven's Land, there is no bad. Not until Genesis 2 does the narrative give us individuals. The individuals God creates are two: the man and the woman.

Genesis 1 operates on the level of the species. The species to which we belong is brought into being along with the various other species, the only major difference being ordinal. By contrast, Genesis 2 speaks of the creation not of mankind but of an individual man and an individual woman. It speaks in this way of no other creature. The human population of Genesis 2 consists of one man and one woman. So the difference is cardinal. What is the status of the man and the woman prior to their 'good till'-date, the date of the transgression, and what is their status after they disobey the edict concerning the tree of knowledge? Dealing earlier with the transition I said that in the course of it the two lose their innocence. The move from a juvenile to an adult understanding is a dramatic change. It is however a change in the head – a psychological change. I will now extract from the transition a shift of being – a change in the world. The transgression is, I will show, linked to the man's and the woman's coming to be mortal, not just to their dawning awareness that an appointment with the reaper is indelibly inscribed in their diary. Something similar, we will then see, is dramatized in *Antigone*.

The Genesis 2 narrative presents us with an individual man and an individual woman. More than the members of the species of Genesis 1, they are less than the particulars of Genesis 3, whose days in Eden are numbered. The ontological status of the pair in Genesis 2 is, we may say, not clear. Playing on Hamlet, one might characterize them as being, *vis-à-vis* us, less than kin but more than kind. Creon's Thebes is a political version of Genesis 2, conceived as a very tight extension of Genesis 1. (The large arc of our discussion has prepared the ground for the linkage of Thebes and Eden. The Garden is hacked out of chaos. The city is hacked out of War.) Antigone's transgression is like the transgression that occurs at the very end of Genesis 2. The Bible, by mentioning 'bad' in Genesis 2 without applying it to anything, signals that Genesis 2 is only a temporary stop for men and women. Just so, Sophocles is opposing the arrangement in Creon's Thebes, which freezes the development at a stage comparable to Genesis 2. The Bible is in effect written from the standpoint of Genesis 3 as normative; the political thinking of Greece, if Creon is taken as its mouthpiece, is written from the standpoint of Genesis 1 as normative. Creon's transformation amounts to his being brought into coincidence with the biblical God who, after the transgression, 'made garments of skins for the man and for his wife, and clothed them' (Genesis 3:21).

We do not think of animals as we think of ourselves. Animals we think of as, primarily, members of species. With one salient exception, we think of them along the lines of Genesis 1, not of Genesis 2. To see that this is so, and to grasp what it means, consider the following.

Some years back, the bison herd of Wood Buffalo National Park, a protected natural habitat straddling the border between the Canadian province of Alberta and the Northwest Territories, was perceived to be under pressure. For the health of the herd, the wildlife ecologists determined, a reduction of the numbers was indicated. Park rangers, equipped with high-powered rifles, culled 30 per cent of the animals.

Imagine, by parity, recommending a cull of 30 per cent of the men and women in the Indian state of Uttar Pradesh on the grounds that the thinning would benefit the population. Arguably, the human numbers on earth are excessive. Yet before seriously considering such a policy for the planet, we would first entertain the idea of colonizing Mars.

The arithmetic of men and women differs from that of subhuman animals. Subhuman animals we think of in terms of the group or species. For men and women, the particulars count. So animals are replaceable.[21]

One salient exception exists to our thinking of animals in group terms. But it is clear from our overall practice that the way we think about our pets is a borrowed way. In regard to pets – sometimes in regard to domestic animals, if but a few are scratching around the yard or browsing in the nearby field – our thinking is driven by sentiment, as is a child's in regard to a stuffed teddy. To them we extend what applies primarily to ourselves. When the beloved Spot dies, the owners often enough go out and get another dog. Often enough to be revealing about what is happening here, one of the same breed is sought. Not infrequently, the name of the first one is reused. The death of a child is nothing like that. The reuse of the name of the deceased for another child within the same family would be unusual. Many would regard it as heartless – as an attempt to pretend that the first did not die or that nothing happened. In the case of pets, in short, the individuals are treated, albeit only up to a point, as particulars.

Speaking of names, it is useful here to observe that we name our pets, though they are no different from animals to which we do not attach nominal handles unless they happen to be found in a zoo. Note that Eve does not get a name until she leaves the Garden. Afterwards, the text resembles the Doomsday Book.

In Genesis 2, what is the status of the man and the woman? Though, unlike the men and women of Genesis 1, they are individuals, that, we now see, does not quite mean that we are beyond Genesis 1. For pets and domestic animals, though no different from the creatures of Genesis 1, are thought of as individuals. If we look at how the man and the woman are described in Genesis 2, we find that they are pretty much the same as domesticated animals. They have a job to do; and they live with God in God's domain: the garden that is, presumably, attached to God's abode. They are tended to and given instructions. So long as they do their job of keeping and tilling, the word 'good' applies. The man and the woman prior to the transgression, then, are particulars only in a secondary sense.

We need a little philosophy here, to clarify the distinctions. To that end, let's take a stroll down by the riverside.

Meet Eddy Rivers

One expects that the sole difference between men and women and subhuman animals is not that we think of the latter alone on the level of the species. The species, after all, is a collection of individuals. One expects that the fact that we think about subhuman things in species terms has an anchorage in some difference between this individual bear, say, and this individual person. To say what the difference is, let me shift from the species/particular contrast to the contrast between modes and substances.

Both modes and substances are individuals, but only substances are particulars. Think of an eddy in a river. Eddies are not things in their own right. They are, rather, characteristic dispositions of moving water. Yet one can certainly identify eddies, and reidentify them over time. The weather turns cold. The river freezes. After the thaw, you return to the banks where you skipped stones the summer previous: 'There's that eddy again,' you quite naturally say. Choosing a name that goes with the flow, let us baptize what is referred to by the demonstrative phrase 'that eddy.' Using the proper name, you could have said: 'There's Eddy again.' Eddies, then, are individuals. ('Eddies,' in the preceding sentence, is a plural common noun.) But eddies, though quite capable of being treated as individuals, are not particulars. They are, that is, modes. When the rock is removed from the current (the channel, say, is dredged), the eddy is no more. But it has not in any sense ceased to be. There is just a different arrangement of water and solids. In effect, 'Eddy is no more' means 'The waters are flowing in a different way.' It means: 'The waters are no longer swirling in that characteristic manner.'

The discussion of several early chapters defended the view that, so far as (subhuman) life is concerned, the Bible can adapt to Darwin. The discussion of the dominion assigned differentially to men and women in Genesis 1 made out that the subhuman realm has an organic, system-like character. Transposed into the terms we are here using, the position is that subhuman individuals are modes. The primary unit is nature as a whole. If we think along these lines, the Genesis 1 use of 'good' as the sole evaluative term makes good sense. Such are the happenings in the (subhuman) world that nothing is bad. All we have are exchanges of matter and energy: intra-systemic changes.

Men and women in Creon's Thebes are treated along the lines of Eddy. Like swirls of water in a river, they are thought of from the standpoint of the whole in which they are located. To be sure, men and women are individuals. But so are domestic animals. Eddy too is an individual, a non-particular individual. In Creon's Thebes, Polynices is treated, like Eddy, or like a domestic animal, as a non-particular individual. Antigone, the same. Creon's Thebes is a political version of the world of Genesis 1. It would therefore be sentimental to object to Creon's claims about the replaceability of Antigone as a wife and of Haemon as a son. New meaning, this gives, to the notion that men and women are *zooi politikoi*! (I invite the reader to look back at the extract from Plato's *Republic* set out towards the end of chapter 4. The kallipolis of Plato is rather like Thebes. We shall explore the idea.)

Antigone does not think of the Thebans along the lines of eddies. Nor do we. This is what brings about the linguistic impasse.

Death and the Maiden

Vernant was quoted to say that the protagonist of *Antigone* stands for the cult of the dead. The reverse is true. She stands for life. Is it not weird for death, with which Antigone is systematically associated, to represent life? Not in the context of Creon's Thebes. In Creon's Thebes, no one, in our sense of the verb, dies. Haemon had said [826] that Creon would 'make a splendid king . . . of a desert island.' Haemon should not be read as looking forward to a deserted Thebes, all its (main) inhabitants dead – a Thebes rebadged Necropolis. He should be understood to be speaking of the very Thebes that Creon conceives himself to rule. Creon's Thebes has in it no particulars. It's like the Garden at the start of Genesis 2, when the first man and the first woman were domestic animals, though the Garden differs in that the Lord God who presides over it grudgingly approves the impending particularization. Creon's entombment of Antigone is not the death of a particular person. It is just a readjustment of the city, like, to put it very unpleasantly, garbage disposal. (Creon would see it as an act of weeding and tilling his garden.) All acts are from the wider standpoint, and all are 'good.' Antigone's transgression brings about the death. It does so by bringing a particular into existence; or, if that seems too mysterious an idea, by bringing out the particularity.

Creon's condemnation of Antigone is not like our justice system's sentencing of a convict to the gas chamber. Creon is not condemning Antigone to death any more than by ordering someone to move the rock one initiates a process that results in the killing of Eddy. Because he does not conceptualize the city so as to make these acts killings, Creon can allow himself to brick up Haemon's bride in a tomb, and to disown Haemon. The other characters do not go along with Creon, any more than do the man and the woman in the Garden obey God. The deaths in *Antigone* are assertions of particularity. Not, I mean, the state-implemented deaths, but the self-inflicted deaths of Haemon, of Eurydice, of Antigone herself. Similar remarks apply, *mutatis mutandis*, for the transgression in Eden.

There are, then, two ways of being gone. There is the way of a nonparticular individual. There is the way of a particular. The one fits with Creon's city and is comprehensible from its perspective. The other fails in Creon's Thebes to make conceptual sense. *Antigone* dramatizes both ways. Her death being a *fait accompli*, Antigone has two possible fates. She can depart in a manner that subserves the city's ends. She can leave in a way that is 'good.' She can, that is, leave *pro*-the city. Alternatively, she can make her final exit in a manner that subverts the ends of the city. She can leave, that is, *anti*-the city – in a way that is 'bad.' When the curtain falls, she can be either *pro-gone* or *anti-gone*. Her choice is the latter. At the end, she is fully herself. She is Antigone. By her leave-taking Antigone makes clear her particularity, her irreplaceability. Creon learns the truth along the lines that the singer and songwriter Joni Mitchell packages thus: 'You don't know what you got till it's gone.' That is

Antigone's non-musical Note from Underground. Need I say that what Antigone's leave-taking signifies is prefigured, in a more abstract way and with a less decisive result, by Achilles's absenting himself from the Trojan battlefield? Need I remark that Antigone leaves Creon's Thebes as Odysseus leaves Polyphemus's cave, in which he too is entombed and doomed to expire? Their exit visas both give 'Nobody' as the decedent's name.

Our world presents us with a far grislier version of the progone/antigone pair. Here's a short paragraph from a recent Martin Amis novel.[22]

> On the television: a street scene, a loose group of shoppers, hurriers. And then one of them disappeared, leaving a hole in the world, with death tearing out of it.

The death of a suicide bomber is, in present terms, not a real death. *It's* like the passing of Eddy. Those killed by the blast are the ones who really die. Antigone's self-extinction in the vault is the novelist's scene inverted. Life tears out of her death.

The contrast between Genesis 1 and Genesis 2 put us on the trail of Creon's Thebes. This result clears up the biblical case at a place where, in its own terms, it is turbid. In their transgression, and in their departure from the God-assigned position of tillers in the Garden, the man and the woman become particulars; or, if this language of coming-into-being seems ontologically mysterious, they actualize a potential particularity. They come to be fully in God's image and likeness. In doing so, they cease to be non-particular individuals. As particulars, they can now die in the normal sense, as Eddy Rivers cannot. If you do not live, you cannot die. It is, then, a privilege to be able to die. As the word 'privilege' aptly implies, that option is not available just for the asking. Subhuman things, individual but not particular, do not return to dust. *They* never leave it. To put up a monument to Eddy Rivers, one has to be sentimental. For representing something ontologically monumental, Antigone deserves a monument. By her action she shows that she can return to dust in a way that subhuman things cannot.

It is astonishing that, read in the present spirit, what Antigone says at the start of the play [37–42] could be a report of what God says to the man in Genesis 2:

> Such, I hear, is the martial law our good Creon
> lays down for you and for me – yes, me, I tell you –

and he's coming here to alert the uninformed
in no uncertain terms,
and he won't treat the matter lightly. Whoever
disobeys in the least will die . . .

In telling the man and the woman that they will die on the day that they transgress, God is therefore doing ontology, not issuing a threat. He is telling them that they will become particulars; and such particulars alone among things are capable of dying. Which explains why they must be denied access to the tree of eternal life only *after* they transgress. That would be like allowing a square access to a fifth side.[23]

It's a Love Story!

The speech of Antigone's on which the heading of this section and the chapter title are based is highly significant. 'I was born to join in love, not hate – that is my nature.' Who would characterize Antigone as an apostle of love? Tough as nails she is, frigid, to Ismene cold as ice. But love stands for something here. The literary master of the emotion can be conscripted to the explanatory cause. The following Proustian excerpt captures the essential thing: the *exclusivity* of love.[24]

> Among all the modes by which love is brought into being, among all the agents which disseminate that blessed bane, there are few so efficacious as this gust of feverish agitation that sweeps over us from time to time. For then the die is cast, the person whose company we enjoy at that moment is the person we shall henceforth love. It is not even necessary for that person to have attracted us, up till then, more than or even as much as others. All that was needed was that our predilection should become exclusive. And that condition is fulfilled when – in this moment of deprivation – the quest for the pleasure we enjoyed in his or her company is suddenly replaced by an anxious, torturing need, whose object is the person alone, an absurd, irrational need which the laws of this world make it impossible to satisfy and difficult to assuage – the insensate, agonizing need to possess exclusively.

Precisely! Antigone would do for Polynices. She would not (necessarily) do for a child, or for a husband. Love simply does not apply for replaceables, disposables, fungibles, pets, mere individuals. It applies for particulars.[25] Early on in the action, Antigone describes what she is doing as an 'absurdity' [111], and Ismene, directly afterwards, characterizes her sister as 'irrational' [115]. What Antigone says does indeed come across as absurd, Antigone herself, deficient in rationality. But that's how love goes. Love does not join according to a formula. A loves B but not C, even though B and C are of equal virtue, merit, prospects, pulchritude, availability, receptiveness, and so forth. For C to complain that A should flip a coin to choose between C and B is to exhibit misunderstanding. Love joins in a non-rational way. If we liken love's attraction to magnetism, then it's a very unusual sort of attraction, drawing A and B together, but not A and C, even though B and C are discursively indistinguishable. That, again, is precisely what baffles about Antigone's speech. Why a brother and not a child? How do the two relevantly differ? Now we understand. King Lear (II.iv.263) put it well: 'reason not the need.' Or, taking a cue from Marshall McLuhan: the muddle is the message.[26]

In the Talmud (Tractate *Aboth* 5:19) a love that is conditional upon something outside of itself is distinguished from a love that has no such condition. If A's love for B is in this sense unconditional, no condition for it can be stated. There is no 'because.' So it is impossible to say, informatively, why A loves B. That, I have been saying, is what Antigone's action with regard to Polynices comes to or exemplifies. Which means: the beloved is in a radical sense non-fungible or irreplaceable. Which means: the beloved is in some radical sense a particular. The love story is also a political story. Not that politics must be based on love. Rather, politics must be sensitive to the fact that the political actors are beings who (*inter alia*) love.[27]

Antigone [615–617] will have none of Ismene's suggestion that she, Ismene, accompany Antigone to the grave. Her attitude towards Ismene now appears reasonable. She says:

> Never share my dying,
> don't lay claim to what you never touched,
> My dying will be enough.

'A single death is a tragedy, a million deaths is a statistic.' So Stalin cynically said. Had Antigone been joined by many in her opposition to Creon, the play would have looked like an exploration of value-pluralism. The Proust quote, illuminating Antigone's 'born to join in love,' also therefore makes sense of Antigone's pushing away of Ismene. The play's philosophical message would be muffled had the sisters of the house of Oedipus mounted a collective effort. The deaths of two would have been one death too many.

I took exception to the standard treatment of the transgression in the Garden, the treatment that a hasty reading can find in Milton's *Paradise Lost*. As the case may be with the beginning, the end of the poem sounds a truer note. Here's the closing couplet.

> They hand in hand with wandring steps and slow,
> Through Eden took thir solitarie way.

The man and the woman are now particulars. They are solitary – set apart. They proceed along *their* human way, a 'wandring' way, through and beyond Eden, not the way of the 'good' world from which they have come. No subhuman animal could do that.

There is a corresponding speech in *Antigone*. As by now we expect, it has a twist to it. Here is what Antigone says about her departure from Thebes, a match for Milton's representation of the pair who leave Eden. 'I will lie with the one I love and loved by him' [85]. (Whether or not the ambiguity of 'lie' – 'be buried with,' 'embrace' – is an artefact of the translation, it is apt.) One can hear the assertion of the lover in the Song of Songs. 'My beloved is mine and I am his' (2:16).

Pace what Milton writes at the start of Book 1 of *Paradise Lost*, the Bible does not teach 'the loss of Eden' until 'one greater Man' come along and 'Restore us, and regain [for us] the blissful Seat.' It teaches the loss of Eden as necessary for men and women to become what, in biblical terms, they are.

The man and the woman, who comes from the man and is in some extended sense his child, leave Eden together, their eyes open to their condition. Oedipus, blinded, that is, deprived of what he vaunted as god-like vision, leaves Thebes with his daughters, who are also, in an extended sense, his sisters. We shall look at his experience in the coming chapter.

'The son whom you love'

The problem speech of Antigone's has a close correlate in the foundational part of the Bible. It is found in its most concentrated form at a very intense spot in the annals of the Israelites. It is found at the *Akedah:* the story of the sacrifice of Isaac; or, if you like, the story of the test of Abraham. At issue is God's choice of Israel. Why this nation?

Why not some other? This was Rashi's issue, the issue of chosenness. God's choice of Israel is like a parent's non-rational preference for one child over another. God, using the vocabulary of family ties, says to Abraham: 'Take your son child, your only son Isaac, whom you love, and go to the land of Moriah, and offer him there as a burnt offering' (Genesis 22:2). Isaac is not however his father's only son; and no special warmth is evinced in Abraham's relations with the second born. Abraham had indeed pleaded with God for Ishmael. 'O that Ishmael might live in your sight!' (17:18) Abraham is troubled by God's treatment of the boy and of his mother, the Egyptian handmaiden Hagar. Isaac is delivered by Sarah at the age of ninety. Having engineered a non-sexual propagation in Genesis 2, God steps in again here, this time as fertility clinician. Isaac, that is, is *God's* special doing. There is something non-rational at the base of human affairs. That has to do with particularity too. That is what God in the story is trying to teach. The son is not replaceable; not fungible.

Through much of his activity, Abraham resists God, or at any rate moves to a different beat. The complexity of the relations between the two is such that the following remarks are more accurately described as impressionistic than as programmatic.

Key to unlocking the combination between patriarch and sponsor is the fact that God, insofar as his concern is with human reality, is operating always on a level that is national rather than personal. For God, the national *is* the personal. God's preference – a political-type preference, obviously – is for the children of Israel, his people, a nation. What is the nature of the preference? Deuteronomy 7:7–8 gives the answer. 'It was not because you were more numerous than any other people that the Lord set his heart on you and chose you . . . It was because the Lord loved you.'[28] When God speaks of Isaac as the son whom Abraham loves, he is projecting his own (non-rational) preference. Why should Abraham's affections go in the same direction? (If we see Abraham as embodying God's plan, then we will take him to be asking why non-rational preferences should be allowed to count politically. Abraham, that is, is torn. He is struggling to figure out where the national enterprise stands with respect to good and bad.) From the fact that A loves B and the fact that B is not discursively distinguishable from C, one cannot validly infer that A loves C. Jacob loves Rachel. God prefers Leah. Jacob accepts Leah out of obligation. Indeed, Jacob accepts her because that is the condition for securing Rachel's hand. Genesis presents us with the baffling story of Abraham twice misrepresenting Sarah as a sister. On the personal level, this preparedness to barter his wife for his life is contemptible. A survey of Abraham's career shows him to be anything but craven. Without God's encouragement or support, he rides out with a tiny retinue, 'three hundred eighteen' (Genesis 14:14) in all, to redeem Lot, who has been taken captive in the war of the kings that rages in the Valley of the Dead Sea. Abraham is not only a particular person, however, father of his children. Also, he is the patriarch, father of the nation. Is not Abraham's willingness to give up Sarah in the courts of the Pharaoh and of Abimelech interpretable, then, as his preparedness to relinquish his political election?[29] Could this not be interpreted as a red flag about basing politics on the personal? Was Hagar, described not just as a 'slave-girl' but also as an 'Egyptian' (16:1), denied to Abraham? From this perspective, the *Akedah* takes on a wholly different inflection. The test comes over as a super-intense interrogation of the linkage of the personal and the political, an interrogation in which God as much as Abraham is being put to the test. If Abraham sacrifices Isaac, the career of Israel comes to an end before it begins.[30] This is a problem not only for Abraham, but also for God, who had conceived the idea of national greatness in the first place. At the end (Abraham is poised, his knife raised), God is unwilling to allow the sacrifice. God is unwilling to permit the flame of national futurity to gutter and die, as he had been unwilling to permit those potentates to seed the national matriarch's womb with an alien crop. Since God loves Sarah, the bearer of national continuity, God's unwillingness is as it should be. By the same token, Abraham cannot be *condemned* for his preparedness to hand Sarah over. He has comprehensible qualms about the national enterprise. In this extra-personal regard, Abraham's love for Sarah is not unconditional. It is bound upon the deal that Abraham concluded with God – that in return for being God's man his progeny would become a great nation. The same applies in respect of Isaac, the patriarch's son. As human affairs go, national greatness isn't to be sneezed at. Why however must Abraham be rebuked if he thinks better of it? What's wrong with a life anonymous and obscure? Not everyone is cut out to bear the burdens of power. It's not just the onerousness of political office, though. It's also the likely immorality of power – a matter about which Abraham and God had already clashed over the fate of the possible just men of Sodom. Indeed, who can fail to see in the story of the slave-girl Hagar and her first-born Ishmael a pre-play of the Israelite experience in bondage, with Abraham saving the *Egyptian* first-born, whom God was quite willing to abandon?

It may be fortuitous that Abraham's national progeny are known as 'Israelites.' Quite apart from Abraham's also having fathered Ishmael,[31] the fact that the passports of his descendants through Sarah are not inscribed 'Abrahamite' turns out however to be bang on from a thematic standpoint. At the close of the negotiations between Abraham and God over Sodom, after Abraham has systematically reduced the city-saving number to ten righteous inhabitants and is rehearsing his brief for single digits, the text indicates that God has had enough. 'And the Lord went his way' (18:33). Emphasis on the possessive pronoun is heard in the mind's ear. God has *his*, God's, way; but Abraham has *his*, Abraham's. These two ways never completely coincide.

What's wrong with living in anonymity and obscurity? I asked the question as if it were rhetorical. But neither here nor elsewhere does God's way subdue an opposed way by force of force rather than by force of reasons, which reasons, not being logically conclusive, never settle the issue once for all. What's wrong with living in anonymity and obscurity? Perhaps others will refuse to allow a group to live quietly and obscurely. Without national status, and without an exercise of the preparedness to defend it that having the status makes possible, servitude might be on the cards. In the real world, then, the case based on the reasons that are ascribed to God does have to be answered. Isn't servitude preferable to death? The either/or in this case is not exclusive, so it's misleading to represent the matter as one of choice. Servitude opens those in bondage to arbitrary treatment at the hands of their dominators. If donning the mantle of patriarchy offers a prospect of defending and sustaining freedom, the choice on the part of a potential patriarch to live a quiet life rather than seize the opportunity might therefore open such a one to very serious rebuke. If obscurity does not mean isolation (and a reclusive existence is not what the reluctant patriarch has in view), the choice might also result in such a one's living a very unquiet life anyway. Well before the allotted four score and ten are up it might even result in his or her living no life at all.

The issue of the personal and the political is the issue of *Antigone* too. The difference is that in the biblical case, the personal, from as early as Genesis 2, is never in question.

11
Life and Times

ב & א

The opening letter of the Bible – ב – has the shape of an opening parenthesis. According to the rabbinic sages,[1] this manner of setting out encodes a prohibition against inquiry into what preceded 'the beginning when God created' (1:1).

Think what we may of reading a message out of the form of a letter, the attributed idea *is* biblical. Acceding to Moses's request for a theophany, God appends a rider: 'you cannot see my face' (Exodus 33:20). Amplifying the qualification, he adds: 'you shall see my back; but my face shall not be seen' (23). Quite apart from God, Moses, and the exchanges between them portrayed in Scripture, it is true that our access to the beginning is from the end. Reasoning from effect to cause, we seek the best explanation for how things now before us stand. But the sages did not just hold that the full frontal view can be attained only in a roundabout manner. The full frontal view is also, they said, hazardous material. Recall C.S. Lewis's caution against 'tak[ing] the thread of life out of the hand of Clotho.'[2] Understood aright, God's 'no one shall see me and live' (20) is no idle threat. Though the auto-annihilation has not come to pass, unlocking the secrets of the atom *has* given us the capacity to engineer the cataclysm. A similar thing might be said in regard to the genetic code – unlocking the secrets of the Adam. Has its decipherment not supplied the wherewithal for abolishing, that is, arranging the death of, mankind as we know it?[3]

The sages found significance in the Bible's opening with ב, the second letter of the Hebrew alphabet, on account of its shape. Taking my cue from the sages, *I* find significant that 'In the beginning' does not begin with א, the first letter. To explain, let me return to the idea of reform.

Belief in the possibility of making a go of it between crib and crypt underpins the view of men and women as autonomous loci of value. The biblical account of the creation offers support, describing as it does the successful execution of a constructive enterprise. All writings that are charters for living are likely to contain supportive material of this ilk. Think of charters for thinning. Before and after photos are *de rigeur* in diet books.

Such supportive material's inclusion being close to the heart of what makes the writings scriptural, it is not surprising to find it in Homer on the side of the ethos that he sets out in full.

In the *Iliad*, Diomedes scales godly heights. The image of a creature of flesh and blood taking on the immortals and in one supreme spasm besting them might have stilled a warrior's doubts about that for which he or she was living: the achievement of lasting renown through a show of god-likeness. The idea here, a simple idea, is captured by words that are often enough spoken to encourage the self-doubter. 'He or she lost fifty pounds. What's weighing *you* down?'[4]

Quelling a person's doubts about the chances of success is one thing; establishing success as possible, another. After devoting themselves for years to trisecting an angle with compass and straightedge, mathematicians proved the enterprise futile. Might some not have scoffed at the folly of those who took seriously Diomedes's *aristeia*? 'If you believe *that*, then perhaps you'll consider the Hellespont I've got listed for sale.' The fact that a story tells of a thing's being done, the fact that the doing thereof is set down in words on the page,[5] does not mean that the thing can be done outside the telling or off the page. 'After tinkering for several years in his workshop, Fred finally fashioned a *perpetuum mobile*. Now he had only to square the circle and get round his long-suffering spouse.'

To pretend that the gap between asserting and verifying a possibility has been bridged opens the pretender to a scruple, mitigation of which may sometimes be found in the fiction's serving a noble cause. Neither in the Homeric case nor in the biblical one is such a pretense, meritorious or ignoble, being perpetrated. Homer's picture of Diomedes rising does no more than *illustrate* the idea of impressing one's fellows by performing feats. Some of those we live among do in fact make a lasting impact; and they do so without storming the gates of Olympus. As for the Bible, God's agency is *not* represented in an unrealistic way. True, the scale of God's effort beggars any undertaking of ours. Nonetheless, the nature of the effort is not cognitively opaque to us. More importantly, God, in his constructive activity, encounters the same sorts of difficulties that we do.

What about א and ב? That the text begins with the second letter is appropriate; appropriate, because the world did *not* come into being *ex nihilo*. Though of superhuman magnitude, God's agency is not magical.[6]

This realism is a biblical hallmark. It is by no means surprising that God's path is potholed and bumpy. It's not that when one looks at the world through clear spectacles it comes across as a difficult place. The world, the natural world, is neither difficult nor easy. It just is. In Raven's Land, God is at play: no shoes to be shined, no appointments to keep. God's *biblical* dealings with the world correspond from the very start to the activities of the man and the woman after the departure from the Garden. They correspond to our dealings as we struggle along faced with the ultimate deadline. The correspondence is not accidental. God's dealings are modelled on ours. That's why God's path is so rough.[7]

Although realism has a lot to be said for it, the Bible's realism, here as elsewhere, is double-edged. The God-figure of the narrative serves as the (realistic) paradigm of agency. If, as the proposition that the creation does not begin with the scratch of a match implies, God's hand is fettered, then the help that his example can tender is also compromised. A person fearful of crossing the road will not be reassured if another chicken is presented as a model, let alone elected to part the sea of cars and get him or her to the other side without fenders ruffled.

Though not quite a dilemma, this is close enough for discomfort. Either God acts on the world – for example, creates it – from a transcendent position, and hence has an ontologically anchored dominion, or else God, internally bound up with the physical realm, is implicated in its workings. If the former, then the claim that men and women are made in God's image and likeness flies in the face of the fact that we are inextricably enmeshed in space and time. If the latter, then the likeness claim loses its power even to justify confidence in our capacity to act effectively.

None of this is to deny that in conjunction with the proposition that men and women resemble God, the representation of God as an effective agent might meet a psychological need or work wonders as a piece of advertising. Nonetheless, the belief in the possibility of success might be as unfounded as the belief that the blue moon, rather than being rock solid, is Roquefort. There is a lot to be said for getting through the day. Are falsehoods justifiable solely on the ground that they help us get through the day?

God's status as world-maker is important to the self-conception of those for whom the Bible is scriptural. It's an important element of the view that life is inherently valuable. When men and women reflect upon their troublous existences, might they not easily conclude that the idea that they can act effectively in the world is bombastic? How quickly, and how often, their plans come to grief. How modest those plans must be in order to stand a snowball's chance this side of heaven. That God is able to make his impress on the chaos despite not having an absolutely free hand might instil in them (made as they are in God's image and likeness) enough confidence about the possibility of such a thing to give it a go. The difficulty is that God's handcuffs might be decisive. The rest might be a caged bird's bravely twittering within its prison.

Relative to my explanation of the Bible's beginning with ב, Jerusalem is brought into ideological proximity to Athens. In the Greek context, the gods, though immortal, are not transcendent. Born into the world, they have their being in time, as we have ours. Similarly, the idea that God's agency is not a *carte blanche* affair makes that agency (more) like ours from the start of the story of biblical creation. But because there is no extra-physical place in the Greek context, the problem is apt to be felt more keenly there. That, to judge from the written sources, is the case. In this chapter I consider how the matter is treated in the two environments.

But What's the Problem?

A person who goes around denying that men and women have the capacity to act effectively is a candidate for a sandwich board inscribed 'Repent! The end is nigh.' Every day most of us manage to dress, prepare a cup of coffee, commute to work and get through the day's tasks. Over the medium span, many of us climb the corporate ladder, purchase and maintain a house, raise a family, and so forth. Over an even longer one, we (collectively) build cities, dam up rivers to generate power, and send probes to the outer planets. In each of these cases, we have a goal, we devise a plan, we proceed to implement it, dealing with difficulties along the way, and with a frequency above chance (otherwise we would cease trying) we reach the destination.

Making mock of human pretensions, Shelley transcribes an inscription on a fallen monument half-buried in the sands of the desert:

> My name is Ozymandias, king of kings:
> Look on my works, ye Mighty, and despair!

Gibbon inscribes the same idea in lapidary prose (*Decline and Fall*, chapter 71). 'The art of man is able to construct monuments far more permanent than the narrow span of his own existence: yet these monuments, like himself, are perishable and frail; and in the boundless annals of time his life and his labours must equally be measured as a fleeting moment.' We can agree that Ozymandias overestimated. Yet did he not preside over a civilization that had the capacity to erect such a monument? History does not present us only with Howard Schultz and his imperium of baristas. It also gives us Augustus and the Roman Empire.

Even in the warrior context, effective action itself isn't in doubt. The warriors build ships, sail the seas, fashion armour, plan and mount attacks, and so on. The ethical implications, the implications for self-image and value, stem from how all this is rated. The warriors take the view that the prowess displayed in building and sailing ships, in fashioning and using armour, etc., is insignificant relative to the power of the winds, the sun, etc. They do not say that their efforts are ineffective; they say that what they do is small potatoes.

A principle of modal logic states that if something of type T is actual, or if it exists, then T-type things are possible. *Ab esse ad posse valet consequentia.* So what's the problem? In preparing the coffee, do I not show that I am, at least with respect to a performance of this size, an effective agent? What need of a transcendent actor to ratify my capacity?

The modal principle is valid. From the standpoint of aggressive philosophical thinking, that, however, does not settle the issue. One *can* reason the need. Despite my prowess with ground coffee and French press, the question of logical possibility can still be raised. Since my making coffee is a paradigm of an effective action, the question has, obviously, to be raised at a more abstract level. The category of action has itself to be placed under a rational cloud. It has to be argued that we misunderstand and misdescribe as 'effective action' what is transpiring when the java is brewed. Philosophers are well acquainted with such calling-into-question. With respect to the present issue, at stake is the reality of freedom. A traditional way in which the denial of agency comes to expression is through reference to fate. Whether it is couched in terms of predetermination or in the more austere vocabulary of professional philosophers, the position is that the notion of our effective agency is an illusion. Not only is the die already cast when (as we put it) we initiate an action, the result too is fixed prior to the roll.

It will be helpful to have an illustration of philosophical give-and-take over such a matter. Here is a test tube case.

Several centuries ago, reports filtered back from Africa telling of a creature with giraffe-like neck and zebrine stripes. Zoologists in Europe wrote such reports off as having their basis in myth. Before too long, however, informants whose naturalist credentials were unimpeachable observed the okapi on the veldt.

We believe that the winged horse is spawn of the fancy, deceiving elf. Suppose that, one fine day, an explorer emerges from the wilds of northern Greece with just such a creature (dubbed 'Pegasus') in tow. Most of us will begin forthwith to wonder about unicorn and griffin, perhaps even chimera. Enter the philosophical spoilsport, who will not allow *this* horse to take wing. 'What is a horse? Is it not a quadruped? And wings, what are they? In the non-insect realm, are they not variants of a quadruped's forelimbs, as (to give a mammalian instance) in the case of the bat? If so, Pegasus here is a sexpedal quadruped. That's a contradiction in terms.'

Grant, for the sake of argument, the reasoning's cogency. The implication is not that the zoologist's specimen is a mirage. After all, there it is, to be fed and groomed, even perhaps mounted for a spin in the clouds. The implication is that *Pegasus is not a winged horse*. For nothing could answer to the literal description 'winged horse.' By the same token, the position is that what is called 'effective action' is not that at all. No more does pointing to your brewing of the coffee prove otherwise than displaying Pegasus establishes the possibility of winged horses. (Perhaps needless to add, if the explorer's find had been described as a thing with wing-like appendages that otherwise resembles a horse, the philosopher would not have been spurred into action.)

Neither on the side of the Athens that we are considering nor on the side of Jerusalem are the issues raised in a technically philosophical way. Yet both sides are sensitive to the problem. Both deal with the issue by telling stories. Neither sets out pieces of reasoning.[8]

To assert determination amounts to asserting that time is unreal, in exactly the sense that, on the preceding illustration, winged horses are unreal. If what happens 'later' is fixed 'earlier,' the relation between the pair is like that between the premises and the conclusion of a (deductively valid) argument. The explanation for why deductively valid reasoning preserves truth is simple: the conclusion is implicit in the premise or premises. Determinism is in that sense a denial of our low-level sense of time. Newness under the sun is a shadow cast by cognitive limitation. *Everything* is present.

The problem arises with greater urgency on the Greek side. On this side, the gods too are subject to the Fates. Part of the causal order, the gods are caught up in it. On the side of Jerusalem, in contrast, transcendence of that order – God preceding the creation – is at least notionally in play. Indeed, there is more than a greater sense of urgency on the Greek side. There is also quite a bit of panic. Still, the parallelism we have been drawing out is, in a more subtle way, maintained. Given the idea (even the residual idea) of a position external to space-time from which what happens physically can be initiated and influenced, the notion of divine foreknowledge enters. This idea is not however given much credence in the Bible. In the light of what we have learned about the two-way traffic between God and men and women, this is not entirely unexpected.

Controlling Causation

What need of a transcendent agent? If an agent from beyond the physical sphere were trotted out, that would solve the abstract problem about causation and predetermination; solve it, to be sure, at a high ontological cost, and not without raising proprietary difficulties. Nonetheless, it would solve it. Both in the biblical context and in the Greek one, the idea is developed. In neither case does the development go very far or have probative force. Really, an immanent solution, or at any rate an immanent treatment, is needed. I will offer a sketch in the next chapter. Here, the object is to set down, largely in a descriptive manner, how the matter of causation is handled.

The relevant material on the Greek side we have already discussed. The reference is to the story of Zeus and Athena, told in Hesiod's *Theogony*.

A struggle on high pits the settled generation of gods against the young lions. In spite of what the threatened fathers do to remain in charge, they are bested. They are bested because of something they do not budget for. The strife is ended, however, in the third generation. How does Zeus manage the feat where his father and grandfather before him failed? How, that is, does Hesiod describe Zeus's disarming what appears to be fated? Zeus swallows his pregnant wife, of whom we hear no more, and gives birth to Athena through a gash that Hephaestus axes to his forehead.

In the earlier generations, the parental agendas were in conflict. Mothers had worked against fathers. By swallowing Metis, Zeus gathers up the causal threads in himself. The mother, a basic principle of origin and change in Greek cosmogony, is thereby prevented from operating independently of (and hence potentially at cross-purposes with) the father. Needless to say, sexual reproduction being what it is, no one parent has complete control, genetically, of the outcome; though, in an extension of C.S. Lewis's fear, and of Zeus's method, cloning, halving the number of parents, brings such mastery within reach.

I've told a similar story on the biblical side. In the conjectural biography God distances himself from the Babylonian pantheon in which he initially operated. By isolating the cause rather than by unifying the causal factors this also is a way of overcoming outside effects. Zeus's is a proto-shift towards the order more characteristic of monotheism – the latter being a case of reduced divine parentage. The deity of the Bible makes a break from the pantheon of Babylon and founds a monotheistic faith.

Though the story of God's departure from the lower Euphrates isn't in the Bible, within the core language of biblical monotheism are found traces of an exodus from the gravitational field of the regnant belief system. In chapter 9, I observed that the name 'Elohim,' one of the Bible's two main appellations for God, is syntactically plural.[9] The *Shema* – 'Hear, O Israel: the Lord is our God, the Lord is one' (Deuteronomy 6:4) – also reads in an unforced way as an assertion of divine unity.[10]

Kings

Two divinities, two kings of heaven, are represented as exercising control. Neither story is capable of delivering the philosophical goods. Neither gives the Proverbist what the Proverbist needs on the side of perplexity. The passivity on the Greek side is especially disappointing, since Sophocles, in *Antigone*, had made some productive feints. I will now look at the case of an earthly king, called 'Oedipus,' whose story, often taken as a story about fate, bears on the issue.

Oedipus the King, in the order of writing the second of Sophocles's three Theban plays, is often singled out as the Olympus of Greek drama. A powerful play, dramatically speaking, it is. That we the spectators know from near the start of Oedipus's guilt, while he remains in the dark until near the end, imparts to the play its horrifying quality. A person inches towards the edge of a precipice, and we who observe it are unable to call out. In the contrast with *Oedipus the King*, *Antigone*, though it dramatizes a sharp conflict, seems flat. So when I speak of disappointment, the point has to do with philosophical depth, not with dramatic force.

The message of *Oedipus the King* is that men and women live in time and that this has consequences. 'What kind of insight is it that we are born, grow up, and eventually die? Speak of labouring to bring forth a mouse!' The questioner is hasty. After all, the Thebans were unable to solve the riddle, which encodes the same insight. In the context of Greek culture, there is not just a single time. There is the time of the gods, there is warrior time, and there is the time of human beings. Biblically, too, time is not unitary. There is Garden time, and then, outside the Garden, there is what is represented as standard time, human time.

Many of the surviving Greek dramas are concerned with the *polis*. *Oedipus the King* falls into this set. Indeed, the play is a thematic partner to *Antigone*. Oedipus, in *Oedipus the King*, is very much like *Antigone*'s Creon. The one challenges human particularity; the other has a problem with human time. The challenge, we have seen, has political implications. The problem, we shall see, does too.

Cadmus slew the Dragon of Ares, the Dragon of War, whose existence prevented the *polis* from being founded. The meaning of Cadmus's exploit is clear. *Polis* life is peaceful life. War and peace are a twain that never meet. Oedipus confronts the Sphinx, which is preventing Thebes from flourishing. The way the Sphinx functions to stultify the lives of the Thebans is not clear at all. As a consequence, neither is the meaning of Oedipus's victory over the Sphinx clear. Let's figure out what's going on.

Thebes is the *topos* of city-formation in Greek dramaturgy: neither is it fully *polis*, nor is it fully extra-*polis*. In this regard, Thebes is rather like the Sphinx. The Sphinx is preventing Thebes from flourishing. Decoded: the pre-political, mythical way of thinking is not consistent with proper communal life. The Sphinx poses a riddle. The riddle encodes the fact that men and women are temporal beings. They crawl on all fours at sun-up, walk upright at midday, and hobble with the help of a stick as the sun sets on them. The riddle is not answered until Oedipus happens along. What does this mean? It means that Thebes has an improper view of men and women. Improper how? Improper for a flourishing community life.[11]

Once we establish what sphyngian feature applies to Thebes, the Sphinx itself can be returned to that mythological bestiary. The point of the play in regard to the city is that Thebes, as a communal entity, is in some important regard Sphinx-like. That is the thematic meaning of the monster's presence at the gates.[12] Formally, the relationship between the riddle's not having been solved and the city's condition is identical to the relationship between eating of the fruit of the tree of knowledge and mortality. Just as one's eating of the forbidden tree *is* one's being (aware of being) mortal, so Thebes's not responding to the riddle *is* Thebes's being dysfunctional.[13] The problem of flourishing consists in Thebes having a monstrous character relative to, culturally speaking, (what are regarded as) the stable alternatives. The Thebans do not flourish – their city does not flourish – because they do not have a proper understanding of themselves as *zooi politikoi*.

A second unusual instrumentality, the Oracle, plays a role in the drama. Attention to its role enables us to identify that sphyngian characteristic being sought.

Sphinx is tails to Oracle's heads. Not to know the solution to the riddle, sc., to have an improper understanding of men and women, is the same as being receptive to the Oracle. What is an Oracle? An Oracle is a source of information about the future. To foretell the future, one must have knowledge of the future. Otherwise, it's guesswork for which a coin would serve as well as a priestess. To have knowledge of what is to come, one must be in touch, cognitively, with the future. For an Oracle, the future is as present as the present. But future and present are separate. To connect the two is like linking the tail of a lion with the head of a woman.

Laius and Jocasta take the Oracle very seriously indeed. Nonetheless, they attempt to forestall the predicted end. By arranging for the nameless infant to be put to death, they think to snuff out his causality. 'If the child is no more,' they reason, 'he can neither kill the father nor defile the mother.' Oedipus himself, similarly, attempts to master the causation. Informed of the Oracle, and believing his adoptive parents Polybus and Merope to be the parents referred to, he departs Corinth forthwith. 'For' he reasons, 'if I am distant from them, I cannot kill the one or bed the other.'[14]

None of the efforts is effective. Even if Oedipus had been exposed and had died, that would still have been compatible with the Oracle's claim about parricide. Here's the scenario.

Oedipus has succumbed to the elements. Aware of the infant's royal parentage, the shepherd buries the body in a manner that he deems appropriate to the pedigree – on a high place overlooking Thebes. Passing one day, Laius is killed as the large boulder placed atop the grave, shaken loose by the thundering hooves, crashes down onto his carriage.[15]

An unlikely story? But Oedipus's encountering his father at the crossroads during the flight from Corinth is every bit as improbable.[16] It's what we call *coincidence*. The point is not, then, that (what seem to be) unlikely things will happen because they are predetermined or fated. Unlikely things happen all the time. They do, simply because causation has a rippling character. We can thus be sure that many things will occur in the causation of which we, as agents, are involved, but which we have no intention of bringing about – things which we, in cases where the impact is negative, are often regretful, even horror-struck, to hear we had been complicit in actualizing. Would Thales have been gratified to hear that he had a hand in the reconstruction of Solomon's Temple? *Oedipus the King* works with some especially chilling examples. And why not? What point would there have been, from the standpoint of the needs of community, to dramatizing a pronouncement from the crystal ball to the effect that Oedipus has an appointment in Samara with a cup of coffee and a jelly doughnut?

Let me illustrate the issue by describing how a teacher with a dramatic flair might go about teaching *Oedipus the King*. It will be noted that the illustration eliminates the idea of fate or pre-determination from literal play.[17]

Shoes and the Man

Entering the class, the teacher proceeds to peer, with increasing alarm, at the footwear of the students in the front row. 'You,' says the teacher, pointing to a student wearing a pair of Nike runners, 'are a killer.' The same charge is made against each of those present who is sporting running shoes. 'I am surrounded by killers!' the teacher asserts in dismay.

Is the institution another in the horrific litany: École Polytechnique de Montréal, Columbine High School, Virginia Tech? God forbid! Just the usual mixture of keeners up front and the chattering class in the back. The claim is that the students are killers in the way that Oedipus is a killer, and Oedipus did not set out to kill his father. So how is the teacher's claim true? And what's the tie-in with knowledge of feet? The answer is that the running shoes are produced in sweatshops in, say, the Philippines, where the workers, toiling under insalubrious conditions, are sitting ducks for opportunistic disease. Now what is a person to do who cares about this? Students, asked the question, will often say: 'From now on I forswear such shoes. For me only Rockports, Mass. produced.' But the result is the same. For want of buyers of their product, the workers are laid off. Without income, they are once again vulnerable to hunger, sickness, and so forth.[18]

What we do has effects over which we have little to no control, including negative effects that are apt to make the affected parties, if they are nearby, rise up against us. (In today's world, everywhere is close.) Try as we might, we cannot foresee all but a few proximate consequences; and we certainly cannot exercise control over many consequences that we can, if we make the effort, foresee. What's to be done? In the context of communal life, where the negative effects are sources of conflict, we have methods. Automobile insurance is a good representative. The institution keeps the person who (unintentionally) causes the harm at arm's length from the person harmed, while, at some cost to the former and to other premium payers, compensating for injuries and losses that result from the damage.

What's the problem with Oedipus? He gives the answer to the Sphinx and is duly installed on the throne. The hand of the widowed queen, Jocasta, being part of the prize package, he gets that too. But the answer really means that men and women live in time, and do not have control, while Oedipus self-ascribes godlike, trans-temporal knowledge because he supplied the answer. He takes himself to be the tamer of the Sphinx and, believing that he has evaded *its* deliverances, the equal of the Oracle too.[19] To have the answer in the substantive sense is really however to know that one cannot be the equal of the Oracle. So Oedipus is in a self-contradictory situation, a situation resolved only when, at the end of the action, he puts out his eyes, that is, abdicates from his vaunt to god-like knowledge. The only emperor is one who has put out the vile jellies; the emperor of eyes' cream.

Isn't the point about causation valid for anyone, including the hermit? So what does this have to do with the *polis*? The negative results horrify the characters in the play. They are intensely interested in *avoiding* them. The Oracle's pronouncements fill them with dismay. A few paragraphs back, I wrote, give or take a word, the following: 'We can be sure that many things will happen for which we, as agents, are causally (in part) responsible, but which we have no intention of bringing about; which, as in the case of Oedipus, we are not only surprised, but also horrified, to hear that we had had a hand (or foot) in bringing about.' We can be sure that many such things will occur. It may however be a matter of indifference to us, and not because we are psychopaths. Consider Homer's warriors. (In the Greek frame, the warrior way is the stable pre-political way.) They don't care about peaceful existence, about political existence. More accurately, this kind of existence is even unknown to them. Living for eternity, the warriors would certainly not have had an answer to the Sphinx. 'A man,' they would have reacted to the answer, 'doesn't kneel. A man stands tall.' Nor would that have mattered. Infancy and dotage are alien to their value system. To them, infants and dotards are like static on a sound recording. It is no wonder that the Sphinx is posted at the gates of Thebes. Had it taken up a station in the Greek encampment at Troy it would have gone hungry. To those bivouacked there the Sphinx's riddle is irrelevant.

The story of Oedipus's crimes and punishment has a sequel. Though bleak in mood, *Oedipus at Colonus* presents the protagonist working through the shock of his self-discovery. Banished from Thebes because of the parricide and incest (such pollution cannot knowingly be abided), Oedipus ends up in Athens. (Colonus is a suburb of Athens – where, in fact, Sophocles was born.) Theseus, king of Athens, accepts Oedipus into the city. The Fates, who previously doomed Oedipus, have spun around. Now they bless him. And, says Theseus, he will be a blessing to Athens. How is Oedipus blessed, and in what way is he a blessing? Why does he need a blessing? Though what we have here is specific to Oedipus's circumstances, it's just like Genesis 1. In Genesis 1, men and women receive a blessing. The man and the woman in Genesis 1 need a blessing because their route is open-ended. Given ignorance of the future and the inexorable spread of causation, Oedipus needs a blessing if he is to live peacefully among others. To manage the serious frictions that the unintentional causing of harm to others is bound to engender, those who live communally, and at peace, have to set up institutions such as our civil courts. Less formally, to live with themselves they must be able to forgive themselves for the bad things that they have done unintentionally to others, and to live with others they must be prepared to forgive the latter for the harms that they have suffered when those harms have not been inflicted maliciously.

So, just like the Sphinx, Sophocles's title *Oedipus the King* is three-in-one. Oedipus is a king, ironically, who doesn't know. Like King Solomon, he is unaware that his wisdom cannot save him. But Oedipus is a king, in the proper sense, for giving up on that. Also, he serves as a model for Theseus. In that third sense he is a ruler, a yardstick for ruling.

The Quadrupedal Tripedal Biped

While the positive output of *Oedipus* disappoints, the way the exploration goes couldn't be more gripping. The interplay of plot and theme is spectacular. The play works by presenting Oedipus as himself a Sphinx.

It turns out that not only is Oedipus a riddle to himself, but he is, again like the Sphinx, a distorted exemplification of the riddle. The viewer of the action knows that Oedipus is the guilty party. That heightens the horror. But the viewer doesn't quite understand something that Oedipus himself discovers. So there is a revelation on the part of the viewer too. All this is achieved by a series of puzzles that the play, in its plotting, involves.

Oedipus's life trajectory turns back on itself: a grotesque parody of the dream of homecoming; an unholy mother and child reunion. The chorus says the following of Oedipus [1340–1343]:

> But now for all your power
> Time, all-seeing Time has dragged you to the light,
> judged your marriage monstrous from the start –
> the son and the father tangling, both one –

Could there be a reference in the last line to the feud of generations in Hesiod? Rather than pursue the thought, let's turn our attention to another, happier, family get-together.

The turkey is on the table. The patriarch is yet again holding forth about his life: exposure in the trenches and war wounds as a raw youth, living abroad after being discharged, overcoming obstacles on the road back home, rising to the top as a captain of industry. Then, pointing to the missus, he says: 'On that late summer day, as I first entered the kindergarten classroom, I met mother.' A claim of this kind applies to Oedipus – albeit in a literal, revulsion-inspiring sense. Oedipus meets his wife at birth; at which event, of course, she figures not as another newborn in the delivery room who years later will become his bride, but as his biological mother.

The quoted sentence illustrates the trope of prolepsis. The speaker applies at one point of time a description the correctness of whose application is based in what occurs only at some later time. Save for a precocious youngster reared in a society where marriages are prearranged, 'I met my wife in the nursery' could not have been spoken assertively when the speaker was five years old. Only an oracle could have spoken it.

A second example. 'I'm turning into my father.' This figure of speech is also relevant to Oedipus, and not just as a trope. Not only does Oedipus meet his wife in the delivery room, he nearly literally turns into his (own) father when he takes his place in her bed.

Oedipus, to couch it in these terms, is a living and breathing prolepsis; and, Sophocles is (at the very least) saying that the proleptic is a monster. Oedipus's self-blinding consists, from this perspective, in severing his future from his present; leaving the future where, one might argue, it belongs. Which is what Jocasta, just prior to his self-revelation, tells him [1077–1078].

> Live, Oedipus,
> as if there's no tomorrow!

This is not the counsel of *carpe diem:* live in the moment. It's the claim that things come to us out of the dark, that we must budget for the fact that the future is not present to us.[20] Jocasta's counsel applies as much to herself as to Oedipus. In trying to arrange the infant's death, she made opposite assumptions about the future. Perhaps for that reason she consigns herself, once the truth is out, to the timeless.[21]

Four more plot line oddities in *Oedipus the King* confront the reader. The first concerns the name of the protagonist, the second and third concern central elements of the action, and the fourth has to do with the *dramatis personae*. While the idea of literalized prolepsis is pretty exotic, the key to the play consists in recognizing that these oddities too, though available to the literal-minded, are cognate.

Oedipus is so-called, by Merope and Polybus, the rulers of Corinth who adopt him, because of the edematous condition of his feet – a result of the limbs' having been pinned together when, soon after he was born, his Theban parents consigned him to the elements. No principled reason exists why Oedipus should have wondered about the name. How many bearers of 'Philip' among us are aware that the name means 'horse lover'? Yet though one would not therefore regard it as a flaw in the artistry that the significance of Oedipus's very name is a key piece of the puzzle the proper positioning of which awakens him to his identity, it is not the case that he takes *no* interest in the handle. Oedipus's name is for its bearer a point of pride. In the first speech of the play, addressing the Theban citizens who have arrived in their time of trial, Oedipus vaunts [7–9]:

> Here I am myself –
> you all know me, the world knows my fame:
> I am Oedipus.

Oedipus *has* interpreted his name. He links it to the act that gave him his fame, viz., solving the Sphinx's riddle about the nature of man. The riddle, of course, concerns man's feet.[22]

Though Oedipus did not acquire immediately at birth the name that precedes him, endearments aside he won't remember being called anything else, and his memory will certainly go back to a Corinthian adolescence. How then could he link the name with the event that put his name in lights as Thebes's sapient saviour? The foul foot, that is, comes very oddly into play.

The world of an artistic work is not a world of accident. One expects that the coincidence (as it may initially appear) in the case of Oedipus has some thematic pay-off.

This, then, is the first of the oddities. Oedipus eventually fingers himself as the perpetrator of the abominations that the Oracle foretold. The identification is secured partly through the dawning recognition that his name has to do with the condition that affected his newborn feet. A good gumshoe, he puts two and two together. 'If *that* is what the name commemorates, then the drunken lout's blurt that Polybus and Merope were not my natural parents was probably accurate.' So, Oedipus concludes, he himself may well be guilty since, as he knows, he slew a royal at the crossroads shortly after departing Corinth. At a crucial turn in the play, the meaning of 'Oedipus' is made clear to its bearer. 'Your ankles were pinned together,' explains the messenger from Corinth [1133].

> And you got your name from that misfortune too,
> the name's still with you. [1135]

Why does Sophocles see fit to present Oedipus's self-awareness as dawning via a change in his understanding of the name? Wouldn't it have sufficed for his attention to have first been drawn *on this very occasion* to the name's incriminating origin?

What we confront here we have previously encountered in the case of Odysseus. Just as Homer is making a thematic point with 'Outis,' so too is Sophocles, with 'Oedipus.' It's not, as some classicists have stated, that names were regarded as magical in those days. Sophocles's point is the opposite. It's that Oedipus's treatment of the name as causally explained by a later event only makes sense if all times are effectively simultaneous. Short of the categorical denial of time, this requires the sort of scenario that Hesiod presents, a scenario in which what happens happens over and over, that is, in which time is circular.

The second oddity is equally striking. A fog cloaks the events at the crossroads. In the violence that broke out when Oedipus confronted Laius and his party, Oedipus killed (so he himself reports) 'every mother's son' [898]. It turns out that a second pair of eyes viewed the confrontation. The owner of those eyes had told at the time of Laius & Co. being set upon by (plural) highway*men*. Jocasta [828–829] puts the number at five. Nor was that eyewitness a bystander who just happened to find himself at the crossroads. He was in fact a member of Laius's party. Very much alive, he is therefore a walking refutation of Oedipus's claim to have dispatched the lot. On Oedipus's account, in fine, one encountered several, and only that one survived. On the other account, a larger number accosted the several, and the remainder on the side of the latter was one. No single event can match the discordant arithmetic. 'One can't equal many' [934].

To be sure, either or both of the parties can be mistaken. The second witness even has a motive for perjury. It would likely have gone badly for him had it been suspected that to save his skin he skulked off during the attack. And it is more likely that the accusation of dereliction would have been made had there been only a single attacker. This *could* make sense of the discrepancy from *his* side. It does nothing however to rationalize Oedipus's saying, inaccurately, that he did in all the members of the party.

Sophocles could easily have told the story differently. The eyewitness could have been journeying from Daulis to Corinth. There are grounds for thinking, then, that in telling the story as he does Sophocles is telling us something.

I pass now to the second unusual feature. Pollution grips the city of Thebes because the killer of Laius is on the loose. The situation is even worse: not only has the killer not been apprehended, but a search has not even been mounted. As I indicated, the citizens arrive at Oedipus's door to beg for his help in this regard. But the killing of Laius occurred long years earlier. Oedipus is now the revered ruler of Thebes. His children are grown. What took so long? Presumably, the point is not Asclepian or Hippocratic, that pollution has a protracted incubation period.

An easy answer suggests itself. To fall far, Oedipus had to fall from a height; and Rome isn't built in a day. The unities of time and place and action that Aristotle enunciated being conventions of classic tragic theatre, the story of Oedipus's climb to eminence in Thebes has therefore to be understood.

Though the answer comes easily, those who accept the resolution must feel it to be a dramaturgical failing that Sophocles's plot should involve the oddity. True, rising takes time. But whose time? If the end is fated, it takes no time. For the gods, for an Oracle, there is no tomorrow, though not in Jocasta's sense. To them, the future is present. And to this there is a realistic side. You smoke a pack a day. Thirty years on you present with emphysema.

The Sphinx had posed an ambiguous question, not just an enigmatic one. In fact, the Sphinx carries the ambiguity in its very body. Suppose you are asked: What has the head and breast of a woman, the wings of an eagle, and the body and tail of a lion? You are apt to be unclear as to whether the questioner is looking for one thing that answers to all three specifications or for several things among which the listed parts are distributed. The answer, that is, might be: a circus act comprising a woman, a bird, and the king of the beasts. The Sphinx itself constitutes of course another answer – of the other sort. Like the latest household utensil touted on the infomercials, the gadget that grates, dices, and chops, the Sphinx is 3-in-1. The sphyngian question has three elements too. And the answer is again 3-in-1. But note the difference. The 3-in-1 in the first case is space-like; in the second, time-like. Oedipus has understood the answer in the former way. He had misunderstood human time. (He regards himself as Zeus-like in his knowledge.) And he, too, is Sphinx-like in this regard. Like the Sphinx, Oedipus is monstrous. He is at one and the same time several immiscible things: his father's child; his mother's spouse; his children's sibling. Tiresias says three times that Oedipus is the murderer. In the light of the discrepancy, the repetition is a nice stroke. Oedipus is the murderer thrice over. He is a 3-in-1 murderer.

The threefold accusation is a nice stroke. Sophocles is, it seems, gripped by its niceness. For he turns the tragedy into a veritable thicket of threes. Always at the margin of our awareness as we work through the action is the Sphinx's riddle with its three stages of human life. In the play itself we find Oedipus's rhetorical claim to the Chorus Leader that the 'third best' approach to divining the wishes of Apollo would under the circumstances be as good as the others [321]; Creon's assertion that he is the 'third' of the royal family, after Oedipus himself and Jocasta, and that the three are 'equals' [649]; the fateful meeting spot, 'where three roads meet' [790]; the fact that the infant born to Laius and Jocasta was cast out when 'he wasn't three days old' [791]; again the meeting of the 'three roads' [805] and the 'triple crossroads' [884]; Oedipus's mention of 'three generations' of lineage [1166]; the three flocks of the messenger and the shepherd [1246–1247]; and the 'three whole seasons' they spend there [1248].

As to the fourth oddity, again Sophocles seems to go out of his way to underscore it. As we saw, one person other than Oedipus survived the violence at the crossroads. *Prima facie* unaccountably, he turns out to be the person who was charged with disposing of the infant Oedipus. And in the course of the interrogation it emerges that the messenger sent from Corinth to inform of Polybus's death is the very person who bore Oedipus to Corinth. Why two characters for four roles? It was, we know, usual for a single actor to play several roles in the productions. For the number of actors was limited. But here we have single characters in the play playing several roles. Wouldn't the spectators, who knew the conventions well, have remarked the fact?

Once again, Sophocles is weaving plot and theme. The characters exemplify the idea that there is nothing whatever amiss in people playing distinct roles. A shepherd can also be a guard. Why not? What makes for a Sphinx-like character is a mixing of parts that should be kept apart, for example, spouse and child.

In an oft-declaimed poem, Robert Frost describes a triple crossroads. Two roads diverge in a wood. The speaker tells of being 'sorry I could not travel both / And be one traveler.' Oedipus's sorrow stems from his having done what the speaker sorrows at being unable to do.

Will the Real Œdi Stand Up?

Let's play the identification game. The category: 'Big shots from the classical canon.' Let's call the person you are trying to identify 'Œdi.' Here are the clues. Œdi (pronounced 'Eddy') is renowned for figuring out riddles. Œdi is exposed to the elements by his blood relatives, and left for dead, because of a prediction, from a vatic source, to the effect that he will do them harm. Strangers then save him from the otherwise hopeless condition, and take him off to a distant place, far from home. Later, he saves a polity from perdition by solving a riddle, and is as a result adopted into the court, where he rises to eminence and authority and is given a new name. Our man has an intense interest in the fate of his natural father, for whose death, he is told, he is responsible. Œdi gets into serious trouble because of an inappropriate sexual liaison with the wife of a person to whom he is subordinate. Œdi intensely grills a number of people and issues unfair threats to them, making accusations of spying and conspiracy. As his story is told, Œdi is both father and brother to his sons.

Who is this person? Given what precedes, the expected response (quite apart from the suggestiveness of 'Œdi') is: 'Oedipus.' But the description was framed with one eye on the Bible's Joseph. Joseph is an interpreter of dreams. His brothers cast him in a pit after he reports a vision of his future ascendancy over them. Passing Midianite traders then extract Joseph from the pit, where he would otherwise expire, and sell him to Ishmaelites, who transport him to Egypt. In Egypt he interprets the dreams of the Pharaoh, thereby saving the land from the ruinous consequences of a seven years' famine. He is as a result elevated to a position second only to the Pharaoh himself. Rebaptized with a local name, he is made a virtual son. Joseph's fundamental homewards-looking concern is for his father, Jacob, in whose welfare and life he is intensely interested. 'Is your father well, the old man of whom you spoke? Is he still alive?' (43:27) Because he resisted the seductive advances of the wife of Potiphar, he had earlier found himself, due to her vengeful perjury about his comportment, in the lock-up. In examining his brothers, he makes a variety of harsh and unreasonable threats. Jacob, at the end of the story, adopts Joseph's sons, Ephraim and Menasseh, who in a sense are therefore both Joseph's children and the children of his father, that is, his brothers.

Though the parallels are amusing,[23] I do not set them out just to elicit a chuckle. Had that been the motivation, I would not have omitted to say that both characters operate in the vicinity of a Sphinx, and that a problem with lower extremities is present in both stories.

The stories of Oedipus and Joseph connect in more than the superficials. There are indeed deeper reasons why the two *should* be counterparts. Oedipus ends up in Athens; the classical promised land. Joseph's main stage, too, is far from where he belongs, and is presented, as Thebes is presented, as disreputable. It follows that to reach their respective destinations both have to resist and move beyond the conditions in which they find themselves. It would be monstrous for Joseph to treat Egypt, his home away from home, as his primary domicile; and Oedipus's monstrosity consists in his excessively close relationship with the place he comes to regard as his second home.

As such stories go, Joseph's story is healthy, even upbeat. While we approve of Oedipus's eventual rehabilitation in the vicinity of Athens, that does nothing to mitigate the horror we felt at what had befallen him in Thebes. For all the ups and downs Joseph, by contrast, leads a charmed life. Its complex elements mesh into a whole that does not have a fissure in its middle, that does not self-destruct, and that requires no correlate of the therapeutic couch. I want to show that the reason for this (once we discount the providential explanation) is that Joseph has an understanding of time that is appropriate to human reality. Joseph is in effect Oedipus's healthier half.

Remembrance of Things Future

Positively Proustian by contrast with the jerky and episodic chapters that precede, the story of Joseph occupies the last third of Genesis. I will focus on the strand of the complex narrative that treats the issue of interpretation of oracular signs and time in a concentrated way.

Having resisted the advances of Potiphar's wife, Joseph finds himself in the lock-up along with the retainers, incarcerated for unspecified misdemeanours. Each of the retainers dreams a dream, each according to his specialty; the butler dreams of wine; the baker, of bread and cakes. The dreams are structurally isomorphic. 'In my dream,' recounts the butler,

> there was a vine before me, and on the vine there were three branches. As soon as it budded, its blossoms came out and the clusters ripened into grapes. Pharaoh's cup was in my hand; and I took the grapes and pressed them into Pharaoh's cup, and placed the cup in Pharaoh's hand. (40:9–11)

Save for the ending, the baker's dream is structurally identical:

> I also had a dream: there were three cake baskets on my head, and in the uppermost basket there were all sorts of baked food for the Pharaoh, but the birds were eating it out of the basket on my head. (16–18)

Joseph offers to interpret. In both cases the trios represent three days. In both cases, the Pharaoh will lift the servant up once a time of that duration has elapsed. Only, while the butler will be restored to favour, the baker will literally have his head lifted: he will be hanged, and the birds will eat of him!

Given the structural parity of the dreams, how are the contradictory fates justified? What does the episode have to do with Joseph and Israel?

Close reading of the dreams discloses the key difference. Though formally indistinguishable – the text accentuates the indistinguishability by attributing to the retainers 'a dream' (40:5) in the singular[24] – the two are isomorphic *only* in a formal sense: three of this, three of that. Once the temporal dimension clocks in, a difference emerges. The butler's dream has a cinematographic quality. The vine puts forth buds, which *then* ripen into grapes, which are *then* pressed and fermented, and so on. The baker's dream is, by contrast, photographic: still or static. Where the baker's awareness is, in fine, space-like, the butler's is time-like.

Two facts confirm that this is how the dreams are designed to play off each other. The baker's métier lends itself as readily as the butler's to the idea of process. You must sow and weed and irrigate and reap, grind and mix and knead. So the failure to tell the baker's story as a story of planting and tending, of milling and baking, has to be deliberate. Also, the baker only divulges his dream after he has heard the favourable interpretation of his companion's. He is, that is, fixated on the end, the outcome.

The distinction between the metaphorical reading of the baker's dream and the more literal reading of the butler's might seem to be telling us that oneiromancers, like those who must construe the words of an oracle, have to read between the lines. This is not the message. The message is about life. What we have, in the shadow of the most famous Sphinx, is a proper answer to the Theban riddler. 'Be aware that the later develops gradually out of the earlier; and that what is latent in the earlier is not enfolded therein as the theorems of a mathematical system are implicit in the axioms.' The problem with the baker is that he telescopes all the stages into one. But the end stage, the final stage, is death. To run the stages together is to meet *his* fate.

Close examination of the plot of the story that finds Joseph in jail confirms this to be the message. Joseph is, in a functional sense, the fourth patriarch. His perishing in the lock-up would end the national saga. So far as the plotting goes, springing him requires that word about his aptitude as a dream-reader reach the Pharaoh. The butler, restored to the buttery, delivers the intelligence, apprising the Pharaoh of Joseph's talent when the Pharaoh tells of his bafflement by the disturbing dreams of lean kine and fat, of sere and plump ears of corn. But the episode also introduces, as I shall now begin to explain, the main thematic line, of the dialectics of continuation.

A number of the story's plot-features are thematically significant. The retainers are castrates. (The word I myself have been rendering 'retainer' is, literally, the noun 'castrate.' The NRSV gives 'officer' (40:2). Commonly enough in Eastern lore, non-female servants in the king's retinue are surgically emasculated. Joseph would not have got into trouble with Potiphar's wife had he been in the neutered state.[25]

Obviously, the word may have come afterwards to apply to any court functionary. If so, the Bible writers are again, as we shall understand in a moment, displaying a remarkable subtlety.) The relevant medium of consciousness is the dream. The butler deals in wine, capable of inculcating and sustaining a dream-like state. The tipsy are, as it were, daydreamers.

Once a further fact about the Hebrew is noted, the story quickly yields up most of its message. The Hebrew words 'remember' and 'male' are cognate. That they have the same root is not, semantically speaking, an accident. Given the widespread idea, endorsed, notably, by Aristotle, that the male is the prime generative agent in reproduction, and given that a memory is a trace, there is a natural link between being a potent male and leaving something behind. One's offspring are what remains of one; they are one's trace.

The deeper significance of the episode now emerges, and the thematic significance of some of the more baroque details, details that may at first sight be seen as the authors' exercise of pleasurable invention for its own sake, is clarified. Joseph asks the butler to 'remember me when it is well with you' (40:14). But as soon as he is sprung, Joseph's service vanishes from the butler's mind. Only after 'two whole years' (41:1) is his memory jogged – by the Pharaoh's oneiric plight. Why so long? The butler's memory is defective: he is only a partial male. Once this is clear, the main lesson of the whole episode regarding time can be put in a number of memorably apophthegmatic ways. All of the following are echoed in the original, the first two in the language itself.

- Begetters are not forgetters; forgetters are not begetters.
- Not to remember is to be dismembered.
- Carry on or carrion.
- Those who are hung up will be hung up.
- Those who are not well-hung will be well hung.

There is more subtlety than even such formulations capture. While remembering is essential (I repeat that the silver cord unwinding from Abraham is cut if Joseph is not remembered), the instrument is the dream. The remembering, that is, must not be too vivid. One must not be connected to the future in a way that fixes the future in terms of the present; that would determine it, in the mathematical sense, functionally. Prior to his self-immolation Oedipus suffered from this sort of total present-ness. The figurative meaning of 'lifting' applies to the butler, not to the baker. But the figurative is present only *in potentia* in the literal. Extracting it requires suppleness, flexibility, openness, creativity. In the story, that flexibility is assigned to dreams. Appropriately, the butler's specialty, as I already remarked, is a psychedelic: wine.

To remember not at all is to be dismembered. As the case of Holocaust survivors indicates, memory can also however be had in excess. Total recall binds one to the past; makes one its hostage. To develop, one must not be arrested. This is a kind of down-to-earth version of the present-ness of which the Oedipus story is critical. Wanted, then, is the mean between the cult of the novel and (the specialty of the Egyptians) the mummified past, antiquarianism.

These lessons resonate with the post-Genesis Bible narrative. Freed from Egypt, the Israelites hanker after the fleshpots of their captivity. It's the age-old nostalgia for the good old days, even if, as is frequently the case, these were in reality not-so-good old days. A constant formula of the Bible, after Genesis, when the consciousness of the nation is dominated by the Egyptian experience and the Exodus, is the need to remember that one had been a slave in Egypt and had been delivered from bondage by the Lord. The point here is that some of the Israelites remember too well. They are the slaves of the past, as they were slaves, arrested in their national development, in Egypt. The desire to go back is the refusal to accept liberation. Thus, in the first biblical appearance of this theme, God stations 'cherubim, and a sword flaming and turning,' (3:24) at the gates of Eden to bar the man and the woman from a homecoming of an improper sort. A middle path is needed between total amnesia and total recall – between, in our terms, the Eden-dweller and the warrior.

Oedipus's self-blinding is a metaphorical version of castration, which itself is a metaphor for accepting that the future is to us dark. For purposes of dealing with the Oracle and the Sphinx, Oedipus would have done well to enlist the services of Joseph. Indeed, for purposes of gaining the self-understanding that he needs, Oedipus could not have done better than to apply to Joseph's father. The psychoanalyst must complete analysis before offering his or her services to others. Jacob has the credentials, his lameness, acquired in the course of attempting to find out *his* identity, being a less dark version of Oedipus's loss of sight.

Oedipus 'solves' the riddle. He is in his person the key that fits into and opens the lock, because he himself, doomed in his inflated self-regard to tumble, is adjusted perfectly to the tumblers. What walks, and walks, and walks? It's the baker's language. What Oedipus learns is that what walks on four *later* walks on two and *later* walks on three. Like Lear, Oedipus is most noble when he is most broken. Achilles, too, came down to live in time.

So too, I have argued, did one other member of our cast of characters.

Jacob did not get an answer when he wrestled with the angel. Later in the Torah (Exodus 3:13–14), Moses makes the same request, and in this case God is forthcoming:

> If I come to the Israelites and say to them, 'The God of your ancestors has sent me to you,' and they ask me, 'What is his name?' what shall I say to them?' God said to Moses, 'I AM WHO I AM.' He said further, 'Thus you shall say to the Israelites, I AM has sent me to you.'

The name can also be (and sometimes is) rendered in the future tense: 'I WILL BE WHAT I WILL BE.' Though the present-tense rendering is primary – God is the principle of particularity; God's 'I AM' is an assertion of the ontological irreducibility of this particularity – the future-tense version does make a point that is implicit in the present-tense one. The Bible's movement is downwards: to earth, where men, inspired with God's particularity, pursue their lives as humans. This requires that the future be taken out of the hands of those who claim the kind of access to and control of the future that is tantamount to a denial of its reality. God's self-naming is thus in effect an answer to the Sphinx's riddle.

Oedipus the King ends with the chorus chanting a stock piece of Greek wisdom: 'count no man happy till he dies, free of pain at last' [1684]. Like the short choral speeches that end many Greek tragic plays, this one sounds like a flourish, a plausible explanation for whose presence is found in the religious context of performance.[26] As for the sentiment itself: it is quite true that our happiness depends on happenstance. To appreciate that our lives are governed by luck – that this is the predicament that we alone among creatures find ourselves in – requires no special insight. It cannot however be concluded that short of mastering chance (the prerogative of the gods, and perhaps even not of the gods, they too being subject to the Fates), our lives are crapshoots. The message of the play, as I read it, like the message of the Bible, is that it is up to us to take such steps as we can, and that we can take some steps. That our efforts cannot ensure that we live happy lives does not imply that our efforts are futile, or that the right response to the predicament is fatalism. For those efforts, communal ones in the main, can ensure that the lives we live are at least ours.[27]

The title 'Oedipus the King' is partly ironic. 'I am Oedipus,' the protagonist had stated at the very start [9], asserting, on the basis of his removal of the Sphinx, his superior status. '*I* can assist you in your troubles.' 'I am Oedipus,' he asserts again, a broken man, at the end [1496]. 'Learn from my fall, and you might do better. Set your lives on a proper footing.' 'Let there be light,' the biblical God commands at the outset. And the end? I quote again from Elijah's anti-theophany: 'a sound of sheer silence' (1 Kings 19:12). When God next speaks to Elijah, he asks: 'What are you doing here, Elijah?' It's a genuine question, not a rhetorical one. 'Do you really think that I can do something for you?' The advice that God then tenders (advice about practical politics) Elijah could have come up with himself.

We shall now look at a thinker who believes that only knowers of the sort that Oedipus comes in the play to see that he is not should be kings. We shall see that this thinker does not advance such a view while leaving everything else as it is. This thinker reverts to Genesis 1 from Genesis 2 and takes a position on which being is prior to becoming. To this thinker a whole world of thinking has become a swollen footnote.

12
Misbehaviourism

Philosophia's Choice

'This is the first time I was ever in a city where you couldn't throw a brick without breaking a church window.' So said Mark Twain after a visit to Montreal. A brickobolus in fourth century BCE Athens stood a similar chance of shattering the reflections of philosophers. Schools where the discipline was instructed and practised dotted the city, quite a few of them located in the leafier suburbs distant from the hubbub of the agora. Aristotle's Lyceum. The colonnaded promenade or painted porch – the Stoa – where Zeno taught. The Garden of Epicurus. The archetype of these institutions was Plato's Academy, set up c. 385 in a private grove within a garden that had been deeded to the citizens of Athens by a certain Academus upon whom, according to a legend of the city's earliest days, the god Apollo had originally bestowed the land.

'All of Western philosophy is footnotes to Plato.' A witticism about the profession of philosophy in ancient times could be tacked on as a footnote to this, Alfred North Whitehead's most memorable contribution to Bartlett. 'Prospective philosophers had to make a choice: Plato or Aristotle? Aristotle was no exception. Faced with the choice,' the witticism concludes, 'he chose Plato!' There is a good deal of truth in the barbed jest, and not just as regards Aristotle and/or antiquity.

Save for a cameo appearance or two, Plato, colossus on the stage of Greek culture, has so far been excluded from our festivities. Let's now invite him to the party. Will Plato suit the company, or will he, like Eris at the nuptials of Thetis and Peleus, sow discord? Plato too, it happens, drops onto our plates something inscribed as was Eris's apple, and invites us to bite. He offers us the kallipolis, the fair city of the *Republic*.

Early on, Plato's claim about Homer's cultural significance was quoted. Socrates, Plato's spokesperson, mentions the many in his day who 'praise Homer and say that he's the poet who educated Greece, that it's worth taking up his works in order to learn how to manage and educate people, and that one should arrange one's whole life in accordance with his teachings.'[1] Just in case one suspects that Plato, axe ground and at the ready, builds Homer up in order to cut him down, here is the dispassionate judgment of a modern scholar.[2]

> It is not my claim that the *Iliad* is a definitive statement of Greek religious consciousness; it is not a testament, a gospel or torah. There were many other aspects of the religion of the Greeks, who at various times and places created and believed in religions of fertility, or righteousness, of ecstasy, and of salvation. But the *Iliad* is the most important book of the Greeks; while it is not in the ordinary sense a religious book, it embodies religious attitudes which were important to the Greeks and went far towards making them Greek.

What was it in Homer the absorption of which made the Greeks Greek? Reading Plato, one is at a loss. Since Plato so frequently marches Homer in for a roughing up, this is surprising. More than surprising, astonishing, is the fact that the philosophical tradition has been content to leave the blank blank. Comb the vast literature on Greek philosophy for an exposition of Homer that constitutes a solid platform for assessing Plato's indictment, and that's what you will draw. Over the past few years, I have even conducted a straw poll, asking many professional philosophers to specify what Plato objects to in Homer. Almost always mentioned is the soap opera on Olympus and the fact that Homer writes poetry. True, Plato thinks that by encouraging disrespect for the gods exposure to Homer could have a socially disruptive effect. True too, according to Plato artists *qua* artists don't know what they're talking about. But the second of these would apply equally to a poet who sang of the natural world that it is, as Plato himself holds,[3]

> but a spume that plays
> Upon a ghostly paradigm of things;

As for the first, where is the obvious falsity in the proposition that the forces of nature comport themselves in what from our perspective are capricious and mutually conflicting ways? Would *Protagoras*, had he been asked, have put his approval on the basis that Homer poetically pictured the gods as reigning like cats and dogs?

More anon about Homer's depiction of the gods and Plato's opposition to it. Here and now, the point is only that students of philosophy weaned (as back in the day I was) on Plato's early and middle dialogues lack an independent notion of what Homer holds, positively holds, about men and women. Could a diet too heavy on philosophy courses be at fault? I doubt that a few offerings from a classics department would have cleansed the palate. When they are not pursuing a literary or linguistic interest, the experts here see the *Iliad* as a story that rubs our noses in the horrors of war, not as encoding a view of the human condition.

Leaving Aristotle out of it, the witticism about philosophia's choice hits, it seems, the bullseye. To judge from the treatment of Homer, philosophers have chosen Plato. In itself, the choice is fair enough. They have however chosen by default. This is not fair at all.[4]

A Conjecture

What is it about the epics that strikes Plato as foul? Why does Plato not hit Homer more straightforwardly?

Homer's views were expounded in chapter 6. To state that Homer's position on the nature of men and women differs from Plato's is to understate. The two are incommensurate. If Homer is (as Redfield asserts) instrumental in making the Greeks Greek, Plato is out to remake them in a different image and likeness. In the continuation of the sentence from the *Republic* quoted at the outset Plato himself puts a word to the – as he sees it – non-negotiable difference. Socrates advises Glaucon to 'agree' when he encounters those who praise Homer as 'the most poetic of the tragedians and the first among them' (607a). Homer, in some sense of 'tragic,' takes that kind of view. In Plato's judgment, the troubles that assail men and women are not in the world. They stem from ignorance. They are in the head.

Philosopher and Bard are playing for high stakes – the hearts and minds of the Greeks.[5] Could this explain the slant of Plato's criticism? Given Plato's commitment to giving reasons, I am loath to take the position that when it comes to Homer he follows the principle that all's fair in love and war. Yet it cannot be denied that Plato's model of hospitality is more Polyphemus than Abraham.

It's puzzling. Here, to make sense of Plato's approach, is a conjecture that attracts a lot of credence from its capacity to make sense of Plato's handling of the epics without obliging us to pin on him a charge of bad faith.

In addressing the epics, Plato does not focus on what is new, that is, the reformed view of men and women as autonomous. He takes his lead from the pre-reformed warrior ethos, that is, the side of Homer dimly consonant with his own thinking. It is perfectly reasonable for Plato to do this. Homer did not after all refute the ethos. Logic forced no one to follow Achilles off the fields of glory into the quotidian. And, arguably, it *was* this side of Homer that was demotically picked up.

Reviewing what we have seen in Homer, let me show that if we seek structure beneath the gore, the warrior ethos reveals itself to be quite Platonic.

In the *Iliad*, Homer presents, on the warrior side, an encompassing value system. For the warriors, Life = War. The idea that to be alive is to battle is in part an expression of a heightened sense of life's fragility. How could something so flimsy be of primary value? That is the dominating thought. Yet despite their understanding full well that though here today they are gone later today, the warriors do not react by raising the white flag. They fight, that is, they live vigorously, for the sake of something of greater value than life itself. That greater thing, the thing that for them has primary value, is survival; survival in (public) memory. The warriors regard their individual lives only as *instruments* for securing the latter. The warriors are thus performing through their doings what in the culture is an *imitatio deorum*, by which they hope to achieve (and are regarded as capable of achieving) a simulacrum of what is had by the gods *qua* gods: immortality.

Three structural pillars of Platonism are these: the ontological principle that the timeless is more basic than the temporal (the Forms have primacy over the corrodibles that inhabit space and time); the epistemological principle that the contents of mind are more basic than physical furniture (the Forms are the primary objects of knowledge); and the value-theoretic principle that the worth of the mutable is less than that of the durable (the Forms are better than the changeable phenomena). All three principles are visible in the warrior conception of things. The timeless is above the temporal. Timelessness is given a mental location – in (public) memory. Worth is judged by relative proximity to immortality.

I will now bear the conjecture out by critically annotating a few things that Plato says in the *Republic* about Homer. Observe that each of the passages that Plato quotes and alludes to played a key role in *our* explorations of the Homeric view.

Plato Homeromastix

The first passage, from the *Odyssey*, could just as well have been directed against the extended speech to the ambassadors in Book 9 of the *Iliad*. Odysseus, encountering Achilles during a visit to Hades, speaks to him the following words [11:547–553]:

> . . . Achilles,
> there's not a man in the world more blest than you –
> there never has been, never will be one.
> Time was, when you were alive, we Argives
> honoured you as a god. And now down here, I see,
> you lord it over the dead in your power.
> So grieve no more at dying, great Achilles.

How does Achilles react? Odysseus proceeds [554–558]:

> I reassured the ghost, but he broke out, protesting,
> 'No winning words about death to *me*, shining Odysseus!
> By god, I'd rather slave on earth for another man –
> some dirt-poor tenant farmer who scrapes to keep alive –
> than rule down here over all the breathless dead.

Life of whatever sort, however mean, is preferable. In *Republic* Book 7, Plato half-quotes this claim. He (516d) has Socrates say that the philosopher would

> prefer to 'work the earth as a serf to another, one without possessions,' and go through any suffering, rather than share the . . . opinions [of ordinary, unreconstructed, folk] and live as they do.

As a gloss, this is laughable, doing to Homer what Aristophanes, no doubt to Plato's great distaste, did to Socrates. True, Plato had earlier quoted Homer's original verbatim. (His audience will certainly have known the original.) But on that occasion too he had ignored Homer's meaning. The passage, Plato had said, is offensive because it 'disparage[s] the life in Hades' (386c), the idea being that doing this would dishearten soldiers on the battlefield. Achilles is not however blowing the whistle on Hades as the BBB might do on Florida swampland advertised as Shangri-La to prospective retirees from Quebec. He is unfavourably contrasting the very thing that has paramount value for a warrior with the often drab and workaday lives that most of us, beyond the bounds of the warrior ethos, live. As to whether those who regard their lives as intrinsically valuable are more likely to flee than fight, that is an empirical question.

Note, however, that Plato's 'gloss' makes good sense if the point is that the *polis*, the locale of peaceful life, is the central value. Which, as we have seen, is the (unreformed) position of Sophocles's Creon.

We return to that passage about the carpenter (406d–407a):

> When a carpenter is ill, he asks his doctor to give him an emetic or a purge to expel the trouble, or to rid him of it by cautery or the knife. But if he is advised to take a long course of treatment, to keep his head wrapped up, and all that sort of thing, he soon replies that he has not time to be ill and it is not worth his while to live in that way, thinking of nothing but his illness and neglecting his proper work. And so he bids good-bye to that kind of doctor and goes back to his ordinary way of life. Then he either regains his health and lives to go about his proper business, or, if his body is not equal to the strain, gets rid of all his troubles by dying.

One might bid goodbye to an unfulfilling job. One might leave a relationship that has soured. But Socrates's topic is life itself, not just this unpleasant happening or that regrettable turn. Our lives, Plato's mouthpiece is saying, are for doing what it is that we do. Failing the ability to do it effectively, those lives should be relinquished.

What does Socrates mean by 'that way of life'? What kind is 'that kind of doctor'? That way of life *is* our life; we struggle along. That kind of doctor is the common-or-garden kind, of the body or of the heart, striving to make it go better with us. The case of Nestor, the Old Soldier among the warriors, is revealing here. As it happens, Nestor's view is just like Plato's. Nestor regrets that, no longer able to fight, he is still around. But while Homer gives this view respectful expression, the *Iliad* rejects it.

Homer begins the shift towards locating primary value in the individual with Athena grabbing a distressed Achilles by the tresses. While a considerable way to go remains even after the meeting with Priam, for Achilles there is no going back.[6]

The Trojan king begs for the return of the body of his son. As we have already seen, Achilles raises Priam from the ground:

> Come, please, sit down on this chair here . . .
> What good's to be won from tears that chill the spirit?
> So the immortals spun our lives that we, we wretched men,
> live on to bear such torments – the gods live free of sorrows.

Casting off his moiety of divinity, Achilles casts in his lot fully with the human.

Humans are not just clods of clay; nor are they divine. They are in-between creatures – middlemen. And so, Achilles would have Priam sit with him part way between the earth and the heaven.

Plato's comment about losses such as Achilles and Priam have suffered?

> . . . it is best to keep as quiet as possible in misfortunes and not get excited about them . . . First, it isn't clear whether such things will turn out to be good or bad in the end; second, it doesn't make the future any better to take them hard; third, human affairs aren't worth taking very seriously; and, finally, grief prevents the very thing we most need in such circumstances from coming into play as quickly as possible. (604b–c)

Well might Plato have been repelled by Achilles. Achilles also recognizes that grieving must end. After speaking the first line quoted above, *he* had said:

> Let us put our griefs to rest in our own hearts,
> rake them up no more, raw as we are with mourning.

True, life must be lived – and that's no tautology. Life can also be wasted, frittered away. But Plato likens the grieving to the 'weeping and wailing of children when they trip' (604c). The passing of others who are dear to us; our own deaths. Suffering. These are mere pratfalls. The stuff of farce, none of it is worth taking sufficiently seriously to dictate how we evaluate things.

To judge by the exhibits, in criticizing Homer Plato does not go straight at the view of men and women whose dramatic vector is Achilles. He takes issue with Homer by amending several features of the warrior conception. But Homer's basic understanding of human reality leaves that conception behind. Since, as I see it, Homer's case is a considerable one, Plato had better make a case that has at least an equal capacity to compel. The sequel is devoted to considering whether he does.

Relative to the various landmarks we have visited, the Platonic position is on the positive side a mixture of Genesis 1 (where the reality of men and women is subsumed by nature) and Creon's Thebes (where the reality of men and women is absorbed into the *polis*).[7] Backing up Plato's stand is a deep and wide metaphysical analysis. One essential, and highly speculative, feature of the metaphysics will be exposed presently.

A Greek Moses?

Augustine opined that Plato might have 'learnt by word of mouth . . . the contents of the Scriptures.'[8] If Augustine's claim of likeness between Plato and the Bible boiled down to this, that Plato's ambition is sky-high, his accomplishment biblical in scope, no disagreement would be heard from *this* quarter. Plato's is indeed a prodigious performance, the more remarkable performed as it is by a single individual in a single lifetime. Shakespeare and Beethoven come to mind, and even they do not quite measure up. Plato takes on board Homer and Hesiod, pre-Socratic philosophy and classical drama, Athens's rise and fall, the advent of the sophists, and so on. Assembling these materials, Plato slots all of them within a single story. Augustine is speaking however of a likeness of content, and here agreement must be withheld. Plato's thought does have a substantive affinity for *Christian* theological thinking. The Hebrew Scriptures are not the Gospels. Jerusalem is not Rome. The biblical message, Moses asserts, is not in heaven. As I have argued, Homer is my Greek Moses, and Plato holds no brief for Homer.

Christian theology apart, Augustine might defend *his* enrolling of Plato in Jeremiah's yeshiva by highlighting the fact that the world, in the biblical story, is brought to light with men and women in mind, which bespeaks a deeper rationality: made for a purpose, the world answers to recognized and anticipated needs. A central tenet of Plato's metaphysics is that the world is a rational place. This quintessentially Platonic claim is far stronger than the claim of scientists that the world is governed by law-like regularities that patient scrutiny can divine. The Platonic claim is that the world is *intelligible* – that it makes sense in the same way that a hungry person's going to the store to buy a loaf of bread he or she wants makes sense. (Atomic Theory predicts that two atoms of hydrogen will combine with one of oxygen. We expect the combining to occur, and would be surprised if it didn't. Why the valence of oxygen should be 2 is not however intelligible to us.)

The defence, despite a veneer of plausibility, rests on an error. Although the world of Genesis *is* designed with men and women in mind, that world is *not* the sum total of being. The world of Genesis is the Land of Men and Women. It is not Raven's Land.

We could say that the biblical God is to the natural world as men and women are to the human world (to houses). To invert this, saying that the natural world is like a house, is to beg the question at issue. It is not false that a house is to men and women as a nest is to birds. It hardly follows that the nest is constructed with a purpose.

The Intelligible World

Plato holds that the world is intelligible. Here, from the *Phaedo*, is a passage which adumbrates the position – a capsule intellectual autobiography that Plato puts into the mouth of Socrates.

Socrates reports that he was first attracted to views like those that Thales advanced. However, as he turned his attention to human affairs, these views came to seem inadequate. 'One day,' Socrates relates (97b–98e), 'I heard someone reading, as he said,' from a book of Anaxagoras,

> and saying that it is Mind that directs and is the cause of everything. I was delighted with this cause and it seemed to me good, in a way, that Mind should be the cause of all. I thought that if this were so, the directing Mind would direct everything and arrange each thing in a way that was best. If then one wished to know the cause of each thing, why it comes to be or perishes or exists, one had to find what was the best way for it to be, or to be acted upon, or to act. On these premises then it befitted a man to investigate only, about this and other things, what is best. The same man must inevitably also know what is worse, for that is part of the same knowledge. As I reflected on this subject I was glad to think that I had found in Anaxagoras a teacher about the cause of things after my own heart, and that he would tell me, first, whether the earth was flat or round, and then would explain why it is so of necessity, saying which is better, and that it was better to be so. If he said it was in the middle of the universe, he would go on to show that it was better for it to be in the middle, and if he

> showed me those things I should be prepared never to desire any other kind of cause. I was ready to find out in the same way about the sun and the moon and the other heavenly bodies . . . I never thought that Anaxagoras, who said that those things were directed by Mind, would bring in any other cause for them than that it was best for them to be as they are. Once he had given the best for each as the cause for each and the general cause of all, I thought he would go on to explain the common good for all, and I would not have exchanged my hopes for a fortune . . .
>
> This wonderful hope was dashed as I went on reading [his book] and saw that the man made no use of Mind, nor gave it any responsibility for the management of things, but mentioned as causes air and ether and water and many other strange things. That seemed to me much like saying that Socrates' actions are all due to his mind, and then in trying to tell the causes of everything I do, to say that the reason that I am sitting here is because my body consists of bones and sinews, because the bones are hard and are separated by joints, that the sinews are such as to contract and relax, that they surround the bones along with flesh and skin which hold them together . . .

I daresay that none among us would be satisfied to be told that the desk at which he or she is working is in the study because the wood of which it is fashioned is in the study. We would also want to know how it got to be where it is and why it is there, and among those Socrates lumps with Anaxagoras are many whose answers would have satisfied us. Socrates alludes to Anaximander's claim that the earth does not move because it is *meteôros*. This is quite different than saying that the earth is immobile because its composing stuff is stationary. Socrates might well ask *why* the earth is at the centre. To this the answer might be that *something's* got to be at the centre. Were something else at the centre, *it* would be stationary. Still, Socrates has a point. The question 'Why is such-and-such the case?' often does not get a satisfactory sort of answer unless some purpose or intention is mentioned. This is so where the actions of men and women are the subject matter.

Plato, to extrapolate from the passage, is turning the tradition of Thales upside down.[9] Rather than maintaining that men and women are complex magnets, he is taking the position that magnets are mini-men and mini-women. Thales would collapse the Proverbist's four into his three. Plato is collapsing in the other direction. He is mapping the whole, nature + culture, onto its second term, culture, where Thales is mapping the whole onto the first term. This puts Plato at odds with the biblical view. The Bible finds the world of men and women intelligible, albeit perplexing. It does so by restriction to the world that they make. Plato is saying that men and women fit into an independently intelligible world that is not of their making. They themselves are little pieces of intelligibility. Plato's approach is not anthropofocused; and his position is not anthropocentric.

We now have a better handle on why Plato trains such intense fire at Homer's representation of the gods. Taken at face value, that representation likens the happenings in extra-human nature to the actions of beings who have minds. Zeus often does with thunderbolts what the purchaser does with the bread that he or she obtains – make toast. Socrates's complaint about Anaxagoras's mode of natural explanation doesn't therefore arise. So far, for Plato, so good. The problem is that Homer's gods are unruly. Individually, they do not behave in consistent, predictable ways. As a group, they do not act in concert. And that is, to Plato, objectionable.

Up to a point Plato has science on his side. Up to that point the Bible is an ally. Unless we, men and women in the street, look at the largest and most obvious periodicities – day and night, the round of the seasons, the phases of the moon, the wheel of the stars – nature comes across to us as disorderly, both on the level of its parts and as a whole. Careful interrogation of the surrounding world over time has enabled us to penetrate beneath phenomenal confusion to, in many cases, underlying order. The Greek natural philosophers were much more right than wrong about that. And the Bible agrees. We should, according to the Proverbist, who has observed the ants as closely as Aristotle,[10] persevere in that interrogation.

Plato asserts that reality is intelligible. Not just a postulate, this for Plato is a basic metaphysical truth. It goes far past the scientist's working hypothesis that irregularities on the perceptual level are complex constellations of underlying regularities. A heavy burden of proof falls on Plato's shoulders in regard to this supposed truth. For it is quite speculative. So heavy is the burden that no one could reasonably be expected to salute on the basis of Plato's authoritative voice.

Why isn't the science enough for Plato? The example of the Proverbist shows that perplexity about the human and a respect for a scientific view of the natural world need not war like Esau and Jacob. At any rate, it has not been established that, conceptually speaking, the Proverbist's ensemble is incoherent. If Plato's speculative addition is accepted, that, at a deeper level, penetrates beneath the Proverbist's partition. This is vital for Plato. To penetrate is to supply an independent basis for cultural criticism – for evaluating some 'ways' as defective. If successful, it renders culture accessible to Greek philosophy.

Plato is committed to explaining away the Proverbist's perplexity. An example from a later philosopher who very much chose Plato over Aristotle illustrates the manner in which he does so; or, better, since Descartes's success is as subject to debate as Plato's, signposts the route along which he is committed to doing so. In Part VI of the *Meditations* Descartes writes (58): 'a clock constructed with wheels and weights observes all the laws of nature just as closely when it is badly made and tells the wrong time as when it completely fulfils the wishes of the clockmaker.' A bad clock is as perfect a piece of nature as is a good one. Its 'badness' *qua* timepiece has nothing to do with running afoul of some natural order. Considered from the natural point of view, nothing fails of perfection. From that point of view, imperfection can be given, at most, a statistical sense. Just so, the variation in the behaviour of men and women that is the datum for the Proverbist's perplexity is like the variation in the time behaviour of timepieces.

This, packaged in biblical terms, is a reversion to the world of Genesis 1 from the world of Genesis 2, where 'good' *and* 'bad' apply. A clock that does not tell time is not a bad clock in the Genesis 2 sense of 'bad.' The Thebes of *Antigone* is a political version of Genesis 1. Just so, from the Theban standpoint a transgression of Creon's edict is a sign of defect in the transgressor. We should not be at all surprised to find that in Plato's world, as in Genesis 1, everything is good. Plato's world is presided over exclusively by the Form of the Good. There is no Form of the Bad. In Genesis 2, good and bad are heads and tails: you can't have one without the other at its back.

We come back, then, in dealing with Plato, to the issue of the disobedience of the man and the woman in the Garden. This gets a direct treatment in Plato's account of the behaviour of the citizens of the kallipolis. I will now set out the contrast between Plato's view of human action, and the biblical one. It will emerge that Plato's is a view of action that removes mind from the picture. The conception of men and women in any substantive sense as having minds is inconsistent with how Plato understands the agency of men and women. Or, as the Bible puts it: the man and the woman in Genesis, up until the transgression, are pieces of nature and/or domestic animals. The minders of the Garden are mindless.

One last point before the final push. Crucial in Plato's position, from the present standpoint, is not the Theory of Forms as a position in ontology. The idea of the world as a system, an organic-type whole, is a sufficient platform for pursuing our issue.

Plato's Action Theory

Plato analyses action, from the side of the subject, in terms of desires and beliefs. The breadbox is bare. You've set your heart on a sandwich for supper. No other desire, for example, to watch the five p.m. news on TV, is stronger. According to Plato, you will make the move to go and get a loaf. To be sure, you might not succeed. A neighbour might buttonhole you as you exit your door. You might total your car *en route* to the store and end up as an item on the five p.m. Perhaps you forgot that it's a bank holiday. Nonetheless, from *your* perspective, the course of action – grabbing your coat and hat and setting out – follows.

Suppose you stay put. Did you find some bread in the freezer that you had forgotten? Did your sandwich craving abate? Did you hear that the store is toast, a fire having gutted the mall? If any of these is so, then the belief/desire constellation has changed, and your staying put falls into line. What Plato will not allow is that you just decide, you simply choose, to stay put. This makes as much sense, from his perspective, as a stone levitating when released outside an upper-storey window does from ours.

The position is that no autonomous factor called 'will' mediates between, on the one side, desires (in the example, the desire for bread) and information (in the example, the various bits of data about the world and about your condition), and, on the other side, action. Plato's slogan here is well known to students of Plato: to *know* the good is to *do* the good. In fine: the behaviour that emanates from the agent is tightly determined by desires and beliefs. When the relevant desires are in effect and the relevant pieces of information are believed, non-performance requires an external explanation.

The issue of will is a vexed one. Pre-analytically, we regard ourselves as doing what we do, at least sometimes, because we choose. True enough, our choices usually track our desires and the information that is at our disposal. An external observer who is well informed about a person's wants and beliefs can with a fair degree of accuracy anticipate what he or she will (try to) do. Nevertheless, what usually occurs does not, we think, have to occur. We hold that the sheer exercise of choice can *invest* a specific course of action (or inaction), *endow* that course of action (or inaction), with value. By deciding, under the mentioned circumstances, to stay put, I am *making* that course of action (or inaction) more valuable than the course that is otherwise indicated.[11] Plato cannot effectively respond by saying that since the decision alters the situation there is no conflict with his view. Decision *follows* belief and desire. *That* is his view. On his view there is no independent decision. I am saying (and what I am saying, I say, is what we believe) that decision is an *independent* factor, and that, as such, it can in principle serve a valorizing function.

Doesn't saying that my act of will invests or endows the chosen course of action with value cave in to Plato? Is it not thereby conceded that whatever the internal goings on my choice is, as Plato maintains, locked to what I regard as good? It does not and it is not. We have here a play on words, not an argument. To say that X is good from where I stand because I choose it is not to say that X is deemed better by me, 'better' in *Plato's* sense, than all other courses of action that occur to me as options. Consider the words 'I'd rather have done X.' One who asserts the words does not mean 'I deem X to be better than the course I followed.' Rather: 'Given the opportunity to do it all over again, I would choose X.' We see no inconsistency in someone's claiming that though her life worked out satisfactorily by virtue of having completed medical school, as her parents wished and as the vocational counsellor advised, she would rather have joined the circus. This does not mean that the life under the big top is deemed to be the sort of life that would have given more fulfilment, more happiness, than ministering to the sick and/or earning lots of money and garnering esteem and respect. It means, or at any rate *can* mean: 'I'd rather have chosen my course.' To convert this into 'I'd be happier having made the choice,' and then to point to 'happier' as supportive of Plato, is to confuse two senses of the term. The doctor can perfectly intelligibly say that she would have been happier to have made the choice to have become a doctor than passively to have followed the course designated by her mother and father and approved by the vocational expert, viz., to become a doctor. In saying this she cannot be saying, nonsensically, that the life of a doctor would have been more fulfilling than the life of a doctor. She is saying that she would have preferred (= would have been happier) choosing it.

Plato grants of course that men and women can do the wrong thing. He thinks that left to their own devices, frequently if not most of the time they will. That is why the institutions of the kallipolis are so coercive. Yet Plato does not grant as a possibility what is expressed in the

Latin phrase '*Video melior, proboque deteriora sequor.*' He allows only that men and women are often misinformed about what is good or better or best.[12] As Plato sees it, if I determine that relative to my purposes some course of action is overall the best, then, irrespective of whether I am right about this, I cannot not (try to) do it.

The important consequence is plain. Actors being fallible, to say that action follows knowledge is to say that action follows what passes from an actor's point of view for knowledge. Often, indeed very often, our beliefs are false. Often, very often, we act on misinformation. Rooting around in his wife's purse for a few coins to feed the meter, Charles snags a scrap of paper on which 'I love John' is inscribed. Though he is not aware of this, he has ripped off part of the whole note: 'I love John's apple pie.' Even if what one does is locked tightly to what one believes, it cannot be concluded that Charles will confront the wife in a rage. For he will also hold many other beliefs. Perhaps he is of a forgiving nature. Perhaps he has his own tart or crumpet on the side. Nonetheless, since (discounting external interference) what one does is certainly a function of what one supposes to be true, unless and until Charles is supplied with correct information his actions will be out of synchrony with the facts. Should he immediately confront his wife, even as a sheepish grin replaces his snarl she might start to question the quality of his trust, and this, to quote Dolly Parton, could spell the first letters of D-I-V-O-R-C-E. Now Plato holds that most men and women lack true belief, let alone knowledge. Unlike Ms Parton, most men and women are by nature insufficiently endowed, and for most men and women no procedure of intelligence augmentation is available. Knowledge is available only to the few who are intellectually equipped. It is the prerogative of the philosopher. Accordingly, what most men and women do, their decisions on what to do, must be alienated from them and reposed in other hands – the hands of the knowers.

It's a neat package. The world is a unitary place. Each thing belongs in some slot, a slot that suits its nature. But the human things, who have the power of thought, may misunderstand their natures, and their positions. This misunderstanding can result in disorder. Proper order depends on knowledge of the structure of the whole, knowledge that only a select few have the capacity to achieve. Only a few are able, so to speak, to digest the fruit of the tree of knowledge of the Good. The idea that one's life course is a matter for voluntary decision, and that making such choices is of the essence of the lives of men and women, Plato rejects. We may *think* of ourselves that way. If we do, we are, according to Plato, thinking falsely. So, as I put it, the alienation of decision from the less knowledgeable follows. If they resist, they must be forced.

The *Republic* argues that men and women who live in accordance with the plan will live lives that are happiest: fulfilled and contented. Doing what they do well, they will not be frustrated. Any other course is likely to yield more frustration. It's an attractive argument, and rings of some truth. We now know where it fails – where, I mean, *our* opposition is focused. In important part, we regard the lives we live as having the value they do *because* we choose them. Repudiating volition as he does, Plato would deny that this makes sense. *This* denial is the dead centre of the web.

One might wonder whether Plato could consistently hold such a view. Whitehead, making a pair for Bartlett, expressed the doubt, though against science. 'Scientists animated by the purpose of proving that they are purposeless constitute an interesting subject for study.'[13]

Going beyond Homer to the core of myth that Homer taps, let me show how Plato contradicts himself in the *Republic*. In the closing Book, Plato tells the Myth of Er.[14] In Plato's recounting, the life position of a citizen of the kallipolis turns out to be a function not only of his or her specific endowments and qualities and aptitudes, which is how the political construction was explained in the non-mythic part of the dialogue, but also of a choice that he or she makes. The position that each individual ends up in is only spun into finality by the fates after the individual selects from among the options. The problem is that if one reaches the spinners late, the available options may be limited to life positions that few would choose. If Plato doesn't recognize the problematic legitimacy of the kallipolis, why would he tell the story this way? If he recognizes that, must he not regard legitimacy as anchored in the consent of the players? This is however inconsistent with the formal account in the dialogue, where the questions are these: What kind of life will be a good life for the individual? How ought the rulers to act in order to maximize the chances of that kind of life being lived? To say that the life that is chosen will be the best life, or to make the choice part of the package, is to reject Plato's politics.[15]

The Schema of the Particular

I return now for a fuller philosophical treatment of the distinction between individual and particular. To this end, let me use a third noun phrase, 'concrete thing,' meaning 'object localized in space and time; object with relatively discrete spatio-temporal boundaries.'

Take a concrete thing that is thought of functionally, for example, an automobile. It is unimportant that the thing is an artefact. Important is that it is thought of as a role filler. The heart, or the liver, neither of them manufactured, would also do. The parts of the automobile, for example, the air filter, are understood relative to the whole – relative, specifically, to the function that the whole serves. Now the air filter is itself a concrete thing. It is a quite different concrete thing from the left front tire. When the air filter ceases to perform the function for which it is designed, the mechanic will not proceed to replace it with the other part. Any (other) concrete thing meeting the air filter's specifications *qua* air filter will however do just fine. The owner of the automobile does not care which of the (new) Frams is installed. When this indifference holds, let me refer to the concrete thing as *an individual*. When a concrete thing is such that another such thing will not do, let us speak of it as *a particular*.

I began by spelling out the meaning of 'individual' in terms of the idea of function. Individuals are concrete things that are fungibles. Reverting to Noah's floating menagerie: it makes no difference which (flesh-and-blood) bison is present on the voyage; important is only that some bison or other be aboard that satisfies or meets certain general specifications – that, to phrase it in a flatter language, falls under certain concepts. The one that is present must not, for instance, be sterile. The bison, in the Flood story, is therefore an individual but not a particular.

The idea of an individual as just now explained is the idea of a concrete thing that fills some function. Latter-day developments in philosophical logic can be exploited to extend the idea of an individual beyond the functional, in this colloquial sense of 'function.' The more refined idea – the more 'logical' idea – is the idea of an individual as the argument of a function. From a purely lexicographical standpoint, the double usage of 'function' may be fortuitous. Even if it is, there is actually a thought in the double-usage. The idea that it is immaterial which concrete thing does the job, providing some concrete thing or other does, is reflected in the (logical) idea that the ultimate ground for distinguishing concrete things from one another, and hence the ultimate sense of thinghood carried by the concept of a concrete thing, is spatio-temporal position. It follows, as P.F. Strawson's classic treatment in *Individuals*[16] confirms, that philosophical logicians understand concrete things to be in principle such that any number can satisfy the same general conditions – that is, can give the same value when plugged as arguments into the same functions. What else does this mean than that relative to those conditions it is a matter of indifference which of the things one has? So 'function,' in the sense in which I used it in the preceding sentence but one, a sense tracing back to Frege, is no mere homonym of 'function' in the more street-level sense with which we began.[17]

Equipped with the refinement of the idea of a function, we can set particulars more cleanly apart from individuals. For a helping hand, I reach out to Immanuel Kant.

In the *Critique of Pure Reason*, after completing the deduction of the categories, Kant raises a difficulty about their application to the empirical realm. This is a problem, he explains, because *qua* unabstracted from the empirical, the categories are quite heterogeneous with the contents of sense-experience. To bridge the gap Kant introduces what he calls 'schemata.' These have a character halfway between the formal content of the categories and the full concreteness of the objects of sense-experience. Now one is entitled to wonder whether Kant's problem could be solved along these lines. That which is midway between A and B is still, for being at some distance from A and at some distance from B, heterogeneous with both. As the case may be, the idea of schematization is useful for present purposes. Let us simplify what Kant says and see schematization as the provision of less formal (yet still non-empirical) content to more formal structures. Temporal sequence according to rule might thus be the schematization of causation, itself seen as closer to the logical idea of truth-conditionality as expressed by the '$\supset$' or the '$\rightarrow$' of the propositional calculus. My claim, in these terms, is that the schema of the particular is not just the principle of numerical (sc., spatio-temporal) difference. The latter is the schema of the individual. The schema of the particular is the interior. Individuals are distinguished by being outside of one another. Particulars are distinguished from individuals by having insides.

This implies, analytically speaking, that individuals, *qua* functional, have no interiors. The only distinctions between them are those capturable in conceptual terms; what remains of the inside is nothing other than instantial status. And this is nothing.

A 'religious' way of stating the difference between men and machines is that men have souls. Now souls are, pretty much *ex vi terminorum*, not spatial. But that, we can now argue, is only a way of speaking, encouraged no doubt by the needs of salvation. The truth is that the instantiator has a character that resists being unpacked by more concepts. The soul is a principle of particularity. To accept the sharp distinction between individuals and particulars is thus to accept the soul.

In discussing the Bible's description of men and women as standing to the rest in the distinctive relationship of 'domination,' I explained that the characterization of men and women as created in God's image and likeness is the reverse side of the same coin. Just as God is outside of the creation as a whole, so men and women are outside of it in that respect. The explanation focuses the point nicely. Being outside, how can men and women yet be part of the (natural) creation? The answer is: they have insides. From the standpoint of the (natural) creation, their insides are outside. In the biblical narrative, Genesis 2 describes their coming to have insides. '[T]he Lord God formed man from the dust of the ground, and breathed into his nostrils the breath of life' (2:7).

A Fish Story

The point about interiority is a point of difference between the Bible and Greek philosophical thinking (of the latter of which Plato is, as I stated, representative in the relevant respects). Insight into this can be gained by considering the matter from the perspective of developmental psychology.

In a bible-esque reflection on the complexities of life and mind, though one with a decidedly anti-biblical slant, Adam Gopnik describes his young daughter's response to the death of a pet fish. When the fish is surreptitiously replaced by a brother swimmer, nearly enough an identical twin, Olivia, quite aware that the original is no more, reacts as follows.[18]

> 'He looks [exactly] like Bluie,' she admitted. 'He looks like Bluie. But he's not Bluie. He's a stranger. He doesn't know me. He's not my friend, who I could talk to.'

The same goes of course for the dolls, the furniture, the clothes, the special blanket. These, often given names, are invested with souls. Lost and replaced, each would elicit a like reaction.

A fish is a paradigm individual; it is not even residually a particular. Accordingly, the parents can correctly (albeit futilely, so far as the unhappy child is concerned) point out that the substitute is every bit as good. From the standpoint of the parents as logicians, Olivia's response is identical to that of an adult acquaintance who complains when the grimy air filter in his or her car is replaced. 'But the new one isn't the same.' Since all that counts for such a concrete thing are the conditions satisfied, the complaint bears witness to the kind of sentimentality that leads the car owner to christen the family station wagon 'Betsy.'

If Gopnik's piece just reported an experience of the sort that long-suffering parents will all recall, the story wouldn't advance the discussion. But Gopnik writes as a thinker, not as a parent.

> Children, small children particularly, don't just have more consciousness than the rest of us. They believe in consciousness more than the rest of us; their default conviction is that everything might be able to think, feel, and talk.

These words embody a revealing mistake. Bluie's tale provides no grounds for asserting that Olivia believes in consciousness more than do grown-ups, though that is what the philosophy behind Gopnik's thinking ventriloquizes out of him. The quoted formulation implies that once the belief about Bluie is rectified, Olivia will believe in consciousness less. The truth is different: Olivia spreads consciousness more liberally about. She believes in more consciousness than do (most) adults. Once she makes the correction, Olivia will believe in consciousness in a narrower range of cases. She won't believe less in consciousness; she will believe in less consciousness. This is what the Bible is endorsing in creating men and women twice. Olivia will, that is, graduate from Genesis 1 to Genesis 2.

The point is that what Olivia says, though inapt to the case in which she says it, the case of Bluie, is *not* however inapt generally. Not, anyway, if particulars and individuals are different.

In the course of the article, Gopnik expresses his preference (44) for a specific position in contemporary philosophy of mind, Daniel Dennett's:

> There is no 'consciousness' apart from the working of all our mental states. Consciousness is not the ghost in the machine; it is the hum of the machinery. The louder the hum, the more conscious you feel.

Consciousness, in other words, is rooted in the material exemplification of neurological processes.

I will look more closely at this view in the next section. The present point is that Gopnik takes talk of the soul as connected with the idea of sloughing off the coils of physicality. No doubt, some religions, committed to the survival of bodily death, think in this way. But it is not how the down-to-earth Bible marks its anti-Thalean line.

Matter Relativized

In many respects Aristotle's position has more of a biblical look than Plato's. Aristotle appears for instance to stick up for, where his mentor trashes, the particular. But at the end of the day the difference between the pair turns out, as per the witticism, not to be a strong one – not, anyway, so far as the 'for instance' is concerned.

I distinguished particularity from individuality. No such distinction is present in Plato. No such distinction is *metaphysically* available to him. This is no oversight. For deep reasons, Plato works to disallow such a distinction.[19] On Plato's metaphysical anatomization the concrete thing is just the (spatio-temporal) localization of a suite of general characteristics.

Aristotle's metaphysical analysis of concrete things introduces an element absent from Plato's analysis, viz., matter. The availability of matter for the anatomization of being seems to make room for the particular/individual distinction. Isn't Aristotle in a position to say that some of the reality of the concrete thing lies not in the general, sc., the Forms, but in the ineluctably non-general matter?

As opposed both to his sainted mentor Socrates, who seems never to have slept, and to his most famous pupil, who was peripatetic, Plato has a penchant for beds. To answer the question, let us recline with him.

Plato's metaphysical analysis of an actual bed, a concrete thing, proceeds in terms of the Form, Bedeity, and the Reflection (of the Form) in the spatio-temporal Receptacle. Suppose now that a concrete bed has a grainy texture. The texture has no status from the standpoint either of the Form, Bedeity, or of the Receptacle, the latter being just a spatio-temporal vessel or container, featureless apart from its voluminousness. Aristotle, it seems, can accommodate. Over and above the Form and the spatio-temporal Reflection, he has Matter. Given that Bedeity is realized in Matter, and given that Matter possesses its own proprietary features, an explanation is available. Characteristics like the graininess 'had' by concrete things do not trace back to – do not reflect what is the case on – the level of Forms. They are ineluctably linked to the concrete, and hence to particularity.

These distinctions are not hard and fast. Depending on the starting point, one and the same element of one and the same concrete thing can get classified either as Matter or as Form. An installation artist might be interested in the graininess that the bed exhibits. Finding in the bed what he or she seeks, the artist might duly suspend it from the rafters. That it is *a bed* that is appropriately textured is immaterial; the artist would be equally content with a similarly grainy cabinet or piece of driftwood. In fact, the difficulty of suspending the bed (because of its bulk) might constitute a 'hum' in the installation, a roughness in its artistry, just as too much graininess might make the bed a defective platform for snoozing. The bed, in the former case, is Matter relative to the texture, which gets analysed as Form. The texture is em-bedded. The graininess, in the latter case, is Matter relative to the bed *qua* Form. Bedeity is en-grained. Where is the particularity here? All there is is individuality. In Plato's metaphysical terms, it is all one whether the individual is a grainy piece of wood that happens to be a bed, or a bed that happens to have a grainy texture. In either case, we have the same instantiated suite of features.[20]

Matter, the Aristotelian addition to the metaphysical analysis of concrete things, turns out itself to be a shifting and variable notion – a functional one. This problem for Aristotle transposes, *mutatis mutandis*, to Dennett. Dennett's distinction between neurology and machinery is relative too. Dennett locates the hum identified with consciousness in the material in which the neurology is actualized – in the machinery. This corresponds to the furniture maker's locating the hum in the graininess of the wood. But the installation artist would locate the hum in the em-beddedness of the grainy fibre. For the boudoir joiner, the graininess is extraneous to the Form; for the artist, the Bedeity is.

We require a stronger, non-relative distinction, though that does not mean reviving the ghost in the machine. The idea of the interior is stronger, since no individual has an interior. This is not, as philosophers put it, an intentional distinction – a distinction between one and the same thing considered in two ways. It is a *real* distinction; or, at any rate, a realer distinction than that.

Aristotle, I said, chose Plato. Professional philosophers will ask: what alternative was available? Let me sketch an answer.

As the Form is to Platonic metaphysics, so the primary substance is to Aristotelian metaphysics. Primary substances are basic existences; they have basic ontological status. Had Aristotle asserted that particulars are the only true substances, that would have him humming in the biblical choir. True, it would have given Aristotelian philosophy a subjectivistic, or idealistic, slant, quite opposed to Platonic realism, since men and women are the only particulars. But what of it? Moreover, our discussions of nature as a system, and of natural individuals as eddy-like, support the identification.

By sheer chance, the metaphysical vocabulary of Greek philosophical thinkers, a vocabulary that Aristotle inherits, contains a pun that points in just such a direction. The Latin form 'substance' is a direct rendering of the Greek 'ὑποκείμενον.' Both mean, literally, 'understanding.' (A substance is that which stands under.) The claim, then, is that only a being that has the capacity to understand is a substance. And such beings are particulars.

City and Psyche (I)

I turn to the contrast between the biblical position on mind and the philosophical one. I begin with the latter, as it arises out of the parallel that Plato draws in the *Republic* between the structure of the polis and the structure of the psyche.[21] Remarkably enough, the Bible draws a similar parallel.

Scholars on opposite sides of the Bible/philosophy divide tend to contemn (when they deign to look at) the activity across the frontier. The failure of all the parties to appreciate that both Plato and the Bible link their discussions of the mind to their treatment of communal life is therefore multiply unfortunate. Since the internal city/psyche linkage on the biblical side is very obliquely stated, those who devote themselves to Holy Writ would, by operating comparatively, be helped to deepen their understanding of what Scripture has to say on a matter of intense interest not only to philosophers but generally. As for students of Plato, while *they* have access to extra-philosophical materials on the Greek side that endorse views quite like those in the Bible, the relevant anti-Platonic content of the materials is also recessive.[22]

In the *Republic*, Plato asserts that the structure of the psyche is isomorphic to that of the *polis*. The *polis* being larger, it constitutes, he explains, a better basis for examining and analysing the psyche.

Plato handles the structure of the *polis* in straight functional terms. When the parts do their respective job, there is justice. A just *polis* is, like a well-maintained automobile, a properly functioning system of parts. The parts in the case of the *polis* are its citizens.

Plato is not just *considering* the men and women who make up the *polis* functionally, as we, when a war is being waged, consider enlistees or conscripts as (fungible) soldiers and sailors. Plato is reducing the men and the women to the functions they fulfil in the city. They are nothing more than the localized jobs and duties and callings.

The passage describing the carpenter, quoted twice already, is fully explicit about this exhaustive functionalizing. It serves as an excellent platform for drawing pertinent conclusions about mind. The carpenter thinks of himself on the most basic level as a worker in wood; his self-identity is bound up with joining in the overall structure. The carpenter is, so to speak, that air filter of ours invested with the power of thought. Just as the (normal) car owner will tearlessly replace the automotive part when it ceases to fulfil its role and is past fixing (it is dysfunctional, and cannot be repaired), so the carpenter is content to have the carpenter (sc., himself) replaced under the corresponding conditions (he is terminally sick, or incapacitated without prospect of rehabilitation). The carpenter, in effect, is an individual, not a particular. That's how *he* sees it.

The sick carpenter is just like Descartes's defective clock. Telling time incorrectly, it would understand for whom the bell tolls, and not insist on ticking people badly off by ticking badly on.

Just as Genesis 1 takes a too rigid view of the boundaries between the species, so does Plato (whose thinking is on the same level as Genesis 1) draw the lines that divide the function fillers or political classes too sharply. That Plato comes close to likening the idea of an auxiliary's becoming a worker to the idea of a cat's going to the dogs is, however, an inessential feature of the construction. The *Republic*, after all, is no more than a blueprint. The carpenter's delineation of his options – 'Awl or nothing' – is, even in Plato's own terms, too stark. A grimy air filter, its vehicular utility a fading memory, could after all serve as an efficient planter, the built-up deposits extraordinarily conducive to the germination of avocado pits. So it would be wasteful to toss it out (= have it die) once its ride is at an end. By the same token, a no longer limber joiner could quite possibly be repositioned in the economy, perhaps as a blue-bibbed Walmart greeter.

I moderate Plato's account to disarm objectors who might otherwise complain that I am catching him out on optional formulations. The softening leaves unaffected the deeper, the basic, point: the citizen identifies himself or herself with the function or functions that he or she fulfils. The citizen is a fungible.

What follows? The consciousness of the carpenter makes no sense. It makes no sense *because the carpenter is an individual and not a particular*. The carpenter is, again, an air filter invested with the power of consciousness. Since the air filter is an individual, that is, nothing more than instantiated function(s), what is the point of the investiture? I am asking here a question about what consciousness does, what it is good for, not about what it is – neural activity, hum of machinery, or whatever. Consciousness of one's condition is pointful only if there is some alternative to that condition. Think of it in evolutionary terms. The development of consciousness would be of no survival value (it might easily have perditional value) if it just amounted to dwelling on the inevitable. Think Hamlet. ('Don't think, Hamlet, act!') But that is not the primary way of putting it. An air filter would not lament its condition. Neither does the carpenter, in Plato's rendering, lament his. It is not that they are stoical. If that were so, non-stoical counterparts could be envisaged, and for Plato that would constitute a great difficulty. Nor is it that they are saintly. The explanation resides in the fact that in neither case does lamentation make sense. Try, by parity, to make sense of the number 3's bewailing its primehood. The fact that the carpenter could serve as a Walmart greeter when his useful life with hammer and saw is done changes nothing. In Plato's construction, greeting customers is not an alternative-for-the-functioning-carpenter. So it is at least pointless to ascribe consciousness, save in the manner of a Disney cartoon. Or, to put it at once more formally, more generally, and categorically: consciousness does not belong to individuals. Principles of operation they have. Minds they do not have.[23]

What goes for the carpenter goes for all the inhabitants of the kallipolis, philosopher kings and queens included. They too are self-identified functionally. They too do not, then, think. They too are mindless.

As Plato understands it, the psyche is, like the *polis*, an organized system of function fillers. Our main conclusion follows. All the elements of the psyche being understood functionally, the pysche, whatever principles govern its activity, involves no consciousness. The result is pretty much the same as Dennett's: the psyche is a mental machine without consciousness in any proper sense.

Thales redux!

City and Psyche (II)

The Bible says a lot about the city. What it says diametrically opposes what Plato says. Plato is of the view that to gain an understanding of the psyche one can look at the city. The Bible is of the same view. Their positions on the city being in sharp opposition, so too are their positions on the psyche.

The city appears early in Genesis: immediately after the story of Cain and Abel. Indeed, the incorporation of the city is internal to the story of the brothers. The city, then, is linked to the part of the narrative that works the side of the particular. What the Bible says about the city therefore differs from the story that it would tell of the beehive or the anthill. These would be dealt with on the species level; in the orbit of Genesis 1, and dealt with, I am sure, in a purely Platonic way.[24]

In the first biblical mention thereof, the city does not fit in an orderly way into the wider whole in which it exists. Cain builds the city in the Land of Nod, east of Eden, 'away from the presence of the Lord' (4:16), the Land to which God banishes him after the killing of Abel. Equally pertinent are the linkage of the son with the city and the naming of the city after the son, Enoch.

The naming of the city after the son gives the deep parallel with Plato. The city somehow has the character of the son, as, in Plato, the structure of the city is isomorphic to that of the psyche. The city, writ large, is Enoch. It is called by the same name.

The city name 'Enoch' is theoretically revealing, just as is Plato's 'kallipolis.' The Greeks subscribed to a view of the world as a cosmos; as is suggested by the cognate of English 'cosmetic,' the word 'cosmos' speaks of a pleasing unity and order. Not only does Plato inherit such a view, he also powers it up considerably. Not only, according to Plato, does the cosmos exhibit unity and order. Also, its unity/order is rational – the product of intelligence. Plato's city is 'kalla,' that is, 'beautiful,' not just because life there is pleasant. The name is apt to the city because *it* is properly unified/ordered. On the basis of the few allusions to the Bible, the city's ordering is, we appreciate, seen in an entirely different and much darker, not to say more lurid, light. The city does not fall within the ambit of the judgments 'good' that pepper Genesis 1. The city has not yet arisen in Genesis 1. It, a distinctively human creation, belongs to the Genesis 2 part of the narrative. 'Enochville,' then, has very different associations than 'kallipolis.' The label cannot apply until the polarity 'good and bad' is in operation. The city, and the particular, are somehow deviant from the standpoint of the world in which they are situated. To elicit those different associations, I have to examine the biblical text more closely.

The narrative gives two lines of humankind, both on the Genesis 2 side of the story, one going from God through Adam and Eve to Abel and Cain, and onwards from Cain. The original line is called 'the sons of God.' The other, substitute line, denominated 'the sons of man,' begins with Adam and Eve, proceeds through Seth, the substitute for Abel, and then onwards.

The names along the two branches systematically echo one another, as the reader may confirm by comparing Genesis 4:17–19 with Genesis 5:3–25. The significant echo for us is that between Enoch (son of Cain, third in the original line) and Enosh (son of Seth, third in the substitute line). The name 'Enosh' is a (Hebrew) variant on a deeper denomination for Adam, viz., 'the man.' The singular 'man' in Hebrew is 'ish.' 'The man' is 'ha-ish.' The plural, 'men,' is 'anashim,' which displays the 'n' that is part of 'Enosh.' A synonym for 'anashim' is 'bnei-enosh,' which also means 'mankind.' (Translated part by part, 'bnei-enosh' comes to 'sons [or: children] of man.') While the first man is called 'ha-adam,' 'ish' is already understood to lie behind it. This emerges clearly when the first woman is created. Fashioned of the rib of the man, 'ha-adam,' she is called by the feminine form of 'ish,' viz., 'ha-isha.'

The vital thing for here is the fact that 'Enoch' and 'Enosh' are aligned. And since 'Enosh' is another way of saying 'man,' the city that Cain built may be heard to have the name. The city is named 'Man.' 'Enoch' too is, as we have seen, significant. An 'enoch-person' is a person who is educated/acculturated. In a subtle sense, this is even better than 'Enosh.' For mankind was created in Genesis 1. But no culture. The Genesis 1 story is biological. Culture emerges only in Genesis 2.[25]

The Platonic city is isomorphic with the psyche. So is the biblical one. The biblical isomorphism accentuates the unnatural; the failure of cosmic fit. The shocking story of Sodom and Gomorrah imparts the clearest sense of this; though, as I say, the heightened deviancy of these places just magnifies an idea present throughout the Genesis 2 story. Writ large and in an extreme fashion, the deviations of Sodom and Gomorrah magnify the deviations of Adam and Eve in the Garden. Adam and Eve, in the Garden, are proto-particulars. By transgressing, they reveal their particularity.[26] No such transgression can occur in Genesis 1. If the stars should tumble from the sky, that – assuming that human intervention has no part in it – would just result, after a time, in a new equilibrium. No one would care. If an ice age should descend, that too – assuming, again, that chimneys, tailpipes, and the like have no major hand in precipitating it – would not be a transgression of the cold on the hot. What happens in nature is, as per that advertisement, 'all good.'

We are not here, to repeat the Nietzschean phrase, beyond good and bad; we are beneath good-and-bad.

The theoretical implications are by now discernible. The particular, the human particular, and the human particulars' most characteristic human product, the city (= culture), do not fit into the wider (natural) whole. From the standpoint of Genesis 1, and hence from the standpoint of the foundations of Greek philosophical thinking, human beings are transgressive: they are monsters. Consciousness, then, is a principle of particularity; of anti-functionality. This particularity is unavailable philosophically. From the philosophical standpoint, transgression or monstrosity gets analysed – analysed away – as deficiency. Transgression and monstrosity are rationalized in terms of dysfunctionality. The Bible's view is very different. Ontologically, men and women are particulars. Because of what they are, or essentially, they are transgressors; they are, because of what they are, or essentially, dysfunctional. They are non-fungibles. From the biblical perspective, talk of transgression and dysfunctionality in respect of men and women is not relative talk; nor, despite the Bible's constant moralizing, is such talk ineluctably moral or evaluative. Most important for us: it is as transgressors, as monsters, that men and women are thinkers. It is as these things that men and women are irreducibly particular, that they have insides. Although cognitive consciousness can go with the natural flow, it is primarily an instrument of opposition to that flow, and cannot be made full sense of in terms of the principles that constitute and govern that flow.

It comes as no great surprise that those who argue for mind often look to us like theologians and/or employ a religious-sounding idiom. This is a forced result of the limitations of philosophy, not a sign of eschatological commitments of dubious intelligibility, let alone thralldom to myth and superstition. It's not that savage or non-philosophical thinking vitalizes, and that philosophy, in hand with science, overcomes the savagery. What the savage thinker does responds to something that is the case, and science (or philosophy) loses it.

Anti-Philosophical Greek Reflections on the Particular

Plato's parallel is, expressly, between the structure of the psyche and the structure of the *polis*. There is however no reason why social arrangements of other sorts, even social arrangements that precede the *polis*, cannot exhibit the latter structure. Though not political, the warrior society of the Greeks at Troy has such a structure too, the supreme commander (Agamemnon) at the head, the warriors who lead the foot soldiers (Ajax, Odysseus, Nestor) in the middle, and those tasked with constructing ramparts, manning siege engines, and slogging it out in the trenches at the bottom. But Homer develops the side of the issue that Plato suppresses, the transgressive side. Homer's *Iliad* is a tale of a dysfunctional warrior, Achilles. Achilles repairs to an inside place, his tent, and in that place thinks himself out of the ambient, dominant, ethos. Achilles's thinking is the opposite of the carpenter's. Achilles is a 'sick warrior of the Achaeans.' Thought of by the culture to which he belongs in functional terms, and hence regarded as a monster, Achilles does not think of himself functionally. Achilles *vis-à-vis* the Achaean side is like Antigone *vis-à-vis* Creon's Thebes. They are particulars, not just individuals.

The Sphinx glowers over Thebes. Devouring those who try to enter when they fail (as they invariably fail) to solve the riddle, the Sphinx prevents the city from flourishing. The riddle that the Sphinx poses amounts to: 'What is man?' Oedipus solves the riddle, thereby opening the way to the city, the city being, as the Bible puts it, an offshoot of man. Why Oedipus? Why a parricide and a violator of the taboo against incest that is a veritable hallmark of civilization? Oedipus is, in a salient way, a monster among men and women. The problem of the city, the problem of culture, the problem of civilization, is to accommodate the monstrosity – to construct institutions that enable men and women, having the character that they have, to live together. Oedipus is appropriate, then, because he cannot, once he figures out his personal puzzle, deny or gloss over the monstrosity. Having had his face rubbed in the monstrosity, he cannot finesse it or beautify it away. Plato, who tried to fit men and women back into the natural world, answered the Sphinx's question incorrectly. For his kallipolitans he has carpentered a structure in which, while biologically alive, they are dead as humans. Not even the philosopher-rulers can do their thinking for them. They too are fungibles, not thinking things.

The kallipolis is improperly described. It is not a *polis,* a political entity. It is more like a garden, like the one planted in Eden, in the east. Political entities, properly so described, exist only outside Eden. The same goes for men and women.

Conclusion: On the Carmel

'The eloquent and dramatic epic poem captures the terrible anger of Achilles over a grave insult to his personal honour and relates its tragic result – a chain of consequences that proves devastating for the Greek forces besieging Troy, for noble Trojans, and for Achilles himself.' With a critical eye on plot-focused understanding of the kind described in this announcement of a new translation of the *Iliad*, I made the case in these pages that Homer's epic is more than an archaic Greek *Johnny Got his Gun* or *All Quiet on the Western Front*, rubbing its readers' noses in the horrors of war; more than a psychological exploration or character study of its complex protagonist and his equally complex opposite number; more than a colourized dramatization of real or imagined happenings on the margins of the Greek world in what from the poet's perspective was the distant (though still resonant) past. To stop with such readings is to miss the deeper message – a message concerning ultimate issues of human nature and identity. It is because it conveys a message of this depth that Homer's epic had scriptural status among the Greeks. Nor, *pace* the writer of the announcement, is the *Iliad* tragic or devastating in *authorial* intent. Dark? Certainly. Its darkness is however crepuscular. The distant cockcrow of a cultural awakening, the epic presages the 'Let there be light' of, as it happens, the world that the first biblical man and the first biblical woman – and we, to whom the self-conception as human beings that the Bible attributes to the transgressors of Eden has been passed down – are born into and inhabit. Like the slashing and burning that God would had to have done in order to create the Garden, the epic's devastations are preparatory for a new edifice, the human edifice, in which we – or most of us – dwell. Similar remarks apply, *mutatis mutandis*, to the tragedies of Sophocles.

But though Homer and Sophocles are pointing in the direction of the conception of men and women as human beings, forces on the Greek side obstruct the forward movement. Because of the force of these forces, there is indeed on the Greek side no rounded depiction of that conception. The *reforming* tendencies (as I called them) of Homer and Sophocles are not productive of a reformation. The notion of particularity, essential for the reform to go through, is absent. So the tendencies can seem as if they are the products of wishful thinking. For a rounded depiction of the human conception, it is necessary therefore to look elsewhere. Which brings me to the second objective of the project, and explains why I have produced an essay on Athens *and* Jerusalem.

The second objective – a Jerusalemite counterpart to the handing over of central and representative literary texts of ancient Athens to those who reflect on the dominant Western conception of human nature and identity – is to redeem the core part of the Bible from those of a religious cast of mind without in the process leaving its view of men and women vulnerable to summary dismissal from the side of science.

At the heart of the Bible is found a humanist conception very like the one that Homer, in a culturally much earlier environment, and Sophocles, addressing the pressures on the forming human self-conception from the side of the *polis,* are gesturing towards and to some extent working out. The value that God is appealed to in the Bible to stamp 'Approved,' the value of his carbon copies – human beings – is a value that, *au fond*, the Bible supports independently of the appeal. That is, so far as its anthropological component is concerned, the theological aspect of the Bible is theoretically dispensable. Jacob's ladder is not a skyhook. It is set up on the earth. Antecedent dismissal of the Bible's anthropology on the grounds that it has sky-high commitments is therefore dogmatic. Also, the Bible's tight focus on human reality, which is in itself methodologically unexceptionable, removes it from head-to-head competition with scientific cosmology. Accordingly, the path is clear to harvesting the Bible's insights about the nature of men and women without premature obstruction from the side of science. This is not to say that the two do not clash. Which brings me to the third and final objective.

The third major goal builds on the second: to save the souls of intellectual traders in abstraction who devote themselves to the human compartment of being from Platonic footnotedom. Salvation turns on the distinction drawn between individuals and particulars. So far as the texts we have considered are concerned, the anti-Platonic action is found in its most concentrated form in the play between the Bible's two creation stories. The ontology of Genesis 1 is restricted to individuals: the Proverbist's three. The world of Genesis 2 numbers particulars among its contents too: the Proverbist's four. To account for human reality, do we need Genesis 2 in addition to Genesis 1? The Bible responds to the question affirmatively, Plato (and science) negatively. Philosophy, as the influence of evolutionary theory on disciplinary activity of late confirms, has a strong tendency to choose Plato.

The three objectives do not make up a miscellany. The first identifies a tendency in Greece, on the non-philosophical side. The second locates in the Bible a fairly full account of where that tendency is tending. The third pinpoints and spells out the nature of the major situational challenge to that tendency, showing that the Bible writers are aware of it and detailing how they meet it. Less abstractly put: Homer and Sophocles are gesturing towards the idea of human particularity. Philosophy challenges the idea. The Bible works out that idea quite fully, in the process providing a counterweight to philosophy. (This indicates that the essay that I have produced is not just on Athens and Jerusalem. It is on two *aspects* of Athens and Jerusalem.)

Why go with the Bible rather than with philosophy? I strove to show how fruitful the distinction between particulars and individuals is, interpretively, explanatorily, and analytically, in respect both of the biblical view and of the non-philosophical Greek materials. With regard to the attempts by philosophy to domesticate, by reduction, what is thereby explained and analysed, viz., the characteristics of the reality of men and women that would be advanced as setting them apart from (the rest of) nature, the philosophical side remains vastly programmatic, acceptance of the truth of its pronouncements a leap of faith. There is another option. Philosophy might dismiss the idea of particularity as a fantasy, either on the ground that it is not coherent, or on the ground that nothing out there answers to it. The latter ground, if no reduction is effected, is sheer assertion. And what is the former if not a tendentious way of saying that the resources available to philosophers cannot rationalize it? As the Pythagoreans learned, much to their chagrin, the fact that a number cannot be expressed as a fraction does not mean that it is not real.

A few thinkers, some occupying the highest seats in the official philosophical pantheon, share the view – or at least key elements of the view – that men and women are particulars, and that this particularity sets them apart. Kant, a giant among these giants, was several times brought into the discussion in a positive way. He was for instance saluted in the course of the exploration of how Homer dramatizes Achilles's move towards the view of men and women as human beings. Homer, I said, does what Kant does, but in a dramatic, non-formal, manner: he gets morality going among the mortal. Relevantly to the *terminus ad quem* of this shift, Kant draws a distinction between two realms of being. The physical world is *phenomenal;* men and women, though one foot of theirs is planted in space and time, are also *noumenal.* In a simpler vocabulary: men and women have a foot outside the system that is nature. Now God, though active in ways that have spatio-temporal effects, is paradigmatically beyond space and time. So what Kant says might just as well be put by saying that men and women, alone among physical things, are 'inspired with God's breath.' Indeed, what Kant says is better put that way. Without extra-formal flesh of the sort that Homer and the Bible supply – for example, in the claim that men and women have dominion, in the claim that they need a blessing, in the claim that they are transgressors and misfits, and so on – all of which can be made good sense of from the standpoint of our everyday experience, Kant's bare assertion of noumenal status boils down to saying what men and women are *not* – they are not (fully) natural – and this, by itself, is saying too little to be informative with respect to what we seek information about. How does one argue from 'Items of kind H are beyond space and time' to 'Items of kind H have intrinsic value' or 'Items of kind H are ends in themselves'? Kant's rarefied formulation strands him somewhere between Genesis 1 and Genesis 2. Genesis 2 supplies the answers. Men and women, though they live in nature, are not parts of the system. They are particulars. They have autonomy of the whole. They therefore have (or have the possibility of having) a different kind of value.

Kant is not a Platonic-type thinker. Like the Proverbist, Kant acknowledges a gulf in being between nature's nature and human nature. But in the manner in which he handles the distinction he too, as the rarefaction indicates, is drawn into Plato's orbit. For the gulf is so deep and wide that it is difficult to see how the two sides could interact, as certainly a proponent of such a view believes that they do. What might a less formal set of 'critical' works look like? The works would, I suggest, have a markedly anthropological appearance. The less formal Kant would delineate and defend the distinctiveness of men and women starting from a position within the arena of experience, as Homer does in the *Iliad*, and as the Bible does in Genesis.[1]

The Western view of human nature is under pressure today. Quite a few inside the culture, more outside, have a bead on it. I will close with a few remarks about the biblical conception's links to liberalism and democracy.

Return to the puzzle about the biblical treatment of the Tower of Babel. Why would God interfere with the Tower builders' effort when they are working to supplant a non-monotheistic view? At first sight, it looks as if God is acting out of jealousy or malice or mean-spiritedness.

The answer supplied is that the tight unity that features the Tower enterprise, a totalitarian unity, is objectionable to the Bible. It leaves no room, as subhuman nature leaves no room, for particularity. This is indeed the case. The objection stands however in need of defence and justification. To bring out the need, let me state the puzzle in a different way.

Monotheism is the view that there is one God. That God presumably has one view. So how do monotheism and anti-totalitarianism link?

The basis for the answer will in all likelihood strike the reader as incredible. The biblical view is *not* at the most basic level monotheistic, as the adjective is usually understood. At the most basic level the biblical view is *theistic*. The operative contrast between the biblical way and the way that the Bible takes exception to is not the contrast between monotheism and polytheism. Operative is the contrast between theism and belief systems of the kind that spawn what the Bible styles *idolatry*. (A corollary is that neither are the positions almost invariably labelled 'polytheistic' theistic, nor is the multiplicity of deities in them of fundamental significance. Even if Zeus were the only inhabitant of Olympus, Olympian religion would not be monotheistic. It would be mono-idolatrous. But, of course, 'theism' is not a biblical label.)

The proposition that monotheism, as usually comprehended, is not of the essence of the Bible runs up against the expert claim, with which I expressed agreement, that 'the genesis of the biblical way is bound up with the beginnings of the monotheistic concept.' It is however easy to understand that the clash has a verbal source. The non-biblical religious belief system of Greece is standardly labelled 'polytheism.' I never met a person in the least reluctant to classify or hesitant about classifying the Olympian belief system under that head. Speaking of the Babylonian creed, I myself used the term. If a verbal contrast is wanted to set the biblical position apart, 'monotheism' is virtually unavoidable.

Theism is the view that deities have a personality structure like that of men and women. It is the view that gods are each of them persons.

(I will get to the 'mono-' of 'monotheism' presently.) In truth, the Greek religious position is not theistic, from which it follows that its classification as 'polytheistic' is conceptually misleading. The assignment of personhood to the Olympian gods is very superficial indeed. The assignment is what I would for once pejoratively call 'primitive.' Or: if the assignment is not superficial, then the Olympian position has in it an element to which it is not entitled. No explanation is needed for why non-theistic gods are indifferent to men and women. They are indifferent in exactly the way that the sun and the wind are indifferent. If the Olympian deities are persons, an explanation is required. But none is ever given. From the biblical standpoint, adherents of the position (from which position Plato's critical reconstruction derives at least half of its momentum) qualify as idolaters. Elements of nature, anthropomorphized, are treated by them as objects of worship. It is for this attitude – bowing down to stones and trees – that the Bible reserves its most withering scorn. (See Deuteronomy 4:15–20.) This is not to say that the awe that the forces of nature inspire in us is inappropriate. It had better not be to say that, since awe is often what we feel quite apart from reading the Romantic poets. It is to say that the awe must not be translated into worship. According to the Bible, the 'must not' is anchored in an ontological truth: persons alone are capable of understanding and hence of responding (or of not responding) out of understanding. It is only in the second instance the slight to God on the part of idolaters that the Bible rides out against. In the first instance it is the misunderstanding on their part, misunderstanding not only of God but also, since they too are like God, of themselves. Elijah, who ridicules the idea that a non-person can answer a prayer, proves better able than the Baal's acolytes to get nature to do his bidding. He puts a match to the combustibles on the altar, rather than supplicates to them. Supplication to non-persons, the episode is saying, is childish.

The Tower builders are unifiers. But their effort of unification opposes the idea of nature as unsystematic. They are, in effect, Mesopotamian Thaleans, albeit on the social science rather than natural science side. They endorse the view of the whole as a system, and hence are committed to regarding men and women as parts of the system – as non-particular individuals. In this they are joined by Plato.

Theism is the view that the deity is a (or: the deities are) person(s), like men and women. The God of the Bible is a theistic deity. The God of the Bible is, given the symmetry of 'a is like b,' like us. The point is not the empty, purely formal, one: whatever we are like, whatever God is like, we share characteristics. The point is substantive: though we have a physical basis, we are not (pieces of) nature; we are irreducible to nature. God is like us; God is not like a natural force – the latter being the Greek view of deities. And the point, equally importantly, is that each one of us is like God, and vice versa. It is not mankind that resembles God. Each man and each woman does. The claim, to make the kind of sense it has to, requires of course that there be but one God. The 'mono-' element of monotheism is, we therefore see, an upward reflection of how each of us regards himself or herself, viz., as a particular, substantially distinct from every other member of the species. Accordingly, no fundamental reason exists why the biblical position could not have been polytheistic, where 'polytheistic' means 'having a pantheon comprising a multiplicity of substantially distinct persons.' There is no more reason for that than there is a reason why in the human realm there cannot be a multiplicity of particular men and women. And from this may be inferred, in a quick step, the danger that biblical thought would see in the idea of an ineffable and inexpressible God. This – from the Bible's perspective, a passage beyond theism – would, if transposed into a creedal system, be an invitation to and recipe for disaster in the human sphere. From the Bible's perspective the associated theology counts as God-less. If God is great, that is because God has given up that kind of greatness.

The one-ness of the biblical God is the one-ness of a person, neither more nor less robust. Even the central creedal profession of the Israelite communion, the *Shema*, can be read as asserting this. By contrast with any natural thing, which can be factored in many ways, God is essentially one. The one-ness is that of (in my labelling) the particular. To be a monotheist, then, is to believe in the fundamental diversity of particular men and women: the several ones cannot coalesce or agglomerate into a genuinely unitary one; they can (only) create a community of ones additively. It seems paradoxical to say that the profession of belief in one God is the profession of belief in the proposition that each member of the family of man counts for one. To see that it is not paradoxical is to see a very basic thing about the Bible. Insofar as the Bible advances the view that informs the way of thinking about ourselves that is ours, it is also to see a very basic thing about us.[2]

The confusion of the languages at Babel is not (just) a measure to bring the enterprise down. It is (also) an expression of what the Bible thinks positively about human reality. The multiplication of languages at Babel is a heightened representation of the root divergence among particular men and women. On a larger scale, it reprises the creation of the (particular) man and the (particular) woman in Genesis 2. It is the creation of beings who stand over and against nature, beings whose language is not – or, more accurately, whose languages *are* not – the (single) language of nature.

This view of human nature allows all manner of real-world political arrangements, from the anarchic and libertarian over to the rigidly collective and (in the strictly political sense) totalitarian. But it is one thing to arrange matters in (say) a totalitarian way because one believes that men and women are parts of a system, another to do so in aid of some practical economic or political goal, for example, to defeat an enemy or to build a tower. The same distinction applies *mutatis mutandis* at the other end of the spectrum. Not every anarchist holds a biblical view of human nature. Some endorse kinds of arrangements more palatable to liberals because they believe that such arrangements minimize costly and disruptive friction. The trouble with this sort of cost-benefit analysis commitment to democratic and liberal arrangements is obvious. The costs might easily rise while the benefits remain the same.

The Bible recognizes all this, does so very fully and very firmly and very articulately. That is confirmed by the fact that 'I am the Lord your God . . .; you shall have no other gods before me' prefaces the Ten Commandments (Exodus 20:2–3; Deuteronomy 5:6–7). The point is not that our compliance is required out of a desire to please or exacted due to fear of punishment. It is that an injunction against, say, taking another life, or taking someone else's property, only makes non-prudential sense if the life in question is an independent life, if the someone who owns the property is an independent entity. In the subhuman realm, night does not steal from day, nor does winter kill summer. In the realm of the 'other gods,' the Commandments do not get a non-prudential foothold.

*

Elijah has quite an entourage in his showdown with the pagan prophets on the Carmel. That the story of the confrontation is told as a story of one against many is not just a dramatic choice. The confrontation is a concretization of the debate between idolatry and theism. And that debate comes to much more abstract expression in the Bible's conceptually dominant story of God's creation of human beings.

'Enough,' Elijah challenged the throng on the Carmel, 'with the fence-sitting. Walk either in the Lord's way or follow Baal's.' With a little bit of showmanship *en route,* I extracted from the scriptural writings of Jerusalem and Athens the not inconsiderable positive basis for tilting fence-sitters towards the side of the Lord, the side of the Proverbist – the anti-Platonic side where Homer and Sophocles are, however insecurely, found. Whatever decision is ultimately taken, the speed with which those who have climbed down onto Baal's side get from eukaryotic revolution to French Revolution, from the flagellated paramecium to the complex negotiations of advanced human culture, is a version of the bone that the humanoid in Stanley Kubrick's movie *2001* throws aloft. A few twirls to the strains of a Strauss waltz, and it transmutes into a spaceship. A considerable injustice is done in this way to the subtlety and power of the word out of the two cities, the word that the distinctive reality of men and women lies between Ham and HAL.

Notes

Introduction

1 'Bible' refers throughout to the Hebrew Scriptures. Unless otherwise indicated, quotations in English draw upon the New Revised Standard Version [NRSV]. A full reference for this source (under 'Bible'), as well as bibliographical data for all sources/editions/translations referred to or quoted from, is supplied in the Bibliography.

Chapter 1

1 Emily Dickinson, 986.
2 Core scripture does single out the lion among beasts and the eagle among flyers, as we still do. In Jacob's blessing of his sons, Judah, who will later have pride of place among his brethren, is likened to a lion (Genesis 49:9). God self-applies the image of 'eagles' wings' (Exodus 19:4) to his deliverance of the Israelites from Egypt.
3 Observe the contrast with Deuteronomy 4:17–19.
4 The Proverbist's use of the singular 'way' in regard both to three and to four obscures *why* four is closed to understanding. The reason is that in regard to four alone there is more than one way. Despite the circuitousness, Genesis's manner of making the point is clearer. According to Genesis, men and women, distinctively among creatures, need (and get) a blessing. They need it because they can stray. (I shall address this matter in detail in chapter 4.) The plural 'ways' would in other words be conceptually appropriate in respect of the Proverbist's four but not in respect of his three.
5 Barnes, *Early Greek Philosophy*, 16.

6 Consider here the closing sentences (154–5) of Nobel physics laureate Steven Weinberg's popular book on the origins of the universe, *The First Three Minutes:* 'Men and women are not content to comfort themselves with tales of gods and giants, or to confine their thoughts to the daily affairs of life; they also build telescopes and satellites and accelerators, and sit at their desk for endless hours working out the meaning of the data they gather. The effort to understand the universe is one of the very few things that lifts human life a little above the level of farce, and gives it some of the grace of tragedy.' The tales to which Weinberg condescends often express what men and women think of their lives, not what they hold, foggily and prescientifically, of the (extra-human) universe and its origin. In part by examining such tales, I am trying to work out the meaning of a few accounts of the condition of men and women in 'the daily affairs of life,' and to show that the sense that they make, sense that gives very lttle comfort, is live and compelling.

7 Barnes's understanding of Homer and Hesiod is mistaken. They are not proto-philosophers. We shall see that their interest, like the Proverbist's, is focused on four. This is not to say of the body of myth lying behind Homer and Hesiod that it is unlinked to three. It *is* to say that the linkage does not interest them.

8 Barnes, *The Presocratic Philosophers*, 17. The descriptive section headings in the book are all drawn from Genesis.

9 The anthropomorphic character of the Greek deities is a very superficial feature. In the sharply contrasting biblical position, it is impossible to abstract the human-type personality from God; which is not to approve the image of a bearded giant atop a throne. Typologically, Greek religion is therefore over on the pagan side, while the biblical belief system is theistic. The difference between pagan and theistic is brought out by observing that, psychological duty apart, petitionary prayer doesn't make much sense in the Greek context.

10 The thinking of the time might have been lost as the materials were reworked later. The evidence is however that the earliest writings were preserved without radical change. I shall deal with this technical matter later.

11 No one acquainted with the early panels of Genesis could fail to observe that praise is lavished here upon Solomon for requesting precisely what was forbidden to Adam and Eve and what they were punished for taking. The text also makes clear that they took something that God has. 'See,' the Lord says, just prior to the expulsion from Eden, 'the man has become like

one of us, knowing good and evil' (3:22). Indeed, Solomon, in requesting wisdom, likens himself (7) to 'a little child.' Whoever is responsible for the text is alluding to Genesis; doing, then, what the Proverbist also does with his three and four. The parallel commands us to think more closely about the prohibition and banishment.

12 The strongest Hebrew word for 'sin' means something like 'fall short' or 'miss,' as in 'fall short of the mark' or 'miss the target.' An archer can miss by more or less. Sinning, then, is not a yes/no affair.

13 As we have seen, it is also in large part due to Aristotle, a jewel in the Athenian diadem, that we know what little we know of Thales. Very likely, then, the prediction is known to us due to its military application. Thales's prediction of the eclipse saved Thales from being eclipsed.

Chapter 2

1 In quoting from the *Iliad* and from the *Odyssey* I specify locations by book and line(s), usually (as in this case) between square brackets. The line numbers refer to the translated versions.

2 Matthew might be making the same point as David. But the Gospel's words can be taken in the way that I am taking them here, and taking them in this way enables me to bring out David's answer.

3 Isn't the Greek position open to a reverse objection? Can't a powerful A care for an impotent B? Once the non-theistic character of the Greek position is underscored, the objection evaporates. David requires an answer in accordance with which A here must care for B.

4 I am referring here to latter-day, analytic, philosophy. The rise of philosophy at which we looked in the preceding chapter is not, save *per accidens*, the rise of an analytic way of thinking.

5 The notion of self-regard here is normative. God is not just a model of self-regard. His reflexive approval is justified. It should be plain why David requires this. A man or woman might think nothing of himself or herself. The Greeks, again, could not see that the gods' disdain for them was groundless. They had, as we say today, low self-esteem. This negative self-image continued to influence their thinking even after the gods were to some degree cast out.

6 Clement, *Miscellanies*, 5.109. A relevant fragment is quoted in Barnes, *Early Greek Philosophy*, 95.

7 None of this devalues *source criticism*, as it is technically known. Distinguishing the strains yields valuable historical information.

8 Paris is as I say attentive to the fair sex before Achilles is born. Indeed, he thinks of women as wives. He must therefore be in his late teens at least. Since Achilles's son Neoptolemus participates in the final phase of the war at Troy, Achilles has to be at least thirty. Hector is Paris's older brother. We thus have Achilles, a man in his prime, chasing down Hector, a man in late middle age. My point is that none of this affects Homer's story telling. Details of myth and legend about Troy are of secondary concern to him.

9 The quotation is from xlix. Next quotation: ibid.

10 When, following the death of Solomon, the unified kingdom that David had fashioned split, the northern entity, cut off from Jerusalem, established new centres of worship; new sacrificial altars. A few such sites were even erected after the destruction of the Temple – for example, in Leontopolis in Egypt. Did the Leontopolitans make use of the Bible?

11 In the document, as I read it, the tendency of things to go wrong in God's world was given an explanation anchored in the foundations of creation. One way forward under the circumstances was to sequester the rot down low and project the triumph beyond historical space and time. The writers of the Hebrew Scriptures ('The Old Testament') resisted this apocalyptic line. Taking for the most part a piecemeal approach, they remained historical and non-hysterical in their thinking.

12 Two points should restrain those who would dismiss the line being taken here out of hand on the grounds that what had been written hundreds of years earlier couldn't have been suitable for dealing with the problem. First: the redactors probably omitted a lot that was unsuitable. Second: the earlier producers too will certainly have had enough experience of a gley ganging for it to inflect their writings. The story of the Flood of Noah (which the redactors did not make up) narrates the dashing of a comprehensive divine plan. The split of the kingdom after Solomon is a mine of non-mythic material.

13 The story might track a real historical movement. Even if it does, the Bible (by which I mean: the text as it was put together in the decades after the Temple's destruction – more on this in a moment) is formulated in a way that turns Babylon into a notional or conceptual (as distinct from a geographical) place. The Bible in effect does to Babylon what the classical tragedians of Greece do to Thebes.

14 A rather Prometheus-like character, God is, enlightening humans (in both senses). I develop the parallel in chapter 5.

15 Genesis contains a second non-natural creation story, a non-monotheistic one. Of this the Bible is highly critical. I will explore it in chapter 4.

16 What I say here resonates with God's experience in Genesis 1. God also has to deal with a limitedly responsive world.

17 The Bible makes the point minus the censoriousness when it has Abraham (21:33) planting a tamarisk in Beer Sheva. Why would a tent dweller plant a tree? In setting down roots, Abraham might well have asked 'Am I my own keeper?' In Hebrew, 'tamarisk' is an anagram on (the root of) 'question.' (Magically, 'tamarisk' includes 'ask.') In planting the tamarisk, Abraham might be planting that question. As to why Cain is criticized, I will address that later.

18 This explains why the Eden phase is more sharply differentiated in the text from the Cain/Abel phase than the latter is from the city-dwelling phase that follows. The first man is not the first shepherd. Cain, in the verses immediately after the one just quoted, is represented as the first city father.

19 The phrase 'till and keep' does not quite fit with this reading, especially as the Hebrew for 'till' is based on the verb that is usually translated as 'work.' (In English, we also say 'work the ground.') The writers are in something of a knot. The man and the woman are enjoined to continue God's work. But that work, Garden making, is more than just the expenditure of sweat to stay alive. The story, in effect, serves two inconsistent functions. Anthropologically, the activity in the Garden is gathering, which simply sustains the gatherer. But the Garden, a cultivated place, contrasts with nature.

20 'What,' the reader will ask, 'about the issue of disobedience?' In eating of the forbidden fruit the man and the woman do not comply with God's commands. Just so, God tells Cain that the world on which he does his work will eventually be as uncompliant to him as the man and the woman, on whom God did *his* initial work, are to him: 'when you till the ground, it will no longer yield to you its strength' (4:12).

21 Alter, *The Five Books of Moses*.

22 According to Cynthia Ozick, Alter's 'welter and waste' is 'one translator's own little miracle' ('And God Saw Literature, That It Was Good'). John Updike ('The Great I Am') sighs 'Eheu' to the same rendering, though on literary rather than on philosophical grounds. Ozick's remark, quoted below, is from the correspondence pages of *The New Republic*.

23 Though 'to wonder' would be natural, and less figurative, the verb here differs from the one that the Proverbist uses.

24 The great scriptural commentator Rashi observes the psychological connotations of 'tohu.'

25 A line from Plato's *Gorgias* beautifully illustrates the ease with which one whose mode is epistemological rather than ontological can employ the phraseology of Genesis. Callicles suggests that Socrates's style of thinking is poor preparation for his day in court. '[Y]ou . . . would not know what to do, but you would reel to and fro and gape openmouthed, without a word to say' (486b).

26 'Boohoo' is phonetically better – a winsome echo of 'bohu.' Alas, the English word voices a negative reaction and in that regard doesn't quite fit. It is perhaps more than just amusing to call up here James Joyce's account of early consciousness in *Portrait of the Artist as a Young Man*. The elements of Joyce's evocation are roughly congruent with those of Genesis 1. Light and dark. Wet and dry. Parental figures looming out of the murk. An early sense of yea and nay.

27 This would have been clearer had Eden involved hunting as well as gathering. The contrast with Abel would have come out more clearly. But the Bible has an ulterior reason for deferring the meat-eating stage.

28 Observe how the Proverbist alludes to the Genesis 1 creation story (heavens and earth) at 3:19 and to the Genesis 2 story (groundwater and dew) at 3:20. Consistently with the thesis that the whole is anthropofocused, the Proverbist, without making any distinction between the two, proceeds to offer counsel with respect to distinctively human reality and characteristically human interrelations.

Chapter 3

1 It is conjectural whether the English verb 'to babble' traces back etymologically to the biblical story. As the case may be, the idea of mutual misunderstanding and the idea that what the other says is gibberish are connected.

2 In transliterated Akkadian, 'bab-ilu.'

3 A system involving a multiplicity of deities must have the characteristic. Functionally, a group of gods in full agreement on all matters would be indistinguishable from a single, unschizophrenic, god. 'I am of two minds, each of which is in agreement with the other.'

4 If Abraham leaves for the reason that the reform is too flattening, isn't he moving back in the direction of the Babylonian belief system? The question will be answered below, through a more complex analysis of the Tower enterprise in which 'not acknowledging God-likeness' is given a precise meaning.

5 There is another way to look at it. Lot, we are told, is an orphan. In adopting him, Abraham exhibits a range of admirable qualities, and the Bible wishes to represent Abraham as a paragon. But the Bible also tells us that Abraham left for Canaan when he was 'seventy-five years old' (12:4). Later we learn that Sarah, his wife, is roughly the same age. Childless at the time of the departure, it would therefore have been entirely reasonable for Abraham to see Lot as, possibly, the next in line. Observe that God does not say in chapter 12 that the nation will spring directly from Abraham's loins.

6 Note the echo of 11:2, which locates the Tower enterprise. Lot is moving back towards a position with similar coordinates to the one that Abraham had exited.

7 Of Lot's *line* we do hear more. Through Moab, one of the issue of his couplings in the cave, the line winds down to King David, God's favourite. (See Ruth 4:18.) Is the choice of David a shift away from the line of Abraham back towards the line of Lot? As the case may be with David and Abraham, the Bible does in a sense come back to Lot as it comes back to the raven. It comes back to the raven in the company of a person who in fact stands to the line of Abraham in the same way as does Lot, viz., Job. We shall pay a visit to Job in due course.

8 God had solemnly undertaken not to cause another Flood. What about (say) the South Asian tsunami of 2004? Were the Tower builders right to show distrust? The issue of the raven, we shall see, supplies the answer.

Chapter 4

1 In *The Art of Biblical Narrative*, Robert Alter states that an aesthetic motive, as opposed to a thematic one, often lies behind aspects of the text. Thus, 'I do not think . . . that every nuance of characterisation and every turning of the plot in these stories can be justified in either moral-theological or national-historical terms. Perhaps this is the ultimate difference between any hermeneutic approach to the Bible and [my] literary approach . . . : in the literary perspective there is latitude for the exercise of pleasurable invention for its own sake, ranging from "microscopic" details like sound-play to "macroscopic" features like the psychology of individual characters' (46). To pin on those who deny a free-standing aesthetic motive a commitment to the thematic significance of *every* nuance would be like saying that the weave of the canvas is pertinent to the painter's intent. Alter means that the text contains in a substantial way thematically inert elements – that is, features of the story that have nothing to do with 'moral-theological or national-historical' matters. I disagree. The 'literary approach' is at any rate dangerous. It can lead to thematically significant features being missed. Alter asserts, for instance, that the alliterative character of the Bible's opening phrase is literary. In chapter 2 of this book, a thematic construal was supplied. Since, presumptively, a construal of this sort has always to be preferred, a construal of this sort must always be sought.

2 The name 'Jemimah,' which appears at Job 42:14, means 'dove.' Literally, 'Jemimah' means 'of the days.' The phrase tells us what kind of bird the dove is.

3 Pointing to the phrase 'to and fro' (8:7), some readers might quarrel with my gloss of the text, on which the raven does not return to the ark after it first departs. 'To and fro' is not inaccurate to the Hebrew, and it *can* convey the sense of going away from the vessel and then returning *to* it. Though my feeling is that 'hither and yon' captures better the sense, I would not insist on it. The thematic contrast that I see in the Bible's treatment of the two birds does not require me to do so. Observe that it is only with respect to the (returning) dove that Noah 'put out his hand and took it in' (9). The raven, upon to-ing from its fro-ing, isn't permitted to re-enter. Why not? The answer, as before, is that its place, the land that it inhabits, is not for men and women. It remains the case, then, that in sending the raven out Noah is not sending it out on a human mission. We can split the difference here by saying that though the raven would as lief leave, it has for the meantime nowhere else to go and like all living things is programmed to preserve its life.

4 For the genealogical details, see Robert Sacks, 'The Book of Job: Translation and Commentary,' 144. The family tree's seed is planted at Genesis 22:21.

5 Philosophically, even this formulation is suspect. In speaking of survival as 'good' for the tumour, as a 'victory,' are we not projecting from our own case?

6 I mention Abraham, since the issue of justice is explicitly debated with the patriarch. The parallel with Noah, the second Adam, is stronger still. Compare Genesis 6:9. The extinction of the world during the Flood cannot be put on the basis of increasing sinfulness among animals. Further in regard to the lesson that Abraham learns at Sodom, I assume that the irony – the painful irony – is not lost. It's a very good idea for a political leader to be cognizant of the realities of exercising power. But Abraham's progeny were themselves collaterally damaged, as the Assyrians and then the Babylonians steamrollered over their corner of the world. The words that God was just now quoted to say about Job to Satan – 'Have you considered my servant? There is no one like him on the earth, a blameless and upright man' – apply equally to Abraham. After the words about Job comes the test. Abraham's progeny were also tested, often through no fault of their own, by political events, and they, as opposed to the fictional Job, were not restored to their earlier position. The real world is stingy with happy endings.

7 The question bears on the issue about Genesis 1:1 that drew Rashi's comment. The question goes against Rashi's reading of the verse.

8 In chapter 37 one of Job's comforters makes an argument that at first hearing sounds so much like God's in chapter 38 as to make the latter seem redundant. Closer attention reveals that Elihu *is* arguing epistemologically. '[N]o one can look on the light, when it is bright in the skies' (37:21). God's answer is new, then, because of the ontological content. Commentators systematically miss the distinction. For instance, Marvin H. Pope, in the Introduction to the Anchor Bible Job, xxii, repeats himself in glossing Elihu's remarks in chapter 37 and God's answer to Job in chapters 38 to 41.

9 The translation into Genesis would be: 'Why did you think that the raven, sent aloft, would return?' God has his messengers, the angels, who do his bidding. Men and women have their homing pigeons, who do *their*s. But God also has Satan, with his own agenda.

10 In *God: A Biography* Jack Miles declares (87–8) that the biblical God lives no life apart from his concern with men and women. My reading of the creation story in Genesis as the story of the characteristically human is in accord with this claim. Scripture is however aware that reality has an extra-human part. *Pace* Miles, God is concerned with that too, though not in the Pentateuch. It is also not quite true to say, as Miles does, that '[God] has no history, no genealogy, no past that in the usual way of literature might be . . . introduced . . . to explain his behaviour' (87). In chapter 5, below, I will sketch God's (lost) biography.

11 Yuval Lurie, *Cultural Beings: Reading the Philosophers of* Genesis, offers an insightful philosophical treatment.

12 The usual interpretive line consists in saying that in Genesis, men and women are appointed stewards over nature. I can see no basis for denying that their stewardship is of an entirely self-interested variety. They are to care for nature because *their* flourishing depends on it.

13 If the unit is taken to be rhinoceros + tickbird + tick, one could avoid saying of the elements taken pairwise that the good of the one is the bad of the other. But this just shows how different the human case is, since in the human case very few would take anything other than the individual man and the individual woman as the true units. Certainly, in starting up the species from a fully individuated and particular man and woman, Genesis 2 is identifying itself with this line.

14 A textual sign that Genesis 1 is beyond naturalism is the appearance of the phrase 'very good' in the last verse, verse 31. The phrase suggests at least this: there is a graduated scale of goodness. Such a scale gestures towards the absence of goodness at one end.

15 The *legal* establishment of ownership over land recurs throughout Genesis. Thus Abraham's establishment of proprietary rights to a well that he dug (Genesis 21) and his purchase of the Machpelah burial site (Genesis 23). Thus Jacob's separation of his land from the land of Laban (Genesis 31).

16 Menand, 'Holden at Fifty,' 87.

17 History has not been an effective teacher. According to David Ahenakew, a leader at one time of the Aboriginal people of Canada, Hitler was right 'to fry' six million Jews, since the Jews had taken control of Germany. The storm of protest elicited by his remarks (made in December 2002 to a reporter for the *Saskatoon StarPhoenix* after a speech to the Federation of Saskatchewan Indian Nations) soon found Ahenakew tearfully retracting. Such views do not come from nowhere. Looking very deep, we can see that the theory behind paganism is at work here. The theory is that there is a single metaphysical scheme that captures everything. Men and women are not ontologically distinctive, only different. Tapping into this source, Ahenakew later in fact drained back his tears. Ahenakew's models are clear. The Jews, he said, are 'a disease.' The word 'disease' tells the tale. Dutch elm disease, crossing the waters in ships, decimates the elm population of southern Ontario. Starlings are introduced into North America from Europe and wreak havoc. Just so, Jewish bankers (yellow starlings in Hitler's Germany), the yellow peril, and so on. Compare the following lines from Toronto's *Evening Telegram*, 22 September 1924: 'An influx of Jews puts a worm next the kernel of every fair city where they get a hold. These people have no national tradition . . . They engage in the wars of no country, but flit from one to another under passports changed with chameleon swiftness, following up the wind the smell of lucre.' This country's national anthem begins: 'O Canada! Our home and native land . . .' Members of the myriad cultures who have settled here sing the words with real conviction. The decision to make their lives here, to make Canada their home, makes them native here. The idea that the members of the First Nations alone can intone the anthem is a felt absurdity, whatever literal truth it has. In effect, the condition attributed by Ahenakew to Jews is the normal condition of men and women.

18 For the basic information, see http://nps.gov/archeology/kennewick.

19 The quotation is from page 19.

20 The magnificent work is the showpiece at the University of British Columbia's Museum of Anthropology. I would conjecture, from the forelimbs in each case, that Reid is quoting the Michelangelo panel that I now refer to.

21 That the seventh day (Genesis 2) also gets a blessing confirms the reading. Monday is washday. Thursday is market day. The sabbath is a day of

rest. It is not *for* anything. Note that God does not react with 'good' after the creation of humankind. In effect, men and women are, in the relevant sense of 'good,' good-for-nothings. The fact that the blessing is given to the fish after God does respond to their appearance with 'good' signals that the blessing is in this case something of a fish story.

22 Observe that Job's comforters are eventually criticized for insisting that he must have done something wrong. Lightning can strike a total innocent. If the Bible denied that, it would be unserious. But there is nothing amiss with focusing on non-natural problems. Job's final speech echoes – deliberately, it certainly seems – Proverbs 30:18. 'I have uttered what I did not understand, things too wonderful for me, which I did not know' (42:3). In effect, he did not appreciate that his tribulations are comprehensible quite apart from his innocence. They fall under the Proverbist's three, not under his four.

23 The Hebrew rendered as 'having dominion' has the harsh sense of the English 'coming down hard upon.' Trampling or crushing would be on the high side of domination. In moderation – for example, Woodhouse for dogs or Le Notre for shrubs – domination might be fairly benign. NRSV's 'subdue' (ibid.) functions both in the harsh sense ('subdue an opponent') and in the mild one ('speak in subdued tones').

24 I am not saying that the particular deer that is brought down benefits. This does not however mean that the particular deer does not benefit. It is hard here to speak sensibly of benefit. The idea gets a firm foothold only if we anthropomorphize. By contrast, whatever sense one gives to the claim that the human population benefits by the death of a particular person with low IQ or congenital defect, that person *certainly* does not benefit.

25 It is therefore semantically unobjectionable that in English translations the definite description 'the man' gets transmuted into the proper name 'Adam.'

26 Further to my claim in chapter 2 that the world might contain or might come to contain a creature that will at some point in time put an end to us, we can appreciate that the word 'dominion' that the writers employ mixes two different ideas. One is the idea that some among the creatures are 'on top' of others: the lion is the unpredated predator. The other is the idea that some among the creatures are strongly distinct from others: men and women, as particulars, are unlike the rest. Might particulars perish at the hands of non-particulars? Why not? We today tend to overlook the distinction because of our unprecedented ability to change natural processes. But of such a thing the Bible writers knew nothing. As for technological

prowess, theirs was rudimentary. So, again, the use of the idea of dominon in Genesis 1 is dependent on the conceptual resources of Genesis 2.

27 This could explain the sharp contrast between the processes of creation in Genesis 1 and in Genesis 2. In Genesis 2 the creatures are represented as, in germinal form, differentiated at the start. The seeds need only sprout. In Genesis 1 it's more a matter of relatively stable patterns emerging in a churning whole. If so, then, once again, the Genesis 1 description of the creation in terms of distinct realms of animals, plants, and so on, exploits the conceptual resources of Genesis 2. Arguably, the beginning of Genesis 5 *deliberately* signals the priority of the second creation account. Prefatorily to setting out the genealogy of Adam (who belongs firmly to the world of Genesis 2) along the line of Seth, the text intermixes Genesis 1 formulations regarding the emergence of men and women with Genesis 2 formulations. Genesis 5:1–2 – 'When God created humankind, he made them in the likeness of God. Male and female he created them, and he blessed them and named them "Humankind" when they were created' – corresponds to, even quotes, Genesis 1:27. The pronoun translated as 'them' in 5:1 is in fact singular: 'him.' So 'humankind' in its first occurrence is better rendered as 'a man.' The occurrences of 'them' in 5:2 match the original. So 'humankind' is appropriate. Chapter 5 thus mentions both the particular and the kind, and subordinates the latter. An associated difference is that while 'male and female he created them' is part of 1:27, in chapter 5 it inhabits a verse of its own. The separation is necessary in chapter 5 (though not in chapter 1) because in the world whose story chapter 5 narrates a particular person from which each of us stems, viz., Adam, is first created, not the kind, humankind, to which we all belong.

28 The Wikipedia entry – http://en.wikipedia.org/wiki/Ham_the_Chimp – for the first higher organism, a chimpanzee, sent aloft in the American space program, gives dates, as they are given for Yuri Gagarin, Alan Shepard, and Marc Garneau. 'Ham (August 1956? – January 19, 1983).'

29 See this book's chapter 12n16.

30 I am not going back here on the thesis that Genesis is not cosmogonic. I am making the point in the easiest way. Indeed, on the psychogenic reading, the point about name giving makes even better sense than it does on the cosmogonic one.

31 The genealogy gives Irad as the son of Enoch. The first syllable of 'Irad' is the word 'city.' So the writers are intent on ensuring that the reader gets the point.

32 Observe that the imperative about the tree of knowledge is not quite categorical. In the day that you eat of this tree, God says to the man, you shall die. So if the man (or the woman to whom the man conveys what God

says) is prepared to accept the consequences, God would have to agree that their transgression is not a violation of what he says.

33 If the 'killing' of Abel is not the offence, why is Cain criticized? God had asked: 'Where is your brother Abel?' (4:9). The nature of the offence calls out from Cain's response (ibid.): 'I do not know; am I my brother's keeper?' Cain's insouciant *denial* of responsibility for the impact of his revolution on Abel is the problem. The phenomenon that the Bible is addressing in moral terms is perennial. Though the tape recorder, the switching circuit, and the supermarket eliminate their livelihoods, they do not eliminate the men and women who made a living as stenographers, switchboard operators, and deliverers of eggs and milk. An obligation exists on those who take over not to let these men and women fall through the cracks. Cain knows perfectly well where his brother is. He hears Abel's plaint from the soup line, the mean streets, and the gutter: 'Brother, can you spare a dime?'

34 As earlier explained, 'Babel,' the Hebrew form of 'Babylon,' parses as 'bab-el,' that is, 'gate of god.' The (more historical) link between the inauguration of monotheism and the Tower is evident. The builders, their lives having been made difficult by the confusion of voices from on high, are trying to batter down the gate of the godly domain – cp. the storming of the Bastille – in order to take the citadel. If we credit the conjectural history, the problem is merely accentuated. Why would God scotch the Tower enterprise if the objective is to overcome a belief system at odds with monotheism?

35 The Bible even puts 'one' in 11:1 in a plural form.

36 Michael Chabon, *The Final Solution*, 64.

Chapter 5

1 The term '*Achsenzeit*' was coined by Karl Jaspers. In *The Origin and Goal of History*, the philosopher asserts (1) that the period so labelled 'gave birth to everything which, since then, man has been able to be.'

2 Positions related as reformed and unreformed must be on roughly an equal footing in quantity or scope and quality or depth of articulation. The move from confusion to clarity is not a reform. A child, in rising to cognitive erectness, does not replace an immature view with a mature one. A sculpture is not a reformed block of marble.

3 Scholars debate whether the *Iliad* and the *Odyssey* were the work of a single hand. The validity of the reasoning here is independent of whether in the matter of the epics' authorship one has unitarian or separatist sympathies.

4 In its written form, the Hebrew language is consonantal. If English were like Hebrew in this respect, 'bread' would appear in writing as 'brd' and would thus be ambiguous as between 'bread, 'broad,' 'bride,' 'braid,' 'bird,' 'bored,' 'bard,' 'barred,' 'beard,' and so on. Obviously, for the reader of Hebrew, context plays a large role in disambiguating. The brd that is hatched (to illustrate with English) must have wings. The brd that is sliced is more likely to be made of flour than to suck nectar from a flower. Over the course of time a few letters with an intermediate, vowel-like, character were introduced into written Hebrew as an aid to reading. The full system of vowel markings currently in use (mainly in poetry, in writing for children, and for adult acquirers of Hebrew as a second language) also developed about a millennium and a half after the Bible was first put together; developed, largely, as a way of removing ambiguities from Holy Writ.

5 The case of Abraham, the first son of Terah, is a departure from the general biblical bias against the firstborn. The fact confirms the present point. God's world in Genesis 1 is not a second try. Abraham's move in Genesis 12 is unprecedented. When the text is read more closely, the sharpness of both breaks is considerably dulled.

6 This is my general secularist axiom. I should add that the 'reflection' does not have to be mirror-like. It's just a matter of what happens on high being motivated from down low. The representation of what happens on high, as in Plato, can be a standard-setting model that cannot fully be met by objects composed of physical stuff.

7 Hammurabi's Code has some elements in common with the biblical view. It contains, for instance, the *Lex Talionis*: 'An eye for an eye.' Some scholars see a real-world link with (the historical correlate of the Bible's) Abraham, who is called by God out of Hammurabi's Mesopotamia. (Scrabble players will see the patriarch's name in the lawgiver's.) The intriguing idea, then, is that Abraham's departure from that part of the world is precipitated by a desire to ground the newly encoded moral precepts more firmly, in less contested soil.

8 Audibly, too. Pronounced 'yavan,' the word is in Modern Hebrew the appellation of Greece.

9 It astonishes that Prometheus's comeuppance – chained to a rock, his liver is eaten by a vulture – involves an organ the English word for which is cognate with 'life.' How did that jingle for Carter's Little Liver Pills go? 'Life not worth living? It might be the liver.'

10 I indicated earlier that Athena's intervention is Protean. The word 'both' confirms the point. The reference is to Hera, who, Athena explains, has sent her. But Hera's contribution is to the Greek warriors' effort. Athena's

is different. As in Hesiod's story, Athena is acting here as the instrument of radical change. Whether or not the coincidence of imagery is deliberate, it is apt that in both cases the intervention involves the head.

11 What in fact came to pass might not have eventuated. And 'came to pass' is itself unstable. A few thousand years hence, from the perspective of some much different culture, the judgment might be that the promises, which have a temporal dimension, were not kept.

12 Athena not only is the inspiration for change in Greece. She is also associated with the polis called 'Athens.' This second affinity is more like God's for men and women in the Bible.

13 The reverse holds for Abraham. It is important to the narrative that the patriarch be a paragon. That is why the episode of Abraham's misrepresenting his wife as his sister seems so odd. An interpretation consistent with both Abraham's nobility and the episode's oddity will be supplied in chapter 10.

14 Authorship of the famous Psalm 23, 'The Lord is my shepherd,' is astutely attributed to David in this regard.

15 David is not in the end permitted to build that house. This feature of the story may reflect (what was regarded as) the historical fact that Solomon built the Temple. David, the Michelangelo of *this* piece (one imagines an architectural firm named 'Ben Jesse and Buonarroti'), does however blueprint the structure. The preceding story suggests that this is thematically significant. If David is a parallel for God, then someone else *should* build God's house. For just as David's house, so far as national continuity goes, builds on the taking of another's wife, so God has taken his (national) bride, Israel, from another. It would be a bad example for such behaviour to be rewarded too quickly. Observe, again, that Abraham has to be forced to abandon what from the standpoint of his patriarchal status is an inappropriate spouse.

16 The Bible contains a great deal of this kind of wordplay. Here is one example. *Jacob*, at a crossroads in his relations with his dispossessed brother, Esau, comes to a ford in the river *Jabbok* (Genesis 32:22). (Despite the 'k' and the double 'b' in 'Jabbok,' the word has the same consonants as 'Jacob.') Jacob, by contrast with his father Isaac, has to come to terms with his other side.

17 There is a more substantive basis, too, for the identification. Hadad is linked (35) to David's progenitor, Moab. And other telltale signs are present. Esau is called 'Edom,' which is cognate with 'red.' This sets up a linkage between David, who is redheaded, and Adam of the red clay. See chapter 3n7.

Chapter 6

1 A third point might be that while men and women are parts of the physical world, they are not just more of nature. If so, the point feeds the Proverbist's three and four.

2 Finley, *The World of Odysseus*. The book originally appeared in 1954.

3 The Greeks themselves tended to see the epics as historical.

4 There are in fact two soliloquies in the *Iliad*. I will return to the fact.

5 A simple example of a point that looks factual but is conceptual will help here. Consider the assertion 'All positive integers are small.' This looks like a generalization. If taken that way, it would be disputed. 'Agreed, 7 is small. But 1,234,655 is large.' The defence of the claim would run thus: 'A positive integer is small if there are more positive integers greater than it than smaller.' On this definition of 'small,' each and every positive integer is small. Note that a meaning analysis backs up the philosophical position.

6 969 lies between the squares of the adjacent natural numbers – 31 and 32 – that stand on opposite sides of 1000. (The Bible *is* attentive to the powers of 10. Thus 1 Samuel 18:7: 'And the women sang to one another as they made merry, "Saul has killed his thousands, and David his ten thousands."')

7 Unlike the Christian heaven, Hades is not an alternative.

8 The case of Nestor, King of the Pylians, offers confirmation. The Old Soldier of the piece, he is mildly self-embarrassed because of his age. '[I]f only I were the man I was,' he sighs [4:367].

9 I say 'energetically' rather than 'violently.' The case of Paris shows that there is more than one way for a swordsman to thrust; to parry too, for that matter.

10 Leaving the trace in the public memory does not require besting the gods. As Hector's 'let me die' claim confirms, it does not even require bellowing over a fallen opponent. After all, even the hurricane that is off the Saffir-Simpson Scale eventually abates. The classicist C.J. Rowe (*Plato*, 177n8) treats 'emulating the gods' and 'competing with the gods' as synonymous. Diomedes both copies and competes. *But his case is represented as unusual.* The warrior ethos mandates the first (which is more accurately understood as 'measuring oneself against the gods'), not the second. Hector is trying to measure up to the gods in his activity, not to best them.

11 In Sophocles's *Ajax*, the protagonist, driven mad by the failure to inherit, butchers a herd of cattle, mistaking the animals for the warriors on whom he is out to revenge himself. This is an exploitation of two scenes in the *Iliad*: the Book 1 scene where Achilles, furious at the loss of Briseis, draws his sword against Agamemnon, and the Book 23 scene where Achilles, wild with grief at the loss of Patroclus, sacrifices twelve Trojan captives,

along with horses and dogs. Sophocles's suggestion is that after the clang of armour subsides, he who continues the bloodshed does not understand the difference between beasts (whose value is instrumental to us) and human beings (whose lives have intrinsic worth). A warrior in our midst would seem to us insane.

12 Gopnik, 'Last of the Metrozoids,' 86–7. The team is about to take the field competitively for the first time. Gopnik, who has assumed the coaching duties, does not give the motivational speech, but Brad Pitt, playing the part of Achilles in the movie *Troy*, does.

13 In Hebrew as in Latin, the word 'angel' means 'emissary.' The ambassadors who visit Achilles are angels from the regnant value system, trying to get him to look upwards.

14 No Hebrew speaker would initially take the word in the original as meaning 'awesome.' The Authorized Version has 'dreadful.' The darker renderings – 'awful,' 'dreadful' – are confirmed by Jacob's state. The narrative tells us that he 'was afraid' (ibid.).

15 The reading is not anachronistic. A word with the same root, translated in the NRSV as 'physicians,' appears at Genesis 50:2. The physicians in this case are Pharaonic functionaries with expertise in embalming – deceptively enlivening the dead.

16 Some sages seem to have been disturbed by the way the story is told. In Yalkut Shimoni, 1 Kings, 18, it is suggested in respect of verse 26 that God thwarted a plan by the prophets of Baal for a hidden confederate beneath the altar to ignite *their* sacrifice!

17 I am alluding to the apocryphal story of Thales having made a fortune in the olive trade. He did so (the story goes) by gaining control of the olive presses in the spring of what he correctly forecast, extrapolating from climatic regularities, would be a particularly bountiful year. See Aristotle, *Politics*, 1259a5–20. The idea that Elijah proceeds by guile is not new. John Gray, *Kings I & II: A Commentary*, 401, reports: 'One rationalistic commentator suggested that not water, but naphthah or some such substance susceptible to spontaneous combustion was used. R.H. Kennet went further and suggested that a burnished reflector was also used. If such hypercriticism is worthy of reply we may object, with Rowley, that the Baal-prophets would be especially vigilant, and would be as much *au fait* with such elementary science as Elijah' (410). This response assumes the Bible to be factual reportage. Whatever historical kernel it contains, the Bible does not however emerge from the hands of the editors and redactors as history. The tale carries a moral and a philosophical message. To sustain his position, Gray would have to know the guiding motive. As most do, he takes it to be, in the usual sense, religious. But religiosity, as I hope my general line

makes clear, is itself a problematic notion in the Bible. Far from its being 'hypercritical' to say so, it is 'hypocritical' to be primed in advance against saying so.

18 Norman Simms, 'Is Judaism a Jewish Heresy?'

19 Yehezkel Kaufmann, *The Religion of Israel, from Its Beginnings to the Babylonian Exile*, maintains that the manner in which opposition to idolatry appears in the Tanakh indicates that the writers were not responding to the real thing. Kaufmann's pungent phrase is 'vestigial fetishistic idolatry.' At the core of Kaufmann's position is the view that monotheism is a Mosaic development and hence precedes (and in its essentials is uninfluenced by) the experience in Canaan after the return from Egypt. The commandment against idolatry as stated in Exodus 20:4–5 and in Deuteronomy 5:8–9 seems to be in accord with Kaufmann's view, as does the description of idolatry in Samuel. But see n24 below. Kaufmann, in my view, is reading the text too historically.

20 Maimonides, *Guide for the Perplexed*, III:32.

21 Though evidence that the story of bondage and deliverance is historically accurate is scarce, it seems plain that the Israelite communion did contain within it a hieratic element that came from Egypt. 'Moses' is a name of Egyptian provenance, as are the names of Moses's sister, Miriam, and his nephews, Aaron's grandsons, Phinehas and Hofni. Moses is of course a Levite; and Aaron is the first in the line of priests, the cohens.

Chapter 7

1 *Dubliners*, 225. Lying immobile beside his sleeping wife in the chill box of a dreary Dublin hotel room, Gabriel has just learned that his own life's forward progress has been arrested. Greta's affections, he discovered earlier that evening, are frozen in an adolescent relationship with a dead suitor. Joyce, by dramatizing the case of a literary type who has failed to break free of Ireland's grip, is speaking of his own need, as an artist, to leave his native land and his father's house.

2 For his unrelenting attacks on the epic poet's artistry, Zoilos, a grammarian and literary commentator from Amphipolis who lived in the 4th century BCE, came to be known as 'Homeromastix,' that is, 'scourge of Homer.' ('Zoilos' is used in stratospheric English with the meaning 'carping critic.') In this instance, the objection has some merit. Would it not be enough for the monster to promise a reward in return for the drink? Why require the sommelier's name too? This confirms my upcoming point, however. To introduce 'Nobody,' Homer is stretching his plot onto a thematic bed that is too long for its natural limbs.

3 In calling the one-eyed and literal-minded beast 'Polyphemus,' that is, 'multi-tongued,' Homer is having a bit of fun. (The latter half of the name is visible to English speakers in the word 'blasphemous.') It's like calling the head of a gang of thieves who can't shoot straight 'Brains.' But Ajax, no brute, is also Polyphemus-like. He too loses a match with the flexibly minded Odysseus.

4 Some translations render it as 'Noman.' The well-known Latin form is 'Nemo.'

5 In the poem 'Ulysses,' Tennyson responds to the feature of Odysseus that I am referring to. Odysseus cannot hack the life of a politico. Using as a cue Tiresias's prophecy that Odysseus would die far from home, among 'a race of people who know nothing of the sea' (*Odyssey* 11:140), Tennyson has him setting sail with his hearties and journeying beyond the Pillars of Hercules, into the unknown, to test life at the extreme, and to do so entirely for the sake of doing so, far from the gaze of others. 'Made weak by time and fate, but strong in will / To strive, to seek, to find, and not to yield.' This is less reflective than existential. 'A man like this,' the narrator of a Primo Levi short story writes of his friend Carlo, 'when he's dead, he's dead forever. He's not the kind you tell stories about or build monuments to; he's all in his actions, and, once those are over, nothing remains' ('Bear Meat,' 41). Dante, whom Levi idolizes, takes a rather Tennyson-like view of Odysseus. Perhaps Dante influenced Tennyson. In *Survival in Auschwitz*, Levi himself, who was forced to test life *à outrance* in the death camp, quotes a canto from *The Inferno* that takes Tennyson's Ulysses beyond 'and not to yield.'

6 Polyphemus's cave might be likened also to the *poêle*, with Odysseus in the role of the meditator. The parallelism goes only so far. Trapped in the cave, Odysseus does what he always does: uses his wits. His wits are his identity. In the tent, Achilles is a changed man. He has removed the armour of his erstwhile identity. He now trains against that identity the considerable intelligence that up to then had been welded to it.

7 In what sense does Achilles best Zeus? Though by the end of the *Iliad* we have witnessed a change, we do not quite know how to answer. There are two things here. Whatever the epic initially contained, or whatever its original thrust might have been, classical Greece had already transitioned to peace as the norm. So the poem, if it slanted in some other direction, was likely edited and adjusted so as to impart that message, just as the Bible was adjusted to the calamity of 586 BCE. Also, it is quite true that the 'victory' of Achilles over Zeus in the epic is incomplete. Once again, the classical age moved the van forward. We shall be exploring the specifics in the sequel. I might just remark that Homer gives Zeus some words that vaguely prefigure the change that Zeus thought he could avoid. Speaking of Achilles as he is about to return to the fray, Zeus says: 'Now, with his rage inflamed for his friend's death, / I fear he'll raze the walls against the will of fate' [20:35–36].

8 Quoted by Knox, 29, in the introduction to the edition of the *Iliad* that I am using. 'Force as man's instrument' is ambiguous. Does force control man, or does man use force as an instrument? The ambiguity may be an artefact of the translation. If so, it fortuitously captures the truth that Weil misses. If not, Weil's (ambiguous) language knows better than she does. I cannot forbear adding a more personal comment. What does Weil understand by force? Knox sets out her explanation (ibid.). Force is 'what makes the person subjected to it into a thing.' He proceeds. 'She wrote these words in 1939; . . . but before [the article could be published] Paris was in the hands of the Nazis and her compatriots, like all Europe, were subjected to force and turned into things – corpses or slaves.' Many were enslaved; many incinerated. But the unfortunates were not shackled and reduced to ashes by force. *People* robbed them of their freedom and marched them to the incinerators. Others, indeed, and many of 'her compatriots,' turned neither into corpses nor into slaves. They became turncoats. Weil's words are in this context repellent. 'What could the French collaborators have done?' they seem to ask. The question insults those who resisted and whitewashes the worst of our natures. Weil won't have known in 1939 of collaboration. Still, that Knox should not take exception to the broader context is more than insensitive.

9 Meditation I, in *The Philosophical Writings of Descartes*, 12.

10 The naive reader of Descartes will scratch his or her head too. The meditator accepts the following principle (ibid.): 'hold back my assent from opinions which are not completely certain and indubitable just as carefully as I [hold it back] from those which are patently false.' Assent is to be withheld, then, from the proposition that a car is racing down the street on a collision course with me (I could be hallucinating) just as it is to be withheld from the proposition that the moon is made of green cheese.

11 I want to stress that Achilles is not speaking ironically.

12 It's an amusing thought that the stone, being too large to pass, causes a royal bellyache that keeps Kronos permanently off *that* throne. In fact, after he is vanquished Kronos is persuaded to disengorge what he had swallowed. The stone, which he vomits up first, Zeus installs at Pythos, beneath Parnassus, 'forever to be a marvel and a portent for mortal men' (500).

13 An extension of the claim that Homer is imaginatively exploiting the myth of Zeus and Thetis consists in seeing Athena's encouragement of Achilles as a third instalment of the *Theogony*'s representation of the mother's making common cause with the son to supplant the father. Might Athena not

be identified with Metis, whom Zeus has swallowed? Isn't Achilles the son that Zeus would have had he followed his inclinations?

14 Observe that the end of strife is linked to Zeus's unifying potentially divergent forces within himself. The movement to peace has a monotheistic slant.

15 I have steered a fairly wide berth around the shoals of classical scholarship. I must here mention one technical issue. The meaning of the word that Fagles translates as 'third born' is contested. Some see in 'Tritogenia' a reference to Triton, the idea being that Athena has a distant origin in some early, even non-Greek, pantheon, where she is (like Thetis) linked to water. Athena is, then, 'water born.' The issue for us is however the reception of Homer from the time of Pisistratus and onwards; and its reception by, in the main, Athenians. From this perspective, Fagles's rendering is appropriate. The recipients, who knew Athena as born of (the sky-god) Zeus, would have been responsive to the pun.

16 In agreeing to send Patroclus out, Achilles speaks the warriors' language. He does not say that Patroclus's death is something he would personally regret. '[Y]ou will only make *my* glory that much less' [16:106].

17 In 'Philosophy as a Humanistic Discipline,' Bernard Williams focuses from a meta-philosophical standpoint on the non-formulaic character of such changes. Having in effect ceded to science the area that philosophy traditionally claimed for itself, he is struggling not to have the discipline go the way of phrenology. Here, then, is where Williams locates what I call 'perplexity.' But what about the humans who go through the non-formulaic changes?

18 Autolycus, Odysseus's maternal grandfather, gave him the name with the idea of being *at odds* in mind. See Book 19 [458–464]. Jacob's name derives from the adjective meaning 'crooked.' Esau's heel, which Jacob grasped in an effort to be born first, is right-angled, as unstraight as a line can be. Famously, Odysseus is described in the opening line of the *Odyssey* as 'the man of twists and turns.'

19 'Esau' means 'hairy.' The name of the chief suitor, Antinous, means 'a deceptive facsimile of rationality.'

20 Plotwise, the episode is part of Jacob's attempt to master his fear about an impending meeting with his brother Esau, whom he has not seen since he finagled the blessing. The episode corresponds to Odysseus's meeting with Ajax in Hades. In the end, the encounter with Esau goes better than Jacob anticipates, and much better than Odysseus's meeting with Ajax. In both cases, the justice of the succession is in question and, though more in the biblical case, the mettle of the successor.

21 The text is fairly explicit. In Genesis 26 Isaac, like both Abraham and Jacob, sets out for Egypt because of a famine in the land. But he goes only as far as Gerar in Philistia. There, blessed by the Lord, he 'sowed seed . . . and in the same year reaped a hundredfold' (12). Isaac's experience falls somewhere between that of the inhabitants of Eden and that of those who contend with a hostile world on its own terms.
22 Most versions of the Documentary Hypothesis identify a priestly strain in the biblical narrative.
23 At Exodus 33:11, God is said to commune with Moses 'face to face.' Jacob names the place of the wrestling match 'Peniel,' 'for I have seen God face to face' (Genesis 32:30).

Chapter 8

1 Milton, arguably, defends a humanist view against what a literal-minded reading of Genesis suggests. He does not, if so, take the line that immortality ever was an option; that it results, as Milton's nearly exact contemporary Thomas Browne puts it in the essay 'Of Death,' from 'the error of our first parents.'
2 It is well worth observing that the text doesn't support this conversion. The text says: the man and the woman, now that they are knowledgeable, are (in that respect) like God. When it is added that their access to the tree of life must therefore be barred, only an independent view of God as eternal prevents this from being read as requiring the barring on the grounds that should they gain immortality they will lose their God-likeness.
3 In Greek myth, Poseidon and Apollo, as the quotations above indicate, are said to have raised Troy's ramparts for Laomedon, son of Ilus, who is also mentioned [7:525], and Poseidon is said to have flooded the city when Laomedon did not pay for the labour as he had promised. This, then, would be a use of myth by Homer, not a mere quotation of it. What follows concerning Athens supplies a firmer basis for what I am claiming here.
4 Williams, *Shame and Necessity*, 104.
5 In one respect, there *is* more to the action than fighting. But the 'more' in question is not far off across the sea. Troy (inside the walls) is itself part of the action. As I will explain in the next chapter, Troy, though it has wives and young children none of whom bears arms or straps on armour, cannot however be said to be outside the fighting in the sense that Williams intends. Troy, we shall see, is as odd a city as the Trojan War is odd as a war, and *its* oddity bears the same message, *mutatis mutandis*, as does the oddity of the war.

6 It is as it should be that prior to his return to the fray Achilles does not eat the food of the warriors. He is given what nourishes the gods. This, then, is a variation on the myth of Thetis and Peleus. Athena again does the work: 'she instilled / some nectar and sweet ambrosia deep in Achilles's chest' [19:417–418].

7 A different, more philosophical, explanation for the need to bar access to the tree of life after the transgression will be offered in chapter 10.

8 Thus its prevalence as a medical emblem. The association of snakes with healing crosses cultural frontiers and tracks back to the rim of recorded history. The statue of a Minoan mother goddess bearing a snake in each outstretched hand (c. 2000 BCE) is a good illustration predating the archaic Greece of Homer and the roughly contemporary Near East of the Bible. But the winged staff entwined by a pair of snakes – the caduceus – commonly employed today as a medical insignia is in fact part of the paraphernalia of Hermes, the divine messenger, god of travellers and of great changes. The use of the emblem by the medical profession is mildly amusing, since salient among the changes that Hermes is associated with in Greek mythic lore is the transition from life to death. (In the final book of the *Odyssey* Hermes leads the suitors' ghosts 'past / the Land of Dreams . . . / [to] where the dead, the burnt out wraiths of mortals, make their home' [24:13–15].) So it is much as if the physician's shingle bore the name 'Killam' or 'De'ath.') In fact, a different Hellenic deity is associated with medicine: Asclepius. The latter also has a snake-entwined standard as part of his livery. Asclepius's staff, which has only one snake, is forked. While the US Public Health Service makes use of the caduceus, the American Medical Association's icon, like that of its Canadian and British counterparts, is Asclepian. Given the similarity of trappings, the lower profile of Asclepius among Olympians no doubt lies behind the confusion. A snake of bronze attached to a pole is connected to healing in the Bible. See Numbers 21:8. This snake, Nehushtan, serves as the symbol of the Israeli Medical Association.

Chapter 9

1 Seth L. Schein, *The Mortal Hero*, 141.

2 The *Iliad* contains a list that has a greater *prima facie* resemblance to Fitzgerald's. But the reason for setting out the catalogue of fighters in Book 2 is explicitly stated. It has to do with the value system of the warriors – the imperative of being remembered. The randomness of *this* list is quite incidental to its point; it could have been set out alphabetically.

3 Knox, who manages to suggest that Homer is the first Greek writer to mention the city, can justifiably assert no more than this: the *Iliad* is the earliest surviving work in which a city is mentioned, Troy being that city. From the standpoint of reflective thinking, Thebes, which we shall visit in the sequel, has a much better claim to be tagged the first Greek city. In many respects, Troy resembles Olympus.

4 The point is made in the *Iliad* with the exchange between Diomedes and Glaucus, who discover a background bond between their two families. 'Splendid – you are my friend,' says Diomedes [6:257], after Glaucus has told of his birth and lineage. None of this makes sense in the heat of the battle. The exchange is a dramatization of a level beneath that on which the action of the epic occurs.

5 I state again that the *Odyssey* is not compelling in this regard. The ingenuity of Odysseus is more the issue than the rise of a new way. The real legatees of the *Iliad* are the dramatists of classical Greece.

6 It may be felt that Priam has not had nearly enough of a part in the epic, nor the right kind of part, to justify representing him as going through the same change as Achilles. I am inclined to agree. In having Priam *resist* the invitation to sit beside Achilles, Homer is I think indicating that Priam is not Achilles's counterpart. It is, if so, as a grief-stricken father that Priam comes to Achilles and as a grief-stricken father that he departs. The 'mutual recognition' between the pair that I speak of just below is, then, a projection of Achilles's, not an existential reality.

7 'Ballad of Hector in Hades.'

8 Quite a few scholars, for a variety of reasons, have felt that the last part of the *Odyssey* is a later addition. See Knox, Introduction to the *Iliad*, 7. Observe that the *Iliad* begins with Athena's intervention, and the very end of the *Odyssey* finds her intervening again. In both cases, the interventions are to prevent bloodshed and strife. This itself is a sign that matters have not been moved decisively forward.

9 Compare Proust's domestic evocation of Homer (I quote one of several passages): '"Saint Loup with the helm of bronze," said Bloch, "have a piece more of this duck with thighs heavy with fat, over which the illustrious sacrificer of birds has poured numerous libations of red wine.' *Remembrance of Things Past*, 832.

10 In Aeschylus's *Agamemnon*, the first of the trilogy making up *The Oresteia*, Clytaemnestra, having killed her husband Agamemnon, as natural justice requires (for he had sacrificed their daughter Iphigeneia to placate the god), speaks (1603–1605) of a day when she will 'have purged / our fury to destroy each other – / purged it from our halls.' It's not quite the

purgation of the fury that the institutionalization of punishment gives; it's the substitution of justice for vengeance.

11 'Nimrod,' though it has the Hebrew meaning 'opponent,' which might be rendered in Greek as 'agonistes,' is of Babylonian origin. The cities that Nimrod is credited with founding – 'Nineveh, Rehobothir, Calah, and Resen between Nineveh and Calah' (10:11–12) – are real. Though the Bible does not mention it, there is also a city called 'Nimrud.' Just as Cain named a city after his son, so Ham, father of city builders, does, in a sense, the same. Since there never was a city called 'Enoch,' it seems that the Bible writers, in having Cain give this name to the first biblical city, and in suppressing what they would have understood to be a historically real link between Nimrod and 'Nimrud,' are making a first of a second. In regard to Genesis 10:9, one might therefore take 'before' in a straight temporal meaning, which would cohere with the sense that what the text includes lies between assertion and quotation. The point would be that God of the Bible appears after Nimrod and his civilization.

12 Lewis, *The Abolition of Man*, 59. Noah's other sons stand to the reader of the text, then, as the goddess of wisdom does to Achilles in Book 1 of the *Iliad*.

13 Rushdie, *The Satanic Verses*, 325, slightly edited.

14 Observe that the problem that the Bible finds in Sodom is not present in Hector's Troy.

Chapter 10

1 Thebes was the capital of Athens's rival state Boeotia. It was natural for the dramatists, who worked in Athens, to use it as a contrast and a foil, as New Yorkers might use Chicago, or Montrealers, Toronto.

2 'Cadmus,' connected in meaning with 'first' or 'original,' is of Semitic provenance. Eden, the birthplace of men and women, is planted 'in the east' (Genesis 2:8). 'East' here, signifying the starting point, is cognate with 'Cadmus.' The mythic Cadmus is often traced back to Phoenicia.

3 Given that Athena is linked with the setting up of the Areopagus, the first Athenian court of law, God stands to the city much as she does. It will not be found surprising that it is Athena who advises Cadmus to plant the dragon's teeth.

4 Though the idea of objective institutions of justice in a world of nomads is not logically inconsistent, the close association of justice and farming makes good sense. Judicial authorities, to be legitimate, have to be accepted, and their acceptance has to be generally known. Otherwise, why would disputants appear before them for mediation or take their

deliverances seriously? Also, some centralization of administration is necessary. Without a modicum of permanence, these things are unlikely to be up and running.

5 As noted earlier, political geography of biblical times includes a city called 'Nimrud.' So here too we have a naming after a founder.

6 To say in Hebrew that a person is enoch–ed (מחנך) is to say that he or she has learned manners. *À propos* the dragon's sown teeth: in Hebrew, the word 'gums' is cognate with 'educated' or 'trained.' The idea, I imagine, is that the gums support neat rows of teeth. A farmer is, if you will, an orthobotanist.

7 In the Bible, God too steers clear of cities and has many scruples about city founders and urbanites. Lot has to work a lot harder than Abraham to persuade the angels to accept his hospitality.

8 Euripides's *Bacchae* tells of the god Dionysus entering without knocking. In his usual fashion, Euripides is skewing the main line. It could hardly be held that Poseidon, or Ares, is unfairly excluded from the city. Euripides's position is that Dionysus has a genuine claim to belonging. Euripides's point, expressed in the terms of the myth of Cadmus, is that the Dragon has a cu[s]pid or two as well as m[ol]ars.

9 The Bible contains the same general idea. Consider the visit of the angels to Sodom. To be sure, the contrast in the Bible is sure to be more moderate, since God is not identified with nature.

10 Kitto, *The Greeks*, 106.

11 Below, I revert to the technical distinction of chapter 4 between *individuals* and *particulars*. The *mot juste* here is 'particularism.' But until the distinction needs explicitly to be set out, I stick to what comes naturally.

12 Vernant, 'Tensions and Ambiguities in Greek Tragedy,' in *Myth and Tragedy in Ancient Greece*, 41.

13 References to death and to the dead fill *Antigone*. The passages so far mentioned and cited involve several such. Vernant is therefore right to factor it into his interpretive effort. But Antigone's death, we shall see, has a meaning in the play that can be understood properly only in contrast to Creon's understanding of life. Those who link Antigone with death do not observe closely enough that it is *Creon* who makes the association. Thus, at 875–6, he identifies 'Death' as 'the one god [Antigone] worships.'

14 Both Homeric epics quote the story of Oedipus. In the more extensive of the two quotations, in the *Odyssey*, Oedipus's mother, called 'Epicaste,' is described as having hanged herself because of the abominations, 'leaving her son to bear / the world of horror a mother's Furies bring to life' [11:316–8]. And that's the end. Evidence exists of an epic, *The Oidipodia*,

from which the various elements found in later writers might derive. But that poem's content can't be much less conjectural to Knox than it is to me.

15 It is common for the playwrights to draw upon Homer. I mentioned Sophocles's *Ajax*. There is however a difference between the dramatists' use of Homer and their use of myth. They take up where Homer leaves off. The myths are often much farther in the background.

16 See Zeitlin, 'Thebes: Theater of Self and Society in Athenian Drama.'

17 In the political frame, a more emotive version of 'replaceable' is 'disposable.' A useful neutral word is 'fungible.' The term has currency mainly in the commercial sphere. A $10 bill is a fungible. Since all $10 bills have the same buying power, only a sentimental (hence economically irrelevant) ground can explain why you would protest a teller's handing you one rather than another. For instance, the serial number may be even, and you have a phobia against even numbers. The jugs of milk of chapter 2 are fungibles.

18 The first three verses of Genesis 2 sum up Genesis 1. Genesis 2 effectively begins at verse 4, which corresponds to Genesis 1:1.

19 The exchanges between Creon and Antigone are very like those between the ambassadors and Achilles. Nor does the likeness come down just to the mutual incomprehension. A change occurs through Achilles in the root idea of human finitude. Death, as we understand it, comes into the world. So Achilles is in a more substantive sense too a precursor of Antigone. I believe, however, that the biblical connections are in this instance more revealing.

20 The word I translate as 'bad' the NRSV gives as 'evil.' Hebrew does not justify the rendering.

21 For a glimpse of the real world underbelly of these abstract formulations, consider the following lines by Hannah Arendt (*Origins of Totalitarianism*, 438). 'Total domination, which strives to organize the infinite plurality and differentiation of human beings as if all of humanity were just one individual, is possible only [by] fabricat[ing] something that does not exist, namely, a kind of human species resembling other animal species whose only "freedom" would consist in "preserving the species." Totalitarian domination attempts to achieve this goal both through ideological indoctrination of the elite formations and through absolute terror in the [concentration] camps.' The internal quotation paraphrases an entry in Hitler's *Tischgespräche*.

22 Amis, *Yellow Dog*, 150.

23 Another, and more aggressive, way of looking at it suggests itself. Prior to the transgression, it would not have made a difference if the man and the

woman partook of the tree of life. The text never in fact says that they do not. In banishing the pair, God says that 'now' (3:22) they must be blocked from doing so. This is consistent with their having eaten of the tree of life before they became particulars.

24 Proust, *Remembrance of Things Past*, 252.

25 It strengthens the point that in Proust's story Swann, whose lovesick agonies are being anatomized, falls for a very shallow woman. 'To think,' as Swann exclaims to himself at the close of the story of his courtship (ibid., 415), 'that I've wasted years of my life, that I've longed to die, that I've experienced my greatest love, for a woman who doesn't appeal to me, who wasn't even my type!' That's what Creon says to Haemon: 'Antigone is not your type.'

26 *À propos* Lear's 'reason not the need,' just imagine circumstances in which a person *might* from an initial position of indifference be brought, through exposure to syllogistic reasoning, to look after his or her offspring. We would, I think, have to go as far as envisaging a father who, afflicted with amnesia, has to be retrained to parenthood. 'Each person cares for his own offspring. These are your offspring. So you should see to them.' This person's subsequent treatment of the children, if the re-education took hold, would be rather like an employee's *vis-à-vis* an employer. 'You are a paid employee. Employees are paid to work. So you must do your job.' But, plainly, the thing in the former case is abnormal, not to say pathological. Fatherhood, though hard work, is not a job. Our amnesiac, going through the motions, would be *paternal*, not a *pater*. One can, by the same token, act lovingly without loving.

27 The expunging from a community of love, or the refusal to recognize what love ontologically presupposes, goes along with a wholesale change in interpersonal or social psychology. In the novel *Black Box*, Amos Oz brilliantly tabulates the contrasts: 'Esteem takes the place of friendship. Self-negation replaces respect. Obedience instead of participation. Subjection instead of brotherhood. Enthusiasm takes the place of emotion. Shouts and whispers substitute for speech. Suspicion instead of doubt. Torture instead of joy. Repression instead of longing. Mortification instead of meditation. Betrayal instead of leavetaking. The bullet instead of an argument. Slaughter instead of dissension. Death instead of change. Purging crusades instead of death. "Immortality" instead of life' (175).

28 In an effort to moderate the problems that the claim of God's preference raises for the Israelites (and their descendants), some say that the choice

carries a heavy burden for the chosen. But this doesn't moderate enough. If the Israelites were chosen because God wanted his way propagated, then his choice is conditional. It's like choosing a spouse on the grounds that the chosen one will be a good provider. That is not however the dominant sense of Scripture.

29 What runner in a competitive race would stop to lend a hand to another runner who has stumbled? Since Lot is a competitor, isn't the rescue in the valley an expression of a reservation about patriarchy? If so, Abraham's treatment of Sarah and the action in the case of Lot are of a piece. In both cases, Abraham is acting on his own initiative, not doing what God would want. And in both cases, God is not having it. (A different reading of the redemption of Lot can be based on what I say in chapter 3n5.)

30 To read the Akedah as dealing with a national, not a personal, death would be quite in keeping with what we have learned of the treatment of endings in Genesis. The 'death' of Adam and Eve is the end of innocence. Cain's 'killing' of Abel signifies the superannuation of the herder. The death of Isaac on the altar would be the end of the Israelite national enterprise. Lot's claim that he will die unless he is permitted to settle in Zoar is the claim that city life will end. Let me add that a serious problem affects the 'religious' reading of the Akedah. At Sarah's advanced age, Isaac's birth is a medical miracle. If God can work miracles, why would the death of Isaac conflict with God's keeping his promise? Couldn't God arrange for another son?

31 Abraham also fathers a host of other national patriarchs. See Genesis 25:2.

Chapter 11

1 Genesis Rabbah, 1:10.

2 The curse that Ham draws for having viewed his father's nakedness belongs to the same category. After the Flood, Noah is the new Adam, the source of all mankind. Ham's brothers keep their gaze averted from the father's dishabille. They 'walked backward and covered [his] nakedness' (9:23). One imagines that the Lord God, walking about Eden in the cool of the day, is not wearing clothes. The man and the woman presumably do see God in all his glory. (Exodus 33:22 explicitly states that Moses will not see God's glory, which suggests the anatomical construal.) Since, however, they lack knowledge, that is, they do not understand, the sight of the generative principle is allowed, just as parents might permit young children to see them in the buff.

3 Though anachronistic, this second construal is exactly the kind we should expect. See the penultimate footnote in chapter 10.

4 It can also go the other way. A creed that teaches the futility of human endeavour is likely to offer some sharp portrayal of things going badly wrong, or going nowhere. 'Even X failed. So you are sure to fail too.'

5 Or even in pictures. Think of the Escher drawing of a self-feeding watercourse in which water flows always downwards. Such a thing is at least physically, and quite possibly logically, impossible. Yet we would apply the words 'self-feeding watercourse &c.' to describe what we see.

6 Still in the interpretive spirit of the sages of Genesis Rabbah, I have yet another reason. The name of the second letter, 'beth,' is the associative form the word meaning 'house.' Thus 'Bethlehem,' meaning 'house of bread.' ב is in fact an ideogram of a house. The Bible's opening thus signals that the core concern is with human reality.

7 Leaving Raven's Land out of it, one might allow that Genesis 1:3 is God's single moment of Eden. I might add that it is quite appropriate from the present perspective that Genesis 2, which places the man and the woman in the Garden, begins with א!

8 How strong anyway is the extra-formal difference between arguing that X is possible and telling extensive stories of X? Parmenides mounts the internal philosophical attack on time. Change, he in effect argues, is a winged horse. (The reasoning, I should add, has to be extracted from some fairly enigmatic poetry.) In the dialogue named for Parmenides, Plato advances a metaphysical view that combines Parmenidean fixity (the Forms are timeless) with Becoming (the physical world, whose contents are reflections of the Forms, is itself temporal). But how does saying that change involves an element of changelessness show that change makes sense? If it showed that, could one not say, thereby refuting the argument about winged horses, that such things combine equinity with wingedness? Isn't the Eleatic's argument that, like roundness and squareness, the mutable and the immutable *cannot* be combined? Plato is also (just) telling a complex story; one that, as it were, saves the appearances. Let me make clear that I am disagreeing here with a certain meta-philosophical view about how positions like Plato's are defended, not with the position itself. 'Complex' should not be underestimated. Suppose we look very closely at that Escher drawing. At some level of granularity, will we not find that we will no longer agree to describe the water at every point as flowing downwards? Those who find the narrative mode of Homer and the Bible and the dramatic mode of Sophocles philosophically ineffective should give more thought to these matters.

9 The word used to vocalize the Tetragrammaton (the second major appellation), 'Adonai,' is the first-person singular possessive form of the plural of 'Lord.' It means: 'my Lords.'
10 This translation is mine. The NRSV has: 'The Lord is our God, the Lord alone.' The Hebrew word rendered 'alone' informs the end of the first day of creation. Again in my translation: 'and it was evening, and then it was morning, one full day [had been completed]' (1:5). 'Alone' or 'only' could not fit here in place of 'one.' Of course, even with 'alone' or 'only' the *Shema* see-saws between 'the only deity is our God' and 'God is the only deity that/who we acknowledge as ours.' The latter is compatible with a multiplicity of divine beings.
11 A second relevant question: Why Oedipus?
12 The riddle isn't spelled out in the play. That it is thematically relevant is confirmed by the mention, in Oedipus's first speech – the opening speech of the drama – of children, old men, and people generally. The words of the priest, in the second speech, raise confirmation to verification: 'You see us before you now, men of all ages' [17]. Recall that at Troy, on the Greek side, there are only adult men.
13 Dysfunctional by what yardstick? The yardstick calibrated to classical Athens. This is confirmed in the third of the Theban plays.
14 In a bizarre reflection of the taboo that Oedipus violates and of the measures that he takes to ensure its non-violation, Exodus 23:19 commands: 'You shall not boil a kid in its mother's milk.' Subsequent elaboration of this prohibition generated an outright ban on consuming milk with meat, even chicken with goat's milk.
15 Greater ingenuity would be needed in respect of the Oracle's claim that Oedipus would sleep with his mother. Think of frozen sperm from a donor who has since died.
16 As I shall illustrate below, the play is full of improbabilities; deliberately so, I maintain.
17 The upcoming section adapts ideas from Williams's *Shame and Necessity*.
18 The same sort of scenario would play out with respect to almost any item of clothing; or, indeed, artefact. Suppose you, a right-thinking coffee drinker, insist on fair trade. The result may be that workers on non–fair trade plantations lose their employment. Incidentally, the teacher in my classroom confection is in all likelihood a killer too. He or she need only look down at what he or she has laced on. Shades of Oedipus!
19 The speech of the priest, quoted in an earlier footnote, is a dead giveaway. 'You see us before you now, men of all ages' [17]. That is exactly what

Oedipus claims for himself, the oracular capacity to see all the ages 'now,' and hence to control the future.

20 Tiresias is consistently advising restraint. He vaguely corresponds, as a religious figure, to Elijah on the Carmel.

21 A recent movie, *Minority Report,* deals with the issue. A set of 'precogs' are regarded as capable of predicting crimes. The authorities, reading the precogs' minds, track down and deal with those fingered as future perpetrators before the crimes are committed, sometimes by killing them. The question arises: Without knowledge of the actual commission, can this be justified? What is the truth value of 'X is a future perpetrator of Y' before Y occurs?

22 The Greek for 'swollen foot' and for 'I am a foot knower' are similar.

23 'Œ' is self-explanatory. Why 'di'? 'J' is a diphthong. The first of its sonic elements is 'd'. (The 'd' occasionally emerges from hiding. 'James,' for instance, is 'Diego' in Spanish.) The English surname 'Jago' is a variant of 'Iago.' So 'j' converts with 'di.' Amusingly, the sounds making up 'Joseph' (i.e., 'd-i-o-s-e-ph') almost permute into 'Oedipus.' Since the first letter of the Hebrew 'Joseph' is given by 'y,' a reader of the original would not, unfortunately, join in the fun.

24 The NRSV misses this, putting 'they both dreamed' for the Hebrew 'they both dreamed a dream.'

25 'Eunuch' means 'bed guard.'

26 The same words end Euripides's *The Phoenician Women*. The endings of *Antigone* and *Oedipus at Colonus* have a similar sound. Knox (413) reports that the speech is regarded by some scholars as a later addition.

27 I will explain in the next chapter that unhappy lives can be lives that we are happier living than happy lives.

Chapter 12

1 The same view about Homer's significance, slanted towards the younger element of the populace, and advanced approvingly (Socrates is just reporting), Plato puts into the mouth of Protagoras. Once schoolchildren have mastered their alphas and betas, their teachers 'set the works of good poets before them on their desks to read and make them learn by heart, poems containing much admonition and many stories, eulogies, and panegyrics of the good men of old, so that the child may be inspired to imitate them and long to be like them' (*Protagoras* 326a). That Plato has a sophist, indeed the most important one, speak approvingly is obviously significant. It shows where Plato stands.

2 James M. Redfield, *Nature and Culture in the Iliad*, 245.

3 The lines following are from Yeats, 'Among School Children.'

4 Let me offer a representative confirming instance. The point about how the gods are portrayed is the sum total of Christopher Rowe's evaluation in his contribution to the *Routledge History of Philosophy*, vol. I, *From the Beginning to Plato*, ed. C.C.W. Taylor. See in particular 438–9. It is revealing that the scholar who contributes the most extensive discussion of Homer to the *Routledge History of Philosophy*, Robin Osborne, specializes in ancient history. (Rowe too is a classicist by training and trade.) I would not expect, or for that matter want, a philosopher *qua* philosopher to contribute a major piece on Homer in a *literary* context. This, however, is an encyclopedic work on philosophy. Still, given Homer's marginal position in the philosophical firmament, it doesn't surprise me that the editor has enlisted a classicist. What is more surprising is that the classicists recruited are so passive in regard to Plato's handling of Homer. Osborne's extensive discussion of Homer (16–25) gives not an inkling of the philosophical themes of the epic that I have elicited. For a classicist, a little philosophy is, it seems, a dangerous thing.

5 That Plato was invited to Syracuse to implement his ideas testifies that the competition wasn't entirely in Plato's head.

6 The death of Patroclus is an important stage in the shift. In the *Symposium*, Plato distorts Homer's sense badly, and does so, as per my conjecture, by linking it with the warrior view. 'Do you suppose,' Diotima asks Socrates, 'that . . . Achilles [would have] avenge[d] Patroclus . . . if [he] had not believed that [his] courage would live for ever in men's memory, as it does in ours?' (208d). Achilles is intent on getting even for Patroclus's death. He is gripped by self-loathing because he is responsible for his friend's fall. The first of these is not a warrior's motivation; the second, not a warrior's emotion.

7 Why is it that Plato, who attacks Greek tragic writing, mentions Sophocles only in passing, and then (329b–d) by relating an anecdote that, only if one is half-asleep, could be taken to have a pro-Platonic slant? We have a possible explanation. Unlike Homer, Sophocles does not sympathetically advance the pre-reformed view.

8 Augustine, *City of God*, Book VIII, chapter 11. Needless to say, Augustine is referring to the (so-called) Old Testament.

9 Plato puts the quoted words into Socrates's mouth. Scholars debate whether the flesh-and-blood Socrates held views about the extra-human world. According to Aristotle (*Metaphysics* 987b1–5), Socrates 'bus[ied] himself about ethical matters and neglect[ed] the world of nature as a whole.' He focused, that is, on *distinctively* human affairs. Though not much to go on, this implies that the historical Socrates was not more interested in the Proverbist's three than the Proverbist himself. If so, it is Plato who has Socrates choose Plato.

10 For the Proverbist's view of the anthill, see note 24. Aristotle comments on ants in *Historia Animalium.*

11 The language here is tricky. Asked why I do A rather than B, I might say: 'Because I want to do A.' This looks like (and may sometimes amount to) 'I desire A.' But it may also mean 'Because I choose to.' That is: 'I prefer A to B' might equate with 'I choose A.' Here is a usefully articulate passage from Anthony Powell's novel *The Soldier's Art*. The novel's narrator, Nick Jenkins, finds Charles Stringham serving as an officers' mess waiter in the British Army in the Second World War. This Jenkins sees as a position unsuitable for his old school friend. Stringham proceeds to explain himself. 'I wouldn't go so far as to say that I'm actively enjoying what I'm doing at the moment – but then how little of one's life has ever been actively enjoyable. At the same time, what I'm doing is what I've chosen to do. Even what I want to do, if it comes to that' (78).

12 The belief part, as this makes clear, is not only about means to satisfy desires. If I am informed that smoking causes cancer, that might change my desire for a cigarette. So beliefs affect desires.

13 *The Function of Reason*, 16.

14 He is, in fact, retelling the Myth, tailoring it to suit his purposes. The received version of the Myth is found in Homer. In Book II (379d–380a), Plato mentions the original, and slights Homer's portrayal of fate and of the gods' role in it as a 'foolish mistake.'

15 Homer's anthropological views, though not themselves political, are not politically inert. The way we think of political actors links with how we view political action. The valuing of the individual's life cannot easily be separated from the defence of the individual's freedom to live that life as he or she sees fit. This explains why Plato takes Homer on in a dialogue devoted to political existence, even though the epics contain nothing of the polis in its political sense.

16 The book is subtitled 'An Essay in Descriptive Metaphysics.' For Strawson, 'individual' is a generic term. Anything with clear identity conditions qualifies. Among individuals, some are particular, some general. The former are those whose identity conditions make reference to spatial location and temporal position. That is Strawson's metaphysical analysis of particularity. As I use it, 'particular' is irreducibly a term of ontology, not of metaphysics. Metaphysics, though equal to the individual, cannot by nature accommodate (in my sense) the particular. A close reading of *Individuals* discloses that Strawson needs the ontological idea. The need can in fact be felt throughout his philosophy. But he is, as a philosopher in

the tradition, committed to the adequacy of metaphysical analysis. For an extended discussion, see my '"And the spirit of God hovered on the face of the water": An Introduction to the Bible for Philosophers.'

17 For Frege's classic analysis, see his 'Function and Concept.'

18 Gopnik, 'Death of a Fish,' 42–7. The first two quotations are from 46.

19 The basic reason, which will be brushed in the next section, is that the presence of the distinction would in principle disrupt the unity/orderliness of the world.

20 In 'Matter and Rationality,' I argue that the Aristotelian material element has epistemological, not ontological, status.

21 This is not a change of subject from philosophy of mind to politics and sociology. As we have seen, as Greek culture moves from the archaic to the classical period, issues of human reality get refocused on polis life. Men and women did not begin to have souls (= to be particulars) when they became polis dwellers. I will explain at the end how what is said about the polis and the psyche can be generalized backwards to pre-political culture.

22 I am referring to Homer, to Hesiod, and to the classical dramatists. Plato is fully conversant with their writings. His dialogues are replete with quotations and allusions. Chapter 10 established that Plato was deliberately undermining – 'philosophizing' – Sophocles's position; which means: transposing it back from the logical field of Genesis 2 to that of Genesis 1.

23 'I am firmly persuaded that a great deal of consciousness, every sort of consciousness, in fact, is a disease' (*Notes from Underground*, 7). Dostoyevsky's protagonist is railing against the deterministic conception of men and women. Within the confines of that conception, he exults in dysfunctionality; does so, since from a subjective standpoint dysfunctionality is a cog's closest approximation to genuine particularity: autonomy and separateness.

24 Ants are mentioned, and a comparison with the human collective that flatters the anthill is drawn, in Proverbs 6:6. 'Without having any chief or officer or ruler, [the ant] prepares its food in summer and gathers its sustenance in harvest.'

25 Hebrew 'Enoch' is less like 'Enosh' than the English translations make it seem. Since the names in the two lines are counterparts, and since it is the easiest thing in the world to create echoing names if all that counts is phonetics ('Georgie' and 'Porgie'), the sonic distance in this instance draws attention to a point that, arguably, the writers wish to make, viz., that Genesis 2 men and women, 'bnei-enosh,' are by nature cultural beings, 'enochs.'

26 'Transgression' has strong moral connotations. The word should be read in a morally neutral way. The distinctively human product, the city, is the result of not fitting into the natural order of things. It is a disruption of functionality. This is just, writ large, the case with the human particular. A 'standard' reading of the story of Eden locates 'the problem' in human free will. It is easy to see in free will a disrupter of (external) order, and hence a sign of an 'inside.' I have pursued *this* line, and again explained how the Platonic position is theoretically opposed, in 'Inhumanity and Polity: An Essay on Plato's *Republic*.'

Conclusion

1 I sketch such a revision, and argue that several instabilities in Kant's own (more formal) presentation even point to his commitment to something like the distinction between Genesis 1 and Genesis 2, in 'Transcendental Idealism: What Jerusalem has to say to Königsberg.'

2 In Mishnah Sanhedrin 4:5, in a fashion that reflects both the view that individual life is the locus of primary value and also the view that the distinctness of each individual is implicit in the biblical story, Rabbi Judah haNasi, the chief redactor of the Mishnah, the first major compilation of the Jewish oral tradition, writes (c. 200 CE): 'Therefore was the first man, Adam, created alone, to teach us that whoever destroys a single life, the Bible considers it as if he destroyed an entire world . . . Also, man [was created singly] to show the greatness of the Holy One, Blessed be He, for if a man strikes many coins from one mold, they all resemble one another, but the King of Kings, the Holy One, Blessed be He, made each man in the image of Adam, and yet not one of them [exactly] resembles his fellow.'

Bibliography

Aeschylus. *The Oresteia*. Robert Fagles, trans. Harmondsworth, England: Penguin, 1979.

Alter, Robert. *The Art of Biblical Narrative*. New York: Basic Books, 1981.

– *The Five Books of Moses*. New York: Norton, 2004.

Amis, Martin. *Yellow Dog*. Toronto: Vintage Canada, 2003.

Arendt, Hannah. *Origins of Totalitarianism*. San Diego: Harcourt Brace, 1973.

Aristotle. *Metaphysics*. W.D. Ross, trans. Oxford: Clarendon Press, 1924.

– *Poetics*. R. Kassel, trans. Oxford: Oxford Classical Texts, 1965.

– *On the Soul*. J.A. Smith, trans. Oxford: Oxford Classical Texts, 1956.

Augustine. *City of God*. Henry Bettenson, trans. Harmondsworth, England: Penguin, 1984.

Barnes, Jonathan, *Early Greek Philosophy*. Harmondsworth, England: Penguin, 1987.

– *The Presocratic Philosophers*, 2nd edition. London: Routledge, 1982.

Bible. *New Oxford Annotated Bible*. Bruce M. Metzger and Roland E. Murphy, eds. New York: Oxford University Press, 1991.

Chabon, Michael. *The Final Solution*. New York: HarperCollins, 2004.

Descartes, René. *Meditations on First Philosophy*. In Volume II, *The Philosophical Writings of Descartes*, John Cottingham, Robert Stoothoff, and Dugald Murdoch, trans. Cambridge: Cambridge University Press, 1985.

Dinesen, Isak. *Out of Africa*. New York: Random House, 1937.

Dostoyevsky, Fyodor. *Notes from Underground*. Constance Garnett, trans. New York: Classic House, 2008.

Euripides. *Hippolytus*. In *Euripides I – Four Tragedies*. David Grene, trans. Chicago: University of Chicago Press, 1956.

Finley, M.I. *The World of Odysseus*. London: The Folio Society, 2002.

Frege, Gottlob. 'Function and Concept.' In *Translations from the Philosophical Writings of Gottlob Frege*. Peter Geach and Max Black, trans. and eds. Oxford: Blackwell, 1960.

Glouberman, Mark. '"And the spirit of God hovered on the face of the water": An Introduction to the Bible for Philosophers.' *Iyyun, The Jerusalem Philosophical Quarterly* 60, 2011.

– 'Matter and Rationality.' *Apeiron* 11, 1977.

– 'Transcendental Idealism: What Jerusalem Has to Say to Königsberg.' *Dialogue: Canadian Philosophical Review* 49, 2010.

– 'Inhumanity and Polity: An Essay on Plato's *Republic*.' *Iyyun, The Jerusalem Philosophical Quarterly* 49, 2000.

Gopnik, Adam. 'Death of a Fish.' *The New Yorker*, 4 July 2005.

– 'Last of the Metrozoids.' *The New Yorker*, 10 May 2004.

Gray, John. *Kings I & II: A Commentary*. Philadelphia: Westminster Press, 1964, 1970.

Hesiod. *Theogony, Works and Days, Shield*, 2nd edition. Apostolos N. Athanassakis, trans. Baltimore and London: Johns Hopkins University Press, 2004.

Homer. *The Iliad* and *The Odyssey*. Robert Fagles, trans. Bernard Knox, Introduction and Notes. Harmondsworth, England: Penguin, 1990, 1996.

Jaynes, Julian. *Origin of Consciousness in the Breakdown of the Bicameral Mind*. New York: Houghton Mifflin, 1976.

Jaspers, Karl. *The Origin and Goal of History*. London: Routledge & Kegan Paul, 1953.

Joyce, James. *Dubliners*. Harmondsworth, England: Penguin, 1992.

Kaufmann, Yehezkel. *The Religion of Israel, from Its Beginnings to the Babylonian Exile*. Moshe Greenberg, abridgement and trans. Chicago: University of Chicago Press, 1960.

Kitto, H.D.F. *The Greeks*. Harmondsworth, England: Penguin, 1957.

Levi, Primo. 'Bear Meat.' In *A Tranquil Star*. Alessandra Bastagli, trans. New York: Norton, 2007.

Lewis, C.S. *Abolition of Man*. New York: HarperCollins, 2001.

Lurie, Yuval. *Cultural Beings: Reading the Philosophers of* Genesis. Amsterdam and Atlanta: Rodopi, 2000.

Menand, Louis. 'Holden at Fifty.' *The New Yorker*, October 2001.

Miles, Jack. *God: A Biography*. New York: Knopf, 1995.

Ozick, Cynthia. 'And God Saw Literature, That It Was Good.' *The New Republic* 4, October 2004.

Oz, Amos. *Black Box*. Nicholas De Lange, trans. London: Flamingo, 1988.

Plato. *Gorgias*. W.D. Woodhead, trans. In *Plato: Collected Dialogues*. Edith Hamilton and Huntington Cairns, eds. New York: Pantheon Books, 1961.

– *Phaedo*. In *Five Dialogues*. G.M.A. Grube, trans. Indianapolis: Hackett, 1981.
– *Protagoras*. W.K.C. Guthrie, trans. Harmondsworth, England: Penguin, 1956.
– *Republic*. G.M.A. Grube, trans. Revised by C.D.C. Reeve. Indianapolis: Hackett, 1992. Also: F.M. Cornford, trans. Oxford: Oxford University Press, 1945.
– *Symposium*. Walter Hamilton, trans. Harmondsworth, England: Penguin, 1981.
Pope, Marvin H. Anchor Bible, Job. Garden City, NY: Doubleday, 1965.
Powell, Anthony. *The Soldier's Art*. London: Mandarin Paperbacks, 1966.
Proust, Marcel. *Remembrance of Things Past*. Volume I. C.K. Scott Moncrieff and Terence Kilmartin, trans. Harmondsworth, England: Penguin, 1985.
Redfield, James M. *Nature and Culture in the Iliad*. Expanded edition. Durham and London: Duke University Press, 1994.
Rowe, C.J. *Plato*, 2nd edition. London: Bristol Classical Press, 2003.
Rushdie, Salman. *The Satanic Verses*. Toronto: Vintage, 1997.
Sacks, Robert. 'The Book of Job: Translation and Commentary.' *Interpretation* 24, 1997.
– 'The Lion and the Ass: A Commentary on the Book of Genesis.' *Interpretation* 8, 1980; 9, 1980; 10, 1982; 11, 1983; 12, 1984. archive.org/details/RobertSacksACommentaryOnTheBookOfGenesis.
Schein, Seth L. *The Mortal Hero*. Berkeley: University of California Press, 1984.
Simms, Norman. 'Is Judaism a Jewish Heresy?' Unpublished ms.
Sophocles. *The Three Theban Plays: Antigone, Oedipus the King, Oedipus at Colonus*. Robert Fagles, trans. Bernard Knox, Introduction and Notes. Harmondsworth, England: Penguin, 1984.
Speiser, E.A. Anchor Bible, Genesis. Garden City: Doubleday, 1964.
Strawson, P.F. *Individuals*. London: Methuen, 1959.
Taylor, C.C.W., ed. *Routledge History of Philosophy*, Volume I, *From the Beginning to Plato*. London: Routledge, 1997.
Updike, John. 'The Great I Am.' *The New Yorker*, 1 November 2004.
Vernant, Jean-Pierre. 'Tensions and Ambiguities in Greek Tragedy.' In *Myth and Tragedy in Ancient Greece*. Jean-Pierre Vernant and Pierre Vidal-Naquet, eds. Janet Lloyd, trans. New York: Zone Books, 1988.
Weinberg, Steven. *The First Three Minutes*. Updated edition. New York: Basic Books, 1988.
Whitehead, Alfred North, *The Function of Reason*. Boston: Beacon Press, 1971.
Williams, Bernard. 'Philosophy as a Humanistic Discipline.' *Philosophy* 75, 2000.
– *Shame and Necessity*. Berkeley: University of California Press, 1993.
Zeitlin, Froma, I. 'Thebes: Theater of Self and Society in Athenian Drama.' In *Nothing to Do with Dionysos?* John J. Winkler and Froma I. Zeitlin, eds. Princeton, New Jersey: Princeton University Press, 1990.

Index